Russell Shorto is a journalist and author of two previous books of non-fiction, *Gospel Truth* and *Saints and Madmen*. He lives in New York's Hudson Valley.

Acclaim for *The Island at the Centre of the World:*

'Magnificent ... done with relish, wit, imagination (but never at the expense of known facts), a subtle grasp of larger historical and cultural movements, a dramatist's or a screenwriter's sense of narrative suspense, a portraitist's sense of character ... little short of sensational ... Shorto's book deserves to be a bestseller: it is narratively irresistible, intellectually provocative, historically invaluable. But beyond that, it has a big-heartedness about people and events that makes it an inspiration not only for democracy, for history, but for scholarship too' Simon Callow, *Guardian*

'Once in a while a book appears that entirely changes the perspective of the general reader on a place, or on a series of historical events. Russell Shorto's *Island at the Centre of the World* is just such a landmark book ... reads like a thriller ... [like] the similarly ground breaking *Longitude*' Professor Lisa Jardine, *The Times*

'Rattling well-told tale ... a terrific popular history about a past that beautifully illuminates the present' *Sunday Times*

'Often reads more like a novel than a history ... both the characters and the colony are brought to life in an absorbing, enjoyable book' *Literary Review*

'A great story ... Shorto is an accomplished historian ... I was completely convinced: if people absolutely have to build empires, it's hard to imagine more charming empire builders than the Dutch' Tom Payne, *Daily Telegraph*

'Russell Shorto's remarkable book ... It is Shorto's thesis, developed through more than 400 compulsively interesting pages ... that during the brief decades of its Dutch colonial existence the infant Manhattan had already found, once and for all, its tumultuously eclectic soul ... The research has clearly been formidable ... the result is a book that New York aficionados will find fuels their enthusiasm' Jan Morris, *New Statesman*

'Masterly new history . . . Why has the Dutch side of our national story remained so obscure for so long? . . . New York history buffs will be captivated by Shorto's descriptions of Manhattan in its primordial state . . . he writes at all times with passion, verve, nuance and considerable humor . . . Shorto's basic premise is undeniable. The legacy of tolerance from the Dutch colony in Manhattan would be extended . . . deep into the dark fields of the Republic' *New York Times Book Review*

'A dramatic, kaleidoscopic and, on the whole, quite wonderful book . . . one of those rare books in the picked-over field of colonial history, a whole new picture . . . With his full-blooded resurrection of an unfamiliar American patriot, Russell Shorto has made a real contribution' *New York Observer*

'A tour de force, written with a rare clarity, a sense of irony and wry wit. It is a masterpiece of storytelling and first-rate intellectual history' *Wall Street Journal*

'*The Island at the Centre of the World* ranks among the best books ever written about New Amsterdam, the Dutch settlement on Manhattan that would become New York City. Shorto's prose is deliciously rich and witty, and the story he tells – drawing heavily on sources that have only recently come to light – brings one surprise after another. His rediscovery of Adriaen van der Donck, Peter Stuyvesant's nemesis, is fascinating' Edwin G. Burrows, Co-author of *Gotham: A History of New York City to 1898*, winner of the Pulitzer Prize for History

'Russell Shorto's dramatic adventure tale about the settling of Manhattan will transform the way we look at American history. The Dutch colony, founded just three years after the Puritans landed in Massachusetts, quickly became the gateway for the pluralistic mix that would define a new nation. Shorto's book recounts the fascinating struggle between Peter Stuyvesant and the lesser-known but more influential Adriaen van der Donck, whose appreciation for individual tolerance laid the foundation for our Bill of Rights and helped to create our national character. It's also the story of the remarkable age of exploration led by Henry Hudson and others who spread the culture of the European Renaissance to a distant wilderness. Based on a wealth of documents that archivists began translating 40 years ago, Shorto has produced both a triumph of scholarship and a rollicking narrative. The result is an exciting drama about the roots of America's freedoms'
Walter Isaacson, author of the *New York Times* bestseller *Benjamin Franklin*

The Island at the Centre of the World

The Untold Story of Dutch Manhattan and the Founding of New York

RUSSELL SHORTO

BLACK SWAN

THE ISLAND AT THE CENTRE OF THE WORLD
A BLACK SWAN BOOK: 0 552 99982 2

Originally published in Great Britain by Doubleday,
a division of Transworld Publishers

PRINTING HISTORY
Doubleday edition published 2004
Black Swan edition published 2005

1 3 5 7 9 10 8 6 4 2

Map by Laura Hartman Maestro

Set in 11/13pt Granjon by
Falcon Oast Graphic Art Ltd.

Black Swan Books are published by Transworld Publishers,
61–63 Uxbridge Road, London W5 5SA,
a division of The Random House Group Ltd,
in Australia by Random House Australia (Pty) Ltd,
20 Alfred Street, Milsons Point, Sydney, NSW 2061, Australia,
in New Zealand by Random House New Zealand Ltd,
18 Poland Road, Glenfield, Auckland 10, New Zealand
and in South Africa by Random House (Pty) Ltd,
Endulini, 5a Jubilee Road, Parktown 2193, South Africa.

Printed and bound in Great Britain by
Cox & Wyman Ltd, Reading, Berkshire.

Papers used by Transworld Publishers are natural, recyclable products made from wood grown in sustainable forests. The manufacturing processes conform to the environmental regulations of the country of origin.

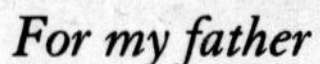

For my father

Contents

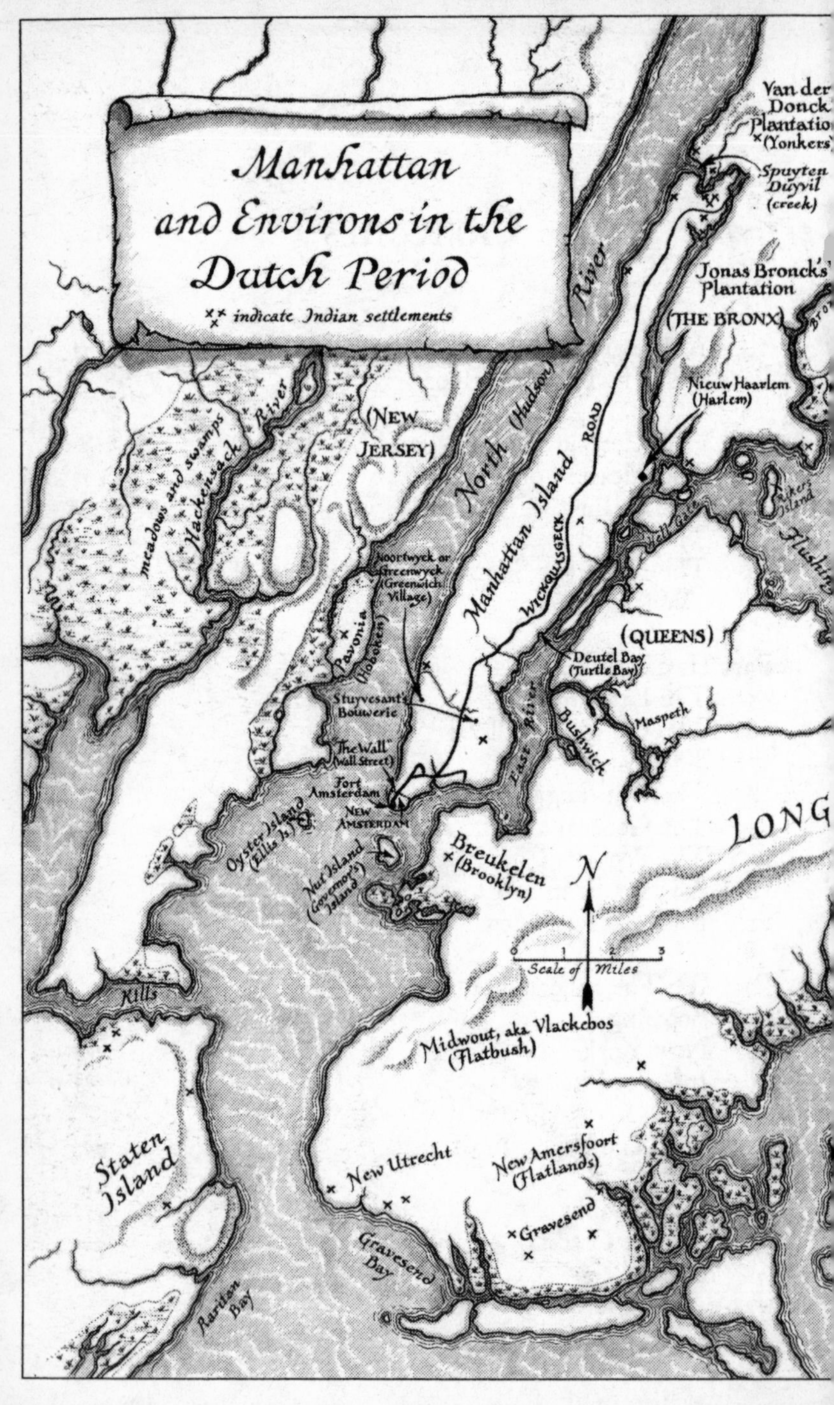

Manhattan and Environs in the Dutch Period
indicate Indian settlements
Van der Donck Plantation (Yonkers)
Spuyten Duyvil (creek)
Jonas Bronck's Plantation
(THE BRONX)
Nieuw Haarlem (Harlem)
North (Hudson) River
Manhattan Island
WICKQUASGECK ROAD
meadows and swamps
Hackensack River
(NEW JERSEY)
Noortwyck or Greenwyck (Greenwich Village)
Pavonia (Hoboken)
Stuyvesant's Bouwerie
"The Wall" (Wall Street)
Fort Amsterdam
NEW AMSTERDAM
Oyster Island (Ellis Is.)
Nut Island (Governor's Island)
Breukelen (Brooklyn)
East River
Bushwick
Maspeth
Deutel Bay (Turtle Bay)
(QUEENS)
Hell Gate
Flushing
LONG
N
0 1 2 3
Scale of Miles
Kills
Midwout, aka Vlackebos (Flatbush)
Staten Island
New Utrecht
New Amersfoort (Flatlands)
Gravesend
Gravesend Bay
Raritan Bay

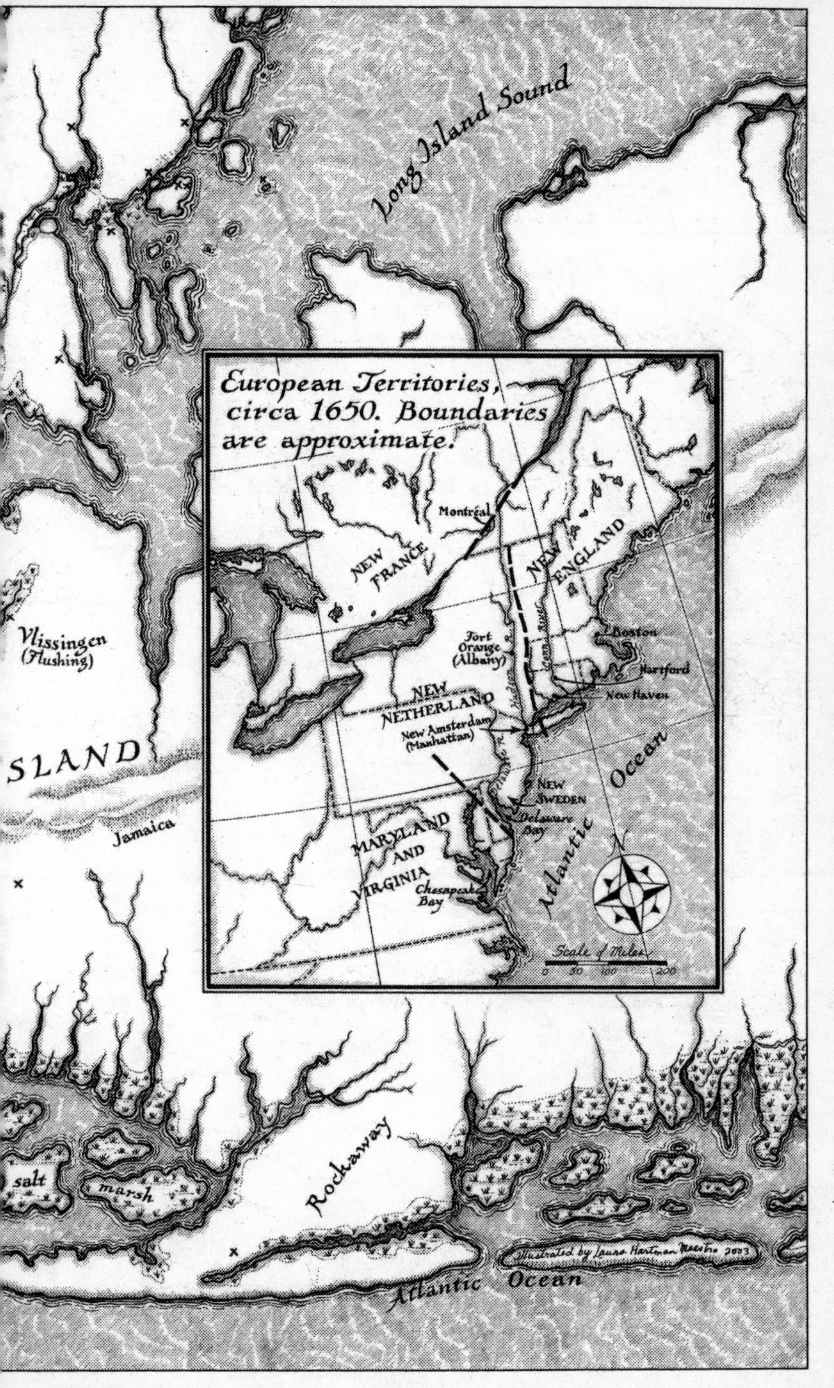
Long Island Sound
Vlissingen
(Flushing)
SLAND
Jamaica
salt
marsh
Rockaway
Atlantic Ocean
Illustrated by Laura Hartman Maestro 2003
European Territories, circa 1650. Boundaries are approximate.
Montréal
NEW FRANCE
NEW ENGLAND
Fort Orange (Albany)
Boston
Hartford
New Haven
NEW NETHERLAND
New Amsterdam (Manhattan)
NEW SWEDEN
Delaware Bay
MARYLAND AND VIRGINIA
Chesapeake Bay
Atlantic Ocean
Scale of Miles
0 50 100 200

Acknowledgements

This book would not exist without the work of Charles Gehring, who, as director of the New Netherland Project, has devoted thirty years to translating the manuscript Dutch records of the New Netherland colony. But published translations aside, for more than two years he has welcomed me into his workspace, opened his files to me, offered advice, made introductions and helped in dozens of other ways. Over Vietnamese lunches and pints of microbrew beer, on the Albany waterfront and along the canals of Amsterdam, he has been my guide. My greatest thanks to you, Charly.

I also owe a debt of gratitude to Janny Venema of the New Netherland Project, for similar help mixed with friendship. She spent days transcribing as-yet-unpublished manuscripts for me. She gave me a primer in how to read seventeenth-century Dutch handwriting. She made the town of Beverwyck, long since swallowed up by the city of Albany, come alive for me.

Of the many others who helped me, I would like to thank Jeremy Bangs and Carola de Muralt of the American Pilgrim Museum in Leiden, the Netherlands, who gave me a sense of the texture of seventeenth-century Dutch life and a magnificent afternoon-long tour of their one-of-a-kind museum. Patricia Bonomi, professor emeritus of history at New York University, offered guidance as I set out on the project and encouragement as I approached the end. Peter Christoph of the New York State

Library shared with me his reminiscences about his discovery of the Dutch manuscripts and efforts to get them translated. Diane Dallal, archaeologist with New York Unearthed and the South Street Seaport Museum, helped me to visualize New Amsterdam amid the canyons of lower Manhattan. Firth Fabend, historian and author, helped on many fronts, especially in understanding how 'Dutchness' changed in North America from the seventeenth century onwards, and in assessing the colony's legacy. The Friends of New Netherland invited me to speak at their annual meeting in 2003, thus providing me with a chance to air some of my ideas about the Dutch colony. Willem Frijhoff of the Free University of Amsterdam, distinguished historian and authority on New Netherland and its people, is a man of great generosity who offered brilliant, timely advice and encouraged me in my focus on Adriaen van der Donck. Elisabeth Paling Funk, Dutch-born scholar and authority on Washington Irving, helped me to disentangle history from myth, and translated some seventeenth-century poetry for me. Wayne Furman of the New York Public Library, as well as the staff of the library's New York History and Genealogy division, accommodated me throughout my research. I'm grateful to Joyce Goodfriend of the University of Denver, authority on early New York, for good conversation on history and historians, for advice and pointers, and for introducing me to Jack's Oyster House in Albany. Anne Halpern of the National Gallery of Art assisted with research on the portrait of Adriaen van der Donck. Leo Hershkowitz, professor of history at Queens College, who has written with equal elegance about both the Jews of New Amsterdam and Boss Tweed, knows New York history as few people on earth do, and gave me the benefit of his perspective. Maria Holden, conservator at the New York State Archives, gave me a primer on the Dutch documents as artefacts: on paper, ink and methods of preservation.

On a sun-dazzled Fourth of July morning on the terrace of the Stadscafe in the city of Leiden, Jaap Jacobs of the University of Amsterdam broadened my view of seventeenth-century American colonial history, helping me to see it not merely as foreshadowing later American history but as part of European history and the global struggle between England and the Dutch Republic; I am also grateful for his elegant writings on New Netherland and on the concept of tolerance in the seventeenth century, and for conversation on the prickly figure of Peter Stuyvesant, on a biography of whom he is currently at work. My thanks to Joep de Koning, probably the world's foremost collector of maps of New Netherland, for conversation, for insights, and for giving me a chance to roam among his matchless collection; to Dennis Maika of Fox Lane High School, Bedford, New York, whose dissertation on and insights into the significance of the 1653 municipal charter and the subsequent boom in the colony were instrumental in shaping my own thoughts; to Simon Middleton of the University of East Anglia, for pointers on early modern republicanism in the Netherlands and for his encouragement as a fellow Van der Donck enthusiast; to Peter Neil, director of the South Street Seaport Museum; to Chip Reynolds, skipper of the *Half Moon*, for taking me aboard and giving me a feel of the ship; to Peter Rose, authority on seventeenth-century Dutch food, for culinary assistance; to Thomas Rosenbaum of the Rockefeller Archives, Pocantico Hills, New York, who afforded me access to that institution's remarkable collection of seventeenth-century Dutch notarial records; to Ada Louise van Gastel, for her work on Adriaen van der Donck and her encouragement; to Hanny Veenendaal of the Netherlands Center in New York City, for giving me a grounding in the Dutch language and for assisting in translations and in reading old Dutch documents; to Greta Wagle, who welcomed me into the family of New Netherland aficionados, put me in touch with people, and has been generally delightful to know; to Gerald de Weerdt, curator of 't Behouden Huys Museum, Terschelling, the Netherlands, for sharing insights on Dutch seafaring; and to Laurie Weinstein, Western Connecticut State

University, who helped in my attempts to understand Dutch–English–Indian interactions.

A separate thank-you to Firth Fabend, Charly Gehring, Leo Hershkowitz, Joep de Koning, Tim Paulson, Janny Venema and Mark Zwonitzer for reading the manuscript and offering excellent comments and critiques. The book is greatly improved by their input, though of course any errors remain my own doing.

My thanks also to Coen Blaauw; José Brandão, Western Michigan University; Marilyn Douglas, New York State Library; Howard Funk; April Hatfield, Texas A&M University; L. J. Krizner, the New-York Historical Society; Karen Ordahl Kupperman, New York University; Hubert de Leeuw; Harry Macy, editor of *The New York Genealogical and Biographical Record*; Richard Mooney, *New York Times* editorial board, retired; the staff of the New York State Library and Archives; Hennie Newhouse, Friends of New Netherland; Don Rittner; Margriet de Roever, Gemeentearchief Amsterdam; Martha Shattuck; Amanda Sutphin, New York City Landmarks Preservation Commission; Martine Julia van Ittersum, Harvard University; Cynthia van Zandt, University of New Hampshire; Loet Velmans; David William Voorhees, of The Holland Society of New York and managing editor of *De Halve Maen*; and James Homer Williams, Middle Tennessee State University.

Thanks also to my team. Anne Edelstein, my agent and friend, plucked the rabbit of an idea out of my brain and made this all happen. Laura Williams gave advice in the early stages. Anne Hollister and Elisabeth King fact-checked the manuscript with scrupulosity and style. Tim Paulson listened to my initial rambling, inchoate idea, pushed me to carry it forward, and was there along the way with smart counsel. Bill Thomas, my editor at Doubleday, championed the project from the beginning and managed throughout to support it with the excellent combination of overflowing enthusiasm and sharp critical judgement. Thanks also to Kendra Harpster, John Fontana and Christine

Pride of Doubleday. In London, Marianne Velmans, my editor at Transworld, brought her Anglo-Dutch perspective to bear, and critiqued the manuscript with great insight. Gillian Somerscales caught errors and otherwise improved the text.

Finally, my wife, Marnie Henricksson, endured the years of this project, shared the good times of it with me and saw me through what were some definite not-so-good times. She is the love of my life and I owe her everything.

So much for the living. From time to time during the course of my work on this book I've had the flickering sense that the spirits of Adriaen van der Donck and Peter Stuyvesant were hovering somewhere nearby; the first, perhaps, interested by the notion of being plucked from historical oblivion, the second maybe by potentially being rescued from the status of historical cartoon. There is one other spirit I've felt as well, a less obvious one. I would like to express my gratitude to the late Barbara W. Tuchman: for providing a model of a writer committed to history and narrative both; for being among the first popular historians to recognize, in her final book, *The First Salute*, the overlooked contribution of the Dutch to early American history; and finally and perhaps most importantly to me, for making a bequest to the New York Public Library in honour of her father, which resulted in the establishment of the Wertheim Study Room, where much of this book was researched.

The Island at the Centre of the World

Prologue
The Missing Floor

IF YOU WERE TO STEP INSIDE A LIFT IN THE LOBBY OF THE NEW York State Library in Albany, you would discover that, although the building has eleven floors, there is no button marked 8. To get to the eighth floor, which is closed to the public, you take the lift to floor 7, walk through a security door, state your business with a librarian at the desk, then enter another lift and go up one more level.

As you pass shelves of quietly mouldering books and periodicals – the budgets of the state of Kansas going back to 1923, the Australian census, the complete bound series of *Northern Miner* – you may be greeted by the sound of German opera coming from a small room in the south-eastern corner. Peering around the doorway, you would probably find a rather bearish-looking man hunched over a desk, perhaps squinting through an antique jeweller's loupe. The hiddenness of the location is an apt metaphor for the work that is going on here. What Dr Charles Gehring is studying with such attention may be one of several thousand artefacts in his care – artefacts that, once they give up their secrets through his efforts, breathe life into a moment of history that has been largely ignored for three centuries.

This book tells the story of that moment. It is a story of high adventure set during the age of exploration – when Francis

Drake, Henry Hudson and Captain John Smith were expanding the boundaries of the world, and Shakespeare, Rembrandt, Galileo, Descartes, Mercator, Vermeer, Harvey and Bacon were revolutionizing human thought and expression. It is a distinctly European tale, but also a vital piece of America's beginnings. It is the story of one of the original European colonies on America's shores, which was eventually swallowed up by the others but never wholly digested.

At the book's centre is an island – a slender, wilderness island at the edge of the known world, which, as the European powers sent their navies and adventurer–businessmen roaming the seas in history's first truly global era, would become a fulcrum in the international power struggle, the key to control of a continent and a new world. The story encompasses the kings and generals who would plot for control of this piece of property, but at its heart is a humbler assemblage: a band of explorers, entrepreneurs, pirates, prostitutes, and assorted flotsam and jetsam from different parts of Europe who sought riches on this wild island. Together, this unlikely group formed a new society. They are the first New Yorkers, the original European inhabitants of the island of Manhattan.

We are used to thinking of American beginnings as involving thirteen English colonies; to thinking of American history as an English stock onto which, over time, the cultures of many other nations were grafted to create a new species of society that has become a multi-ethnic model for progressive societies around the world. But that isn't true. To talk of the thirteen original English colonies is to ignore another European colony – the one centred on Manhattan, which pre-dated New York and whose history was all but erased when the English took it over.

The settlement in question occupied the area between the newly forming English territories of Virginia and New England. It extended roughly from present-day Albany, New York, in the north to Delaware Bay in the south, comprising all or parts of what became New York, New Jersey, Connecticut, Pennsylvania and Delaware. It was founded by the Dutch, who called it New Netherland, but half of its residents were from elsewhere. Its capital was a tiny collection of rough buildings perched on the edge of a limitless wilderness, but its muddy lanes and waterfront were prowled by a Babel of peoples – Norwegians, Germans, Italians, Jews, Africans (slaves and free), Walloons, Bohemians, Munsees, Montauks, Mohawks and many others – all living on the rim of empire, struggling to find a way of being together, searching for a balance between chaos and order, liberty and oppression. Pirates, prostitutes, smugglers and business sharks held sway in it. Right from the start, in other words, it was *Manhattan*: a place unlike any other, either in the North American colonies or anywhere else.

Because of its geography, its population and the fact that it was under the control of the Dutch (even then its parent city, Amsterdam, was the most liberal in Europe), this island city would become the first multi-ethnic, upwardly mobile society on America's shores, a prototype of the kind of society that would be replicated throughout the country and around the world. It was no coincidence that those who, on 11 September 2001, wished to make a symbolic attack on the heart of American power chose the World Trade Center as their target. If what made America great was its ingenious openness to different cultures, the small triangle of land at the southern tip of Manhattan Island is the New World birthplace of that idea, the spot where it first took shape. Many Americans today – whether they live in the heartland of the continent or on Fifth Avenue – like to think of New York City as so wild and extreme in its cultural fusion that it's an anomaly in the United States, almost a foreign entity. This book offers an alternative view: that when you go beneath the level of myth and politics and high ideals, down to where real people live and interact, Manhattan is where America began.

The original European colony centred on Manhattan came to an end when England took it over in 1664, renaming it New York after James, Duke of York, brother of King Charles II, and folding it into its other American colonies. As far as the earliest American historians were concerned, that date marked the true beginning of the history of the region. The Dutch-led colony was almost immediately considered inconsequential. When the time came to memorialize US national origins, the English Pilgrims and Puritans of New England provided a better model. The Pilgrims' story was simpler and less messy, and had fewer pirates and prostitutes to explain away. It was easy enough to overlook the fact that the Puritans, having fled to American shores to escape religious persecution, instituted in their new territory a brutally intolerant regime, a grim theocratic monoculture about as far removed from what the country was to become as one can imagine.

The few early books written about the Dutch settlement had a brackish odour – appropriately enough, since even their authors viewed the colony as a backwater, cut off from the main current of history. Washington Irving's early nineteenth-century 'Knickerbocker' account – a historical burlesque never intended by its author to be taken as fact – muddied any attempt to understand what had actually gone on in the Manhattan-based settlement, and its existence was reduced by popular culture to a few random, floating facts: that it was once ruled by an irascible, peg-legged governor and, most infamously, that the Dutch bought the island from the Indians for 24 dollars' worth of household goods. Anyone who wondered about it beyond that may have surmised that the colony was too inept to keep records. As one historian put it, 'Original sources of information concerning the early Dutch settlers of Manhattan Island are neither many nor rich [for] . . . the Dutch wrote very little, and on the whole their records are meager.'

Skip ahead, then, to a day in 1973, when a 35-year-old scholar named Charles Gehring is led into a vault in the New York State Library and shown something that delights his eye as fully as a chest of emeralds would a pirate's. Gehring, a specialist in the Dutch language of the seventeenth century (an obscure topic in anyone's estimation), had just completed his doctoral dissertation and was casting about for a relevant job, which he knew wouldn't be easy to find, when fate smiled on him. Some years earlier Peter Christoph, curator of historical manuscripts at the library, had come across a vast collection of charred, mould-stippled papers stored in the archives. He knew what they were, and that they comprised a vast resource for American prehistory. They had survived wars, fire, flooding and centuries of neglect. Yet, remarkably, he doubted he would be able to bring them to the light of day. There was little interest in what was still considered an odd byway of history. He couldn't come up with funds to hire a translator – and in any event, there were few people in the world who could decipher the writings.

Christoph eventually came into contact with an influential American of Dutch descent, a retired brigadier general with the splendid name of Cortlandt van Rensselaer Schuyler. General Schuyler had recently overseen the building in Albany of Empire State Plaza, the central state government complex, for his friend Governor Nelson Rockefeller. Schuyler put in a call to Rockefeller, who was by now out of office and about to be called on by Gerald Ford to serve as his vice-president. Rockefeller made a few telephone calls, and a small amount of money was made available to begin the project. Christoph called Gehring and told him he had a job. So it was that while the nation was recovering from the mid-life crisis of Watergate, a window onto the period of its birth began to open.

What Charles Gehring received into his care in 1974 was twelve thousand sheets of rag paper covered with the crabbed, loopy script of seventeenth-century Dutch, which to the untutored eye looks something like a cross between our Roman letters and Arabic or Thai – writing largely indecipherable today even to modern Dutch speakers. On these pages, in words written 350 years ago in ink that has now partially faded into the brown of the decaying paper, an improbable gathering of Dutch, French, German, Swedish, Jewish, Polish, Danish, African,

American Indian and English characters comes to life. This repository of letters, deeds, wills, journal entries, council minutes and court proceedings comprises the official records of the settlement that grew up following Henry Hudson's 1609 voyage up the river that bears his name. Here, in their own words, were the first Manhattanites. Deciphering and translating the documents, turning them from the raw material of history into a resource accessible to historians, was, Dr Gehring knew, the task of a lifetime.

Twenty-six years later, Charles Gehring, now a 61-year-old grandfather with a wry grin and a soothing, caramelly baritone, was still at it when I met him in 2000. He had produced sixteen volumes of translation and had several more to go. For a long time he had laboured in isolation, the 'missing floor' of the state library building where he works serving as a nice metaphor for the way history has overlooked the Dutch period. But within the past several years, as the work has achieved a critical mass, a modest renaissance of scholarly interest in this colony has grown up around Dr Gehring and his collection of translations. As I write, historians are drafting doctoral dissertations on the material, and educational organizations are creating teaching guides for bringing the Dutch settlement into accounts of American colonial history.

Dr Gehring is not the first to attempt a translation of this archive. In fact, the long, bedraggled history of the records of the colony mirrors the way history has treated the colony itself. From early on, people recognized their importance. In 1801 a committee headed by none other than the vice-president, Aaron Burr, declared that 'measures ought to be taken to procure a translation,' but none were. In the 1820s a half-blind Dutchman with a shaky command of English came up with a massively flawed longhand translation, which then burned up in the famous 1911 fire that destroyed the state library. In the early twentieth century a highly skilled translator undertook to translate the whole corpus – only to see two years' worth of labour go up in the same flames. He suffered a nervous breakdown, and eventually abandoned the task.

Many of the more significant political documents of the colony were translated in the nineteenth century, and these became part of the historical record; but without the rest – the letters and journals and court cases about marital strife, business failures, cutlass fights, traders loading sloops with tobacco and furs, neighbours stealing each other's pigs; in short, without the stuff from which social history is written – this veneer of political documentation only reinforced the image of the colony as wobbly and inconsequential. Dr Gehring's work corrects that image, and changes the picture of American beginnings. Thanks to his work, historians are now realizing that the Dutch colony centred on Manhattan had, by the last two decades of its existence, become a vibrant, viable society – so much so that when the English took over Manhattan they kept its unusually flexible and accommodating structures in place, thus ensuring that the character of the earlier settlement would live on.

The idea that the Dutch made a key contribution to American history seems novel at first, but that is because early American history was written by Englishmen, who, throughout the seventeenth century, were locked in mortal combat with the Dutch. Looked at another way, however, the connection makes perfectly good sense. It has long been recognized that the Dutch Republic of the decades after 1600 was the most progressive and culturally diverse society in Europe. As Bertrand Russell once wrote, regarding its impact on intellectual history, 'It is impossible to exaggerate the importance of Holland in the seventeenth century, as the one country where there was freedom of speculation.' The Netherlands of the time was the melting pot of Europe, its policy of tolerance making it a haven for everyone from René Descartes and John Locke to exiled English royalty to peasants from across Europe. When this society founded a colony based on Manhattan Island, that colony was characterized by the same freedoms – of thought, belief, movement, trade – that existed in the home country. Those features helped make New York unique, and, in time, influenced America in some elemental ways. How that happened is what this book is about.

*

I came to this subject more or less by walking into it. I was living in the East Village of Manhattan, a neighbourhood that has long been known as an artistic and countercultural centre, a place famous for its nightlife and ethnic restaurants. But 350 years earlier it was an important part of the unkempt Atlantic Rim port of New Amsterdam. I often took my young daughter around the corner from our apartment building to the church of St Mark's-in-the-Bowery, where she would run around under the sycamores in the churchyard and I would study the faded faces of the tombstones of some of the city's earliest families. The most notable tomb in the yard – actually, it is built into the side of the church – is that of Peter Stuyvesant, the Dutch colony's most famous resident. Around the mid-seventeenth century this area was forest and meadow being cleared and planted as Bouwerie (or farm) Number One: the largest homestead on the island, and the one Stuyvesant claimed for himself. St Mark's is built near the site of his family chapel, in which he was buried. Throughout the nineteenth century New Yorkers insisted that the church was haunted by the old man's ghost; that at night you could hear the echoed clopping of his wooden leg as he paced its aisles, eternally ill at ease at having had to relinquish his settlement to the English. I never heard the clopping, but over time I began to wonder – not so much about Stuyvesant, who seemed too forbidding to be the object of such speculation, but about the original settlement. I wanted to know the island that those first Europeans found.

Eventually, I got in touch with Charles Gehring. I learned about the extraordinary documents in his keeping, and about the organization – the New Netherland Project – he had founded to promote interest in this neglected period of history. In the autumn of 2000 I attended a seminar he sponsored on the topic, and encountered dozens of specialists who were exploring this forgotten world, unearthing pieces of it that hadn't seen the light of day in centuries. They were digging into archives from Boston to Antwerp and turning up hitherto forgotten journals, voyage diaries and account books. The age of exploration itself was expanding under this new examination. In my interviews with Dr Gehring and others, I realized that historians were fashioning a new perspective on American prehistory, and also that no-one was attempting to draw together all the disparate elements, characters and legacies into a single narrative. In short, no-one was telling the story of the first Manhattanites.

It turns out, in fact, to be two stories. There is the small, ironic story that originally attracted me: that of men and women hacking out an existence in a remote wilderness that is today one of the most famously urban landscapes in the world, who would shoulder their muskets and go on hunting expeditions into the thick forests of what is now the skyscrapered labyrinth of midtown Manhattan. But go deeper into the material and you begin to appreciate the broader story. The origins of New York are not like those of most other American cities. Its first settlers were not isolated pioneers but characters playing parts in a drama of global sweep, a struggle for empire that would range across the seventeenth century and around the globe, and which, for better or worse, would create the structure of the modern world.

Moving back and forth from the individual struggles detailed in the records to the geopolitical events of the day, you can sense the dawning of the idea that would lead to the transformation of Manhattan into the centrepiece of the most powerful city in the world: that, of all the newly claimed regions whose exploitation was rapidly changing Europe – from the teeming cod fisheries off Newfoundland to the limitless extent of the North American plains and the sugar fields of Brazil – this one slender island, sitting in the perfect natural harbour on the coast of a vast unexplored land and at the mouth of the river that would become the vital highway into that continent, would prove the most valuable of all. Its location and topography – 'like a great natural pier ready to receive the commerce of the world', as one early writer described it – would make it the gate through which Europeans could reach the unimaginable immensity of the North American land mass. Possess it, and you control passage up the Hudson river, then west along the Mohawk river valley into the Great Lakes and the very heart of the continent. Later migration patterns proved the point; the Erie Canal, which created a water highway from the Hudson to the Great Lakes, resulted in the explosive growth of the midwest and cemented New York's position as the most powerful city in the nation. In the seventeenth century that was still far in the future; but one by one, in various ways, the major players in this story sensed the island's importance. They smelled its value. Thus Richard Nicolls, the British colonel who led a gunboat flotilla into New York harbour in August 1664 and wrested control of the island from Peter Stuyvesant, instantly termed it 'best of all His Majties Townes in America'.

So the story of Manhattan's beginnings is also the story of European exploration and conquest in the seventeenth century. And at the heart of the material I found a much smaller story: that of a very personal struggle between two men over the fate of a colony and the meaning and value of individual liberty. Their personal battle helped to ensure that New York, first under the English and then as an American city, would develop into a unique micro-civilization that would foster an intense stew of cultures and a wildly fertile intellectual, artistic and business environment.

One of the protagonists in this struggle, Peter Stuyvesant, has been portrayed by history as almost a cartoon character: peg-legged, cantankerous, a figure of comic proportions who would do his routine, draw a few laughs, and then leave the stage so that the real substance of American history could begin. But much of what was known about Stuyvesant before came from the records of the New England colonies. To New England, the Dutch colony centred on New Amsterdam was the enemy; so the portrait of Stuyvesant accepted by history was that drawn by his greatest detractors. In the New Netherland records, by contrast, Stuyvesant comes across as a complex, living individual: a tyrant certainly, but also a doting father and husband; a statesman who exhibits steel nerves and bold military intuition while holding almost no cards and being surrounded by enemies (English, Indians, Swedes, foes from within his own colony, even, in a sense, the directors of his sponsoring company in Amsterdam); a man who abhors unfairness – who publicly punishes Dutch colonists who cheat the Indians in business deals – but who, with the harshness of a hard-line Calvinist minister's son, tries to block Jews from settling in New Amsterdam. He is a tragic figure, undone by his own best quality, his steadfastness. But Stuyvesant didn't act in isolation. The colony's legacy revolves also around another figure of the period, a man named Adriaen van der Donck, who has been forgotten by history but who emerges as the hero of the story and who, I think, deserves to be ranked as an early American prophet, a forerunner of the revolutionary generation.

But if the colony's end points forward to the American society that was to come, its beginning is dominated by another figure – wilful, brooding, tortured – who harks back to an earlier era. Henry Hudson was a man of the Renaissance, and Manhattan's birth thus becomes a kind of bridge between these two worlds. So the story begins far from the Atlantic shore of America, in the heart of late Renaissance Europe.

All that said, what originally captivated me about the Dutch documents – that they offered a way to re-imagine New York City as a wilderness – stayed alive throughout my research. Above all, then, this book invites you to do the impossible: to strip from your mental image of Manhattan Island all associations of power, concrete and glass; to put time into full reverse, unfill the massive landfills and undo the extensive levelling programmes that flattened hills and filled gullies, to return streams from the underground sewers into which they were forced back to their original rushing or meandering course. To witness the return of waterfalls, to watch freshwater ponds form in place of asphalt intersections; to let buildings vanish and watch stands of pin oak, sweetgum, basswood and hawthorn take their place. To imagine the return of salt marshes, mudflats, grasslands; of leopard frogs, grebes, cormorants and bitterns, to discover newly pure estuaries encrusting themselves with scallops, lamp mussels, oysters, quahogs and clams. To see maple-ringed meadows become numbered with deer and the higher elevations ruled by wolves.

And then to stop the time machine, let it hover a moment on the southernmost tip of an island poised between the Atlantic Ocean and the civilization of Europe on one side and a virgin continent on the other; to let that moment swell, hearing the screech of gulls and the slap of waves and imagining these same sounds – waves and birds, waves and birds, with regular interruptions by wracking storms – unchanged for dozens of centuries.

And then let time start forward once again as something comes into view on the horizon. Sails.

Part I
'A Certain Island Named Manathans'

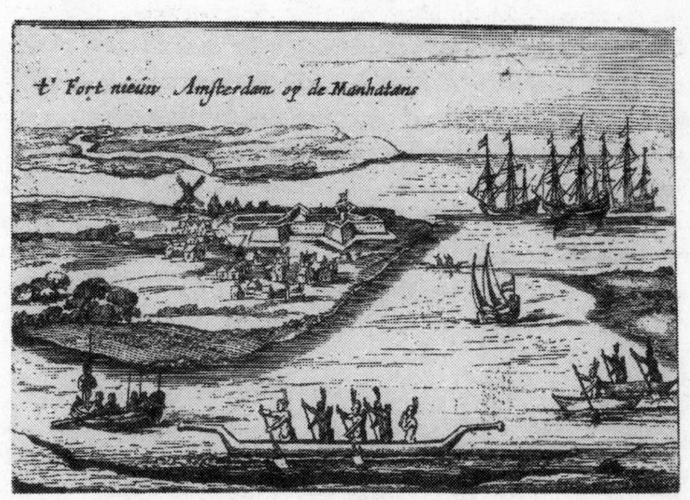

1
The Measure of Things

ON A LATE SUMMER'S DAY IN THE YEAR 1608, A GENTLEMAN of London made his way across that city. He was a man of ambition, intellect, arrogance and drive – in short, a man of his age. Like our own, his was an era of expanding horizons and a rapidly shrinking world, in which the pursuit of individual dreams led to new discoveries, which in turn led to newer and bigger dreams. His complicated personality – including periodic fits of brooding passivity that all but incapacitated him – was built around an impressive self-confidence, and at this moment he was almost certainly convinced that the meeting to which he was making his way would be of historic importance.

He walked west, in the direction of St Paul's Cathedral, which then as now dominated the skyline. But the structure in the distance was not the St Paul's of today, the serene, imperial building that signifies order and human reason, with the spirit of the Renaissance and the Enlightenment shining from its proud dome. His St Paul's had a hunkering tower in place of a dome (the steeple that had originally risen from the tower had been struck by lightning almost half a century before and hadn't been replaced); it was a dark, medieval church, which suited the medieval market town that London still was in the early seventeenth century. The streets through which he walked were narrow, shadowy, claustrophobic, sloping towards central sewer ditches; the houses that lined them were built of timber and walled with wattle and daub – it was a city made chiefly of wood.

Since we know his destination and have some notion of the whereabouts of his house, it is possible to trace a likely route Henry Hudson, ship's captain, would have taken on that summer day, on his way to an appointment with the directors of the Muscovy Company, funders of voyages of exploration and discovery. The widest thoroughfare from Tower Street Ward towards Cordwainer Street Ward was Tower Street. He would have passed first through a neighbourhood that, despite being within sight of the scaffold and gallows of the Tower itself, was an area of relatively new, 'divers fair and large houses', as John Stow, a contemporary chronicler, described them, several of which were owned by prominent noblemen.

On his left then came the dominating church of St Dunstan in the East, and a reminder of his heritage. The Muscovy Company had not only funded at least two of Henry Hudson's previous sea voyages; in its half-century of existence it had numbered several Hudsons on its rolls, including, among its founder members in 1555, another Henry Hudson, who rose from a humble 'skinner', or tanner, to become a wealthy member of society and an alderman of the City of London, and who may have been the explorer's grandfather. So our Henry Hudson was presumably born to the sea and to the company both, and inside this church he was now passing his Muscovy Company namesake lay, beneath a gilded alabaster stone inscribed:

Here lyeth Henry Heardsons corps,
Within this Tombe of Stone:
His Soule (through faith in Christ's death,)
to God in Heaven is gone.
Whiles that he lived an Alderman,
And Skinner was his state:
To Vertue bare hee all his love,
To vice he bare his hate.

If in his walk the seaman chose to make a detour down the hill past the church he would have come to the open expanse of the Thames, where the view upriver to the west was dominated by the span of London Bridge with its twenty stone arches, houses perched precariously along both sides of its course. Directly across the river, beckoning lowly and enticingly, lay Southwark, a wild outland and thus also the entertainment district, with brothels tucked into its alleys and, visible from here, the 'bear bayting' arena, which provided one of the most popular and satisfying distractions for the masses. Beyond it stood the rounded wooden structure of the Globe Theatre in its original incarnation. Indeed, somewhere over on the Southwark side at this very moment, amid the tradesmen, whores, 'sturdye Beggers' and 'Common Players in Enterludes' that populated the borough, Shakespeare himself – at forty-four a near-exact contemporary of Hudson – then at the height of his powers and fame as the leading dramatist of the day, was likely going about his business, or maybe sleeping off a night of sack at the Mermaid with his actor friends Richard Burbage and John Heminges, or brooding over the foolscap sheets of *Coriolanus*, which was written about this time and which, coming on the heels of the great tragedies, may have felt a bit hollow.

Tower Street became Little Eastcheap, which in turn merged into Candlewick and then Budge Row. Hudson's business lay here, in an imposing building called Muscovy House. The medieval look of the London of 1608 belied the fact that England's rise to global empire was under way, and one of the forces behind that rise lay behind these doors. From the bravado of its formal name – the Merchants Adventurers of England for the Discovery of Lands, Territories, Iles, Dominions, and Seigniories Unknown – one might be excused for thinking the Muscovy Company had been founded out of sheer, unstoppable exuberance. The original band of merchants and aristocrats who had formed it just over fifty years earlier included many of the most distinguished men then in London – the Lord High

Treasurer, the Steward of the Queen's Household, the Keeper of the Privy Seal, the Lord High Admiral – as well as sundry other knights and gentlemen. But while global exploration, the great intellectual and business opportunity of the day, had brought them all together, no-one considered the undertaking a swashbuckling adventure. It was desperation that drove them towards new horizons. The England of the 1540s had been a backwater, economically depressed, inward-looking, deep in the shadows of the great maritime empires of Spain and Portugal. Wool was the country's chief commodity, but English traders had been excluded from the major European markets for more than a century. Economic stagnation was bound up with intellectual stagnation: while the Renaissance was in full flower on the continent, English interest in the wider world was slim, and the few long voyages of exploration England had mounted were for the most part led by foreigners, such as the Venetian John Cabot (*né* Giovanni Cabotto). As maritime pioneers, the English lagged behind.

History traditionally links the rise of England in the latter sixteenth century with the accession to the throne of Queen Elizabeth I in 1558. But one could trace it to 1547, when an intellectually voracious twenty-year-old named John Dee did something countless students since have done: spent his summer abroad, and returned flush with new knowledge and insights. After an academic career at Cambridge in which he proved to be something of a mathematical genius, Dee travelled to the University of Louvain in what is today Belgium. The rich summer sun of the Brabant region might have been revelation enough, but Dee soon found himself in a lecture hall gazing at an object that was, to him, transcendent. The teacher was Gemma Frisius, a Flemish mathematician and charter of the heavens, and what Dee saw was a map astonishing in its level of detail, in the new lands it portrayed, even in its lettering. The Low Countries, he discovered, were miles ahead of his island in new learning.

Dee spent long candle-lit nights poring over Frisius' maps with a Flemish scholar named Gerhard Kremer. Kremer, an engraver by training, had, under the academic pen-name of Mercator, begun to make a name for himself ten years earlier by creating a map of Palestine that rendered the Holy Land with greater accuracy than had ever been achieved. Mercator was a genuine Renaissance man – a master cartographer, an engineer of telescopes, sextants, surveying equipment and other highly sensitive measuring devices, the author of a gospel concordance, promoter of the new italic typeface that made map print more legible – and in him Dee found a soulmate. In 1569 Mercator would publish the map that was to give him his immortality, rendering latitude and longitude as straight lines, the meridians of longitude evenly spaced and the distances between the parallels of latitude increasing in size as one approached the poles. It solved a cumbersome problem of navigating at sea, because with it sailors could plot and follow a straight course rather than constantly recalculating their position. (The Mercator projection is still a feature of navigational maps, although at the time it was introduced some mariners were as confused as later generations of schoolchildren would be by the distortions in size it caused.)

In a nice foreshadowing of the complicated intercourse between the Low Countries and the British Isles that would shape the next century, when Dee returned to London he brought with him maps, measuring instruments and globes, created by Mercator and Frisius, that would help spark England's rise to global prominence. What Dee's English colleagues found most intriguing about the maps and globes was an area most people would ignore: the top, what we call the Arctic Circle. Frisius' map, oriented as if looking down from the North Star, showed a distinct open channel cutting across the Arctic, self-confidently labelled in Latin *Fretum trium fratrum*. The sight of the boldly indicated Strait of the Three Brothers must have made Dee's English friends gasp. The Holy Grail for all learned and adventuresome minds was the discovery of a short passage to the riches of Asia. Finding it would repay investors many times over; for the English, it would vault their economy out of the middle ages and into the European vanguard. The legend of the Strait of the Three Brothers was confused even at that time, but it appears to have been based on the adventures of the Corte Real brothers, Portuguese mariners who explored the area around Newfoundland at the beginning of the sixteenth century and who, according to some reports, had sighted, or perhaps even sailed, the fabled passage to Asia before two of them vanished into Arctic oblivion. (Ironically, the Spanish also had a theory about this mythical strait, only they called it the Englishmen's Strait.) Now here it was on Frisius' map, thanks apparently to his contacts with Portuguese mariners; and it was on Mercator's globe as well, labelled simply *fretum arcticum*, Arctic Strait. For the astonished English observers, seeing the thing in print, seeing its coasts and coves delicately but decisively rendered, confirmed its reality.

Fate, it seemed, had brought together the men, the means and the time. The solution to England's twin crises of economy and spirit was *out there*. So the nation's leaders formed a business circle, chipping in twenty-five pounds per share and raising a total of six thousand pounds.

With the principals lined up and funds ready, it remained only to choose the likeliest route – either the one indicated on Frisius' map or one of several others that were now being proposed with equal confidence. The imperative was to find a northern passage, both because such a short cut would render obsolete the Spanish and Portuguese monopoly on the southern hemisphere and because any northern peoples encountered along the way would be more likely buyers for English wool. That an Arctic sea route existed was beyond anyone's doubt. The universal belief among the intelligentsia in something we know to be a physical impossibility in wooden sailing vessels rested on several arguments, such as the one put forth by the Dutch minister of religion and geographer Peter Plancius that 'near the pole the sun shines for five months continually; and although his rays are weak, yet on account of the long time they continue, they have sufficient strength to warm the ground, to render it temperate, to accommodate it for the habitation of men, and to produce grass for the nourishment of animals.'

The name by which the company became known gives away what happened on the first voyage it financed. In 1553 a doughty mariner named Richard Chancellor took the north-eastern route, and while he failed to discover a passage to the Orient, he became the first Englishman of the era to make landfall at Russia. The so-called Muscovy trade that ensued – in which the English found a ready market for their wool, and imported hemp, sperm whale oil and furs from the realm of Ivan the Terrible – was so profitable that for a time the search for a northern route to Asia was largely abandoned.

The company expanded, and so did the nation. Elizabeth acceded to the throne; Drake circumnavigated the globe; Shakespeare wrote. When in 1588 Philip II of Spain launched an invasion fleet bound for England, intending to bring the island into his empire and win its people back to Roman Catholicism, the undersized English navy shocked the world by crushing the Armada. The aftermath of the victory was one of those moments when people suddenly realize they are living in a new era. Theirs wasn't a dark and chilly island after all, the English were informed by their great poet, but a 'precious stone set in the silver sea.'

By the early 1600s, however, the wheel had taken another turn. The queen was dead, and the Russia trade had fallen off. Faced once again with financial crisis, the Muscovy Company's directors made a decision to return to their original purpose. They would resurrect the Renaissance dream and commit themselves anew to discovering a northern passage to Asia.

The man to whom they now turned to renew the quest is not the protagonist of this story, but the forerunner, the one who would make it possible. In the ranks of legendary explorers,

Henry Hudson has been slighted: not celebrated in his time by the English public as Francis Drake or Martin Frobisher or John Cabot had been; not given nearly the amount of ink that history has devoted to Columbus or Magellan. There is a logic of personality in this. Drake had defined manhood for an era, and the Italian Cabot had a feckless charm (he was in the habit, after his celebrated return from the New World, of promising people he met in taverns that he would name islands for them), but when we come to Henry Hudson we see only a dark and moody figure hovering behind the records, one seemingly more comfortable in the shadows of history. A new appreciation for the Dutch colony in North America, however, compels a reappraisal of the man whose forceful if erratic decision-making rerouted the flow of history.

Nothing is known of the early stages of Hudson's career, but the fact that he is a ship's captain when we encounter him in 1608 indicates that he had by then had a lengthy one. It's reasonable to assume that he had served in the defeat of the Armada twenty years earlier, though we have no information on this. The Muscovy Company tended to take on boys as apprentices and have them work through one or more aspects of the business: bureaucrat, 'factor' (i.e. agent) or sailor. Thus one Christopher Hudson, who rose to the position of governor of the company from 1601 to 1607 and who some historians have thought was probably Henry Hudson's uncle, had worked his way up in the sales and marketing line, serving as a company representative in Germany in his youth. Henry Hudson was in his forties when he stepped into the light of history: a seasoned mariner, a man with a strong and resourceful wife and three sons, a man born and raised not only to the sea but to the quest for a northern passage to Asia – indeed, a man who, brought up from infancy on the legends of his predecessors, probably couldn't help but be obsessed by it.

The fire of obsession was fanned in him, as in the country at large, by a compatriot named Richard Hakluyt. Hakluyt, a consultant to the Muscovy Company, was another of the Elizabethan era's multifaceted characters: part journalist, part popularizer, part lionizer, above all a zealot for the internationalist cause in England. In the 1580s he began gathering log books, journals and other records of voyages, and he published the whole lot of them in repeated waves – the main body under the title *The Principal Navigations Voyages Traffiques and Discoveries of the English Nation*, which came out, with impeccable timing, shortly after the defeat of the Armada – creating a steadily building crescendo of popular enthusiasm for English adventures at sea. The result was to make England aware of itself in an international context, to see itself among the European nations casting outward in a new age, an age of discovery. Hakluyt exhorted his countrymen to be proud that they were living in 'an age wherein God hath raised so general a desire in the youth of this realm to discover all parts of the face of the earth'.

Thanks to Hakluyt, mariners now saw themselves in historical terms. Because of Hakluyt, Hudson – a determined and self-possessed man to begin with – openly hungered for a place on the list that included Columbus, Magellan, Cabot, Cortes and Da Gama. And for Hudson there was only one route to this glory. He would be the one to locate at last – after the failures (glorious failures, but failures still) of Columbus, Cabot, Chancellor, Frobisher, Cartier, Verrazzano – that fabled ribbon of icy blue water, sail through it, emerge into the nutmeg-scented air of Cathay, and single-handedly open the planet wide. He believed he would be the one.

He would be wrong in this. And yet, fate being what it is, his dream of achievement would come true – bounteously, and far more strangely than he could have imagined. Fate would make him the accidental patron saint not just of a grand city that would rise in the future to claim the somewhat presumptuous title of capital of the world but, with it, of a new kind of society that would become a model for the world of a distant century. A wavering but unbroken chain would stretch from him to a far-off mélange of skyscrapers and bodegas, dim sum and hip-hop, supers and subways, limos and eggcreams and finance and fashion – the messy catalogue of ingredients that, stewed together over time, would comprise a global capital, twenty-first-century style. To the extent any individual could, he would be a fulcrum on which history would turn: from a world of wood and steel to one of silicon and plastic.

*

Hudson's first voyage was pure madness. While geographers debated whether the elusive passage to Asia lay to the north-west, via Canada, or the north-east, around Russia, what Hudson attempted in his first command was something fantastically bolder and far more ridiculous than either of these, something that no human being had ever tried: to go straight up, over the top of the world. He was relying on an 'established' theory, first proposed eighty years before by Robert Thorne, a merchant–adventurer who argued that in addition to finding the ice melt away as he neared the pole, the lucky sailor who ventured across the top of the world would benefit from the 'perpetual clearness of the day without any darkness of the night'. Still, while daylight is handy, deliberately to steer a 70-foot wooden boat manned by a crew of twelve and powered only by wind straight north on a direct course for the top of the world, defying the six million square miles of Arctic ice shelf, proposing to slice straight across it and come careening down the other side of the planet – the nerve of it beggars the imagination. No wonder that on the morning of 19 April 1607, Hudson and his tiny crew, including his young son John, whom he was probably in the process of training just as he had been trained, stepped out of the weak spring sunlight and into the dark, ancient interior of the Church of St Ethelburga just inside Bishopsgate (apparently successfully ignoring the tap-houses crowding around the door of the church: the Angel, the Four Swans, the Green Dragon, the Black Bull), took their places among the congregation and beseeched the God of their forefathers to bless their endeavour.

Even more remarkable than Hudson's decision to attempt such a voyage was the fact that he survived it. Slicing through fog and ice, living on bear and seal (at one point the crew fell sick from rotten bear meat), surviving vicious storms and the horror of a whale attempting to surface from under the keel of their ship, they made it above 80 degrees north, within six hundred miles of the North Pole, before Hudson noted drily, 'This morning we saw that we were compassed in with Ice in abundance . . . And this I can assure at present . . . by this way there is no passage.'

By any normal measure the voyage would have been considered a failure, but these were not normal times: it was now the seventeenth century, there was a vast new world out there, and entrepreneurs and ships' captains knew that crossing one false path off the list was a form of progress. Far from considering Hudson's foray a failure (for one thing, his report of 'many whales' off Spitzbergen Island led to a massive and lucrative whaling enterprise there in the following years, and, predictably, the decimation of the whale population), the company, immediately on his return in September 1607, signed him up to attack the problem again the next season.

Hudson spent the winter at his London home, plunging into his charts and letters from fellow mariners and geographers, warming himself at his own hearth and in the company of his family, laying plans, perhaps meeting up with Hakluyt himself – the two had by now become friends – to discuss options. The following season sees him setting off straight away, on 22 April 1608, in the same Muscovy Company ship, the *Hopewell*, this time with a crew of fourteen, sitting in his closet-like captain's cabin, carefully putting pen to the page of his log book as they pull away from the Thames-side docks, heart thrumming with the high adrenaline of setting forth, as he records dutifully: 'We set sayle at Saint Katherines, and fell downe to Blacke wall.'

He had a new course this time: north-east. It had been attempted by others, including his Muscovy Company predecessors, but the directors were still of the belief that it was to the north of Russia that the best chance of reaching Asia lay. Hudson himself may have been doubtful – he had reason to believe the north-west was more likely – but he was willing to follow their wishes. Or so it seemed. The 'failure' of his second voyage is less interesting than what happened on 6 July, after he had concluded it was impossible to continue (on entering the strait he had pinned his hopes on he writes with awe, 'it is so full of ice that you will hardly thinke it'). Unable to find a way around the islands of Nova Zembla (today Novaya Zemlya in the Russian Arctic), he was now 'out of hope to find passage by the North-east', and so proposed to alter course completely, tear up the mission directive from the company and have a go at the north-west. After slaving for ten weeks against the raw elements of the Arctic, his crew, with good sense, baulked at the idea of taking a detour straight across the Atlantic and into a wholly new wilderness. A near-mutiny ensued; Hudson was forced to remove his gaze from the distant horizon of his obsession and focus instead on the human beings in front of him on the deck. He backed down. They returned to London.

No sooner did he arrive than he was busy readying himself for his next expedition. He had momentum now: two voyages in two successive seasons; two routes down, and one to go. He was convinced that he was homing in on the passage, that the puzzle that had occupied Europe for the length of the Renaissance was about to be solved. The answer, it now seemed certain, lay in the misty, all-but-unknown region that was only recently now beginning to be labelled on maps as America.

At around this time – possibly before the 1608 voyage – he received letters from his friend and fellow explorer the considerably larger-than-life John Smith, who had fought in Hungary against the Turks, been captured and sold into slavery in Istanbul, won the heart of his female captor, escaped to Transylvania via Russia and trekked across north Africa – all before his twenty-fifth birthday. Not content with such a record, in 1607 Smith spearheaded the founding of a colony in Virginia that would become the first permanent European settlement on the North American coast (Walter Raleigh's Roanoke colony, which broke ground in 1587, had vanished by the time relief forces arrived in 1590). Here he and his comrades were now living in a hell on earth (only 38 of the 150 original colonists survived the first winter); and from here Smith sent Hudson maps of the North American coast, together with certain theories he had been developing. These were precisely what Hudson wanted to hear and conformed with a theory of his own: that a sea or river somewhere to the north of Virginia gave out onto the Sea of Cathay. (Smith's information seems to have come from Native Americans who talked of a great ocean accessible via the Hudson river – presumably the Great Lakes, which could be reached via portage through the Mohawk river valley.)

Thus we find Hudson where we met him at the beginning of this chapter, shortly after making landfall in late August or early September 1608, about to step into Muscovy House – in starched ruff collar and embroidered jerkin, perhaps, clothing suitable for a formal interview – for his obligatory meeting with the company directors. His mind was apparently in turmoil. On the one hand, Smith's information buttressed his belief that the goal was within his grasp. But Samuel Purchas, a director of the company and, like Hakluyt, a popularizer of England's sea ventures (it is from him that most of our knowledge of Hudson's voyages comes), on meeting up with him one day immediately after his return, found him 'sunk into the lowest depths of the Humour of Melancholy, from which no man could rouse him. It mattered not that his Perseverance and Industry had made England the richer by his maps of the North. I told him he had created Fame that would endure for all time, but he would not listen to me.'

This was completely in character: Hudson seems to have typified the figure of the man of energy and obsession, wracked by periods of despair. As he entered Muscovy House, the reality of recent failure and the possibility of imminent glory must have hammered at his brain from opposite sides. He seems to have thrived on such tensions, such contradictions: seeking to expand human civilization by immersing himself in the void of nature; strolling in the easy centre of culture and society while the too-wild tang of rotten bear meat still lay on his tongue.

We can't follow him inside. The building itself, along with all the records of the Muscovy Company, was destroyed in the Great Fire of 1666. If there was a corporate record of the meeting, of who voted against funding him again and why, it is lost. We can only imagine his shock, then, when they rejected him, gave up on the great quest, abandoned one of their own. Maybe they had grown leery of his monomania and propensity for sparking mutiny. Possibly the Muscovy Company was running out of steam (it would soon be subject to the seventeenth-century version of a corporate takeover by the younger and more vigorous East India Company).

But Hudson had barely enough time to sink into the depression to which a psychologist might have diagnosed him as susceptible before a new, unexpected avenue stretched open before him. Shortly after stepping out of the company's mansion into the glare of a summer day, he found himself accosted by a courtly, discreet, 72-year-old gentleman. Emanuel van Meteren had been born in Antwerp, but when he was fifteen his family moved to London, and here he had lived ever since, acquiring an English education and an English sense of refinement, but remaining essentially Dutch. For the last thirty years he had served as the Dutch consul in London, and was on intimate terms with many of the prominent businessmen, aristocrats and explorers in both countries. He had learned that the Muscovy Company was dropping Hudson – indeed with his closeness to the directors of the company, he may have known before Hudson did.

In the very act of putting his dignified presence before Hudson, Van Meteren revealed the true scope of interest in the mariner's obsession. It wasn't a matter of one ship's captain and the company he worked for. Hudson's quest was tied into the historic current washing over the powers of Europe, the self-conscious need to blast out of the Mediterranean paradigm that had held them through the middle ages and to reach around the globe: to discover, exploit, expand, do business. Van Meteren spoke on behalf of certain Dutch merchants, who were desirous, seeing that Hudson's own countrymen had lost faith, of abetting his ambition. In short, they wanted to hire him.

The mariner apparently suffered no pangs of disloyalty, either to the country of his birth or the company that had nurtured him. Delaying only to attend the christening, in mid-September, of a granddaughter (Alice, child of his son Oliver), Hudson boarded a ship to cross the Channel, having no idea that his contribution to history would come not from discovering the passage to the Orient but as a result of this very twist of fate, this kink in his chain of bold, brilliant and majestically misguided voyages.

2
The Pollinator

IN THE SEVENTEENTH CENTURY, TO ENTER AMSTERDAM WAS to be softly assaulted in the senses. There was the squeal of seabirds and the slap of oars; a stew of smells: cabbage, frying pancakes, the miasma of the canals. There was the sensation, on entering the ultramarine opacity of the canal grid, of gliding into an orderly, enclosed space. The slender-bricked houses made an elegant but modest statement, their gabled tops framing and taming the sky. The cobbled quaysides were alive with workers wheeling barrows or wobbling under the strain of sacks being loaded into lighters; women with billowing skirted bottoms scrubbed stoops and sprinkled them with fat handfuls of sand; everywhere there were dogs and horses and children.

As Henry Hudson arrived in Amsterdam in the autumn of 1608, the world around him was turning. The Spanish and Portuguese empires that had had their way with South America and the East Indies for more than a century were in decline, and two new powers were rising in parallel. The Dutch were growing in might alongside the English, and would peak sooner, giving the world Rembrandt, Vermeer, the microscope, the tulip, the stock exchange, and the modern notion of home as a private, intimate place.

The Dutch, of course, were of the sea; keeping it back was a way of life, and water was their element. They were the continent's shipbuilders, sailors, pilots, traffickers, and this was their key to empire. When the union of Spain and Portugal in 1580 closed off to Dutch traders the port of Lisbon (through which they had long received goods from Asia, which they then resold throughout Europe), the Dutch merchants took the drastic step of stocking their vessels with gunpowder and cannonballs and going directly at the Iberian supply source, the islands of the East Indies, more than a year's journey away by the southern route. They arrived with guns blazing at the Portuguese military and trading posts there, and took them, converting Java, Sumatra and the Malaysian peninsula into outposts of a new empire. When the first successful convoy returned home in 1599, its hulls packed with six hundred thousand pounds of pepper and an equal amount of nutmeg, cloves and other spices, Amsterdammers were stunned at the plenitude; church bells throughout the city rang in celebration. The Dutch rise to world power had begun.

Geography shapes character, and the character of the city Hudson entered was vastly different from the one he had just left. This single point helps to explain why Manhattan, which owes its originating contours to Hudson, would become such a different place from, say, Boston or Philadelphia. One difference between England and the Dutch Republic was contained in the abstract and to our ears wan-sounding noun *tolerance*. England was on the verge of a century of religious conflict that would see royal heads roll and crowds of ordinary citizens flee. The Dutch – traders and sailors, whose focus was always *out there*, on other lands, other peoples and their products – had always had to put up with differences. Just as foreign goods moved in and out of their ports, so foreign ideas (and for that matter, foreign people) did as well. To talk about 'celebrating diversity' is to be wildly anachronistic, but in the Europe of the time the Dutch stood out for their relative acceptance of foreignness, of religious differences, of odd sorts. One example of this could be found in Hudson's new employers, the men who made up the

Amsterdam Chamber of the Dutch East India Company: some Catholic, some Protestant, many of them refugees from persecution in the Spanish-controlled southern provinces or elsewhere who had come to Amsterdam, wedged themselves into society and worked their way up. Over the course of the seventeenth century, the Dutch Republic would give intellectual or religious haven to Descartes, Locke and the English Pilgrims, who lived in Leiden for twelve years before setting out to found a new Jerusalem in New England. The philosopher Baruch Spinoza was a product of Amsterdam's vigorous Jewish community. To this day, Amsterdammers' proud slang term for their city is Mokum, the centuries-old Jewish name for it; and Amsterdam argot for 'see you later' is the Yiddishism 'de mazzel'.

Landscape has a political dimension too, and the low-lying provinces – the Netherlands is really one vast river delta – were always an easy target for invaders. The French expanded into them in the 1300s; then, in 1495, three years after Columbus' transatlantic voyage, Spain added the Low Countries to its empire. As Hudson entered Amsterdam, the United Provinces of the Netherlands had been fighting for independence from their Spanish overlords for nearly four decades, and the long war had toughened them, focused them, made them militarily and economically stronger. Before, they had been a diffuse grouping, each province tending to go its own way; but the Catholic tyranny of Spain – complete with the bloody efforts of the Inquisition to force Protestants to return to the fold – united them. It also gave them a Father of the Country in the person of Willem I, the Prince of Orange, known to history as William the Silent. The assassination of this heroic military leader in 1584 gave Groningen farmers, Frisian horse traders, Zeeland shipwrights, and the cosmopolitan artists and merchants of Amsterdam a common focal point. They also had their own Minutemen, called the Sea Beggars, a scrappy band of sailors who against all odds defeated the precision-drilled Spanish regulars to take back the coastal town of Briel, giving the Dutch their first hope of throwing off the foreign yoke.

Maybe the most striking difference between the Dutch and the English was that the new government formed by the seven United Provinces of the Netherlands during their struggle was something utterly anomalous in Europe: in the midst of the great age of monarchies, stretching from Elizabeth Tudor to Louis XIV, the Dutch carved out a republic. It wasn't a republic in the full Enlightenment-era sense – it wasn't of the idealistic, self-righteously stubborn, 'we hold these truths to be self-evident' model that gave rise to the American republic; it had come into being in a piecemeal way, as towns joined together to protect their interests. But it was a bottom-up system: it came from the people. The French had their intricately intertwined systems of fashion and protocol, the Spanish court its tottering 'magnificent fountain' of patronage, and the English their class system, with an aristocracy rooted in the nation's soul. The Dutch of the seventeenth century distinguished themselves by taking pride in being ordinary. They had a cultural distaste for monarchy and ostentation – as one writer of the time put it, a 'strenuous spirit of opposition to a sovereign concentrated in one head'. They believed in hard work, in earning an honest guilder, in personal modesty. They thought the English preoccupation with witches was paranoia.

The Dutch dressed so simply that foreigners complained that on the streets of Amsterdam it was impossible to tell the difference between a city magistrate and a simple shopkeeper. In the early part of the century Amsterdam had few grand houses; the homes that lined the Herengracht and Brouwersgracht were still modest, single-family affairs. Fantastically for the time, even the prosperous didn't believe in keeping fleets of servants: a wealthy family might have one or two. A French naval commander, boarding a Dutch frigate, was appalled to find its captain sweeping his own cabin. There were noble families, but they had nothing like the power wielded by other European aristocrats. Instead, authority was vested in those who made things happen: businessmen and local magistrates. Over time, human nature being what it is, these men would create a kind of merchant nobility, sometimes even buying titles from cash-poor foreigners, but this in itself underscores the point. Upward mobility was part of the Dutch character: if you were bright and worked hard and took your opportunities, you rose in stature. Today that is a byword of a healthy and dynamic society; in the seventeenth century it was weird.

The whole package – the Founding Father, the young and vibrant republic, the war for independence, the hard-nosed, practical populace that disdains monarchies and maintains a frank acceptance of differences – has a ring of familiarity to it, which was not lost on the American founding fathers of the next century. As John Adams, in his capacity as the first American ambassador to the Netherlands, wrote in 1782: 'The Originals of the two Republics are so much alike, that the History of one seems but a Transcript from that of the other; so that every Dutchman instructed in the subject, must pronounce the American revolution just and necessary, or pass a Censure upon the greatest Actions of his immortal Ancestors.' Some of the similarities are inevitable (don't all rebellions have heroes and martyrs?) but the persistence in America of the most elemental one – a cultural sensibility that included a frank acceptance of difference and the belief that individual achievement matters more than birthright – is, as I hope this book will show, at least in part the result of a kind of genetic transfer from the one culture to the other, a planting of Dutch notions in one vital region of the future United States, from which they would percolate into the American character. And the unlikely and unwitting carrier of this cultural gene was here, this man, in this place.

Hudson was comfortable in Holland;* he may even have spent

* Properly speaking, Holland referred not to the Dutch Republic but to its chief province, with Amsterdam as its hub; the other six provinces in the seventeenth-century state were Utrecht, Gelderland, Overijssel, Zeeland, Friesland and Groningen.

an earlier portion of his life in the country. He had friends here. One was Joost de Hondt, an engraver and mapmaker who acted as Hudson's interpreter in the contract negotiations and in whose house in The Hague Hudson stayed through the winter. Another was the geographer Peter Plancius (he of the polar sun-power theory), with whom Hudson spent long evenings that winter, poring over maps and stray bits of information or hearsay. No man in the Dutch provinces knew more about the shape of the world than Plancius. He was one of those who believed the route to Asia lay to the north-east, but Hudson was adamant that the passage was most likely to be found to the north-west, and he got further support for this from an item Plancius had somehow got his hands on, and which he now gave to Hudson: the journal of the Englishman George Weymouth, who had made a try at the north-west route seven years earlier and had recorded detailed observations.

Like the English, the Dutch had had a longstanding interest in finding a northern route to Asia. Fifteen years earlier, the Dutch explorer Willem Barents had made three attempts at a north-east passage, and even his having frozen to death on his last voyage had not dulled local enthusiasm for the project. The Dutch East India Company had sprung into being as a result of the recent, extravagantly successful voyages to south-east Asia, and would soon field a vast fleet and no fewer than five thousand sailors. It was better organized and had more money at its disposal than the Muscovy Company. If, as the company's intelligence reports had it, Hudson was on the verge of discovering the long-sought northern passage to Asian markets, he was the man they wanted.

But in this they were not alone. Hudson arrived in the Dutch Republic at a decisive moment, when all of Europe was focused on these low-lying provinces. Two years before, in a thicket of masts and gunpowder discharge and carnage, Dutch ships under Jacob van Heemskerck had blasted their way through the Spanish fleet as it lay moored off Gibraltar, providing a coda to

England's defeat of the Armada twenty years earlier and finally bringing the Spanish king, Philip III, to the bargaining table. While Hudson was sitting down to negotiate a contract with the Dutch merchants, representatives from all the nations of Europe were gathered 35 miles away at The Hague to hammer out a truce in which all had a stake. If such an agreement could be worked out it would be tantamount to recognition of the United Provinces as a nation in its own right.

So while Hudson sat at East India House overlooking the green, still water of the Gelderse Kade and negotiating with the Dutch merchants, spies from delegations to the truce negotiations at The Hague were paying close attention, for the two sets of discussions were connected. The main issue of the conference was a truce, but the subtext was the rising Dutch power. The Spanish and Portuguese representatives were still fuming at the Dutch inroads in Asia, and wanted these to be rolled back as a condition of peace. England felt the same. James I, the bookish and ungainly Scotsman who had replaced Elizabeth on the throne, had directed his representatives at The Hague to push for an end to Dutch trading in the east. The VOC – as the Dutch East India Company would become known worldwide, the initials of its Dutch name, de Verenigde Oostindische Compagnie, emblazoned on ships in all ports of the world – had a charter that gave it a monopoly on Asian trade carried out via the southern route only; so if someone were to discover a northern back door to Asia, the company's dominance would be open to challenge. Hence the general eagerness to get to Hudson.

Before the VOC and Hudson reached an agreement, others made a play for him. Pierre Jeannin, who headed the French delegation at the negotiations, dashed off a missive to King Henri IV, informing him of a development that had ramifications for the 'present negotiations to obtain a truce for the States General'. There was word, Jeannin reported, that the Dutch were about to close a deal with the English mariner Hudson, who was on the verge of discovering a short route to

Asia. (Perpetuating the Plancius myth, Jeannin gossiped that Hudson 'has found that the more northwards he went, the less cold it became'.) Jeannin put forward the plan hatched by a renegade Dutch merchant named Isaac le Maire, who proposed stealing Hudson away from the VOC and signing him to a pact with a French-led consortium, and added, 'there are also many rich merchants who will gladly join in.'

By now the English were angry that they had let go of Hudson. But the Dutch merchants got wind of the French activity, and promptly signed a contract with the mariner. The frenzy of activity among the major European players heightens the notion of Hudson as a fulcrum: they all sensed this sailor was *going somewhere*, that the future lay in his direction, and they wanted to go with him.

*

To sea then, launching from near the squat brick tower called the Schreierstoren, where the city walls fronted the water and where generations of Dutch women had stood gazing nervously out, waiting for their men to return. Hudson was ready by the spring, in time for the sailing season of 1609. He had a new ship, the 85-foot *Halve Maen* ('Half Moon'), and a crew of sixteen, half English and half Dutch. He had orders, too: to find a north-*eastern* route. He must have pushed strongly for the north-west, for the company directors pushed back; in the instructions Hudson carried the Dutch merchants warned him 'to think of discovering no other routes or passages' than the north-eastern. In his best fashion, he disobeyed them utterly. After taking a flyer along the coast of Norway in the general direction of Russia, he went along with a gale blowing westward – and kept going. He was about to voyage three thousand miles in the opposite direction from that he had promised to take: behaviour inconceivable in another ship's captain, but for him, pretty standard. Thus, his historic journey was truly of his own doing, even if its result was something beyond his intention.

Having persuaded his crew to reverse course in mid-ocean, he had two options: to follow George Weymouth's journal, which suggested a true north-west passage, navigating the islands and ice floes of what is today northern Canada, or John Smith's notes, indicating that the passage was in fact not north-west at all, but south-west, straight through the North American continent. He followed Smith. After approaching Newfoundland, he hugged the coast southward for six weeks, until he came within 10 miles of the Jamestown settlement of Virginia, and his friend. Then, abruptly, he stopped. He knew perfectly well where he was, for his English first mate recorded in his journal, 'This is the entrance into the Kings River in Virginia, where our Englishmen are.' They were at the mouth of the Chesapeake, where the Chesapeake Bay Bridge now crosses. Hudson was aware that he was sailing for a Dutch concern, and would probably have felt neither welcome nor comfortable docking at the English settlement; he had probably come to this point to fix his position. So, after swinging further south to Cape Hatteras Island, he headed north, and on 28 August came into Delaware Bay – the first European ever to do so. No sooner had he entered the bay than the crew sighted treacherous shoals and sand bars. The captain quickly determined that this river could not be the wide, deep channel that led to Cathay.

And so they continued north: misty mornings, bloody sunsets, a stretch of coast like a long, smooth cut; surf eternally pounding the belt of sand; wild silence beyond. They were aware they were shouldering a new world, impossibly dark, utterly unknown, of imponderable dimension and with no clear means of access.

Then they felt something happening. Rounding a hooked point, they were startled at what they perceived to be the mouths of three rivers. Cliffs rose up – the land 'very pleasant and high, and bold to fall withal'. They were in the outer reaches of New York harbour, riding the coast of Staten Island. Fish streamed thickly around them: salmon, mullet, wraith-like rays. They anchored and went ashore, marvelling at primordial oaks and 'an abundance of blue plums'.

Then, from nowhere, people appeared. They approached the newcomers frankly, dressed in skins, peaceably and with an air of dignity, offering corn bread and green tobacco. In 1801 the Moravian missionary John Heckewelder interviewed a Long Island Indian and published an account of Hudson's arrival from the Indian perspective. The story, supposedly handed down through generations of Delaware Indians, echoes the account given by Hudson's mate Robert Juet of the first encounter, depicting it as peaceable, wary, curious. The Indian told of sighting 'a large house of various colors' floating on the water (Dutch ships were indeed vividly painted with geometric motifs). Like Juet's version, the Indian story has the first meeting taking place on land, after several of the visitors, including their leader, had rowed ashore. The Indian story adds that the leader of the newcomers was dressed in a 'red coat all glittering with gold lace' – a nice and by no means incongruous addition to the portrait of Hudson.

Out came the products. Hemp, dried currants, oysters, beans on the one side; knives, hatchets and beads on the other. Over the next three days, as the ship explored an intricate mesh of islands, bays and rivers, making the rounds of Brooklyn, Staten Island and coastal New Jersey, there would be two violent encounters with Indians, Juet claims initiated by the Indians. People died. One cannot help noting that immediately Europeans entered the watery perimeter of what would become New York City, these two things take place: trade and violence.

Hudson then sailed his small, three-masted wooden vessel into the coliseum-like interior of the harbour – 'a very good harbor for all windes'. From his perch on the high poop-deck, looking down on his crew, he gave the order to proceed upriver. His heart must have quickened as the vista unfolded before him. 'The River is a mile broad: there is very high Land on both sides,' wrote Juet: it was as likely a channel into the other side of the world as one could hope for. Upriver, they encountered more natives: 'a very loving people . . . and we were well taken care of'. Hudson went ashore with them, visiting their circular house made of bark. 'The land is the finest for cultivation that I ever in my life set foot upon,' he wrote. He and his men noted more offerings from the locals: furs.

Then it ended. The river grew narrow and shallow. Its water was sweet, no longer salty. Asia did not lie over there. They turned south again, and there were more skirmishes with the Indians of the southern reaches of the river. It's not certain if Hudson was aware that the land they 'rode quietly' past one rainy night was an island – in the first written record of the name, Juet refers to 'the side of the river called *Manna-hata*'. In any case, while Hudson dutifully noted the possibilities for trade – the grandness of the harbour and the river, the toehold they would give one on the continent – his own gaze never left the horizon of his obsession. He headed for home, empty-handed.

Strangely, Hudson did not sail straight to Amsterdam but put into port in England, at Dartmouth. He may have done so to disembark some of his English crew – once again there had been loud grumbling on the voyage; once again a crew had bickered among themselves while the captain kept his head in the clouds. At any rate, an international skirmish ensued. His contractual obligation was to submit all charts, log books and notes to his employers in Amsterdam, but the English authorities tried to stop him; they detained Hudson bodily, and got a look at at least some of his records. International spies were still following him. 'Juan Hudson,' a Spanish spy wrote to Philip III less than a month after the *Halve Maen* pulled into Dartmouth, 'has . . . arrived here in England and did not give a full report to his employers.' Eventually Hudson managed to pass his log to Van Meteren, who sent it, along with a report, to Amsterdam.

The news of Hudson's river voyage passed through the sieve of Dutch political and business interests. To the sea-minded merchants on the Zandhoek and the Buitekant, Amsterdam's harbourfront, monitoring the offloading of lighters packed with Spanish taffeta, German porcelain, Swedish copper and East Indies spices, looking for the next business opportunity, hopes of a new passage to Asia were forgotten as they studied Van Meteren's report (which was published as a way of announcing to the world that the discovery was Dutch) and learned of the discovery and charting of a water highway into the unexplored continent that was 'as fine a river as can be found, wide and deep, with good anchoring ground on both sides'. It was a bonus that it was lightly inhabited by a 'friendly and polite people'. What jumped out at them, however, were other words, sharp, money-laden nouns – '*Vellen* . . . *Pelterijen* . . . *Maertens* . . . *Vossen* . . .' – the report making a frank promise of 'many skins and peltries, martins, foxes, and many other commodities'.

And so the story comes back to the founding, half a century earlier, of the English fur trade with Russia. It had dwindled in part because the Russian capability for slaughter had outstripped the beavers' sexual abilities. North America held a fresh, seemingly limitless supply. For some time Dutch traders had been trying, unsuccessfully, to insinuate themselves into the French fur trade further north in Canada. Now that would no longer be necessary: they had their own foothold on the continent. The Dutch staked their claim to the territory Hudson had sailed and which the subsequent explorer Adriaen Block charted in 1613 – a swathe encompassing three river systems, which would eventually become the Delaware, the Hudson and the Connecticut, occupying a position on the eastern seaboard of North America to the north of the English territory that Walter Raleigh had named in honour of his virgin queen – and promptly forgot about the mariner himself.

Which was fine because, after the initial furore over his prodigal return, the English wanted Hudson back; and Hudson himself had his eyes still fixed on his prize, now tacking away from the epicentre of history as he pursued it. His obsession was unyielding, making him, finally, a man of the past: of the

Renaissance dream of a voyage to far Cathay. He conned three fantastically wealthy young aristocrats into believing in the imminence of his discovery. Having ruled out John Smith's route, he now staked everything on Weymouth's indication of a passage to the icy north, through what was known as the Furious Overfall (the channel into Hudson Bay, now called Hudson Strait). The three funded him forthwith; he raised a crew and set off, without skipping a beat, the following spring. His calculations and his hunch pointed to it as inevitable: the passage *had* to be there.* He wouldn't take no for an answer. The world would have to kill him to stop him.

And it did. He hadn't reckoned that his crew might not share his conviction, and would do whatever they had to to save themselves. His arrogance was so supreme that he didn't see his end coming. Even as he was being lowered from the deck of his ship into the shallop, hands bound behind his back, dressed in 'a motley gown' as one of the mutineers would later testify (for they took him at daybreak, as he stepped out of his cabin), he remained clueless. 'What do you mean by this?' he asked in bewilderment as they bound him, and they told him he would soon find out. He had egged and cajoled and lashed the twenty-two men onwards, month upon month, as they fought a losing battle against the pack ice, as the shrouds and sails froze above them, as the food ran out and the sightings of bears and seals out on the white strip of the horizon stopped, as they were reduced to clambering ashore and scavenging moss for sustenance. First their gums bled, then their teeth loosened. Toe by toe, frostbite ate its way into their flesh, so that many could no longer stand, their pallets crowding every available space onboard. Finally, they could take it no more.

* For the record, Hudson was right. Roald Amundsen finally achieved the north-west passage in 1906, but by then it was a matter of personal adventure, the commercial possibilities of a northern route to Asia largely extinguished by the brutal realities of the voyage.

Besides the captain, the small party loaded into the shallop comprised the most desperately sick and those that had remained loyal to him, and included his son John, still a boy. At some point after they were set adrift – after the ship had moved away from them into open water, her topsails fattening in a fresh wind, after he had watched her hull evaporate into the white hoar of early morning, leaving their small vessel to the elements, with no food, no water, no source of fire and three hundred thousand square miles of ice-choked sea around them – his iron will must have finally caved in. He would have been left, then, before the cold ate its way into his blood and heart, to endure what must be any man's twin nightmares: watching his innocent child suffer and die because of his own folly, and contemplating the utter destruction of his life's ambition. At some point before his mind closed down he would have acknowledged that his dream of discovery was to die here, as he would die.

The irony of his end came with the surviving mutineers limping back to London, standing trial for mutiny and murder, and then being exonerated on their outrageous but ingenious claim that in fact Hudson *had* found the north-west passage, and that *they* knew where it was. Rather than being hanged, then, the survivors found themselves enrolled by King James, along with some of the most prominent men in London, as inaugural members of a new company, the 'Company of the Merchants Discoverers of the North-West Passage', with a charter to proceed through their new-found strait to commence trade 'to the great kingdoms of Tartaria, China, Japan, Solomons Islands, Chili, the Philippins and other countrys . . .'

The wave of history, which Hudson had ridden so effortlessly for a short while, rapidly engulfed him. He was destined to be a pollinator, bringing the spores of a culture not his own to new soil. Even before he froze to death in the southern reaches of what became Hudson Bay, on the Amsterdam waterfront a young man named Arnout Vogels was in a whirl of activity. Vogels, a thirty-year-old of adventure and drive, had been born in Antwerp to the south, and was one of those who had fled troubles elsewhere in Europe to the safe haven of Amsterdam, in his case after Spanish forces invaded his home town in 1585. He threw himself into business with the zest of one who has grown up amid war and knows how short life can be. He served an apprenticeship for a trading company in the fur business, but longed to strike out on his own. When the report of Hudson's discoveries spread through the dockside offices of Amsterdam's traders, Vogels moved fast. On 26 July 1610, as Hudson was making his way through the massive icy bay where he would meet his end, Vogels shook hands with Captain Sijmen Lambertsz Mau on a deal to trade in the new, virgin territory. The destination was still vague to most European minds, and so on the contract it was stated rather broadly: 'West Indies, and nearby lands and places'. The term West Indies was still being applied to all American regions.

Overnight, times had changed. The idea of a short cut to Asia, once the height of fashion, suddenly seemed passé to men of Vogels's generation. The future was nearer: just across the Atlantic. The Englishman Hudson had scouted the way for enterprising Dutchmen to follow. There was no concern at this date of a competing claim from England. The English had established a shaky beachhead at Virginia, but their New England settlements were still years in the future; Hudson's venture on behalf of the Dutch pre-dated the Pilgrims' landing by more than a decade. So the field was clear, and the refrains of Hudson's report must have repeated themselves in the minds of the Dutch traders: 'skins and peltries, martins, foxes', 'a very good harbor for all windes'. And they had an image to summon up in their minds as a goal, a key, a way into the heart of a virgin continent: 'as fine a river as can be found . . . a mile broad' – a glistening highway to pure possibility.

3
The Island

CATALINA TRICO, A FRENCH-SPEAKING TEENAGER. JORIS Rapalje, a Flemish textile worker. Bastiaen Krol, a lay minister from the farming province of Friesland. By tens and twenties they came in the years 1624 and 1625, pitching on the inhuman waves in yachts, galiots, ketches, pinks and pinnaces, well-crafted but still frightfully vulnerable wooden vessels, banging around in the damp and narrow below-decks, with barely enough room to crouch, with pigs rooting and sheep bleating hollowly at every slamming swell, with the animal reek and their own odours of sickness and sour filth, each clutching his or her satchel of elixirs to ward off the plague, the devil, scurvy, shipwreck and 'the bloody flux'. The very names of their ships – *Fortune*, *Abraham's Sacrifice* – signalled the two poles of hope and fear that governed them.

Three months it took to follow Hudson, four if the winds failed. From Amsterdam the ships made their way across the wide inland sea called the IJ, with its treacherous shoals, to the windswept island of Texel, and then set off into the white hoar of the North Sea. They gave the Portuguese coast a wide berth and skirted the Canary Islands off north Africa, their captains with skill and luck avoiding predatory privateers and pirates (or not: some ships were taken by both). Then, riding the trades, they beat a long, forbidding arc south-west across the blue-grey wilderness of the Atlantic, swinging upwards again north of the Bahamas and along the coast of the new land, the new world, keeping a sharp eye for the hooked peninsula that Hudson noted, and so into the enveloping embrace of the great harbour.

There still lingered, fifteen years after Hudson's trip, and ten years after Shakespeare penned *The Tempest* on the basis of accounts of a voyage to America shipwrecked on a supposedly bewitched isle (Bermuda), the notion that this might be the gateway to the riches of the sultry, pagan, exotically civilized east. It was possible, as far as the travellers knew, that the western shore, which in fifty years' time would be christened New Jersey, was in fact the back door of China; that India, with its steamy profusion of gods and curries, lay just beyond those bluffs. But these were not explorers; they were settlers, and their immediate focus was here, on the river, on their new home. In the decade and a half since Hudson's find, scouts and traders had made good contacts with the Indians of what the Dutch were now calling the River Mauritius, after Maurits of Nassau, son of the assassinated hero William the Silent and now leader of the rebellion against Spain (though another name had already sprung up: as early as 1614, fur traders were paying homage to their forerunner by referring to 'de rivière Hudson'). In their lean and silent canoes the 'River Indians' (as the traders called them – they were variously of the Mahican and Lenni Lenape tribes) came to them from the north, the east, the west, from far out in the unknown vastness, bringing excellent furs in remarkable quantities. There was indeed business to be had, the traders reported. And so a consortium of smaller interests was formed to exploit it in a systematic way.

The truce negotiated between Spain and the Dutch Republic during the year of Hudson's voyage was to last for twelve years. It came to an abrupt end in 1621, and immediately the spear-rattling began among Dutch patriots and entrepreneurs. One energetic businessman, named Willem Usselincx – a birdlike man brimming with religious zeal – had for years championed the idea of Dutch provinces in the New World that would be driven by both commerce and Calvinist fire. 'It is obvious,' Usselincx argued in the series of meetings that led to the establishment of the West India Company, 'that if one wants to get money, something has to be proposed to the people which will move them to invest. To this end the glory of God will help with some, harm to Spain with others, with some the welfare of the Fatherland; but the principal and most powerful inducement will be the profit that each can make for himself.' The new lands, he stressed, were inhabited not by wild-eyed savages but by intelligent natives among whom the Dutch could plant a colony. There were natural products there to be exploited, maybe gold and silver, as well as raw materials 'which are the sinews of war'.

The renewal of war with Spain would support rather than hinder this scheme: Dutch frigates of a privately owned company could be equipped with guns and carry out raids on Spanish ships in Caribbean and South American waters while also conducting trade in New World ports. Privateering – government-authorized piracy on enemy ships – was an accepted wartime activity.

Merchants and politicians were suddenly interested. Wealthy businessmen organized themselves into five regional chambers, each of which contributed start-up funds; the States General, the governing body of the country, added a modest amount, and by October 1623 the West India Company was as flush as any new company in history, with more than seven million guilders in its coffers. The East India Company had exploited Asia to fabulous result; now its new colleague would encompass the Atlantic Rim – its monopoly extended to west Africa, the Caribbean islands, and the coast of North America. It was to be a creature of war as well as trade, and its network of merchants, skippers, sailors, accountants, carpenters, armourers and soldiers infiltrated the new sphere of interest with remarkable speed. By 1626 an inventory of the company's property, addressed to the directors, included:

> 12 ships and yachts destined for the African trade in Guinea, Benin, Angola, Greyn, and Quaqua coasts, with the exported cargoes and expected returns . . .
>
> 1 ship of Dordrecht to Cape Verd, with cargo . . .
>
> 1 ship destined for the trade of the Amazon and the Coast of Guiana . . .
>
> 1 ship of about 130 lasts, 1 yacht well equipped, destined for the trade and colonization of New Netherland . . .
>
> 33 ships . . . which the Company hath still lying here in port, provided with metal and iron guns, and all sorts of supplies of ammunition of war, powder, muskets, arms, sabres, and whatever may be necessary for the equipment, which can be fitted for sea . . .
>
> Moneys . . . which being in the Treasury, will be applied to keep the foregoing ships at sea, not only to injure the King of Spain, but also by God's blessing to do your High Mightinesses and the Company much service, and the Partners good profit.

The North American territory would play an economic role in this scheme; the company would exploit it for furs and timber, and also use it as a transportation hub, with ships cycling from Europe to South America and the Caribbean to the North American harbour and so back home. Of course, settlers were required, and raising them proved to be one of the hardest aspects of the whole complex business of creating an Atlantic empire. Times were good in the homeland, the future looked even better, and Amsterdam was probably the best place in the world to be poor (its almshouses, wrote an English consul with some exaggeration, were 'more like princes' palaces than lodgings for poor people'). To find the number required to sign on for a passage to what was now being called New Netherland, the company had to look among those who were ignorant or desperate or poor enough to leave the deeply civilized bosom of Amsterdam – with its paved streets, its scrubbed floors, its wheels of cheese and tankards of excellent beer, its fluffy pillows and blue-and-white-tiled hearths and cosy peat fires – and venture to the back of beyond, to an absolute and unforgiving wilderness.

But, as always, the country was loaded with refugees, and, by promising land in exchange for six years of service, the company managed to round up a handful of hale young Walloons – French-speaking exiles from what is today Belgium – make sure, like Noah, that they included a female for every male, and hustle them into the Amsterdam council chamber, where they swore an oath of allegiance to the company and the government.

The councillor who administered the oath, Claes Peterszen, was a renowned physician and surgeon, so renowned that while we know him from Rembrandt's viscerally famous painting *The Anatomy Lesson of Dr Tulp* (Tulp, or tulip, being a nickname, from the flower painted above his front door), at the time it was the doctor who, in agreeing to appear in the portrait, helped make the artist famous. We have a nice mental image, then, of the black-dressed, dignified, austere physician–magistrate with his sharp black V of facial hair, representative of the Dutch political and scientific establishment, and before him, in their rough country attire, the young men and women, shifting and twitching with nerves and exuberant raw youth, who were about to start a new society in a wilderness called Manhattan.

And there was raw youth in abundance: four couples were actually married at sea, the ship's captain, Cornelis May (after whom, incidentally, Cape May, New Jersey, is named), doing the honours. Another pair – the ones named at the beginning of this chapter, Catalina Trico and Joris Rapalje – were smarter. Maybe they knew what conditions would be like on board, and didn't relish the idea of consummating a marriage there. They agreed to take part in the wildly hazardous enterprise on the condition that the company marry them first, in a hastier than normal ceremony which took place four days before their ship left

Amsterdam on 25 January 1624. 'Espousé le 21 de Janvier,' the clerk of the Walloon Church of Amsterdam recorded, without wasting too much time getting the names right, 'Joris Raporbie de Valencenne, et Caterine triko.' Being illiterate, both made their marks on the page. He was nineteen, she was eighteen; no parents signed the register, which suggests that both were either alone in the world or alone in that part of the world, which amounted to the same thing. Like many who were to follow, they had nothing to lose.

Considering the stupendous dangers awaiting them, first at sea and then on arrival, it wasn't a union a betting man would be likely to put money on. And yet, sixty years later, when the English colonies of Pennsylvania and Maryland were embroiled in a border dispute and needed evidence of 'Christian' occupation of certain lands along the eastern seaboard, the representatives of William Penn found an old woman to testify who was known to have been among the first European settlers. Catalina Trico, now in her eighties, was a widow, but she and Joris had had a long and fruitful marriage. The records of New Netherland show them among the first buyers of land in the wilderness of southern Manhattan, building two houses on Pearl Street just steps away from the fort, obtaining a milk cow, borrowing money from the provincial government, moving their homestead to a large tract of farmland across the river in the new village of Breuckelen, and giving birth to and baptizing eleven children. Their eldest, Sara, was considered the first European born in what would become New York (in 1656, at the age of thirty, she proclaimed herself 'first born christian daughter of New Netherland'); she was born in 1625, and the same records show in turn her marriage in 1639, to the overseer of a tobacco plantation in what would become Greenwich Village, and, in due course, the birth of her eight children. Throughout the brief life of New Netherland and on into that of New York, the Rapalje children and their offspring would spread across the region. In the 1770s John Rapalje would serve as a member of the New York State Assembly (he rejected revolution and became a loyalist). The number of their descendants has been estimated at upwards of one million, and in the Hudson valley town of Fishkill, New York, a lane called Rapalje Road is a quiet suburban testament to the endurance of a long-ago slapdash wedding of two young nobodies on the Amsterdam waterfront, which, as much as any political event, marked the beginning of the immigrant, stake-your-claim civilization not only of Manhattan but of America.

When the sea-battered ships finally entered the harbour, the passengers gazed out onto a wholly unfamiliar landscape, stranger and more complex than the flat land they had left. In modern scientific terms, the region that would be their new home comprised an intersection of three physiographical provinces – sandy coastal plain, rolling upland hills and craggy metamorphic ridges – much of which had been slashed and gouged by the glaciers of the last ice age, leaving a stippling of stream beds, jumbled moraine and glacial lakes. Sailing silently into the inner harbour, approaching the southern tip of Manhattan Island, the ships glided into a reedy, marshy expanse of tidal wetland (the Mohawk name for Manhattan – Gänóno – translates as 'reeds' or 'place of reeds'), a complicated crossover region of freshwater and marine species, where bay, swamp forest and serpentine barrens bred skying, cawing shore birds – plovers, sandpipers, dowitchers, yellowlegs – as well as thick populations of homely mallards, and also drew migrating flocks of oldsquaws, mergansers and wigeons that blackened the grey November sky. Mussels, conches, clams and periwinkles encrusted the estuaries – along with, most prized of all, oysters, some of which, a settler wrote, are 'quite large and occasionally containing a small pearl', while others were tiny and sweet and another variety was 'fine for stewing and frying. As each one fills a big spoon they make a good bite.' Rising up above the island's reedy shoreline were forested hills: the best guess on the origin of the Indian name that would stick is the Delaware *mannahata*, 'hilly island', though some have suggested that simply 'the island' or 'the small island' is a more accurate translation.

Putting foot to solid ground, the settlers decided they liked what they saw. 'We were much gratified on arriving in this country,' one wrote home.

> Here we found beautiful rivers, bubbling fountains flowing down into the valleys; basins of running waters in the flatlands, agreeable fruits in the woods, such as strawberries, pigeon berries, walnuts, and also . . . wild grapes. The woods abound with acorns for feeding hogs, and with venison. There is considerable fish in the rivers; good tillage land; here is especially free coming and going, without fear of the naked natives of the country. Had we cows, hogs, and other cattle fit for food (which we daily expect in the first ships) we would not wish to return to Holland, for whatever we desire in the paradise of Holland, is here to be found.

In Europe, newspapers as such didn't yet exist, but periodical pamphlets were a major source of news, and no sooner did the first settlers of New Netherland begin writing home than an Amsterdam physician named Nicolaes van Wassenaer started to publish a semi-annual pamphlet of the pioneers' doings in the far-off land. 'It is very pleasant, all products being in abundance, though wild,' he wrote in December 1624. 'Grapes are of very good flavor, but will be henceforward better cultivated by our people. Cherries are not found there. There are all sorts of fowls, both in the water and in the air. Swans, geese, ducks, bitterns, abound.'

At first the company sprinkled its few settlers over a wide area. In the Dutch understanding, laying claim to a patch of territory involved inhabiting it (for the English – and this would later become a point of contention – all that was required was that an official representative set foot on a patch of soil not previously claimed by Christians). Also in the Dutch understanding, water was the key to any piece of land. Thus the company set about dividing its few colonists among the three principal waterways of their territory. What under the English would become the Delaware, which Hudson had considered exploring but quickly ruled out as a route to Asia because of its shoaled bay, the Dutch called the South River, for the good reason that it formed the southern limit of their territory. For most of their time in North America they called the Hudson the North River (mariners – famously conservative and resistant to change – call it that to this day). The other main waterway – what would become the Connecticut river, today bisecting that state – the Dutch called the Fresh River.

These were the highways of the region, the places to which Indians brought pelts, and the means of exploring the interior. The company sent a few settlers to form a small camp on each – a very few. Two families and six single men were shipped north-east to the Fresh River. Two families and eight men sailed down the coast to the South River. Eight men stayed on a small island in the harbour. The rest of the families sailed a further 150 miles up the North River, through the mud-coloured tidal chop, first past majestic palisades of rock along the western shore, then between the undulating humps of the highlands on both sides, to the place the traders reported was the key junction of Indian traffic – where the east-flowing Mohawk, after travelling all the way from the Great Lakes region, careered over 70-foot falls before emptying into the North River. Here the new-comers disembarked and stood defenceless before the towering pines. For shelter they initially dug square pits in the ground, lined them with wood and covered them with bark roofs (a cleric who would come a few years later, when proper houses were being built, sneered at the 'hovels and holes' in which the first arrivals 'huddled rather than dwelt').

Catalina and Joris were in the party initially shipped upriver from Manhattan to the falls, where a fort and trading post were to be constructed. The natives of the country appeared soon after they stumbled ashore, exchanged presents with the ship's captain and made other gestures of friendship. It was disorientating for the newcomers, but the sun had the warmth of spring in it, and the crumbly black earth seemed to cry out to be impregnated with seed. The Rapaljes and the other couples stayed two years at this spot, in autumn harvesting grain 'as high as a man', the next spring whispering prayers of thanks when three company ships arrived whose names – *The Cow*, *The Sheep*, *The Horse* – betrayed their cargo. During the whole time the Indians 'were all quiet as lambs', as Catalina remembered in old age, coming regularly and trading freely with the settlers.

The initial plan was to make an island on the South River, a hundred-odd miles from Manhattan, the capital of the new province. This was based on the decidedly mistaken belief that the climate of what would become southern New Jersey approximated that which the Spanish had found in Florida. The balminess of those reports sounded good to the Dutch, who preferred not to have to deal with the extreme bother of a harbour freezing up in the winter, bringing trade and communication to a halt. The first settlers to arrive there were dismayed to find no palm trees. Worse, the bay did indeed freeze over that first winter, and in subsequent ones too; so attention shifted to the bay to the north, which, thanks to geographical peculiarities, rarely froze despite its latitude.

The knots of colonists, scattered along a distance of some 250 miles, got to work – cleared ground, felled trees, constructed palisade defences, sowed grain. Ships arrived from home. The colonists made deals with Indians and established a system for trade: in 1625 they bought 5,295 beaver pelts and 463 otter skins, which they loaded onto the ships to be sent back to Amsterdam. The ships in turn brought news. In England, James I, the scholar-king who had succeeded Elizabeth – who had unsuccessfully resisted the Dutch rise to power and had tried to ally England with Spain at a time when English hatred of Catholicism was at a fever pitch, but who had also overseen the creation of the King James Bible, one of the world's great literary works – had died. He had been an awkward monarch, with a tendency to drool and a penchant for crude mannerisms, and was never revered as Elizabeth had been. The nation breathed a sigh when his son Charles – handsome, chaste, dignified – took the throne, not knowing that in time their hopes, for him and for the nation, would be dashed in the most violent way and with profound consequences for this far-off Dutch province.

In the United Provinces, too, power had passed on, here from brother to brother. Maurits, Prince of Orange, the stadtholder or chief nobleman of the country, had led the fight against Spain since the death of his father, William the Silent, in 1584. But he had grown weak in recent years, and in 1619 had fatally compromised his legitimacy by resolving a power struggle with the great statesman Jan van Oldenbarnevelt, who had engineered the truce of 1609 and otherwise skilfully steered the fledgling republic through the thicket of European politics, by having the man's head cut off. Maurits's brother, Frederik Hendrik, at the age of forty-one seventeen years his junior, was a brilliant diplomat and military tactician; taking over after his brother's death, he would continue the revolt and bring the nation to the verge of final recognition of independence. Under these new leaders the Dutch and the English, united in their common Protestantism, had signed a treaty of co-operation against their joint enemy, Catholic Spain, which stipulated that each would have access to the other's ports, including provincial ports.

The New Netherland settlers, chests heaving and faces streaked with sweat, would have had to pause in their labours to digest this information as it percolated out to them. They knew perfectly well that a group of English religious pilgrims had settled to their north a few years earlier – 'Brownists' they were called at the time, after the Separatist preacher Robert Browne, to whose principles they adhered – and they hoped for good relations. In fact, they expected good relations. Remarkably, most of the Walloons who made up the majority of the Dutch colony's early population had been refugees in the university town of Leiden (spelled Leyden at the time), the same place that had harboured the English Pilgrims. The Pilgrims had spent twelve years there as guests of the Dutch, in their flight from persecution in England, before leaving it to found a virgin theocracy in the New World.

The initial settlement strategy in the Dutch province was soon derailed by events. Joris Rapalje, his wife Catalina and the other settlers at what was now called Fort Orange (and under the English would become Albany) saw their hard work come to a sudden and grisly end in the spring of 1626. Their settlement on the riverbank was on former hunting grounds of the Mahicans, who had welcomed them. To the north and west stretched the territory of the Mohawks. These two tribes – the first one of the Algonquin-speaking nations, the second one of the five tribes of the Iroquois League – were of different backgrounds and beliefs, with languages as distinct as English and Russian, with different customs and with little respect for one another. They had been fighting an intermittent war for decades, and the appearance of the European traders in their midst revived the conflict and propelled it to a new level. After more than a decade of contact with Europeans, the Indians were in the process of reorienting their lives around the acquisition of foreign products: fishing hooks, axes, kettles, glassware, needles, pots, knives and duffel, the rough woollen cloth that originated in the Flemish town of Duffel and gives us the term duffel coat. Later, of course, guns and alcohol would be added to the list. Mahicans were even relocating their villages to sites nearer to the Dutch, in an attempt to form a trading and defensive alliance. Out of whatever mixture of friendship and self-interest, by 1626 the Mahicans and the Dutch had established a closeness.

This closeness was probably what led Daniel van Crieckenbeeck, the commander of the fort, to ignore explicit orders forbidding interference in inter-tribal affairs, with results that would have repercussions lasting to the present. One spring day in 1626 a Mahican party of more than two dozen men – their hair 'jet-black, quite sleek and uncurled, and almost as coarse as a horse's tail', as one observer described the Indians, with high cheekbones and aquiline noses, 'like us Dutchmen in body and stature', another writer recorded, and probably, given the period and the time of year, wearing deer-skins loosely about their bodies and tied at the waist – came into the palisade of rough-cut logs and asked Van Crieckenbeeck for Dutch aid in their fight against the Mohawks. The man who asked this favour was most likely a tribal leader named Monemin. Van Crieckenbeeck had his orders; the West India Company had clearly instructed Willem Verhulst, head of the province, that 'he shall be very careful not lightly to embroil himself in [the Indians'] quarrels or wars, or to take sides, but to remain neutral.' On the other hand, Van Crieckenbeeck surely felt responsible for the well-being of the handful of young couples, including a number of pregnant women and perhaps some infants, relying on his protection in the midst of the forest and thousands of miles from home. Maybe he also realized that the Indians expected such support to be an integral part of their relationship with the Dutch; and it stood to reason that helping the Mahicans now would yield a firm ally in the future. So he agreed. The Mahicans led the way, and he and six of his men followed, disappearing into the pines.

Three miles from the fort, they were inundated by a storm of arrows. In one swift, bloody assault, a band of ambushing Mohawks put an end to the Dutch–Mahican alliance, and by the way altered the history of the world. Van Crieckenbeeck, three of his men and twenty-four Mahicans, including Monemin, took fatal hits. The Mohawks made a show of their victory, and nicely capped the terror they had caused, by roasting and eating one especially unfortunate Dutchman named Tymen Bouwensz.

Meanwhile, the group that had remained on the North River was also in turmoil. It had been decided that the settlement in the harbour would be on a tiny, teardrop-shaped island that the colonists called Noten (Nut) Island, after the walnut and chestnut trees they found there. The first settlers who arrived camped here, and their cattle were sent to pasture five hundred yards across the bay, on Manhattan Island. Verhulst, who as the colony's provisional director had remained with this group, began causing problems from the start. He meted out harsh and inconsistent punishment for petty offences, infuriating the colonists. He and his wife may also have misappropriated funds or – an even worse offence – cheated Indians. Both because of the founders' Calvinist sense of propriety and out of a practical awareness that it was not a good idea to upset the natives who were surrounding you, the West India Company had sent Verhulst explicit instructions on dealing with the Indians: 'He shall also see that no one do the Indians any harm or violence, deceive, mock, or contemn them in any way, but that in addition to good treatment they be shown honesty, faithfulness, and sincerity in all contracts, dealings, and intercourse, without being deceived by shortage of measure, weight or number, and that throughout friendly relations with them be maintained.' Whatever their exact offences, Verhulst and his wife had set the colonists howling; they wanted him gone.

At the moment this crisis reached boiling point, a ship arrived from the upriver settlement with news of the Indian attack. The colony was barely a year old and already it was descending into chaos, in danger of collapse. It needed a leader, and one stepped forward.

He had grown up speaking German and Dutch was his second language, but his ancestry was French, so his name was pronounced in the French way – Min-wee. He is one of those figures of history about whom everything we know makes us wish we knew more. He had had no military training, but he was an individualistic, take-charge sort who would affect the course of history in more ways than one. His father had taken part in the northward migration of Protestants fleeing Spanish troops and inquisitors, and settled in the small German town of Wesel, near the Dutch border; it was here that Peter Minuit grew up. With no fixed loyalties and a great drive to get ahead, in good upwardly mobile fashion he made his first smart move in life by marrying the daughter of the mayor of the nearby town of Kleve. He and his wife then moved 75 miles west to the larger Dutch city of Utrecht, where Minuit trained to become a diamond-cutter. He found that a dull occupation, though; and, hearing of the formation of the West India Company, he further learned through French-speaking circles that a party of Walloons were signing on as pioneers in a venture to the New World. So one day in 1624 he presented himself at the stately mansion of West India House on Amsterdam's Brouwersgracht (Brewers' Canal), asking for a posting to New Netherland, apparently not as a settler or company official but as a private 'volunteer' businessman scouting for trade opportunities. The directors must have been impressed by his energy, for Minuit appears to have taken ship with one of the first groups of settlers, and the company's initial instructions to Verhulst say that 'He shall have Pierre Minuyt, as volunteer, and others whom he deems competent thereto sail up the river as far as they can in any way do so, in order to inspect the condition of the land.'

Minuit might thus have been among the party that included Catalina Trico and Joris Rapalje when they sailed upriver, and he seems, during this early period, to have gathered a good deal of information about the new land. He then apparently returned to Amsterdam for a time, perhaps to deliver the 'samples of dyes, drugs, gums, herbs, plants, trees and flowers' the instructions asked him to supply, for the records show him leaving the Dutch Republic once again in January 1626, arriving back in New Netherland on 4 May. So he had spent time in the colony, enough time to impress the settlers with his abilities, and then returned to Europe; now he was back again. It would not have been long after his ship, the *Sea-Mew*, passed through the narrows between Staten Eylandt (named in honour of the States General of the United Provinces) and Lange Eylandt (named for obvious reasons) and dropped anchor in the harbour that he would have been met with the bad news.

A newly formed council of settlers met. They put Verhulst on trial, and voted to banish him and his wife from the province. Verhulst did not go gently; he was furious and vindictive, and vowed to return some day at the head of a foreign army and make use of his knowledge of the territory and its fortifications – an interesting threat in the light of what not he but Minuit would do twelve years later.

The colonists then voted Minuit their new commander. Finding himself suddenly transformed from private scout into officer of the province, Minuit acted quickly. The first decision he seems to have made is the one that would have the most profound consequences. The company directors in Amsterdam had tried to supervise the settlement from afar, which was awkward and ineffective, and Verhulst, their man on the scene, hadn't been able to see the obvious problems. There were too few settlers to be spread out across the hundreds of miles of territory; the news from Fort Orange convinced Minuit that safety was a major concern. Nut Island (today Governor's Island) might have been useful as an initial staging area, but it was too small for a settlement of any size. The South River did not live up to its tropical billing. To anyone with a practical and logistical mind it was clear that the island of Manhattan, separated from Nut Island by a channel 'a gunshot wide', answered every need. It was large enough to support a population, small enough that a fort located on its southernmost tip could be defended. Its forests were rich in game; it had flatlands that could be farmed and freshwater streams. It was situated at the mouth of the river to which Indian fur-traders came from hundreds of miles around, and which connected to other waterways that penetrated deep into the interior; it was also at the entrance to the bay, located in a wide and inviting harbour that seemed not to freeze over in winter. It was, in short, a natural fulcrum between the densely civilized continent of Europe and the tantalizingly wild continent of North America. It was the perfect island.

*

So he bought it. Everyone knows that. Peter Minuit purchased Manhattan Island from a group of local Indians for 60 guilders' worth of goods, or, as the nineteenth-century historian Edmund O'Callaghan calculated it, 24 dollars. From the seventeenth century through to the early years of the twentieth, thousands of transactions occurred in which native Americans sold parcels of land – ranging in size from a town lot to a midwestern state – to English, Dutch, French, Spanish and other European settlers. But only one sale is legend; only one is universally known. Only one has had the durability to make it onto Broadway ('Give It Back to the Indians', from the 1939 Rodgers and Hart musical *Too Many Girls*), and, at the end of the twentieth century, into the punchline of a column by humorist Dave Barry ('. . . which the Dutch settler Peter Minuit purchased from the Manhattan Indians for $24, plus $167,000 a month in maintenance fees').

It's pretty clear why this particular sale lodged in the cultural memory, why it became legend: the extreme incongruity, the exquisitely absurd price. It is the most dramatic illustration of the whole long process of stripping the natives of their land. The idea that the centre of world commerce, an island packed with trillions of dollars' worth of property, was once bought from supposedly hapless stone age innocents for 24 dollars' worth of household goods is too delicious to let slip. It speaks to our sense of early American history as the history of savvy, ruthless Europeans conniving, tricking, enslaving and bludgeoning innocent and guileless natives out of their land and their lives. It's a neatly packed symbol of the entire conquest of the continent that was to come.

Beyond that, the purchase snippet is notable because it is virtually the only thing about the Dutch colony on Manhattan that *has* become a part of history. For this reason too it deserves exploring.

So, who were the Indians who agreed to this transaction, and what did they think it meant? The ancestors of the people whom European settlers took to calling Indians (after Columbus, who at first thought he had arrived at the outer reaches of India) travelled the land bridge from Siberia to Alaska that existed during the last ice age, something more than twelve thousand years ago, then spread slowly through the Americas. They came from Asia; their genetic makeup is a close match with that of Siberians and Mongolians. They spread out thinly across the incomprehensible vastness of the American continents to create a linguistic richness unparalleled in human history: it has been estimated that at the moment Columbus arrived in the New World 25 per cent of all human languages were North American Indian.

There are two rival, hardened stereotypes that get in the way of understanding these peoples: the one that arose from the long-standing assumption of cultural superiority by Europeans, who dismissed American Indians as Primitive, and the modern dogma that sees them as Noble and Defenceless. Both are cartoon images. Recent work in genetics, archaeology, anthropology and linguistics makes plain what should be obvious: that the Mahican, Mohawk, Lenape, Montauk, Housatonic and other peoples occupying the lands that for a time were called New Netherland, as well as the Massachusett, Wampanoag, Sokoki, Pennacook, Abenaki, Oneida, Onondaga, Susquehannock, Nanticoke and others who inhabited other parts of what became the states of New York, Massachusetts, Pennsylvania, Connecticut, Vermont, New Hampshire, Maine, Delaware, Maryland and New Jersey, were biologically, genetically and intellectually virtually identical to the Dutch, English, French, Swedish and others who came into contact with them in the beginning of the seventeenth century. The Indians were as skilled, as duplicitous, as capable of theological rumination and technological cunning, as smart and pig-headed, as curious and as cruel as the Europeans who met them. The members of the

Manhattan-based colony who knew them – who spent time among them in their villages, hunted and traded with them, learned their languages – knew this perfectly well. It was later, after the two had separated into rival camps, that the stereotypes set. The early seventeenth century was a much more interesting time than the Wild West era, a time when Indians and Europeans were something like equal participants in a joint habitation of the land, dealing with one another as allies, competitors, partners.

But if the Indians were so clever and in a strong position, why would they sell their land, the most precious thing they owned? Putting the question that way raises a point familiar to every secondary school student of American history: the Indians had a different idea of land ownership from Europeans. With no concept of permanent property transfer, the Indians of the northeast saw a property deal as a combination of a rental agreement and a treaty or alliance between two groups. Indian nations were divided and subdivided into tribes, villages and other communities. They were often at war with or in fear of attack from other groups, and often entered into defensive alliances with one another, which involved sharing certain tribal lands in exchange for the strength of numbers. This practice coloured the way the Indians saw their land deals with the Dutch and English. They would give the newcomers use of some of their land, and in exchange they would get blankets, knives, kettles and other extremely useful goods, and also a military ally. That this was how they viewed land deals is illustrated neatly by several cases – such as one in South Carolina in the 1750s between the colonial governor and Cherokee leaders – in which the Indians refused any payment at all for the land. As they saw it, the protective alliance was payment enough.

This was probably what the Mahican Monemin had in mind when he approached the unfortunate Daniel van Crieckenbeeck: he was asking the Dutch to fulfil what he understood to be part of the bargain in the land deal at Fort Orange, and help him in a battle with his enemies. Van Crieckenbeeck may have realized that this was a part of the Mahican notion of a property deal, and tried to do what was expected of him, in defiance of his orders.

Thus the situation of the Indians. As to the Dutch, the neatness and compactness of the legend of Manhattan's purchase has to do with the lack of attention paid to the Dutch colony by historians, and with what they perceived to be a shortage of information about the settlement. For those hoping to understand the history of the Manhattan-based colony, the great disaster took place in 1821, when the government of the Netherlands, in a truly unfortunate fit of housekeeping (the Dutch have always been fastidious cleaners), sold for scrap paper what remained of the archives of the Dutch East and West India Companies for the years before 1700. Eighteen years later an American agent named John Romeyn Brodhead, working on behalf of New York State, went to the Netherlands in search of documentary material on the Dutch colony and found to his 'surprise, mortification, and regret' that all of it – 80,000 pounds of records – had vanished.

Fortunately, we have another great mass of relevant documents: the official records of the province, twelve thousand pages strong. As outlined at the beginning of this book, the bulk of these records are only now, after centuries of neglect, being translated by Dr Charles Gehring of the New Netherland Project, and it is upon these that much of this book relies. These records have miraculously survived wars, fires, mould and rodents. But they begin only in 1638. None of the province's records prior to that year have survived, possibly because when, like Verhulst, the early governors of the province were dismissed from service they took the records of their administration back to Amsterdam with them to aid in their defence. We are left, then, with a gaping hole at the earliest period of New York's prehistory, which nineteenth-century historians filled in as best they could. They knew the name Peter Minuit, they knew that he was an early director of the province, and they had a tantalizing scrap of paper suggesting that the island had been purchased from the 'Wilden' (Indians) for 'the value of 60 guilders'.

We know more now, and are able to paint a more detailed picture of what went on in spring 1626. In Amsterdam, in the year 1910, a sheaf of papers showed up at a rare books and manuscripts auction. A curator had labelled item no. 1795 'Documents sur la Nouvelle-Néerlande, 1624–1626'. The owner was a man with the formidable name of Alexander Carel Paul George Ridder van Rappard. The antique sheets he put up for sale may have been part of the collection of his grandfather, Frans Alexander Ridder van Rappard, a noted collector. Years more passed before the papers were bought by another collector (the American railway tycoon Henry E. Huntington), translated, published and made available to scholars.* The documents – which had once been a part of the West India Company archives and had somehow escaped the wholesale destruction – comprised five letters and sets of instructions dating from the colony's beginnings. It is from these papers that much of the information in this chapter comes, and these papers that have given a new perspective on what the Dutch thought they were doing with their New World colony. It was long believed, for example, that the colony from the beginning was an unorganized, ad hoc settlement, not so much mismanaged as allowed to grow in a state of near anarchy, and was generally a mess until the English came in and began to make it function. The so-called Van Rappard documents prove otherwise. They show that a great deal of care was devoted to the colony and to the welfare of the inhabitants. It is from them that we know that there was a leader before Minuit, the hapless Willem Verhulst; and that, before he left the Dutch Republic, Verhulst was given

* In 1924 A. J. F. Van Laer, Charles Gehring's predecessor as translator of the Dutch archives, produced a limited edition publication of these records, *Documents Relating to New Netherland, 1624–1626, in the Henry E. Huntington Library*.

explicit instructions to 'carefully note all places where there is any appearance of tillable or pasture land, timber of any kind, minerals, or other things', to do test drillings of the soil, to denote every waterfall, stream and place for sawmills, to note 'inlets, depths, shallows, rocks, and width of the rivers', and indicate the best places for forts, 'keeping in mind that the fittest place is where the river is narrow, where it cannot be fired upon from higher ground, where large ships cannot come too close, where there is a distant view unobstructed by trees or hills, where it is possible to have water in the moat, and where there is no sand, but clay or other firm earth'. The instructions also note elaborate preparations for farming: 'divers trees, vines, and all sorts of seeds are being sent over . . . and of each sort of fruit he shall successively send us samples . . . And with regard to the aniseed and cuminseed which is sent over to make a trial with, he shall sow the same at different times and places, observing at what time and in which place it grows best and yields most.' Thanks to this cache of documents we have a revised picture, of a well-organized Dutch effort, and, in Minuit, of a competent leader wrapping his mind around the problem of establishing a colony.

Another figure emerges from these documents. In July 1626 Isaack de Rasière, a thirty-year-old merchant's son with a taste for adventure, stepped off the *Arms of Amsterdam* and onto the Manhattan shore, ready to begin his duties as secretary of the province. The Van Rappard documents include letters that De Rasière wrote to his bosses in Holland; in one, he reported that the island was home to a small group of natives whom he called the Manhatesen: 'they are about 200 to 300 strong, women and men, under different chiefs, whom they call *Sackimas*'. It was presumably this small band – probably a northern branch of the Lenni Lenape Indians – with whom Peter Minuit concluded his property transaction.

It is true that there is no deed on file anywhere to prove that the sale took place, but many other important records of the period have failed to survive the centuries. We do have an account from the 1670s that makes reference to the deed to Manhattan, so it existed at that time. Most interestingly, we have an excellent, evocative account of the purchase by someone who had no interest in deceiving. When the *Arms of Amsterdam*, which had brought Isaack de Rasière to New Netherland, left Manhattan on its return voyage, it carried a neat collection of items and individuals associated with this pivotal moment in history: first, the banished Verhulst himself, along with his wife, returning in disgrace and anger (but mollified somewhat by certain of the spoils of their adventure: back in Amsterdam he had a tabard, or cape, made of sixteen beaver pelts, while his wife had a tailor fashion a fur coat out of thirty-two otter skins); second, a chest containing the personal effects of the unfortunate Daniel van Crieckenbeeck, including an otter-skin coat and a ring, which were being sent to his wife; and third, a letter from De Rasière to the West India Company directors, in which he detailed the council's decision to oust Verhulst, as well as providing information about the purchase of Manhattan.

This information may have been the deed itself, which might thus have been among the West India Company records that were sold for scrap in 1821 and so vanished for ever. Fortunately, however, Pieter Schaghen, a Dutch official who had just been appointed to represent the government on the company's board, was on the dock when the ship pulled into port, and wrote a letter to his superiors at The Hague giving a detailed description of the ship's contents and news of the province. It is one of the most famous historical documents in the Dutch language and one of the most important records of early American history. It is, in effect, New York City's birth certificate:

High and Mighty Lords
My Lords the States General
At the Hague

High and Mighty Lords:

Yesterday, arrived here the Ship the Arms of Amsterdam, which sailed from New Netherland, out of the River Mauritius, on the 23rd September. They report that our people are in good heart and live in peace there; the Women also have borne some children there. They have purchased the Island Manhattes from the Indians for the value of 60 guilders; it is 11,000 morgens in size. They had all their grain sowed by the middle of May, and reaped by the middle of August. They send thence samples of summer grain; such as wheat, rye, barley, oats, buckwheat, canary seed, beans and flax. The cargo of the aforesaid ship is

7246 Beaver skins
178 ½-Otter skins
675 Otter skins
48 Mink skins
36 Wildcat skins
33 Minks
34 Rat skins
Considerable Oak timber and Hickory.

Herewith,
High and Mighty Lords, be commended to the mercy of the Almighty.
In Amsterdam, The 5th November Ao. 1626
Your High Mightinesses' obedient,
P. Schaghen

Two days later, in an office within the fortress-like Binnenhof at The Hague, a clerk of the States General picked up his pen and wrote a terse memo: 'Received a letter from Mr. Schaghen, written at Amsterdam, the 5th inst., containing advice of the arrival of a ship from New Netherland, which requires no action.'

It is this letter, then, that gives us the purchase price. While it may be a useful whip for belated self-flagellation over the white takeover of the continent from the Indians, being fair to those involved in the transaction means looking at it from their perspective. We can, first of all, dismiss the figure of 24 dollars because it dates to the mid-nineteenth century and has no relationship to buying power two hundred years earlier. Second, Minuit paid not 60 guilders, which the Indians would have found useless, but 'the value of' 60 guilders – meaning goods. What amount of goods was worth 60 guilders in 1626? Calculating relative worth is a task hopelessly fraught with problems. A steel knife might be of relatively little value in Amsterdam or London, of considerable worth to a Dutch settler living in primitive conditions along the North River in America, and of enormous worth to an Indian living what anthropologists today call a 'Late Woodlands' existence.

One way of putting the sale in perspective is to compare the figure with other amounts paid for parcels of wilderness around the same time. In 1630, for example, Peter Minuit, on behalf of the West India Company, bought Staten Island from the Tappans for 'Duffels, Kittles, Axes, Hoes, Wampum, Drilling Awls, Jews Harps, and diverse other small wares'. In 1664 three Englishmen purchased a vast tract of farmland in New Jersey from Indians for two coats, two guns, two kettles, ten bars of lead, twenty handfuls of gunpowder, four hundred fathoms of wampum (belts of strung beads made of seashell) and twenty fathoms of cloth. We can also look at the Manhattan sale in the context of land transfers between Dutch residents. Three years after the Manhattan transfer, the West India Company granted a Dutchman two hundred acres of what would become Greenwich Village in exchange for one-tenth of whatever he produced from the land, plus the promise to 'deliver yearly at Christmas to the director a brace of capons'. And in 1638

Andries Hudde sold Gerrit Wolphertsen one hundred acres of land on Long Island for 52 guilders.

So the sum paid for Manhattan was roughly in line with other prices paid to Indians for land, and while it was considerably less, on a per-acre basis, than what the Dutch paid each other in land deals, it was not off the scale. As a reference point, a West India Company soldier earned about 100 guilders per year – or nearly twice the price paid for Manhattan. The overriding fact was that in its wilderness state New World land was dirt cheap.

On the other side, given their idea of land ownership, the Indians who 'sold' Manhattan fully intended to continue to use the land, and did. Serious study about the Manhattan colony still being in its infancy, new information is liable to turn up at any time, and in the most unlikely places. As historians in the United States have become interested in the colony, some in the Netherlands have as well. Thus a court case that ended in 1663, the record of which had been slumbering since that date in the archives of the Dutch town of Arnhem until it was unearthed and written about by Dutch historian Janny Venema in 2000, gives focus to the fuzzy notion of how American Indians saw land transactions in the seventeenth century. In 1648 Brant van Slichtenhorst was hired by the Van Rensselaers, the largest landowners in the province, to manage their vast estate. Years later, back in the Dutch Republic, he filed suit for expenses owed, and the seven-year case is packed with details about life among the Mohawks and Mahicans. On behalf of his patrons Van Slichtenhorst bought several estates from the Indians during his time in the Dutch colony, and none of these transactions was remotely straightforward. Beginning days before the sale, and continuing for years after, Van Slichtenhorst had to host as many as fifty Indians at a time, feeding them and providing a steady supply of beer, and brandy for the sachems or chiefs. In addition to the sellers and their retinue, in one case there was actually an Indian property broker who also demanded, as part of his commission, to stay '8 or 10 times' at Van Slichtenhorst's home, along with several women. There was always 'great trouble and quarrels with all the Indian people', Van Slichtenhorst complained, 'and great filth and stench, and everything within reach was stolen'. These demands on his hospitality continued not for days or weeks but for *years* after the sale; Van Slichtenhorst would be out surveying the property and come across an encamped party of Indians – upon which, rather than being indignant at the 'trespass', he was obliged, in accordance with their custom, to give them further presents and entertainment. 'I can honestly say that the first three years we have, not even for half a day, been free from Indians,' he wrote. In the long run, of course, the Europeans got their way. But the Indians were far from guileless dupes, and in the short term, which was what mattered at the time, they got considerably more out of a simple land transaction than the amount of the purchase indicates.

We can assume that something similar happened with the sale of Manhattan. When Isaack de Rasière wrote to Amsterdam in 1628, two years after the purchase of the island, he used the present tense, reporting that Manhattan *is* inhabited by Manhatesen Indians, indicating that they had not gone anywhere. The Indians are a constant presence in the Dutch records of the colony. The settlers relied on them. And there was plenty of room; the island was, for the life of the colony, mostly wilderness. It is not until 1680 that the Manhattan Indians are referred to in the past tense, by which time they had, according to some accounts, moved north into the Bronx.

We can only imagine, then, the scene that must have taken place somewhere on lower Manhattan in early summer 1626: Minuit, his aides, soldiers and settlers, the Indian sachems and their retainers; the formal ceremony, with the making of marks on parchment; and surrounding it, for weeks or months on end, the visits, drinking, eating and bestowing of presents, all in the course of concluding a deal that would satisfy both sides, each of which had its own ideas about how it would pan out. And in some sort of follow-up ceremony forgotten by history, accompanied by a document subsequently lost, Minuit would have dedicated his city-in-the-making, and named it, appropriately, after its Dutch parent, some of whose culture and way of being – its openness and its merchant-prince swagger – the grubby little island village would inherit.

That piece of work completed, Minuit would then have boarded a company sloop and sailed upriver to deal with the crisis at Fort Orange. After spending some time there he ordered Catalina Trico, Joris Rapalje and the other settlers to vacate the area. A similar message was also sent to the South River and Fresh River settlers. Minuit was regrouping. From now on Manhattan – New Amsterdam – would be the centre of things.

He then sailed back to Manhattan, arriving in port on a Friday evening, the last day of July. The next morning he met the man who would become his valued assistant: Isaack de Rasière, whose ship had arrived while Minuit was away. De Rasière handed him letters from the directors; the two then fell to discussing whom they should send north to replace Van Crieckenbeeck, Minuit having decided to retain a contingent of soldiers at the fort. They decided to promote Bastiaen Krol, the Frisian lay minister who had come over with Rapalje and Trico. Krol had also been at Fort Orange for two years, and he had become particularly close to the Indians, for De Rasière wrote that they chose him 'because he is well acquainted with the language' of the tribe. So the man whose desire on arrival was to serve the church in the new province would instead be given a musket and a military command. No-one knows with how much fear he accepted the job; he had, after all, seen what had become of his predecessor.

Aside, then, from Krol and the small party of soldiers at the northern fort, the settlers, by now about two hundred of them, were all collected together along the flattish south-eastern flank of Manhattan, looking across the narrower of the two rivers that wrapped around the island to the bluffed shore 500 yards across the water. Under Minuit they worked quickly to turn their encampment into a permanent settlement. Within a year or so they had thirty wooden houses constructed along 'The Strand'. Minuit and De Rasière shared one of these. The one stone building they erected, with a thatched roof made from river reeds, was the West India Company headquarters, where pelts brought from throughout the territory were stored until they were to be shipped home, and where Isaack de Rasière made his office. At the southernmost tip, poised to catch the fullest gusts, a man named François, a millwright by profession, built two windmills: one for grinding grain, the other for sawing lumber.

Minuit also oversaw the construction of a fort. It occupied the south-western point of the island, well positioned to defend it against enemy vessels entering the harbour. The original plan was for a vast structure in which all the colonists would live, safe from the savages of the country. But the savages didn't seem so savage, and anyway it was clearly impossible, given the available manpower, to do anything very grand. Minuit ordered a redesign. The man who had been sent over to lay out the town and build the fort was apparently uniquely unskilled for a Dutch engineer: the original structure comprised little more than heaped earth and began to crumble even before it was finished. It would be torn down and rebuilt over the next several years; indeed, the ramshackle state of Fort Amsterdam would be an issue right up to the moment when Peter Stuyvesant, standing on its unsteady ramparts, agreed to surrender it to the English. The fort's general outlines are apparent today in the 'footprint' of the old Customs House, which more or less occupies its former position, just opposite Battery Park; in one of history's ironies, this spot, which was originally intended to keep Indians out, is now the home of the Museum of the American Indian, arguably the only place on Manhattan in which signs of Indian civilization persist.

As the settlers explored their island, they found it wondrously varied: thick forest studded with great knuckles of protruding rock; grassy meadowlands; high hills rising in the centre and to the north; charging and trickling streams, large reedy ponds. The Indians who traded with them doubled as guides.

Wickquasgeck was the name of a tribe that inhabited portions of the mainland just to the north of the island, as well as some of the northern forests of Manhattan. The Manhattan Indians used the Wickquasgeck name for the path they took through the centre of the island to these northern reaches. Coming south along it, Indians of various tribes reached the Dutch settlement at the southern end of the island. The Europeans could likewise follow it north – through stands of pin oak, chestnut, poplar and pine, past open fields strewn with wild strawberries ('the ground in the flat land near the river is covered with strawberries', one of them noted, 'which grow so plentifully in the fields, that one can lie down and eat them'), crossing the fast-running brook that flowed south-east from the highlands in the area of 59th Street and Fifth Avenue, more or less where the Plaza Hotel stands, to empty into a small bay on the East River – to hunt in the thick forest at the island's centre, and to fish the inlets that penetrated the eastern coast. As it was clearly destined to be the most prominent thoroughfare on the island, when the Dutch widened the path they referred to it as the Gentlemen's Street, or the High Street, or simply the Highway. The English, of course, called it Broadway.*

*

Going on in this way, putting every muscle and every ounce of guile into their own and their settlement's survival, the water's edge approaching and then inching away from their little community with every tide, the Manhattanites might scarcely have noticed what was happening over the next few years. But

* Broadway does not follow the precise course of the Indian trail, as some histories would have it. To follow the Wickquasgeck trail today, one would take Broadway north from the Custom House, jog eastwards along Park Row, then follow the Bowery to 23rd Street. From there, the trail snaked up the eastern side of the island. It crossed westwards through the top of Central Park; the paths of Broadway and the Wickquasgeck trail converge again at the top of the island. The trail continued into the Bronx; Route 9 follows it northwards.

the sails out in the harbour appeared more frequently, the skiffs rowed in from anchored ships (there was no dock yet) bringing more faces, and more varied ones. Ebony faces from the central highlands of Angola. Arab faces creased from north African sandstorms. An Italian, a Pole, a Dane.

Something was happening quite unlike the unfolding of society at the two English colonies to their north, where the rigid Puritans, who arrived in 1630, and the even more rigid Pilgrims, some of whom had been there since 1620, maintained, in their wide-brimmed piety, monocultures in the wild. Manhattan was a business settlement, a way-station on the rising Atlantic trade circuit, and news of its existence spread to places as far afield as the Amazonian thickets of Bahia and Pernambuco in Brazil, the newly founded Portuguese slave trading port of Luanda in Angola, and Stockholm, where an energetic monarch, Gustavus Adolphus, set his sights on making Sweden, long a frozen backwater of Europe, a military and trading power to rival Spain and the rising nations of England and the Dutch Republic.

A trickle had started. In small clusters, the world began coming to North America via this island nestled in its inviting harbour. And while the West India Company had a firm Calvinist stamp to it, which it tried to impress on its colony, the variegated makeup of the settlement itself – which indeed reflected the mix of peoples welcomed to its parent city of Amsterdam – bestowed upon it a persistent raggedness, a social looseness. It was also natural that the vanguard of private enterprise on the high seas – smugglers and pirates – would discover the place and make it a hub of their own activities. All the elements that made it attractive to legitimate trade applied in their case too, with the additional lure of its distance from civilization and the consequent virtual absence of authority.

Days got livelier; with nightfall, the soft slap of waves along the shore was drowned out by drinking songs and angry curses. New Amsterdam was not a city with its own structure of governance but literally a company town: its inhabitants were considered less citizens than employees, and there was no real legal system. So one was invented ad hoc. Every Thursday, in a room within the crudely walled fort, the 'government' conducted business. Proceedings were overseen by Minuit's law enforcement officer, an Englishman from Canterbury named Jan Lampe,* resplendently Rembrandtesque in his official accoutrements of black plumed hat and silver rapier. Minuit, De Rasière and a council of five heard cases and issued orders, which succeeding councils would reiterate and augment, building up a body of frontier law. In 1638, for example, came a series of scolding decrees: 'All seafaring persons are commanded to repair before sunset to the ship or sloop to which they are assigned and no one may remain on shore without permission.' 'All persons [are forbidden] from selling henceforth any wines, on pain of forfeiting twenty-five guilders and the wines which shall be found in their houses.' '[E]ach and every one must refrain from fighting; from adulterous intercourse with heathens, blacks, or other persons; from mutiny, theft, false testimony, slanderous language and other irregularities . . . the offenders shall be corrected and punished as an example to others.'

Multicultural gallivanting was on the rise. Spaniard Francisco de Porte testified before the council that, yes, he was present at the home of Dutch wheelwright Claes Swits the night the Englishman Thomas Beech's wife, Nanne, in the midst of a good drink-up, 'notwithstanding her husband's presence, fumbled at the front of the breeches of most of all of those who were present', causing her husband to fly into a rage and attack one of the men.

Minuit may have been a capable strategist but he was no governor of men, and the slide towards chaos accelerated. De Rasière struggled to maintain order during his tenure as secretary, which lasted until 1628, when he would go back to

* Presumably born something like John Lamp; like many foreign residents in the Dutch colony, he had his name 'Batavianized'.

Amsterdam, eventually leaving again to become a West India Company sugar baron in Brazil. He complained to the directors in Amsterdam of the 'quite lawless' state of affairs, and thought they should know that, with regard to the company's settlers, 'if they are ordered to speak of your Honors with reverence and without using such profane words as they have heretofore been accustomed to use [they] consider that great injustice is done to them.' When De Rasière caught a rough sort named Fongersz engaging in trade with the Indians on the sly, he told the man he would be forced to confiscate property and fine him, to which Fongersz replied, 'I do not consider you are a big enough man for that.' De Rasière added wearily, in his gossipy report, 'The honorable gentlemen can see what regard such a person has for orders and instructions, but I do not consider it to be his fault, since I have seldom seen him sober and doubt whether he has been so during the last three or four weeks.'

The directors could receive such complaints with equanimity. The times were very good for the West India Company. Its principal objective was to make money at the expense of the Spanish, and in 1628 a windfall landed in its collective lap. For the better part of a century the riches that Spain extracted from its South American colonies were sent to the homeland via a regular seagoing pipeline called the treasure fleet, consisting of as many as ninety vessels, making the crossing twice a year. In May 1628 Piet Heyn, a small, pug-faced seaman who had once been captured by the Spaniards and been forced to spend four years as a rower in a Spanish galley, surprised and swept down on the slow, heavily laden *flota* with his thirty-one privateering gunships while lurking in the waters off Cuba. The haul was staggering: twelve million guilders' worth of silver and gold. It was an amount that instantly repaid the company's investors the capital they had risked, and it stoked the fire of the Dutch economy for years. To the people of the United Provinces of the Netherlands, who for decades had been fighting for independence from the once-mighty Spanish empire, it was a signal, as sharp as a pistol shot, of a historic change. The title of a best-selling pamphlet made it plain: *Tekel or Balance of the great monarchy of Spain; in which is discovered that she cannot do so much as she supposes herself able to do. Written on the occasion of the conquest of the Silver-Fleet by Gen. P. P. Heyn*.

Beyond the sea that stretched in front of the settlers, then, the balance of the world was shifting. Heyn's deed seemed proof that the body of the Spanish empire was in decay. Half a world away on the island of Java, Dutchman Jan Pieterszoon Coen was undertaking an oriental version of Minuit's project: the building of a city (Batavia: the modern Jakarta) in an inhospitable wilderness that would be the base for Dutch trade in south-east Asia. In Frankfurt, meanwhile, William Harvey published his *Exercitatio Anatomica De Motu Cordis et Sanguinis in Animalibus*, spelling out his theories on the circulation of the blood, while in Italy the physician Santorio Santorio developed the trick of measuring body temperature using a thermometer. The methodical Dutch system of communication (missives went in duplicate or triplicate on different ships) was slow but ensured that news got through; thanks to it, the Manhattanites knew of developments in the wider world, and felt themselves a part of it.

To the north, the Pilgrim colony was limping along, and Minuit, feeling flush and expansive, decided it was time to establish contact. He sent letters of friendship, along with 'a rundlet of sugar, and two Holland cheeses'. William Bradford, governor of the struggling English colony, replied with thanks, adding that they were sorry they 'must remain your debtors till another time, not having any thing to send you for the present that may be acceptable'. Shortly after this exchange, Isaack de Rasière sailed to New Plymouth in person as official envoy of New Netherland, appearing in the Pilgrims' midst with 'a noise of trumpets' (the Manhattanites feeling a bit of show was called for), and bringing with him 'some cloth of three sorts and colours, and a chest of white sugar', as well as wampum, with which the English had little acquaintance but in the use of which the New Amsterdam traders had become proficient.

At about this time, and perhaps none too soon, a man of God arrived at Manhattan. But if the settlers expected leadership and encouragement from the colony's first minister of religion they were to be disappointed. The Revd Jonas Michaelius might well have won a contest for the moodiest, scratchiest resident of New Amsterdam. In his bitter letters home he complained about the voyage, the settlers ('rough and unrestrained'), the climate, the natives ('entirely savage and wild, strangers to all decency, yeah, uncivil and stupid as garden poles, proficient in all wickedness and godlessness; devilish men, who serve nobody but the Devil'), and the food ('scanty and poor'). 'I cannot say whether or not I shall remain here any longer after the three years [of his contract] shall have expired,' he wrote, adding, 'we lead a hard and sober existence like poor people.' Michaelius could be excused to some extent for his bitterness: the voyage to the new world had taken his pregnant, sickly wife, leaving him alone to care for their two young daughters.

For the time being, New Amsterdam offered some latitude to freelance merchants and traders. The West India Company allowed them to strike deals with the Indians provided the company itself remained the intermediary that would resell furs in Europe; business was being conducted in half a dozen languages; Dutch guilders, beaver skins, and Indian wampum were the common currencies. Among people whose diet was based on cheese and butter, cows were also a highly valued and tradable commodity.

But while beaver furs by the thousands were arriving at the West India Company's warehouse on the Amsterdam waterfront, the settlement was a long way from turning a profit. The directors wanted their North American colony to repay their investment the way the Caribbean salt colonies were doing, and a split formed in the board over how to make it happen. Some of the directors argued that the colony would never work properly without a massive influx of settlers, and that the best way to get people to go out was by allowing wealthy men to establish plantations there. In return for these estates, each patron (*patroon* in Dutch) would transport a population of farmers, smiths, masons, wheelwrights, bakers, chandlers and other workers. The directors who favoured this scheme proposed themselves as patroons. The other directors thought it was a stupid idea, one that would essentially carve the colony into small fiefs and add to the difficulty of dealing with pirates and renegade traders. Peter Minuit injected himself into this argument, supporting the patroon faction. The Revd Michaelius took the other side, and fired off a raft of letters branding Minuit as a dark force who was in the process of cheating the directors. He managed to convince them that the situation was dire enough to justify recalling both Minuit and Michaelius to Holland – which they did in 1631, ordering Krol, the lay minister who had been left in charge of Fort Orange, to serve as provisional director of the colony.

Minuit was filled with rage as he climbed on board the ironically named *Unity*, his gall only increased by the knowledge that he would have to spend the two-month journey in close confines with Michaelius. He had come a long way since leaving the little German town where he was raised, and he wasn't about to take this interruption in his career lightly. In five years he had established a rough but real outpost of European civilization on the edge of an uncharted continent. He had made peace with the Mohawks to the north following the unfortunate Van Crieckenbeeck incident, forging an alliance that would last through the whole of the colony's existence. He had bought Manhattan and Staten islands as well as huge tracts along the Hudson and around the bay of the South (Delaware) River from their native inhabitants while also managing to keep good relations with them. In so doing, he had outlined the perimeter of a New World province that occupied a considerable chunk of the Atlantic coast of North America, extending from the future state of Delaware in the south to the city of Albany in the north, and established a trade that had already sent more than 52,000 furs to Amsterdam. Most importantly, he had pinpointed and begun to develop the colony's capital, a place whose natural strategic importance was by now apparent to him and his fellow Manhattanites, if not to the West India Company directors. Even the vengeful Michaelius, for all his complaints about the place, could see this. 'True,' he had admitted in one of his bilious letters home, 'this island is the key and principal stronghold of the country.'

On a cold day in early 1632, then, Minuit stood on the deck of a ship laden with five thousand furs, fruits of the New World bound to warm the Old, looking out on a sullen, wintry ocean, and plotting his defence. He had no idea of the rude detour on which fate was about to send him, or of its repercussions for the colony he had coaxed into being.

4
The King, the Surgeon, the Turk and the Whore

CHARLES I, KING OF GREAT BRITAIN AND IRELAND, REGARDED horses and Dutchmen with something like equal and opposite intensity. As the famous equestrian portrait of Charles by Anthony van Dyck and the mounted statue of him in Whitehall suggest, he was never more at ease than when in the saddle. His devotion to racing was such that he spent a good portion of every year at Newmarket, making it – as it remains to this day – the headquarters of the sport in Britain. In the year 1632 he came early, leaving London in mid-February for the arduous 60-mile journey. ('Essex miles' were said to be longer than standard, since the roads in that corner of England were in particularly bad repair.) It was a major undertaking because when the king went to Newmarket, so did everyone else: the political, military and economic leadership of the country, as well as the king's household (his personal physician, William Harvey, did his historic work on the circulation of the blood while attending Charles at Newmarket). Charles was devoted to splendour with an almost religious zeal, and his Newmarket banquets had already become legendary, even infamous: in a single racing season, 7,000 sheep, 6,800 lambs and 1,500 oxen would be consumed at the eighty-six tables set daily. When not viewing the heats or entertaining, he spent his days at the royal retreat hunting, playing tennis or visiting his favourite horses in their stables.

As to the Dutch, he despised them. For that matter, he couldn't stand French people (never mind that he was married to a Frenchwoman), and he considered the Scottish, of which he was one by birth, such irritants that he encouraged as many of them as possible to emigrate to Canada. But the Dutch irked him in several special ways. They were engaged in a vigorous revolt, one that they hoped would, through bloodshed, throw off a monarchy and replace it with a republic. Charles passionately upheld the notion of the divine right of kings, and he considered republicanism to be a form of mass hysteria. Of course he believed in freedom for his subjects, he famously explained, 'but I must tell you that their liberty and freedom consist in *having* government . . . It is not their having a *share* in government; that is nothing appertaining to them.' (He gave this explanation to the crowd gathered to watch his beheading.) He was now in the midst of what would become known as the Personal Rule, the eleven-year period in which, having dismissed Parliament because it quarrelled with him, he governed on his own. During this time he would grow steadily more isolated from his country, the court becoming more insular and his own spending and partying progressively more lavish, as members of Parliament fumed and the supporters of the more radical moved towards open rebellion. Eventually, his worst nightmare would come true: his country in revolt, and himself beheaded.

Not only were the Dutch rebels, in Charles's view, mad and dangerous, there was the additional annoyance that currently, in ports around the world, Dutch merchant fleets were putting their English counterparts to the rout. The Dutch were in the process of muscling the English out of the richest source of commerce, the East Indies; Dutch ships now controlled much of the world's trade in sugar, spices and textiles. Ironically, in this arena Charles was hamstrung by his own authoritarian rule: having dismissed Parliament, he couldn't raise the funds he needed to compete.

Adding to his gall was the fact that, despite all of these irritations, Charles was forced to remain allied with the Dutch. Calvinism held sway in the Dutch provinces that were in revolt against Spain, and going back to Queen Elizabeth's time England's policy had been to support the revolt in the name of Protestantism. But the alliance was weakening; Charles himself, the English political leadership and growing numbers of the English people were turning against the Dutch, beginning to see them as the new threat.

Such was the situation, then, as Charles settled in to enjoy the racing season at Newmarket in March 1632 amid the deep thud of hooves beating the earth, the roar of the crowd, the bright flash of pennants against the sky. The king was in his element, richly dressed, with flowing chestnut hair and tapered fawn-coloured beard (the original 'vandyke'), casting a discerning eye over the favourites, placing bets with the Earl of Pembroke, who everyone knew had a bit of a gambling problem. Surely the last thing on earth Charles would care for here was a distracting, importuning embassy from the upstart Dutch republic. When Albert Joachimi, the elderly and dignified ambassador from the States General, arrived in Newmarket asking for an audience, Charles's first impulse was probably to recoil and send him away. But in the current international climate that would have been a political blunder; eventually he agreed to see the man.

The ambassador began the meeting with lengthy diplomatic niceties about the long friendship between the two nations, which he said had recently been disrupted by 'the enemy' seeking 'to foment some misunderstanding'. Charles understood perfectly well the subtext of the man's complaint, and was no doubt amused by the purposely fuzzy use of the term 'the enemy'. It was true that for decades the English had aided the Dutch in their war on Spain. But over two years before, also at Newmarket, Charles had received another emissary, from the Spanish court. This one he had welcomed – in fact, eagerly anticipated, and their meeting had altered the geopolitical landscape considerably.

Besides horses, Charles's other great and abiding love was for art. He had become, in a remarkably short time, one of the world's greatest patrons of the arts, and his personal collection, which included works by Raphael, Titian, Tintoretto, Mantegna and Correggio, added both to his royal lustre and, because of its staggering cost, to the simmering hatred for him among certain segments of the populace. The fact that, in his collecting, he had established an amiable correspondence with the pope, who had given him paintings from the Vatican collection, only increased Protestant suspicion of him. By 1629 Philip IV, the king of Spain, whose resources were nearly exhausted by the Dutch revolt, wanted very much for England to end its support to the United Provinces and decided to despatch an emissary to persuade Charles to sign a peace treaty. In a stroke of ingenuity that historians have credited to his wife, Philip chose as his ambassador Peter Paul Rubens, the most famous and sought-after artist in the world. Rubens, who was also something of a politician, considered himself a loyal Dutchman, but he came from Antwerp, in the Catholic-dominated southern provinces which had chosen not to break with Spain. As Rubens met Philip in Madrid to discuss the mission, his own hope was that if Charles ended English hostilities with Spain the rebel Dutch provinces would give up on their ruinous rebellion and the north and south would reunite. He agreed to the mission.

In England, Charles greeted Rubens with delight. He commissioned the artist to paint the ceiling of the Banqueting House at Whitehall Palace, newly built by Inigo Jones in the modern Palladian style. The central panel of the completed ceiling (today the only work of Rubens still in its intended position) epitomized Charles's ardent monarchic beliefs: amid a swirling stew of cherubs, his father, James, divine kingship personified, rises to heaven. Proving that the English have always had a sardonic wit, Charles's subjects later executed him outside this very room.

Rubens also introduced Charles to his pupil, Anthony van Dyck, who became Charles's court painter; it is thanks to him that we have a gallery of portraits capturing the king's every mood and manner. Charles knighted both men. He also signed a peace treaty with Spain – another step in the movement between Britain and the Dutch Republic away from friendship and towards confrontation. Rubens was elated, and went next to visit his countryman Ambassador Joachimi in London, hoping to persuade him that now the best hope for a unified Dutch Republic was for the rebel government to seek terms with Spain. But Rubens seriously underestimated the resolve of the northern provinces. Joachimi was as much a rebel as those he served, and told the painter the only way the provinces would unify would be if those in the south joined in the war. (They did not, and eventually the Catholic southern provinces became the nation of Belgium.)

It was against this backdrop of England's recent peace treaty with Spain that Joachimi now approached Charles, amid the stamping and whinnying of Newmarket. In using the phrase 'the enemy' in relation to both the English and the Dutch, he was implying that, recent treaties aside, Protestants still had to stick together in the face of the universal foe of Catholicism. ('We cannot perceive that his Majesty is indisposed towards us,' Joachimi wrote to the States General after his audience, 'because we have neither Saints nor Festivals, wherein the Spanish nation is very superstitious.') Specifically, the ambassador wanted the king to put a stop to a recent disturbing practice: since England's treaty with Spain, Spanish ships that had been captured by Dutch privateers were being seized when they entered English ports, contrary to longstanding agreement between the two nations.

The king heard the man out, and with great decorum dodged the issue. Joachimi went away empty-handed.

Less than two weeks later, however, Charles, just returned to Whitehall, was forced to deal with the man yet again. This time Joachimi's diplomatic reserve showed signs of cracking. There had been a new development. Another ship had been seized, but this was not a Spanish ship taken as a prize by the Dutch. It was a bona fide Dutch vessel, Joachimi informed the king, bound for Amsterdam from 'a certain island named Manathans'. Reports indicated that it carried five thousand furs, as well as the former director of the province of New Netherland.

At that moment, two hundred miles to the south-west, Peter Minuit sat in English custody, fuming. As if it were not enough that he had been (to his mind) unreasonably removed from his post, forced to abandon the infant colony he had nurtured and make the long, hazardous voyage home to defend his conduct, after two frigid months at sea the *Unity* had been caught in a storm off the coast of England and forced to make an emergency landfall at Plymouth, where the courtesy generally extended to a troubled ship by a friendly nation was not forthcoming. Crowning the whole bitter turn of events his life had taken, Minuit was taken prisoner. The only salve for him was the fact that his nemesis, the odious Revd Michaelius, was also in English hands.

When word of the seizure reached the United Provinces, the leaders there were at first inclined to believe that, as one official wrote, 'this intrigue was set on foot by the Spanish Ambassador in England.' But as more information came in, they learned that the English had taken possession of the Dutch vessel on the grounds that its cargo had been illegally acquired in English territory. The Dutch were confused – their traders had not intruded on the English colony to the north of their own. Surely, Ambassador Joachimi now put it to His Majesty, there must be some mistake.

But this time Charles would leave no room for the ambassador to be hopeful. Speaking with a lawyerly mix of precision and subtlety, the king told Joachimi he understood there was some dispute over claims to the territory in question, and that he could not release the ship until he was certain of his rights in the matter. The 'answer of his Majesty', Joachimi reported to his superiors, 'though expressed in polite terms and with a friendly disposition, did not please us'.

Joachimi surely understood what underlay the sudden chill in relations. Not only had the Dutch gained mastery over the East Indies trade, Charles was also aware that the New World colonies represented another source of wealth, though the full advantage to be gained from their exploitation lay in the future. He had recently given – as repayment of a favour – a vast tract of the Virginia territory to his father's friend and adviser George Calvert, Lord Baltimore, which his son named Maryland apparently in honour of Charles's wife, Henrietta Maria. And Charles himself had backed the tobacco trade in Virginia.

But the English had a particular reason for contesting the Dutch claim in North America just now. The whole swirl of geopolitical doings involving the two rising powers had recently crystallized in one event – one of those small, far-off, seemingly minor occurrences that would have historical echoes all out of proportion to its size. A few years earlier, on one of the lucrative Spice Islands of the East Indies (today part of Indonesia), the island of Amboyna or Ambon, a bloody encounter had taken place between the Dutch, who had won control of the island and its clove trade, and a colony of English merchants who were allowed to live and work there. Probably in retaliation for a recent English assault on Dutch ships in the Indies, Dutch soldiers on Amboyna tortured and killed ten Englishmen, as well as several Japanese mercenaries, whom they accused of plotting to take over the fort. The English survivors insisted there had been no such plot, and that the Dutch behaviour had been motivated by simple barbarity.

However outraged the English authorities may actually have been by the incident, they spun it ferociously for moral and political advantage. Pamphlets and books appeared in England, with titles like *A True Relation of the Unjust, Cruel, and Barbarous Proceedings against the English at Amboyna*, containing vivid, novelistic descriptions and graphic woodcut illustrations of the varieties of torture to which the men had been subjected, including both water and fire. ('Johnson [was] brought againe to the torture,' ran one breathless account, 'where Beomont heard him for sometime cry aloud, then quiet again, then roare afresh. At last, after hee had beene about an houre in this second examination, hee was brought forth wailing and lamenting, all wet, and cruelly burnt in divers parts of his body.') So great was the uproar over these accounts that, in addition to lamenting the seizure of the *Unity*, Joachimi complained about them as well in his audience with Charles. The ambassador wanted the king to understand that the Dutch considered these books to be slanderous, 'the tendency whereof is only to excite the temper of one people against the other'. But the king would do nothing to stop their dissemination, and so, entering the battle for public opinion in England, the Dutch countered with pamphlets of their own, printed in English, with which they flooded the English market, giving their side of the affair. (They denied burning the men, but admitted using water torture as 'the most assured and civill' and 'a thing customable throughout Europe'.)

The mileage the English got out of Amboyna was astounding. For decades it fuelled the English perception of the Dutch merchants as relentless, bloodless fiends. The Dutch record of atrocities was surely no better or worse than that of the English, Portuguese or other European empire-builders, but believing it to be more barbarous helped assuage English bitterness that the tiny, waterlogged nation had so far outdistanced them in the global race. As late as 1691, more than six decades after the incident, John Dryden would write his play *Amboyna: A Tragedy*, employing as characters all the actors in the actual events, from the monstrous Dutch governor, Harmon ('Bring more candles, and burn him from the Wrists up to the Elbows'), to the heroic Englishman Beaumont ('Do; I'll enjoy the Flames like Scaevola; and when one's roasted, give the other hand').

But the propaganda also had a negative result. So well did the English succeed in portraying the Dutch merchant-soldiers as inexorable that England virtually ceded the East Indies to the Dutch shippers, and refocused its energies elsewhere in Asia. Thus one resonant consequence of Amboyna, echoing through the coming centuries, would be the build-up of British India.

Another was New York. No such colony existed or would exist for decades, but in the thrust and parry of the two empires-in-the-making in the 1620s and 1630s, events on one side of the globe would generate reactions on the other. By now, some in England realized that the Dutch-controlled portion of North America was the linchpin to the continent, and they were determined that the Dutch should not have control of both the East Indies and the vast unknown riches of North America. Legal minds went to work, and the case for overriding the Dutch claim to its territory was developed.

One month after Joachimi's second audience with the king, Charles's formal reply arrived at The Hague. The king declared he had no intention of suppressing books published in England that dealt with the Amboyna massacre (his response to Dutch anger on this score: 'nothing save the balm of justice can heal ulcerated hearts.') Regarding the complaint about the seizure of the ship that had set sail from Manhattan Island, Charles countered it by disputing the Dutch claim to the territory. The Dutchmen and their vessel, he advised, came from 'a certain plantation usurped by them in the north parts of Virginia, which they say was acquired from the natives of the country'. There followed a flurry of attacks on the Dutch claim to Manhattan Island and the territory extending more than a hundred miles to the north and south of it, some quite novel. '[F]irst, it is denied that the Indians were *possessores bonae fidei* of those countries, so as to be able to dispose of them either by sale or donation, their residences being unsettled and uncertain . . . and in the second place, it cannot be proved, *de facto*, that all the Natives of said country had contracted with them at the said pretended sale.' Moreover, the English claimed that they had true title to the land in question, which was 'justified by first discovery'. In this, the

English were stretching the accepted legalities to the point of absurdity – an absurdity that underlies all of the land grabs of the age of empire and exploration. The 'first discovery' was that of John Cabot, who in 1497 made footfall at Newfoundland. By the logic of the concept of 'discovery', when the foot of an explorer made contact with soil that had not previously been settled by humans whom Europeans regarded as having a proper civilization, that soil, and all soil stretching out from it for as far as the metaphysical aura of discovery could be made to stretch, came under the flag of the explorer's sponsoring nation. Even adherents of this magic-wand approach to extending one's domain, however, would have to have marvelled at the claim that because an Italian foot once touched the soil of a portion of land neighbouring North America (Newfoundland is, after all, an island) – and never mind the fact that at the time Cabot thought he was in an uninhabited region of Asia – the entire land mass, millions of square miles extending up to the North Pole, westward to the Pacific and south as far as the Spanish-held territories, miraculously and incontrovertibly became the property of England.

The Dutch didn't buy it. For one thing, they had a different legal basis for ownership. In their scheme, the discoverer also had to occupy and chart the land; thus the decision to send settlers, however few, to each of the three river systems in New Netherland. By May the matter was over; the ship was released. The English had pushed, and the Dutch – who were simply the more powerful nation at the time – had pushed back. Charles had served notice of England's interest in the property in question, but just now he was not in a position to back up his words.

No-one recorded what Peter Minuit said when, on 3 May, he came tramping into the courtyard of the elegant West India Company headquarters in Amsterdam, livid to the point of distraction, and heard that, on top of everything else, the English were now denying the very right to exist of the colony he had nurtured. He probably didn't feel outrage – not after the way the

Dutch directors had treated him. It may be that what struck him most about the international dispute was how unsettled things were, with the ownership of the land being called into question. For at some point after the inquiry into his conduct as director-general of New Netherland – which resulted in his formal dismissal, and which turned on the charge that not enough settlers had been shipped to the colony during his tenure (an outrageous claim, because Minuit had repeatedly pressed for more settlers) – he met with Willem Usselincx, who had been the original proponent of the New Netherland scheme but who, like Minuit, was now disgruntled. The two of them would soon dream up a secret international colonizing scheme of their own, as audacious as it was ridiculous.

*

Two years before it brought Peter Minuit back to Europe and sailed into an international incident, the *Unity*, sailing in the other direction, had delivered to the shores of Manhattan a raw, tough-minded eighteen-year-old named Harmen Meyndertsz van den Bogaert. He came equipped with training that was certain to be of value in a frontier settlement, having undergone the two-year, hands-on apprenticeship (no book work involved) required before induction into the ancient and not especially venerated guild of the 'barber-surgeon'. He apparently did more than trim the beards of New Netherland's residents, and must have impressed people with his nerve in carrying out amputations and blood-letting, because a little after the run-in with the English over the fate of the colony he was given the weighty responsibility of saving it from another European threat.

By now New Netherland had an undisputed second city – or rather, village. In fact, Fort Orange, the trading post at the conjunction of the Mohawk and Hudson rivers where Joris Rapalje and Catalina Trico had spent their first two years, had become the centre of the fur trade. Once peace had been re-established with the Mohawks, the settlers had returned, eager to make up for lost time. From far out in the uncharted west, Indians came down the Mohawk valley with their heavy loads of pelts; the traders bought them, stored them at the fort, then shipped them downriver to Manhattan. They had a strong relationship with the Mohawks now, one that would last the whole lifespan of the Dutch settlement, so the trade seemed secure.

It wasn't. In late 1634, fur traffic on the Mohawk suddenly dried up. The Dutch, whose world-view was based on water, knew the river and lake system of their territory, knew that far out there in the unexplored west lay a series of lakes, which were the main beaver areas hunted by the Indians who supplied them. If the Indians had stopped coming, there could be only one reason: the French, who long before had infiltrated the waterways far to the north and forged fur-trading alliances with Indians in Canada, had moved south into that territory and made new agreements with the Indians there.

At this stage the fur trade was the colony's entire reason for being. For decades to come debts on Manhattan would be paid in the interchangeable currencies of beaver pelts, Dutch guilders and Indian wampum. While they were prized for their fur, beavers were even more sought after for the pelt beneath the outer layer of fur, which was made into felt. Felt hats were both a necessity and a status symbol throughout Europe, from the Puritans' austere black bonnets to the dashing chapeaux of the Dutch officers in Rembrandt's *The Night Watch* and, later, the English top hat. The entire beaver-to-hat process had a fantastic quality to it. On the production end, hat-makers used mercury to separate fur from felt, leading to routine mental illness and, perhaps, to the phrase 'mad as a hatter'. The hats were wildly expensive; the English diarist Samuel Pepys paid £4 5s for one in 1641 – about three months' wages for an average labourer. This in turn meant serious income for the Indian trappers, and for the French, English and Dutch who competed to trade with them. (It also accounts for the image of the beaver still found on the seal of New York City.) The disruption in the beaver trade was serious. Within a very short time, the French outflanking manoeuvre could become a *coup de grâce*. Something had to be done.

Thus it was that Harmen van den Bogaert, now aged twenty-two, got the commission to do what no resident of New Netherland had yet done: travel into the interior of the continent, seek the Mohawks out in their villages and convince them that the Dutch were better trading partners. By sheer luck, the journal he kept on the voyage – which details one of the earliest forays by Europeans from the coast westwards into the North American continent, provides an extraordinarily rare glimpse of thriving Mohawk villages and also includes the first-ever Mohawk dictionary – survived. It was discovered in the late nineteenth century, and only recently studied in depth. It gives a remarkably fresh and vivid view of the eastern Indians, uncoloured by the history that was to follow.

The situation was so desperate that the mission couldn't wait until spring; choosing two men to accompany him, Jeronimus dela Croix and sailor Willem Thomassen, Van den Bogaert set out on 11 December. They left Fort Orange in icy weather, their packs filled with food as well as knives, scissors and other items intended as presents, in the company of five Mohawk guides.

Things started out hopefully enough, as they hiked into virgin pine forest, but it was a bad sign when, in the middle of the first night, Van den Bogaert woke up to find the guides silently preparing to leave camp without them. He and his companions threw their things together and hurried to catch up; later they discovered that the Indians' dogs had eaten the meat and cheese from their packs, leaving them with only bread. There followed days of brutal slog through snow two and a half feet deep, with slashing winds, swirling blizzards, and sightings of bear and elk through the trees.

On the twentieth, chilled to the bone, they came to a stop before a stream that, Van den Bogaert wrote, was 'running very hard with many large chunks of ice . . . so that we were in great danger. Had one of us fallen, it would have been the end. But the Lord God protected us and we made it across. We were soaked up to the waist.' They pressed on, shivering, 'with wet and frozen clothing, stockings and shoes'. Then they reached a hill-top and an amazing sight: thirty-two houses set in a clearing, some of them two hundred feet long, each covered with elm bark, the whole surrounded by a picket palisade. The men had reached their goal: a Mohawk village, and a new civilization. They were welcomed, and given baked pumpkin, beans and venison. In the light of the fire that night, Van den Bogaert cut open Thomassen's leg to relieve swelling brought on by the long march, and smeared the cut with bear grease.

The series of villages they visited in the ensuing days surprised Van den Bogaert with their level of development. In one there were '36 houses, row on row in the manner of streets', each of which held several families. Some of the houses already bore the signs of European contact: iron hinges, bolts, chains. The men found boats and barrels made from bark. They encountered cemeteries, surrounded by palisades 'so neatly made that it was a wonder', the graves painted red, white and black. A chief's tomb they found was large enough to have an entrance, and was decorated with carvings and paintings of animals. In some villages penned bears were being kept and fattened. Each long-house had several hearths.

The people met them with curiosity or fear. Some, encountering them in the forest, dropped their belongings and ran. In one village, however, 'we caused much curiosity in the young and old; indeed, we could hardly pass through the Indians here. They pushed one another into the fire to see us. It was almost midnight before they left us. We could not do anything without having them shamelessly running about us.' The chief presented Van den Bogaert with a mountain-lion skin, which he slept with, only to discover that 'in the morning I had at least 100 lice'.

There was an irony to the reception the Europeans received in some places. At one village a chief eagerly invited them into his house, which was set away from the village proper because he feared the smallpox that was beginning to ravage the Indians of the region. No-one on either side realized that the presence of the illness, which would decimate the north-east Indians over the course of the seventeenth century, was a result of contact with Europeans, who brought diseases to which they themselves were immune but before which the Indians were helpless.

At every village the people called to them in Iroquois, 'Allese rondade!' or 'shoot!' There was a great deal of excitement when the men obliged and fired their weapons – here, preserved in the amber of Van den Bogaert's journal, we catch that fleeting moment when Indian society was aware of firearms but hadn't yet begun to use them. On Christmas Eve, Van den Bogaert watched in awe as their shamans went to work, and recorded one of the most detailed and dramatic descriptions of an east coast Indian healing ritual:

> As soon as they arrived, they began to sing, and kindled a large fire, sealing the house all around so that no draft could enter. Then both of them put a snakeskin around their heads and washed their hands and faces. They then took the sick person and laid him before the large fire. Taking a bucket of water in which they had put some medicine, they washed a stick in it ½ ell long. They stuck it down their throats so that the end could not be seen, and vomited on the patient's head and all over his body. Then they performed many farces with shouting and rapid clapping of hands, as is their custom, with much display, first on one thing and then on the other, so that the sweat rolled off them everywhere.

Eventually the travellers made their way to the most important village, where they would negotiate. The scene Van den Bogaert describes opens like the third act of a Western, in which the white man finally meets the Indians on their terms. The residents formed two long lines outside the gate of the village, and the Europeans passed ceremonially between the columns and through the elaborately carved entryway to the house at the furthest end. The houses here had gables, decorated with paintings. In the flickering firelight, amid much whooping and excitement, the men were fed and fêted.

And then the rough business tactics began.

A secondary tribal leader berated them for not bringing adequate presents. He showed them the presents the French had given, including French shirts and coats. The atmosphere became tense. As the man kept up his verbal assault the others 'sat so close to us here that we could barely sit'. Van den Bogaert counted forty-six people crowded around them in the room. One of the Indians then began to scream, calling them, in Van den Bogaert's translation, 'scoundrels', and his tirade reached such a fury that Willem Thomassen, a hardened seaman, burst into angry tears. Finally, Van den Bogaert hollered back.

At this, the tactic changed. The Indian laughed, suggested there had been a misunderstanding, and said, 'You must not be angry. We are happy that you have come here.' An old man stepped forward and put his hand against Van den Bogaert's chest to feel his heart; he announced with approval that the man was not afraid. The Dutchmen had apparently passed a test. Warily, the visitors dispensed knives, scissors and other presents. Six leaders of the village stepped forward and presented Van den Bogaert with a beaver coat. When they sat down again to discuss business, Van den Bogaert learned that these Mohawks would prefer to maintain relations with the Dutch because they feared the Hurons, with whom the French were allied. The Mohawks offered their terms: henceforth, each beaver pelt would be worth four hands of sewant and four hands of cloth (a hand of sewant, or wampum, being one string of beads stretched from outstretched thumb to little finger). When Van den Bogaert did not reply, an old chief from another of the five tribes of the Iroquois confederation, of which the Mohawks were a part, stepped forward. He required a translator because he spoke Onondaga, not Mohawk, and said, 'You have not said whether we shall have four hands or not.' Van den Bogaert told them he was not authorized to finalize the deal, but would return in the spring with the answer. They accepted this, but the old man cautioned him, 'You must not lie, and come in the spring to us and bring us all an answer. If we receive four hands, then we shall trade our pelts with no one else.'

A provisional agreement was made. The Indians began a chant, which Van den Bogaert diligently recorded. The chant turns out to contain the names of the five tribes of the Iroquois League, through some of whose lands the Dutchmen had travelled, and Van den Bogaert's documentation of it provides the earliest written record of this confederacy, which would play a role in the American Revolution. A rough translation of the chant, given to me by Iroquois linguist Gunther Michelson, is: 'This white man is a magician. He has leave to go around to all the Mohawk, Oneida, Onondaga, Cayuga and Seneca, and lie down safely among them. This is a useful thing for the Iroquois League.' The chant indicates how much Van den Bogaert succeeded in impressing the Iroquois; the reference to him as a magician also dates the encounter to this period in which the east coast Indians, still amazed by the tools the whites used, thought of them as having wondrous powers.

Following the agreement, Van den Bogaert was given a house, presents and thick portions of bear meat. Although he doesn't mention it, he may have been given other things as well, for the detailed list of Mohawk vocabulary he compiled includes the words and phrases for 'man', 'woman', 'prostitute', 'vagina', 'phallus', 'testicles', 'to have intercourse', 'very beautiful', 'When shall you return?' and 'I do not know.'

The three emissaries said their farewells and began the long journey home. In late January they arrived back at Fort Orange, where the people had feared them dead. They had travelled to Oneida Lake – nearly as far as Lake Ontario – and back, through savage weather, powered only by their own feet. It is no accident that their route was the one that generations of Americans and millions of tons of goods would follow westward in the coming centuries, once the Erie Canal was constructed; it was the natural highway connecting the Atlantic coast to the heart of the continent, the reason the Dutch had focused their attention on the Hudson river, and why, beginning with Minuit, they saw Manhattan Island as the logical hub. Van den Bogaert's trip would prove to be pioneering in the fullest sense.

In the spring, the deal with the Mohawks was indeed finalized. The furs began coming again. Van den Bogaert's impact on the colony would not end here; he would later make a final, tragicomic contribution to history. But for now he had done what was asked of him, and the colony could go on.

*

This, however, begged a question: why bother? While the old ambassador and the young explorer-surgeon were doing their utmost to preserve the colony, its parents, the merchant princes who ran the West India Company, were running it into the ground. They disagreed over how to manage it, with the result that it went largely unmanaged. To replace the capable Peter Minuit they chose a dissolute young clerk in the company's Amsterdam offices with no particular set of skills to recommend him, only a dull devotion to the company and a family relationship to one of its directors. Immediately upon his arrival in Manhattan, Wouter van Twiller began proving himself a drunk and a decidedly deficient leader. At times he even managed to combine the two traits. Shortly after he began his duties, and on the heels of the recent trouble with England over the ship carrying his predecessor back to Europe, an English trader sailed into the harbour and anchored in front of the fort. Her captain made clear his intention to sail upriver and trade with the Indians: an open flouting of Dutch sovereignty. Van

Twiller dealt with the matter by boarding the vessel and proceeding to drink with the captain. He became so drunk that David de Vries, a Dutch adventurer who had spent time in the East Indies and now proposed to throw his lot in with the New Amsterdammers, and who had himself just sailed into the harbour, was embarrassed. The English captain then made the bold declaration that he had every right to sail upriver because the river and all the land around it was English. De Vries responded that New Netherland had long been settled by the Dutch, and that their claim was secure. The English captain countered that the area had been discovered by an English explorer, 'David Hutson'. De Vries countered, quite properly, that Hudson had charted the river under Dutch auspices. Van Twiller appears to have stayed out of the conversation.

After lying at anchor several days, the English ship set sail and headed upriver, in defiance of the Dutch leader. Van Twiller moved quickly. He ordered a cask of wine brought to his office in the fort at once, filled bumpers for himself and the soldiers and other company employees assembled there, and cried out for those who loved the Prince of Orange and him to join him in stopping the Englishman. Whereupon, De Vries reported, 'The people all began to laugh at him.'

Van Twiller let the matter go, and the English ship sailed on unhindered. De Vries was incensed. He sat the man down and explained that it was precisely incidents like this that made or broke a colony. 'I said, if it were my matter, I would have helped him away from the fort with beans from the eight-pounders, and not permitted him to sail up the river,' De Vries wrote in his journal, and added that 'if the English committed any excesses against us in the East Indies, we should strike back at them; otherwise one cannot control that nation, for they were of so proud a nature, that they thought everything belonged to them.'

Clearly Van Twiller had some inescapable weaknesses, but it should also be kept in mind that for this period of the Dutch colony's existence the official records are almost non-existent, so that history has relied on bits and pieces, such as De Vries's journal, in order to recreate the times. Thanks to the wave of scholarship now under way, however, new evidence is emerging that complicates the picture. A letter written by Van Twiller in 1635 to the company directors, discovered recently in the Dutch national archives in The Hague by historian Jaap Jacobs, shows Van Twiller building a fort on the Connecticut river (the earliest documentation for the settlement of what would become Hartford), holding the English at bay and trying to deal with his unruly population – acting, in other words, more or less like the colonial administrator he was supposed to be.

But if Van Twiller was not the outright incompetent that history has made him out to be, he was clearly not equal to the challenge of the place. True, by this time the colonists had managed to complete a number of building projects. New Amsterdam now had a downtown arcade of five shops, and dozens of private houses. Ships carried bricks as ballast on the trip from Europe, and the settlers used these – the slender yellow bricks of Holland, which still turn up occasionally in digs in lower Manhattan – in their first houses, particularly in chimney stacks. Ramparts were added to the fort. There was a boathouse and a sailmaker's loft, a guardhouse and soldiers' barracks, and a church.

But there were few residents with the drive, guts and pioneering spirit of David de Vries. Many were pirates or itinerant fur-traders. The most famous New Amsterdam pirate – Willem Blauvelt – used New Amsterdam as his base for plundering the Spanish main (the waters north of South America), mixed piracy with privateering and was a member of the community in good standing, who dutifully logged his voyages with the provincial secretary and whose financial backers included many of the town's leading citizens.

Piracy in turn brought another wave of residents, for the 'cargo' of pilfered Spanish galleons included not only cases of indigo, chests of sugar and sacks bulging with pieces of eight, but slaves bound for the Caribbean salt fields. As privateers brought them to Manhattan, some of the Africans became slaves in the West India Company's service, while others worked for their freedom or were employed as freedmen from the outset. The very names of Manhattan's Africans – Pedro Negretto, Antony Congo, Jan Negro, Manuel de Spanje, Anthony the Portuguese, Bastiaen d'Angola – evoked the tempestuous course of their lives, from capture and enslavement in Africa to purchase by Portuguese traders and forced voyage westwards on Spanish ships, only to be captured once again by Dutch pirates. Decades later, terms of slavery would be more or less standardized in the colonies, but at this point, on the slightly anarchic island of Manhattan, some of these people were among the more stable residents of the island; many would become farmers, carpenters, smiths and barber-surgeons.

The growing and unruly population required servicing. Prostitution became an established strand of the economy (the wife of Tymen Jansen was known to 'commit adultery . . . not for money, but for otters and beavers'). The island spawned taverns and breweries with remarkable speed – at one point in the early years one-quarter of its buildings were devoted to making or selling alcohol. The 'bar scene' seems to have rivalled anything New York City could boast today (and, ironically enough, came to occupy the same general downtown quadrant that accounts for much of today's nightlife): an enraged woman who came upon her husband in a tap-room later wondered in court 'what he was doing with another man's wife . . . touching her breasts and putting his mouth on them'. A man named Simon Root had part of his ear cut off 'with a cutlass' and petitioned the court to get a certificate clarifying that it happened in a fairly routine bar-room brawl and should not be confused with the standard punishment for thievery. The records are rife with murderous assaults, and the colony's leaders favoured extreme forms of punishment – branding, pillorying, whipping, beating with rods, garroting, hanging – in an effort to instill order. Visible punishment of all sorts – removing an ear, boring a hole in the ear or tongue with a redhot poker, 'riding the horse', which involved shackling the evildoer to a wooden horse, often for days at a time, with heavy weights attached to his arms and legs – was prized for its deterrent effect.

Harsh as punishment often was, there was a certain flexibility in carrying it out: people were occasionally let off at the last minute, sometimes in novel ways. On a cold January day in 1641 eight African slaves were brought into the fort, accused of murdering another slave, Jan Premero, 'in the woods near their houses' (an area north of the town set aside for slave quarters – today it is where the United Nations resides). The men admitted to the crime 'without torture or shackles'. But it couldn't be determined which one did the deed, so the court, in its wisdom, decided lots would be drawn to determine who would be put to death, thus letting 'God designate the culprit'. God chose Manuel Gerrit, alias The Giant. A week later, a crowd gathered near the shore for the entertainment of a public hanging. In theory, drawing lots may have satisfied the law; in reality, hanging a possibly innocent man may have been distasteful to the colony's leaders, or maybe they saw it as a senseless waste of a good slave. There is no proof of tampering in what followed, but the results are suspicious. The executioner fastened 'two good ropes' around the man's neck and pushed him off the ladder, whereupon, to the gasps of the spectators, both ropes broke and the man tumbled to the ground unharmed. The crowd clamoured for mercy, and the court granted it. The Giant went free; the system worked.

A scene that appears in the court records from a few years later nicely sums up the atmosphere of casual mayhem, of violence erupting in the midst of ordinary life, that reigned in this period:

> Piere Malenfant, of Riennes [i.e. Rennes], in Brittany, 35 years of age, declares that yesterday evening about nine o'clock, as

> it was getting dark, he came from the farm in company with Paulus Heyman and his wife, he carrying the child on his arm and the woman the gun. Near Damen's house, the sentry, named Andries Tummelyn, called out, 'Who goes there?' He answered, 'A friend.' Paulus Heyman said, 'Good evening, Jonker Nobleman,' to which the sentry replied, 'What do you want, Merchant?' Heyman retorted, 'Lick my ass.'

At this, the Frenchman and the sentry fell on one another with swords; Malenfant was stabbed through the arm and thigh, and came limping into court seeking compensation.

Clearly, the New Netherland settlers were quite unlike their fellow pioneers to the north, the pious English Pilgrims and Puritans who were struggling to establish their 'new Jerusalem', governed by godly morality. Even so, whether the Pilgrims, via the Thanksgiving celebration, or the Puritans made truly worthy role models for the nation that was to come into being in the distant future is at least debatable; throughout this period the Puritans were busy massacring the Pequot Indians in the name of God and persecuting internal 'heretics' (i.e. anyone who didn't subscribe to their brand of Puritanism). One might say the English and Dutch colonies represented respectively the extreme conservative and liberal wings of the seventeenth-century social spectrum. Technically, hard-line Calvinism was the moral force at work in the Manhattan colony; but in the colony's records, expressions of piety are overwhelmed by accounts like that of a woman who, while her husband dozed on a nearby chair, 'dishonorably manipulated the male member' of a certain Irishman while two other men looked on. Excessive rigidity (of the moral kind) was not the sin of New Amsterdam's residents.

There was a kind of duke and duchess of this era of New Amsterdam, who outdid their neighbours for sheer rabble-rousing. Back in Europe, Griet Reyniers had worked as a barmaid at the tavern of Pieter de Winter in Amsterdam. In fact, she practised two professions at once – the mistress of the tavern once spotted her in a back room, 'her petticoat upon her knees', sexually servicing a party of soldiers. It's impossible to say whether the young Wouter van Twiller wandered into her establishment one evening and became enamoured of her. All we do know is that when he set sail for Manhattan on *De Zoutberg* ('The Salt Mountain') to take up his post as leader of New Netherland, Griet was on board too, ready to seek her fortune in a new land. It was a hazardous crossing: the ship was nearly captured by 'Turks', and then it turned the tables and took the prize of a Spanish bark whose hulls were crammed with sugar. Griet was unfazed by the goings-on, and plied her trade at sea – passengers noticed her pulling 'the shirts of some of the sailors out of their breeches'. Landing at Manhattan and finding it, so to speak, virgin territory, she set up shop. She took to walking the Strand, hiking her petticoats to display her wares for the sailors. If she had come as Van Twiller's mistress, it may have been as a result of his finally dismissing her that she was observed marching into the fort one day crying out, 'I have long enough been the whore of the nobility. From now on I shall be the whore of the rabble!' She had a knack for attention-getting publicity stunts; her trademark was to measure the penises of her customers on a broomstick.

Anthony van Salee was known as The Turk; he was a pirate from Morocco, the son of a Dutch seaman-turned-pirate who had become the admiral of the sultan's fleet and married a Moroccan woman. Anthony was brawny, dark-featured and a one-man criminal class. From the time of his arrival on Manhattan in the early 1630s, he made trouble: he threatened people with loaded pistols; he roamed the village drunk and cursing; he was accused of stealing; when Hendrick the tailor called him 'a Turk, a rascal and a horned beast', his anger apparently spoke for many. Even Anthony's dog was trouble: once a black townsman named Anthony the Portuguese filed suit, claiming that the man's dog had 'damaged' his hog. He won.

Perhaps it was inevitable that Griet and Anthony would come together. They married and had children, although, since she kept at her work, it wasn't always clear who the father was. From the supine position of childbirth she once asked the midwife who the newly delivered baby looked like. The woman replied, 'If you do not know who the father is, how should I know? However, the child is somewhat brown.' The couple became fairly notorious in New Amsterdam, but the point is that they were not especially out of the ordinary. In fact, the view that American history has of the Dutch colony centred on Manhattan fits it fairly well to this point: a colourful collection of losers, drifters and rogues, inconsequential and meandering, waiting around for the winds of fate to blow them off the map. The Dutch had succeeded in obtaining a piece of land of inestimable value, but while they were experts at turning that to advantage in other parts of the world, here – the efforts of Van den Bogaert and Ambassador Joachimi notwithstanding – they let it languish.

By now, however, others had recognized the value of the land on this stretch of the Atlantic coast, and were making plays for it. Van Twiller wrote to the English in Massachusetts of his hope that 'as good neighbors wee might live in these heathenishe countryes', but they ignored him – English settlers were already drifting southwards into territory claimed by the Dutch. The Fresh River – the Connecticut river – was irresistible, and in 1636 a preacher named Thomas Hooker led the first group of English religious pioneers south from the Massachusetts Bay colony to set up a community on the river. They called it Hartford.

Then there was an internal play made for a portion of the colony. Kiliaen van Rensselaer was an Amsterdam diamond merchant with interests in land reclamation (a popular and profitable undertaking in the United Provinces) and agricultural innovations. He was also one of the founding directors of the West India Company, and one of the ardent advocates for setting up private plantations, or patroonships, to settle New

Netherland. Through indomitable drive, he got his own planned settlement approved by the board, and in 1630 began the arduous task of gathering colonists to inhabit it. He chose the manager of his estate shrewdly. Bastiaen Krol, the young man who had come over with Joris Rapalje and Catalina Trico, intending to make a career as a minister, had had his plans waylaid several times now. First, Minuit had put him in charge of Fort Orange after Daniel van Crieckenbeeck's death in the Indian ambush of 1626. Then, when Minuit was recalled, Krol found himself given the job of interim director of the colony. When that stint was over, he returned to the Dutch Republic; it was then that Van Rensselaer met him, realized the depth of experience he had gained and offered him a job. Krol carried out his first task brilliantly. Returning to New Netherland, he purchased from the Mahicans the land surrounding Fort Orange, stretching along both sides of the river. Van Rensselaer exaggerated somewhat when he wrote shortly after that his property extended west from the river 'indifinitely', but it did run about nine miles along the river and 'two days' journey' inland. In other words, the entrepreneur had taken a vital chunk out of New Netherland, and it was his intention to treat his colony-within-a-colony as a sovereign fief.

But for sheer bravura, nothing beat the return of Peter Minuit to New Netherland. It so happened that just before Minuit was recalled from his duties and shipped back on the ill-fated *Unity*, the king of Sweden, Gustavus Adolphus – a Lutheran warrior who was in the midst of massive participation in the Protestant-versus-Catholic Thirty Years War in Germany – was looking for new worlds to conquer. Sweden was in the midst of its own golden age, and Gustavus was tired of watching as France, Spain, England and the Dutch Republic exerted their will around the globe. However, Gustavus died in battle just at the time when Minuit made it back to Amsterdam following his ordeal in England. The crown descended, then, to the head of his six-year-old daughter, Christina, who would grow up to become one of the most cosmopolitan and intellectually nimble monarchs in European history; but for the time being affairs were left in the hands of the chancellor, Axel Oxenstierna, who continued Gustavus's policies. The Dutch had long been the major traders in Sweden, delivering the goods of the world to Stockholm, and Oxenstierna came into contact with a Dutch merchant named Samuel Blommaert who was involved in the copper trade in Sweden. This Blommaert was, like Kiliaen van Rensselaer, a director of the West India Company, and one of those angry over what he realized was a missed opportunity in the North American colony. Van Rensselaer's way of getting around the corporate bureaucracy was to finance his own sub-colony; Blommaert's idea was slightly zanier: to defy his own company and country and establish a Swedish colony somewhere within the New Netherland territory. He met Minuit secretly, and a plan took form. Minuit probably knew the Dutch colony better than anyone alive, and knew in particular that its choice South River territory was all but unguarded.

Thus it came about that some time in the middle of March 1638 one of the strangest invasion fleets ever to approach American shores sailed between Capes May and Henlopen, into what would eventually become Delaware Bay, and dropped anchor at a rocky point on a tributary called the Minquas Kill. Kitted out in battle armour and with the blue-and-yellow flag of Sweden flying from the mainmast of his ship, the *Kalmar Nyckel*, looking for all the world like some latter-day medieval knight errant, Peter Minuit was returning to North America – a German native of French extraction and recent Dutch ties, proclaiming a colony on behalf of Sweden in the wilderness that would become the state of Delaware. In the absence of a Dutch resistance force, Minuit was set to make his second imprint on America. Ranged about him on the decks of the two-ship squadron were several dozen Dutch sailors and Swedish soldiers, pikes and muskets at the ready, plumed helmets glinting sunlight. To this day, in gritty, industrial-era homage to that odd arrival, the road that connects the warehouses along the waterfront in Wilmington – the city that grew up around Minuit's landing spot – is called Swedes' Landing.

Dying from within and attacked from without, the Manhattan colony, *circa* 1640, was thus firmly on the road to extinction. It wasn't even a proper political entity: it had no government; its inhabitants were less citizens of a republic than serfs working at the behest of a multinational company. True, it sat on the verge of a vast continent that Europeans were soon to penetrate, motivated by the zeal to expand their horizons in the wake of men like Galileo, Harvey, Drake and Hudson, and also by the desire to flee decades of religion-fuelled war at home. As the geographical key to unlocking the continent, this region would one day help shift the global centre of power – one could argue that it would become the point on which western civilization itself would pivot as it shifted from the Renaissance era to the modern world, from Eurocentrism to a global perspective. But, for all that promise, it was little more than a place of chaos and slop, of bar-room knife fights, soldiers fornicating with Indian women while on guard duty, and a steady stream of wayward newcomers: hard men hoisting themselves out of skiffs and hitting the packed soil of the Strand, purses strung around their necks heavy with Carolus guilders or Spanish pieces of eight, ready to smuggle, drink, trade, whore and be gone. Henry Hudson had ensured that the settlement was established under Dutch auspices, but so far the vaunted character of Dutch society – as a pluralistic, tolerant republic – was in evidence only in a negative way. It might as well have been any nation's dregs clinging to the southern tip of the wilderness island called Manhattan. It was as if the world, having dimly identified this piece of land and water on the edge of the New World as a fulcrum, wasn't yet ready for it, and so let it disintegrate.

It was a community, in other words, sure to die out, one that history could safely forget.

Part II
Clash of Wills

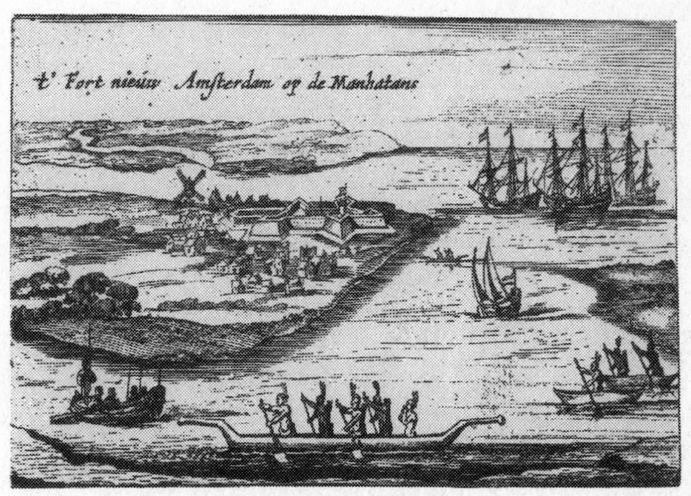

5
The Lawman

SEPTEMBER IS A VIGOROUS MONTH IN HOLLAND. NORTH SEA rains angle down out of charcoal-bottomed clouds. Broad bands of blue sky appear, and the world becomes bathed in smoky light. Suddenly the sun comes on pure and full, shocking the painted-and-varnished shutters on brick facades, threatening to pierce the green murk of the canal surface, bringing ordinary humans close to bursting out in mad spontaneous song. And there is the wind, a constant presence, like an insistent hand on the back, inviting or pushing the inhabitants: *move, make sail, go.*

In September 1638 a newcomer entered the town of Leiden. He had come from his home in the city of Breda, 40 miles to the south in the distant and largely Catholic region called Brabant, which, while a part of the Dutch Republic, did not have the status of a full province. If he was anything like other newcomers, he couldn't have failed to be impressed by what he found in Leiden. Even in a country known for its neatness this handsome brick village stood out in the seventeenth century, its alleys and canalsides manicured, the pavement literally scrubbed, the soaring whitewashed walls of its church interiors crisply set off by dark beams. In fact, it was not a village at all – by 1622 its population had reached 45,000 – but it retained a provincial simplicity. The massive sailcloth arms of windmills punctuated the sky not just on the outskirts but right in the town centre. The streets through which the young man walked would have swarmed with children at play – an oddity at this time in Europe. The prevailing thinking elsewhere, in this age of Puritan grimness, was that childhood was a time when chaos and devilry might sweep into the soul, and thus that children should be checked, submissive, subdued, kept under sober adult supervision. The Dutch approach was the opposite; they hugged and coddled their children, ignoring the scorn of outsiders and following their own experts. '[C]hildren should not be kept on too tight a rein, but allowed to exercise their childishness, so that we do not burden their fragile nature with heavy things,' advised the physician Johan van Beverwyck, the Dr Spock or Benjamin Weil of his day, whose book *Treasure of Health* was a bestseller. So – as the boisterous street scenes of Jan Steen's paintings illustrate – children ran free, and the streets echoed with their play.

A cosmopolitan intensity built as one approached the canal called the Rapenburg – taverns and music halls, curling columns of tobacco smoke from the inhabitants' pipes. Crossing a little pedestrian bridge over the canal, the newcomer would have met up with crowds of his colleagues – other young men massing on the cobbled quayside before a handsome two-storey building with leaded glass panes. The entrance was through an arch in the brick wall to the north. This was the main building of the University of Leiden, the premier academic institution in the Netherlands and a major European centre of learning. Into this building the young man walked on 24 September 1638 to set down as required his name, Adriaen van der Donck, his age, twenty, his home province, and the degree for which he was about to begin studying: law. In seventeen years he would be dead, in a distant land of which, at this point in his life, he may never have heard. He would cause a stir in America and Europe, but in time it would diminish. Few people in history would remember him. But he would make a mark. He would bring the seed of the best and noblest aspect of seventeenth-century

European civilization to fresh soil a world away, where something remarkable would grow. He would play a decisive role in the creation of a great city and a new society.

He was young, strong and forthright, with a deep intellectual bent balanced by a roaming hunger for adventure. His family had stature in Breda – one relative had served as a steward in the court of William the Silent, another had held high rank in the Dutch army – and he came to the university with a certain pedigree. Four decades before, in the early days of the war against Spain, an event had occurred in his home town which by this time had become legend. Breda had been one of many towns in the hands of Spanish occupiers. William the Silent, hero of the Dutch revolt, had recently died, and the Spanish were gaining territory as they marched through the southern reaches of the Low Countries, when a daring Trojan horse manoeuvre turned the tide. A contingent of seventy Dutch soldiers concealed themselves beneath layers of turf in a peat boat and floated past the Spanish troops guarding the entrance into Breda. Once inside the gate, they led an uprising that resulted in the town's recapture. The man behind the *turfschip van Breda* was Adriaen van Bergen, grandfather and namesake of Van der Donck. Van Bergen was still remembered as a hero in Breda decades later; the family shared in the patriotic lustre, and young Adriaen van der Donck wore the association as a badge of honour.

The university also had ties to the early days of the rebellion. The town of Leiden had withstood a Spanish onslaught in 1574, and as a reward for the bravery of its fighters William the Silent chose Leiden as the site of the grand university that he believed the Dutch provinces needed if they were to become a nation. In a remarkably short time the university achieved a status equalling that of Bologna or Oxford, and became just what William had envisioned: a breeding ground for the new nation's top scientists, politicians, lawyers and religious figures.

The Dutch spirit of tolerance pervaded the town. Scientists and writers from all over Europe came to have their books published at Leiden, whose printers were cheap, highly skilled and largely free from censorship. Indeed, no statistic gives a better indication of the Dutch role in the intellectual life of the time than the estimate that over the course of the seventeenth century the Netherlands produced one-half of all books published worldwide.

At the time Adriaen van der Donck arrived, about one-third of Leiden's population was composed of refugees from war and religious persecution. In a century marked by religious conflict, Brownists, Baptists, Walloons, Huguenots, Fifth Monarchy Men and Ashkenazi Jews came here, as well as to other cities in the Dutch Republic, to live and worship. When, early in the century, William Bradford and his fellow Pilgrim leaders, who had fled persecution in England, wrote asking the town whether they might settle there, the magistrates promptly wrote back: '[We] refuse no honest persons ingress to come and have their residence in this city, provided that such persons behave themselves honestly, and submit to all the laws and ordinances here.' The Pilgrims arrived in 1609 – the year that Henry Hudson initiated the Dutch claim to its North American territory – taking up residence in the warren of streets surrounding the massive, gothic Pieterskerk, engaging in trades and practising their faith. They took advantage of the freedom of the press and began printing tracts attacking King Charles's religious restrictions, which they smuggled into England. When Charles's ambassador complained, the town magistrates shielded their new residents, further entrenching the king's low opinion of the Dutch. Ironically, it was the Dutch tolerance of religious differences – precisely the thing that had drawn them – that eventually drove some of the Pilgrims away to the New World. They feared that living among practitioners of ungodly faiths would dissipate them. And indeed, when the first group of forty sailed to Cape Cod in 1620, several hundred more stayed behind, many eventually blending into the melting pot of Dutch society.

Tolerance was more than just an attitude in the Dutch

Republic. Following the bloody religious persecution of thousands in the previous decades at the hands of the Spanish, the Dutch provinces had broken new ground in writing into their 1579 de facto constitution the guarantee that 'each person shall remain free, especially in his religion, and that no one shall be persecuted or investigated because of their religion.' This sentence became the ground on which the culturally diverse society of the seventeenth century was built. But, as in so many societies – think of the early United States, a slave-holding nation that believed itself to be rooted on the principle of freedom – the guiding rule was often broken. In the 1620s a debate on the meaning and wisdom of tolerance had raged through the Dutch provinces. At its centre was a clash that had taken place here, at Leiden University, between two iconic theologians, as one strand of a wider debate about Calvinist teachings. The hard-liner, Gomarus, and his followers, having surveyed a continent scarred by religious war, saw in it proof of the dangers of diversity, and argued that strength came from conformity, that repression of non-Calvinist religion was good for the soul and the state both. Gomarus' opponent, Arminius, and his camp countered that Christian principles of charity compelled tolerance of religious differences, and forbade the persecution of those who had different views. A much-quoted forerunner of Arminius named Sebastian Castellio phrased it with persuasive Christian elegance: 'Many will be damned on Judgment Day because they killed innocent people, but nobody will be damned because he killed nobody.' Besides, the Arminians pointed out, diversity was good for business.

Out of this struggle came an elaborate written rationale for tolerance of religious diversity. Its climax – really, a watershed in human thought – came with Arminius' follower Simon Episcopius declaring in a series of carefully reasoned arguments that the strength of a state derived not from maintaining a single, firmly held faith, as was almost universally believed in Europe, but from allowing its citizens freedom of worship and intellectual inquiry. It is impossible to imagine today how revolutionary this assertion was, how intoxicating it felt to those who championed it, and how deeply it affected Adriaen van der Donck and his generation of scholars. By the time Van der Donck enrolled to study at Leiden, the tolerance advocates held sway, and the staggering successes of the golden age only strengthened their case.

Tolerance was a boon to the university itself, giving it an advantage over other academic institutions in Europe, helping it to become a major international centre of learning in the space of a few decades. In any era scholars and scientists depend on freedom of thought and expression as fire on oxygen, and in much of seventeenth-century Europe the oxygen was growing thin. Galileo had faced the Inquisition only five years before. His *Discourses and Mathematical Demonstrations Concerning Two New Sciences*, upon which Isaac Newton would build to establish the laws of physics, was being published at Leiden, at a safe remove from the Vatican censors, in 1638, just as Van der Donck arrived. Top academics from throughout Europe came to teach at Leiden, attracted by the freedom, as well as by high salaries and other incentives the university offered – such as tax exemption on the alcohol they consumed, up to a healthy forty gallons of wine a year and a half barrel of beer per month.

As a result, Leiden in the 1630s churned with history-making activity. Van der Donck soaked up the atmosphere generated by new learning then revolutionizing the fields of medicine, physics and mathematics, and his courses in law and politics would have been imbued with Dutch ideas about democracy, monarchy and tolerance. The dominant intellectual spirit of the decade – at Leiden and elsewhere – was René Descartes, the Frenchman whose rationalistic method of inquiry brought philosophy and science into the modern era. Descartes, himself seeking intellectual freedom, had moved to Holland in 1629, and lived for most of the next twenty years in an Amsterdam town house opposite the Westerkerk. He enrolled at Leiden University in

1630 and lived there for a time; in 1636 he returned, seeking a publisher for his new work, and stayed for seven years, becoming easily the most talked-about intellectual in town. The *Discourse on Method* was published at Leiden in 1637, the year before Van der Donck arrived, and it caused a sensation.

It was an epochal moment in which to begin a university education – indeed, one might say it was the moment when modern higher education was born. Scientists, philosophers and theologians (the titles were more or less interchangeable) opened up a furious debate on the most fundamental aspects of their fields. What would it mean to follow Descartes and base reasoning not on 'authority' (Aristotle or the Bible) but on the mind of the thinker and, as Descartes said, its 'good sense'? The famous phrase from the *Discourse* that would resound through the centuries, influencing everything from the Enlightenment political thinking of Thomas Jefferson to modern scientific method – *cogito ergo sum*: 'I think, therefore I am' – had just been voiced. The age of the individual was at hand, and the young Adriaen van der Donck was at its epicentre.

Leiden vibrated with the energy of new forms of inquiry. Its anatomical theatre was one of the first and the most famous in the world, but the frenzy for dissections was so great that it was often overbooked and professors had to hold their anatomical classes, wrote one scholar in 1638, 'in the academic Garden and elsewhere'. Some conducted public dissections in their homes, which they had fitted out with 'domestic amphitheaters'. Dogs vanished from the streets of Leiden as medical students became obsessed with the fad for direct observation and study. Johannes de Wale cut open live dogs and pumped their veins to demonstrate the circulation of the blood – work on which William Harvey relied to refine his own theories. Human cadavers were in great demand. Reinier de Graaf became obsessed by the theory that pancreatic fluid was acidic, and he was known to stimulate the pancreas of a cadaver so that it would produce fluid, and then to taste it, and urge his assembled observers to taste it as well, whereupon he would ask hopefully if they detected an acidic flavour. De Graaf's greater contribution to science came when he proved, by dissecting pregnant rabbits, the then outlandish theory that the ovaries had a role in reproduction. Unfortunately, his discovery was overshadowed by the near-simultaneous discovery by Antoni van Leeuwenhoek, using his microscope, of spermatozoa, which gave a last gasp of life to the theory, stretching back to antiquity, that babies came solely from sperm and the female womb was merely a receptacle.

The university's botanical garden was also a (literal) seedbed of innovation. From it came advances in chemistry and botany, and it was here that, through cross-breeding, the Dutch frenzy for tulips began.* And in the wake of Galileo the observatory was booked up by scholars scouring the heavens for sunspots and evidence to support or refute the theory of planets revolving around the sun.

Van der Donck steeped in this intellectual ferment for three years. In law, just as in science, a revolution was taking place. The very concept of a nation was being redefined. In the aftermath of the Reformation, the medieval notion of a state as existing under the umbrella of 'Christendom', with its laws ultimately reflecting the dictates of the church, had collapsed, and the modern concept of a state as an independent political entity was coming into being. The dominant legal figure of the age, who did more than anyone to set the framework within which nations interact to this day, was the Dutch jurist Huig de Groot, known to history as Hugo Grotius. Grotius is considered the

* Tulip mania reached its height just at the time Van der Donck began his studies. The year before, in exchange for a single tulip bulb, a man paid 4 oxen, 8 pigs, 12 sheep, 160 bushels of wheat, 320 bushels of rye, 4 casks of butter, 1,000 pounds of cheese, 2 oxheads of wine, a silver pitcher and a bed. The government of the province of Holland was forced to pass laws to end the speculation before it ruined the economy.

father of international law. (It is an indication of his prominence in history that a bas-relief portrait of him adorns the US House of Representatives Chamber, alongside those of Moses, Hammurabi and Thomas Jefferson.) Of his two major works, *Mare Liberum* created the principle of international waters, which were to be open to all nations, while *De Jure Belli et Pacis*, written in the midst of a century of unprecedented warfare, laid down principles on which war was justified, and how it ought to be conducted.

Grotius dominated the way law was taught at Leiden, especially among the younger, more practically minded scholars. Judging from his later actions, Van der Donck must have avoided the 'antiquarian law' favoured by the older generation of purely theoretical teachers, which confined itself to examination of ancient Roman texts, and instead have concentrated on what was called 'elegant law', which applied the reasoning of ancient authorities to practical courtroom situations. In this respect he would have been a disciple of Grotius, whose work was also broadly influential because it helped to establish the framework by which the great European powers conducted their affairs – including how England and the Dutch Republic, in their increasingly bitter rivalry over North America and other territories, conducted themselves.

Beyond this, Van der Donck would have been drawn to Grotius because he, like Descartes, based his arguments not on biblical citations but on 'natural law', the idea that right and wrong could be determined by applying human reason – or, as Grotius put it, that an act could be judged 'from its conformity or non-conformity with rational nature itself'. Traditionally, American history has shown the principles of democratic government coming out of the Enlightenment era of the eighteenth century, with origins in the writings of John Locke in the late seventeenth. But in recent decades historians have uncovered the early modern roots of those democratic impulses. Some of Grotius' followers, building on his statement of natural law, applied the same kind of radical verve to their writings as would the generation responsible for the American Revolution. One of those disciples – Piet van der Cun, also known as Cunaeus – taught a radical form of Grotius' political thought in his own career at Leiden, and a collection of young idealists formed around him and perpetuated it. Cunaeus' ideas – that a republican form of government was morally superior to a monarchy, and that enterprises like the West India Company enriched a wealthy few to the detriment of both the state and ordinary people – were in the air during Van der Donck's days at Leiden, and helped mould the thought and attitudes of his generation.

For three years Van der Donck studied at Leiden alongside an international contingent of scholars, took part in debating circles organized by the law professors, maybe joined with his colleagues in complaining, as students will, about the food in the dining hall (smoked fish, hashed meat with cabbage, cheese, bread and butter, beer). In taverns in the evenings, with smoke curling from long clay pipes and Rhenish wine flowing from pewter pitchers, the young men might have applied their debating skills to the all-consuming Galileo-versus-Aristotle and Arminius-versus-Gomarus questions. Then in 1641 he emerged, a 'jurist', an authority on the prevailing system of Roman–Dutch law.

What to do next? He was a man of law. He came from a family of renown. He was a graduate of the top university in the country, and the economy was so robust it was practically exploding. Many possibilities must have been open to him – back home in Breda, in Amsterdam, or at The Hague, the centre of legal and political power in the nation. Instead he opted to leave the country. And not just leave, but to go nowhere, headlong into the void. His country was experiencing one of the greatest flowerings of art and science and one of the most profound economic booms of any nation in any period in history. Its streets were safe, its houses snug, its offices bustling. The cuisine was surely nothing to marvel at, but the beer was fresh and excellent;

pipe tobacco was sold in every conceivable grade and form; even the boxes to store it were available in an infinity of materials and styles. Homes were decked out with rugs from Turkey, Chinese porcelain and Delft tiles; dolls'-house makers' skills were in demand, not for child's play but by proud home-owners who wanted them to create miniature replicas of their dwellings. It was one of the first societies on earth in which ordinary town-dwelling citizens had developed a worldly sophistication. English travellers were amazed to find that not just the wealthy but ordinary bakers and shopkeepers decorated the walls of their homes with paintings; moreover, in an obvious sign of their outward-looking nature, the Dutch of this time were the first (as shown in Vermeer's interiors) to decorate their homes with maps. The Dutch at the beginning of the century were also among the first to separate their homes into public areas (downstairs) and private living space (upstairs). A German visiting a Dutch home was astounded that 'it is not permissible to ascend the stairs or set foot in a room without first removing one's shoes.' It was the Dutch of this era who invented the idea of the home as a personal, intimate space; one might say they invented cosiness. All of this had happened roughly within the span of Van der Donck's life. Fuelled by its global trade, the Netherlands had become a very comfortable place. It was unthinkable that anyone with good prospects would want to leave. So why did he?

It is not beyond reason to suppose Van der Donck took his inspiration from Descartes. The intellectual celebrity would have made a natural model for the young man. He lived in and around Leiden throughout Van der Donck's time there, and, for all his personal reserve, was a polarizing presence; some professors at the university became his disciples while others bitterly opposed his 'natural philosophy'. He had a ruddy attractiveness – dark wavy hair, curling moustache, penetrating eyes – and was a man of action as well as intellect: he had volunteered as a soldier under Maurits, son of William the Silent, and strutted the town with a sword as part of his regular dress. His *Discourse*, which Van der Donck is likely to have read while at Leiden, was remarkably chatty and autobiographical for a philosophical work, and a young man of restless and individualistic spirit would have been drawn to the passage near the beginning in which Descartes, in talking about his own setting forth, declared that 'as soon as my age permitted me to pass from under the control of my instructors, I entirely abandoned the study of letters, and resolved no longer to seek any other science than the knowledge of myself, or of the great book of the world.'

Had Van der Donck wanted to go into overseas trade, the logical route was via the offices of the East or West India Company. But they were too regimented for his nature. As in any large corporations, promotion came slowly and steadily. Van der Donck wanted something more toothsome and wild. Perhaps through his parents, or possibly through one of the pamphlets that served as precursors to newspapers, he had learned of a New World colony-in-the-making, a raw, virgin place that was in need of help. It wasn't the West India Company's New Netherland settlement that attracted him, but the colony-within-a-colony at its northern reaches, the private fief of Amsterdam diamond merchant Kiliaen van Rensselaer. He made an enquiry.

His timing was excellent. Van Rensselaer had steadily enlarged his colony in the eleven years since its foundation, buying additional tracts from the Mahicans; it now covered several hundred thousand acres along both sides of the Hudson River, encircling the West India Company's upriver base of Fort Orange. While the company's own colony centred on Manhattan was floundering, the patroon – a micro-manager of the first order – had tended his settlement with great care. He had sent farmers, carpenters, smiths, wheelwrights and bricklayers, as well as livestock, seed, and bare-root trees and vines; from his base in Amsterdam (Van Rensselaer would never see his domain), he gave voluminous instructions for clearing forest and planting crops. Houses went up and roads were laid. Van Rensselaer was able to write in January 1641 that 'In general, the affairs of the colony are all right, God be praised' – but there was a problem, which stemmed from his success. He had a genuine settlement on his hands now, and it needed a government. While technically his colony was within the boundaries of New Netherland, Van Rensselaer considered it a semi-independent entity. That meant he had to provide his own law and order. Thefts and runaways (farmers who signed on for a specific period of years, and then fled before their time was up) were on the rise.

When Van der Donck wrote to Van Rensselaer, asking to be considered for a place in the colony, the merchant must have been pleased. Getting experienced workers of any kind to cross the ocean and take up a new life in his colony was difficult enough: he was forced to pay substantially more than they would make in the Netherlands, and even then he complained about the quality of person he was able to attract. In the mind of a middle-class businessman who had clawed his way up, Van der Donck's credentials, as a Leiden University jurist, would have shimmered. There was no lawyer in the entire colony of New Netherland; the only university-educated man was the minister in New Amsterdam. It was simply too difficult to interest such people in the posting. Van Rensselaer fired off a letter to one of the minor shareholders in his colony, who happened to live in Leiden: 'When convenient please have inquiry made through Mr de laet or some one else regarding a young man, called vander donck, from the barony of breda, who has studied law at Leyden and is desirous of attempting something connected with farming in our colony; and if there are no serious charges against his character, as one can not always get the best to go thither, we might employ him also in some other capacity.'

Once the two met, Van Rensselaer knew how he would employ the young man. He needed someone who could roam the wilds of his untamed land and hunt down outlaws, and also someone with a legal mind, who could administer justice and settle disputes between colonists. He offered Van der Donck the job of *schout*, a Dutch title that combined the duties of sheriff and public prosecutor. It was a difficult posting, but the young man's credentials would give him stature not only among the colonists on his patroonship but among the tough lot in New Amsterdam as well.

To a young man whose education had come more from books than the real world, it must have seemed like the offer of a utopian adventure: to march into a raw land and create a system of justice, to be the lawbringer for a whole new community. Van der Donck accepted, and in May 1641 he boarded *Den Eyckenboom* ('The Oak Tree'), bound for the New World. In his pocket was a thick sheaf of instructions from Van Rensselaer – but however detailed they were they couldn't begin to cover all that lay ahead.

*

It is easier today to imagine the harbour into which the ship sailed ten long weeks later than it has been at nearly any intervening time. For more than two centuries it would be the gateway to North America and a commercial hub linking the continent with Europe; a traffic-choked intersection at which, in their turn, frigates, schooners, steamships, container vessels and pleasure yachts would belly past one another towards and away from the array of piers that radiated from Manhattan's shoreline like the teeth of a comb. Now there is an odd tranquillity. Sailing into the harbour today, you need only turn your back on the spiny rise of Manhattan and delete from your mind's eye the Statue of Liberty and the mute hulks on Ellis Island and Governor's Island to envision it as it once was. With the water surface rippling nicely and the sails overhead snapping and coughing as they labour, urban noise recedes. For minutes at a time you are alone out here – with leisure to take in the undulating geography of the place, its spread of islands and, as Van der Donck would later note, its 'many and different sea havens'. We can only imagine how inviting its idyllic shelter would have been after long weeks at the mercy of the open ocean. In its breadth and depth the harbour struck Van der Donck, as it had his countrymen, as a kind of New World version of the IJ, the great inland sea fronting Amsterdam, whose lanes, throughout the century, bristled with a forest of masts. These Dutch were a people who knew waterways as others knew forest or mountains. To them, land that was inaccessible by water was useless. Conversely, rich land that was cut by navigable rivers and incised by a commodious bay was the ultimate desideratum. This bay was one of the things that had attracted them here – they felt the latent energy in it; they smelled its potential, how it might become a copy of their great home base across the ocean. For now, it remained what it had been for millennia: a sculpted wilderness of salt water, wind and land. The English would call it New York harbour. To the Dutch it was too elemental even to require that much of a name. As Van der Donck later noted with his scholar's Latin, 'it is named *quasi per excellentiam*, "The Bay".'

The ship dropped anchor some hundreds of yards before the southern shore of Manhattan, with its clutch of gabled houses, its windmill and the walls of its fort clustered along it. The passengers staggered down into a waiting boat and were rowed ashore.

Van der Donck didn't record his first impression of New Amsterdam, and while by any ordinary measure the look of the place could not have been one to inspire confidence, there had been a decisive change for the better in the affairs of the town and the colony in the past year. History's simplistic reading of the Dutch colony centred on Manhattan – that it was an inconsequential gathering of nobodies until the English eventually took over and began to make a thriving settlement of it – is based on the records of the West India Company. The West India Company ran the place, and the West India Company never succeeded in making it financially viable; *ergo*, New Amsterdam never really took off. But that logic overlooks a crucial turn of events. In 1640 the company, driven to drastic measures by the failing condition of its settlement, gave up its monopoly on trade in the region, which had kept the place from developing in any areas except piracy and smuggling, and declared New Netherland a free-trading zone. In this new free-market territory, New Amsterdam would be the 'staple port' through which traders' and merchants' ships would pass, where they would pay duties and be cleared for travel. The effect was electric. Small-scale entrepreneurs in Amsterdam who were willing to brave the hazards of the ocean voyage now had, in Manhattan, a base to exploit – a hub around which the circle of Atlantic trade could turn. Gillis Verbrugge formed a partnership with his son Seth, and launched the first of what would be twenty-seven trading voyages to Manhattan. The business would make Seth a wealthy man, able to support his wife, herself the daughter of a successful businessman, in style. Dirck de Wolff set up a company that shipped manufactured goods to the colonists on Manhattan and brought back furs and tobacco; his profits from this and other international trading ventures bought him an elegant Amsterdam town house on the exclusive Herengracht, or Gentleman's Canal, and a vast country estate in the polders near Haarlem.

On Manhattan itself, the change would have far-reaching results. It gave rise, within the space of a few years, to an intensively active merchant class – people who wanted to buy, sell, grow, spend. Convinced now that there was a future here, they began putting down roots. What is more, the Manhattan merchants defied categorization. The tailor also brewed beer; the baker doubled as a ship's captain. Joris Rapalje, who by the time Van der Donck arrived at Manhattan had been in the colony for eighteen years, worked for the West India Company but also had entrepreneurial interests, selling grain on behalf of farmers at Van Rensselaer's colony, and owned and operated a tavern. The looseness of Manhattan society had its disadvantages, but it also made for greater social mobility than in Europe.

Everyone in New Amsterdam had shares in one shipment of cargo or another. 'Everyone here is a trader,' one resident remarked in 1650, which was both true and unprecedented – as was the opportunity for advancement. Govert Loockermans had arrived in Manhattan seven years before Van der Donck, as a sixteen-year-old cook's mate on a West India Company vessel, desperate to get ahead. As soon as the West India Company monopoly ended, he left its employ and signed on as agent for the Verbrugges, overseeing ships and cargo. Over the next few years he would learn to speak English as well as several Indian languages, buy a farm on the East River, and begin leasing ships and moving cargo around New Netherland and the Atlantic, several times being accused of smuggling. He had a fairly sharp mean streak: in an altercation with Raritan Indians he became infamous when he, in the words of a witness, 'tortured the chief's brother in his private parts with a piece of split wood'. He would die, thirty-eight years after his youthful footfall, in the new city of New York, the wealthiest merchant in the colony, owner of one of its finest homes (which would later become the home of the pirate William Kidd and is today the site of a nondescript office building, 7 Hanover Square), one of the richest men in the New World and one of the purest examplars of the kind of free-form upward mobility that American culture would inherit from its forgotten colony.

In New Amsterdam itself, the opening of trade was already showing results as Van der Donck arrived. Dozens of lots were leased or bought in the months after the monopoly was relinquished. Houses were being built, and within them the level of creature comforts was on the rise. When tobacco farmer Jacque de Vernuis died unexpectedly in October 1640, shortly after signing a ten-year lease and leaving behind a Dutch wife, Hester Simons, the inventory of his property included a grey riding coat, a riding cap, shirts, cravats, coifs, stockings and handkerchiefs, pewter dishes, silverware, iron pots, copper kettles, pine chests, curtains, pillows and pillow cases, blankets, three hogs, a fishing rod, a pair of tongs and 'one brass skimmer'. A humble enough collection, but worlds beyond the hand-to-mouth days of even a few years before.

On arrival, then, splashing in leather boots through the East River shallows where the sloop unloaded passengers (it would be years before a proper pier was constructed), Adriaen van der Donck would have taken a turn through a chaotic, energetic, rough town that was very much in transition. There were perhaps four hundred inhabitants, and it was already one of the most multicultural places on earth; in five years' time a visiting Jesuit priest would report that eighteen languages were spoken in its few dusty lanes. In the summer of 1641 the fort was in a tumbledown state, but there were new houses, some of wood and stone, some of brick, with steep roofs and step gables. From the shore a newcomer would cross over the new Brewer's Bridge spanning the grandly named Heere Gracht (modelling their New World base on Amsterdam, the residents felt the town needed a 'gentleman's canal' – in reality it was a stinking ditch), walk past the five stone houses that formed the shopping district, by the bakery and the midwife's house, and skirt the simple wooden church on Pearl Street ('a mean barn', David de Vries called it), with the minister's house and stable behind. The lanes of the town were riotous with free-ranging pigs and chickens, the farming principle of the period being that one's animals roamed for food, and property was fenced to keep them out, not in.

It was high summer; a Dutchman, unused to the humidity, would work up a sweat as he took in the town. Logic and custom would have him stopping at at least one of the several taverns clustered on the half a dozen principal streets – perhaps in the company of Cornelis Melyn, a wealthy Flemish farmer who had made the voyage with him, and who would become instrumental in involving Van der Donck in Manhattan politics. Continuing on his way, Van der Donck might have paused to chat with a German carpenter named Juriaen, who at that moment was building a house for Frenchman Philip Geraerdy, or to observe the English carpenters John Hobson and John Morris, who were fulfilling their contract with Isaac de Forest for 'a dwelling house, 30 feet long and 18 feet wide, with 2 4-light windows and 2 3-light windows, 4 beams with brackets and 2 free beams, one partition and one passage way tight inside and outside and the entire house tight all around'.

If he needed evidence that there was new life pulsing through the colonial community, Van der Donck need only have watched the ship he had sailed on being unloaded of its cargo, for which various residents had put in orders from Amsterdam and to receive which they were no doubt now waiting expectantly at the waterfront. For Tonis Jansen the sail-maker the crew unloaded one bale of French canvas, two bales of sailcloth, one keg containing 200 pounds of sail yarn. Hendrick Jansen, locksmith, got his order of '4 chauldrons of smith's coal, 30 bars of square iron, 60 bars of flat Swedish iron, 150 pieces of hard iron'. The commissary in the West India Company's store signed off on receipt of his goods, which included casks of brandy, sack and French wine, oil, dried beef and pork, '30 tuns of fine salt', a case of stationery, 290 pounds of candles, and '2 large crates containing 50 winnowing baskets'. No sooner had the ship put into port than Arent Corssen Stam, a merchant from Haarlem, signed a contract with Gelain Cornelissen, skipper of *Den Eyckenboom*, 'immediately to deliver the aforesaid ship ready for sailing, tight, well caulked and provided with anchors, ropes, tackle, sails, running and standing rigging, victuals and other necessaries thereto belonging, and to arm said ship with six cannon and other ammunition in proportion'. He was to deliver a new load of cargo to the English colony of Virginia, there receive another load (probably tobacco), and 'sail with the first favorable wind which God shall grant from Virginia direct to London and deliver the ship's cargo to those to whom it shall be consigned'.

Finally, Van der Donck would have walked into the fort, past the latticework guardhouse and to the director-general's brick house. Here he pulled out a letter of introduction and placed it before Willem Kieft, who had replaced Van Twiller three years before as the West India Company's head of the colony. It was a brief, formal meeting. Then Van der Donck was off again, headed north, 150 miles upriver, to the remote settlement that was to be his new home.

There were maybe a hundred residents in the colony of Rensselaerswyck at the time. The few homes, barns and other signs of human habitation were dwarfed by the staggering expanses of wilderness: the smoking, brooding mountains to the north, the stands of high pine trees, the broad river and the endless sky. Van der Donck met a man about his own age named Arent van Curler, a nephew of Kiliaen van Rensselaer, who had been in the colony for three years and was its manager, and then made for the small wooded island just off the western shore of the river and close to Fort Orange, which had been partially cleared for farms. He had decided to make one of these his home. Soon after, a surreal version of the classic Wild West scenario was played out when, rested and ready for work, high on the thrill of adventure and still buzzing from the foreignness of it all, Van der Donck emerged from his rough, thatch-roofed dwelling into the bright August morning, and, wearing 'a silver-plated rapier with baldric and a black hat with plume', the badges of his office, exhibited himself for the farmers, blacksmiths, wheelwrights and bakers of his domain, as well as for the assorted Mohawks, Mahicans and West India Company soldiers. As he strode purposefully up the road that ran along the river, past the palisades of Fort Orange and by the fields and workshops of the colony, the residents must have gaped. Here before them in one trim, gallant and beplumed package was the cutting-edge quintessence of European education, *c.* 1640, the product of a legal system centuries old, tempered by modern notions that in one form or another, with the compliments of Galileo, Descartes and Grotius, placed man at the centre of things. Here was one of the Republic's best and brightest. They had a lawman.

6
The Council of Blood

BY AN ODD TWIST OF FATE, THE TRAGEDY THAT WOULD engulf the Manhattan-based colony of New Netherland, crippling it and condemning it to eventual defeat in its struggle against its English neighbours, was also the event that brought its residents together and preserved the colony's legacy for future centuries. Fate further arranged it that the nightmare descended in the same month that Adriaen van der Donck, the man who was to lead the political struggle that would preserve that legacy, arrived to seek his fortune in the New World.

The disaster came just when things were looking most hopeful for the residents of New Amsterdam and their comrades scattered across the several hundred square miles of North Atlantic coast that comprised the province. With trade thrown open, new residents were pouring in; a merchant elite was forming; families were intermarrying, putting down roots. It began with what seemed a random, minor event.

Everyone on Manhattan knew Claes Swits. He was a garrulous old man, a wheelwright by trade, who had made the voyage to the New World with his wife and two grown sons. Before boarding their ship, they had put up at the Amsterdam inn of Pieter de Winter, the same establishment where Griet Reyniers had worked as barmaid and prostitute before setting her sights on Manhattan. The inn was a favourite haunt of travellers from Germany; as Swits's surname suggests, he had probably originally come from Switzerland. Like everyone else on Manhattan, he became engaged in several different occupations after his arrival. He leased a 200-acre plantation, called Otterspoor, covering much of what would become Harlem, on which he grew grain and milked cows (as rent he agreed to pay the owner, Jacob van Curler, annually, two hundred pounds of butter and 'the just half of all the grain with which God shall bless the field'). Soon afterwards – perhaps finding that the work was too much for a man of his years – he took on a partner. Claes didn't spend much time on the farm; he was too old, or maybe he just hungered for human contact. He bought a small piece of property on the Wickquasgeck Trail, at about what is today 47th Street and Second Avenue, built a house there, and set up as a jack-of-all-trades. The trail – which, as noted earlier, diverged from what would become Broadway at about 23rd Street and ran up the east side of the island before reconnecting with it in the north – was alive with traffic now: Indians of the Wickquasgeck tribe's several villages, as well as members of other tribes from further north and across the river on Long Island, streaming to and from New Amsterdam; Europeans and Africans moving along it as their farms reached up Manhattan. The territory of New Netherland remained vast and wild, but the island at its centre was rapidly succumbing to settlement. There was a place here on its eastern side, the old man figured, for a traveller's rest.

His house on Deutel Bay* became a popular gathering spot, where people could cluster before a homely fire of an evening, drink and sing, curse and argue, maybe step out into the night and gaze at the moonlight on the C-shaped bay. It was here that

* The 'turtle' in Turtle Bay – the name of the neighbourhood that occupies that area – is a corruption of the Dutch word *deutel*, or dowel; the bay (long since filled in) was so named because of its shape.

Nanne Beech, wife of the Englishman Thomas Beech, had 'fumbled at the front of the breeches of most all of those who were present', touching off a skirmish. On another occasion Ulrich Lupoldt, a West India Company official, while drinking at Claes's house, got into a shouting match with Jan Evertsen Bout, who lived across the North River, over rumours that Bout was having his way with a certain 'black wench'. Claes seems to have been close friends with or related by marriage to young Harmen Meyndertsz van den Bogaert, who had made the journey into Mohawk country in the winter of 1634 to re-negotiate fur prices; Van den Bogaert frequented the man's tavern-home, and underwrote his loans.

The wheelwright was, by several accounts, a harmless and well-liked old man. He knew many Indians by name. It wouldn't have surprised him in the least, one day in August of 1641, precisely as Adriaen van der Donck was settling into his duties as *schout* of Rensselaerswyck, to find a 27-year-old Wickquasgeck Indian at his door with a few furs slung over his shoulder, who said he was interested in trading them for some duffel cloth. Claes knew the young man: he lived in a village to the north-east of the island, and had worked for a time for Claes's son. The wheelwright invited him in out of the August sun, gave him something to eat and drink. And, as the old man bent over the chest in which he kept his goods for trade, the young Wickquasgeck – who is unnamed in the records, which is unfortunate since he was at the centre of a major event in the life of the colony – in a seemingly unpremeditated act, reached for an axe that Claes Swits had leaning against the wall, raised it high, and cut off the old man's head. Then he left.

Random as the murder seemed, there was an inevitability to it. The Indian had no quarrel with Swits. But fifteen years before, in 1626, around the time that Peter Minuit had purchased the island, a small group of Wickquasgeck Indians who had ventured south to trade furs were set upon by some Europeans, robbed and murdered – all except a twelve-year-old boy, who had escaped. For fifteen years he had nursed his revenge, as the Europeans increased in numbers and spread out slowly over the island – and then it erupted, perhaps surprising even him.

The murder on the Wickquasgeck Road was thus an element in the clockwork regularity of movement that governs culture clashes: an event triggers another, across space and time, which leads to greater, bloodier reprisals. The killing of Claes Swits echoed. It echoed, first and most consequentially, in the brain of Willem Kieft. Sweltering in his office in Fort Amsterdam, where he had recently greeted Van der Donck and wished him well in his new position up north, the 44-year-old director of the colony reacted to the grim news with something like exhilaration. It was an odd reaction, but he was an odd man. He had been born and raised in Amsterdam, the son of a merchant and a politician's daughter. He had excellent family connections – Rembrandt featured his cousin, Willem van Ruytenburch, in *The Night Watch* (that's him, right of centre, in the dashing yellow ensemble and holding his scabbard). But Kieft himself was something of a black sheep. He had pursued a business opportunity in France, and had failed at it so decisively, with such financial loss to its backers, that a picture of him was tacked over the gallows in the town of La Rochelle, and he was forced to flee. Fantastically enough, he then wound up somewhere in the Ottoman empire, given the task of ransoming Christians who had been taken prisoner by the sultan. But, according to a pamphlet published in Antwerp attacking his administration, Kieft had turned that mission into a profit-making venture by buying the release only of those captives who had the smallest price on their heads, leaving the others to languish in Turkish gaols and keeping the balance of the money.

Perhaps it was this cleverness that recommended him to the directors of the West India Company as the right man to replace the hapless Wouter van Twiller. More likely it was family connections. He had arrived in 1638, when the province was in disorder, determined to exert the iron authority he believed was necessary to turn the settlement around – never mind that it began turning itself around shortly after his arrival, thanks to the advent of free trade. In fact, his whole problem – the problem of all the colony's directors throughout its lifetime – was the impossibility of the situation. Dutch global expansion during its century of empire was built around not settlement colonies but outposts, which explains why, even though the empire extended as far afield as India, Taiwan and Java, the Dutch language is not spread around the globe the way English is. The English as overlords either planted settlements or, as in India, imposed elements of their own culture on a society. The Dutch preferred to set up military and trading posts at strategic spots and let the locals bring trade goods to them. The trading companies did not see themselves in the business of establishing permanent colonies.

But New Netherland refused to remain a trading post. It was unique among the way-stations of the Dutch empire in that it insisted on becoming a *place*. By some estimates it had, by its end, attracted more settlers from the Dutch Republic than all of the other Dutch outposts combined. Its population wasn't composed entirely of soldiers and company employees, but included many ordinary settlers as well, who liked what they found and were hoping to stay. It had streets and buildings; but more than this, by the 1640s it had developed a style, a way of getting by, which certainly had something to do with the company that ran it but had more to do with the likes of Claes Swits, Govert Loockermans, Joris Rapalje, Catalina Trico, Griet Reyniers and Anthony 'The Turk' van Salee – people who operated around the company, not within it.

The place had a life of its own. And with that came, naturally, a need for political structure. As it was, there was no judicial system; or rather, the system was Kieft. There was no body of case law; he settled disputes however he chose. There was no appeal. Kieft and the other directors of the colony weren't given a mandate to oversee the establishment of a political and legal system; instead, the company shipped them off with a single tool:

military dictatorship. It was an effective tool in the sorts of situations they found themselves in in outposts like Batavia and Macassar, but a hindrance in what was fast becoming a fully fledged society.

The colonial leaders were very slow to understand the distinction, slow to comprehend that the situation on Manhattan Island was fundamentally different from that on other exotic outposts. None of the series of West India Company employees who headed the New Netherland operation ever did truly comprehend it – except the last of them, and by the time he did it was far too late for the Dutch.

Kieft never understood it at all. He was not a politician. He arrived with a directive to turn around a failing corporate venture, and he was armed with one arrow in his quiver: total fiat, the power of life and death. Those within his jurisdiction were not constituents but subjects, serfs. It was an accepted business model in the seventeenth century. For most situations in which the East and West India Companies found themselves, it worked.

Kieft did make an initial gesture towards satisfying the natural need among his populace to feel that they were in some way involved in the company's decision-making. He appointed a council of advisers to assist him. This council consisted of two members. One was Johannes la Montagne, a benign Walloon medical doctor who was well liked and no threat to anyone, including Kieft; as a bonus, he was in debt to the company and so unlikely to go against it. The other councillor was Kieft himself. Kieft further decided that, as director, he would have two votes on the council, and La Montagne would have one vote. Decisions were made by majority rule. Thus Kieft's nod to representative government.

The next order of business was to deal with an immediate outside threat, which came from one of Kieft's predecessors. Peter Minuit, with his Swedish settlement force, had anchored at his chosen spot on a tributary of what the Dutch called the South

River in the middle of March 1638, about two weeks before Kieft stepped ashore on Manhattan. Minuit had calculated the placement of his colony with great deftness. He knew the area (today the Delaware River and lands on either side of it, encompassing parts of Maryland, Delaware, New Jersey and Pennsylvania) well; and, more to the point, he had an exquisite appreciation of the respective claims of the Dutch and English in that part of the continent. He knew that the English still held to their right-of-first-discovery claim, by which, in their eyes, the entire coastline – indeed, the entire continent – was theirs. Practically speaking, however, the English colony of Virginia was well to the south, and thus Minuit hoped to avoid detection by them until his settlement had established itself. As to the Dutch, while the South River territory fell under their claim by means of Hudson's voyage, Minuit knew that the West India Company had been erratic in following up the claim by buying lands along the South River from the Indian tribes that occupied them. He knew what had been purchased and what had not; specifically, that the Dutch had bought title to lands along the eastern shore of the South River (i.e. New Jersey), but not the western shore. Immediately upon landing, then, Minuit gathered the tribal chiefs of the area, held a conclave in the cabin of his flagship, the *Kalmar Nyckel*, and got them to make their marks on a deed. The point was not, of course, to satisfy tribal notions of land ownership, nor did the Swedish government care much about executing legal transactions with natives. Minuit had his eyes on the Dutch; he wanted to forestall any legal arguments they might make by employing their own system of property transfer. Using the skills he had learned in the service of the Dutch, he purchased the land on the west side of the river, below the branching river the Dutch named the Schuylkill – i.e. the future states of Delaware and Maryland and the corner of Pennsylvania that would become Philadelphia – on behalf of the twelve-year-old Queen Christina of Sweden.

A month later, soldiers at the lone Dutch outpost on the South

River spotted Minuit's ship and sent a report to Manhattan, which must have infuriated Kieft. This was a military and diplomatic challenge to Dutch sovereignty by a nation that was supposed to be an ally. And Minuit's role at the centre of it must have particularly irked him. Kieft wasted no time, but sent a communiqué aimed directly at the man who had once held his job. In May a Dutch vessel sailed down the coast, between the capes that to this day preserve the names – Henlopen and May – given them in the Dutch period, into the bay, up the South River and into the tributary called the Minquas Kill, dropping anchor before the rocky outcrop behind which Minuit's men, sweating in the spring air, were digging out the perimeter of their fort. A soldier disembarked and handed a letter to the leader of New Sweden:

> I, Willem Kieft, Director-General of New-Netherland, residing on the Island of the Manhattes and in Fort Amsterdam, under the authority of their High Mightinesses the Lords States-General of the United Netherlands and the Incorporated West-India Company, Chamber at Amsterdam, make known to you Peter Minuit, who style yourself Commander in the service of Her Royal Majesty of Sweden, that the whole Southriver of New-Netherland has been many years in our possession and secured by us above and below by forts and sealed with our blood, which even happened during your administration of New-Netherland and is well known to you. Now, as you intrude between our forts and begin to build a fort there to our disadvantage and prejudice, which shall never be suffered by us and we are very certain, that her Royal Majesty of Sweden has not given you any order to build fortresses on our rivers or along our coasts, Therefore, in case you proceed with the erection of fortifications and cultivation of the soil and trade in peltries or in any wise attempt to do us injury, We do hereby protest against all damages, expenses and losses, together with all mishaps, bloodsheds and

> disturbances, which may arise in future time therefrom and that we shall maintain our jurisdiction in such manner, as we shall deem most expedient.

Since the notice did not overtly promise a military attack, Minuit ignored it: from the beginning he had staked the venture on his belief that New Netherland would have too few soldiers to cover its territory. He finished the construction of Fort Christina, then, leaving the fort garrisoned by twenty-five men, sailed off, full of hope and dash, for Stockholm, where he intended to put together the next expedition for the New World. This one would be populated not by soldiers but by colonists. By now Minuit's plan had expanded. He intended to gather not only Swedish Adams and Eves but also refugees from his native Rhine region, who he believed would leap at the opportunity to escape two decades of war and start a new life on new soil. Having worked so hard and diligently in his first effort as colonizer, only to see it taken away from him, had sharpened his ambition, refined it. He wasn't out for adventure any longer. He was a utopian now: he wanted to build a new society.

But Minuit never made it back to Europe. His dream died when he died, in August 1638, in a hurricane in the Caribbean, where he had sailed to obtain a shipment of tobacco for resale in Europe. Minuit's determination and seventeenth-century-style frontier spirit would, however, have a second legacy in addition to that of Manhattan Island. The little garrison he had left behind at Fort Christina would serve as the base for what, over the course of the next seventeen years, would become a sizeable Swedish colony, extending a hundred miles up the Delaware river valley and encompassing the future cities of Philadelphia and Trenton. Out of Minuit's efforts to exploit this rich, wild valley – and, eventually, the Dutch determination to expel the intruding colony – would grow the queer, little-known footnote to history called New Sweden and its surprising contributions to history.

As Minuit had guessed, Willem Kieft opted for the time being not to mount a serious challenge to the Swedes on his southern flank. For one thing, he had a financial crisis on his hands. The opening of trade resulted in an instantaneous economic boost for the people of New Netherland, but the West India Company didn't benefit. As the directors in Amsterdam saw it, they had given up the monopoly that might ensure them eventual profits, yet were still saddled with administering the colony and protecting its inhabitants. The various agreements they had made with the Indians in their territory required the company to protect them too, in the case of attack by an enemy tribe. The merchant princes put pressure on their in-country director to find a way out of this quandary.

Kieft tried. First he tackled the blossoming currency crisis. Florins, doubloons, pennies, pieces of eight, schellings, reals, stooters, daelders, oortjes, Brabant stuivers, Carolus guilders and Flemish pounds all rattled in the tills of New Amsterdam's taverns and jangled in the purses of its townspeople: the sort of currency chaos that accompanies a highly *laissez-faire*, free-trade economy. And coins weren't even the main means of transacting business. Pelts were offered for everything from a glass of French brandy to a town lot. But the major currency, the most common thing dropped into the collection plate when it came round during the Sunday church service, was sewant. Wampum, as it is now more commonly known, was a much more widely used currency among the east coast Indians than is generally realized today. For tribes from different linguistic groups, it formed a kind of universal language – a way to conclude joint rituals, to seal treaties, to pay homage to dignitaries. The very first Dutch traders to follow in Henry Hudson's wake seized on this medium of exchange and expanded it. They learned which variety of polished beads was most highly prized – that of a purple clam shell that came from the easternmost shores of Long Island – and not only adopted it in their dealings with Indians but became wampum speculators among tribes. With the sudden increase in freelance trade on Manhattan had come a flood of low-grade sewant, and Kieft understood that the accompanying confusion was causing financial havoc. Therefore, on one of the regular Thursday 'council sessions' in which he and Dr La Montagne sat, he issued a directive:

> Whereas at present very bad seawan is in circulation here and payments are made in nothing but dirty, unpolished stuff that is brought here from other regions where it is worth 50 percent less than here, and the good, polished seawan, ordinarily called Manhattan seawan, is exported and wholly disappears, which tends to the decided ruin and destruction of this country; therefore, in order to provide against this in time, we do hereby for the public good, interdict and forbid all persons, of whatever state, quality or condition they may be, during the coming month of May to receive or give out in payment any unpolished seawan except at the rate of five for one stiver, that is to say, strung, and thereafter six beads for one stiver. Whoever shall be found to have acted contrary thereto shall provisionally forfeit the seawan paid out by him and ten guilders to the poor, the same applying to the receiver as well as to the giver. The price of the well polished seawan shall remain as before, to wit, four beads for one stiver, provided it be strung.

Next, Kieft turned his attention to the Indian question. The company did indeed, at considerable expense, supply Fort Amsterdam, Fort Orange and Fort Nassau on the South River with soldiers, who were there to protect the company's interests and its servants, and who were obliged by the land treaties entered into with Indian tribes to offer protection to them as well. Since the company couldn't back out of this arrangement, Kieft hit on what he thought quite a clever notion: to ask the Indians to pay taxes for the service rendered. The idea was too rich to be denied. Thursday came around, and Kieft opened the council meeting with his directive:

> Whereas the Company is put to great expense both in building fortifications and in supporting soldiers and sailors, we have therefore resolved to demand from the Indians who dwell around here and whom heretofore we have protected against their enemies, some contributions in the form of skins, maize and seawan, and if there be any nation which is not in a friendly way disposed to make such contribution it shall be urged to do so in the most suitable manner.

Those residents who had been on the scene long enough to know the tribal groups in the region of New Amsterdam – the Tappans, the Hackinsacks, the Wickquasgecks, the Raritans – reacted with alarm, telling Kieft this was more or less exactly what not to do. The Indians, these residents knew, were far from simple in their understanding of the land transactions they had made with the Europeans. The armful of goods mentioned in each title transfer was not, in their eyes, an outright purchase price, but a token that represented the arrangement to which they were agreeing. Under that arrangement they shared the land with the 'purchaser', and at the same time entered into a defensive alliance.

But while some of the European residents of the colony had surprisingly subtle and perceptive views of the natives who lived among them (an example from Van der Donck's writings: 'their womenfolk have an attractive grace about them . . . and if they were instructed as our women are they would no doubt differ little from them, if at all'), Kieft was not one of them. The sum of his actions and writings shows him, in fact, as more or less set on a strategy of eventual extermination. After being rebuffed, even laughed at, by several chiefs over his demand of protection payments, he seized on a small matter – the theft of some hogs from a Dutch farm on Staten Island – as the excuse for a punitive expedition. Even without knowing the history, one can almost see the chain of events unfolding from there. First there were the ironies: the thieves had apparently not been Indians at all but Dutchmen; the farm belonged to David de Vries, the trader who had tried to shame Van Twiller into behaving like a leader, who was friends with many Indians, who spoke several of their dialects and who, in dinners with Kieft at his quarters in Fort Amsterdam, tried to stop what was coming. 'These savages resemble the Italians,' De Vries warned, 'being very revengeful.'

But Kieft was inexorable. In July 1641 he sent a posse to the Raritan village that his information told him was the home of the thieves; several Indians were killed. On cue, then, the Raritans attacked De Vries's farm, killing four farmhands and burning down the man's house. Kieft then took his turn. He would not, he decided, be drawn into war, but rather would adopt the classic strategy of pitting his enemies against one another. Thursday came (it happened to be 4 July), and he delivered his edict in council:

> Whereas the Indians of the Raretangh are daily exhibiting more and more hostility . . . we have therefore considered it most expedient and advisable to induce the Indians, our allies hereabout, to take up arms . . . and in order to encourage them the more we have promised them ten fathoms of seawan for each head, and if they succeed in capturing any of the Indians who have most barbarously murdered our people on Staten Island we have promised them 20 fathoms of seawan for each head.

The offer of bribery yielded fast results. Shortly after the edict was posted, an Indian named Pacham, of a tribe that had had testy relations with the Raritans, strolled past the guardhouse and into Fort Amsterdam holding aloft – with what he presumably felt was appropriate ceremony and pride – a human hand dangling from a stick. On being admitted with his trophy into Kieft's presence, he declared that it belonged to the Raritan chief who had ordered the attack on De Vries's farm.

Kieft was mollified. He felt pleased that his plan had succeeded, and vindicated in the character of leadership he was providing. 'All men are created equal' was a sentiment of the distant future; in the seventeenth century, as in those before, the different races, religions and genders were seen by one and all as occupying different rungs on the chain of being. To a mind like Kieft's – not especially distinguishable from that of Captain John Mason, who had led the English massacre of the Pequots in Connecticut four years earlier, or Nathaniel Bacon, the Jamestown colony's advocate of Indian extermination – the wild peoples of the world, on whatever continent they lived, understood power, and in the face of it they would assume their naturally subordinate rank. The Raritans showed no signs of retaliating, which proved the point.

The whole business might have ended there. But then, without immediate connection to these events, though perhaps subconsciously kindled by them, the unnamed Wickquasgeck Indian chose this moment to seek vengeance for his uncle's long-ago murder. The decapitation of Claes Swits gave Willem Kieft just the excuse he wanted to launch a full-scale retaliation. The natives had now shown that they could never be trusted; extermination was the only solution.

Waging war requires politicking, and Kieft moved first to gain popular support for his effort against the tribes of the area by asking the residents of the Manhattan area to nominate a council of twelve men who would assist him in deciding on a course of action. He deserves some credit for bringing into being the first popularly chosen body in what would become New York State – one of the first such bodies in the New World – though he had no notion of how this move would backfire on him. The twelve assembled themselves, and chose David de Vries as their president. Also on the council was Joris Rapalje, who, with his wife, Catalina Trico, had stuck it out in the colony, moving from youth into middle age, and had recently begun to prosper. Kieft asked the assembly three questions, which, helpfully, he numbered for them:

1. Whether it is not just to punish the barbarous murder of Claes Swits committed by an Indian and, in case the Indians refuse to surrender the murderer at our request, whether it is not justifiable to ruin the entire village to which he belongs?
2. In what manner the same ought to be put into effect and at what time?
3. By whom it may be undertaken?

To Kieft's annoyance, the twelve did not counsel war. They agreed that 'by all means the murderer according to the proposition of the honorable director should be punished,' but insisted that 'two or three times more a sloop be sent by the honorable director to make a friendly request without threats, for the surrender of the murderer.' The twelve councillors knew they had no power, so they tried to lay road-blocks in the path of their headstrong leader. In the event that all-out conflict with the tribes should be called for, they declared, in what seems to have been a transparent stalling tactic, that the colony should first send for two hundred coats of mail from the home country. Also, since by this time Kieft was developing a reputation for, as David de Vries wrote, calling for war while 'being himself protected in a good fort, out of which he had not slept a single night during all the years he had been there', the council added a gentle stipulation that in the event of any military expedition, 'whereas we acknowledge no other commander than the director . . . therefore . . . the honorable director shall personally lead this expedition.'

Kieft, who had made it plain to the council that it was to be a rubber-stamp body, was furious at its wilfulness. He decided to try again, this time communing with each representative separately, in the belief that removing the security of the group would cause each of the simple farmers and tradesmen to give his approval to the director's plan. But while sailor Jacob Waltingen said he was 'ready to do whatever the director and council may order', and Jacques Bentyn, a West India Company official, gave Kieft a thoroughly satisfactory reply that 'it will be best to kill the Indians so as to fill them with fear,' the majority still wanted to take matters slowly and pursue a course of seeking justice for the specific wrong that had been done.

To add to Kieft's annoyance, the council of twelve, having failed to give the endorsement it had been assembled to provide, then took it upon itself to begin advising the director on other matters. The councillors wanted certain rights for individuals, 'according to the custom in Holland'. They wanted a prohibition on the sale of English cattle. Most of all, they wanted themselves, or some similar body, to become a permanent representative assembly, as existed in even the smallest villages in the United Provinces. Two weeks after receiving these proposals, Kieft responded with a decree:

> And whereas the Commonality at our request appointed and instructed these 12 men to communicate their good counsel and advice on the subject of the murder of the late Claes Cornelissen Swits, which was committed by the Indians; this being now completed by them, we do hereby thank them for the trouble they have taken, and shall, with God's help, make use of their rendered written advice in its own time. The said Twelve men shall now, henceforth hold no further meeting, as the same tends to a dangerous consequence, and to the great injury both of the country and of our authority. We therefore, hereby forbid them calling any manner of assemblage or meeting, except by our express order, on pain of being punished as disobedient subjects. Done in fort Amsterdam, this eighth of February, 1642, in New Netherland.

The attempt at winning popular support for his military

action having backfired, Kieft went ahead anyway, ordering West India Company soldiers to attack Indian villages. So began what became known as Kieft's War, a series of murderous attacks and counterattacks that would continue for several years. The ugliest assault came on the night of 25 February 1643. David de Vries had once again stayed at the director's home inside Fort Amsterdam, where he sat across the dinner table from Kieft and tried to argue him out of the attack. Kieft stated that he 'had a mind to wipe the mouths of the savages', to which De Vries replied that Kieft had no right to act on his own, that

> such work could not be done without the approbation of the Twelve Men; that it could not take place without my assent, who was one of the Twelve Men . . . that he should consider what profit he could derive from this business . . . But it appeared that my speaking was of no avail. He had, with his co-murderers, determined to commit the murder, deeming it a Roman deed, and to do it without warning the inhabitants in the open lands, that each one might take care of himself against the retaliation of the natives, for he could not kill all the Indians.

The two men had now finished their meal. Kieft did not reply directly, but told De Vries to go into the new great hall he had had built in the fort. There, De Vries found the soldiers massed for their attack. Two parties were formed: one to march 2 miles to the north-west to launch a raid on a small group of Indians camped at Corlaer's Hook (today the Lower East Side of Manhattan), the other to cross the river and attack a larger group camped in the area of the plantation called Pavonia, at what is now Jersey City, New Jersey.

De Vries found the business disgusting. These Indians, of the Wickquasgeck and Tappan tribes, had come to the Dutch seeking sanctuary from Mohawks further north, having fallen behind in tribute payments and as a result having been attacked in their villages. 'Let this work alone,' De Vries said to Kieft. 'You will also murder our own nation, for there are none of the settlers in the open country who are aware of it.' But the soldiers went off on their missions. De Vries stayed in the director's quarters that night, sitting up all night by the kitchen hearth, watching the blaze, and waiting. Around midnight, 'I heard a great shrieking, and I ran to the ramparts of the fort, and looked over to Pavonia. Saw nothing but firing, and heard the shrieks of the natives murdered in their sleep.' Shortly after this an Indian couple, whom De Vries knew, appeared inexplicably inside the fort. They had managed to flee the massacre, which in the confusion they thought was being done by Mohawks. De Vries told them it was Dutchmen who were annihilating their makeshift village, and that Fort Amsterdam was the last place they should come for refuge. He helped them escape into the woods. In the morning, De Vries heard the returned soldiers boasting that they had 'massacred or murdered eighty Indians, and considering they had done a deed of Roman valor, in murdering so many in their sleep'.

De Vries then recorded in his journal an account of the massacre that later appeared in a pamphlet published in the Dutch Republic, written by anonymous inhabitants of the colony in hopes of making their countrymen aware of the abuse of power taking place in the North American colony:

> [I]nfants were torn from their mother's breasts, and hacked to pieces in the presence of their parents, and the pieces thrown into the fire and in the water, and other sucklings, being bound to small boards, were cut, stuck, and pierced, and miserably massacred in a manner to move a heart of stone. Some were thrown into the river, and when the fathers and mothers endeavored to save them, the soldiers would not let them come on land but made both parents and children drown . . . Some came to our people in the country with their hands, some with their legs cut off, and some holding

> their entrails in their arms, and others had such horrible cuts and gashes, that worse than they were could never happen. And these poor simple creatures, as also many of our own people, did not know any better than that they had been attacked by a party of other Indians – the Maquas. After this exploit, the soldiers were rewarded for their services, and Director Kieft thanked them by taking them by the hand and congratulating them.

The pamphlet that De Vries copied, called *Broad Advice*, probably exaggerated the horrors, but its exaggerations help make the point that the colonists opposed the war against the Indians, and, in fact, were so shocked by the folly and danger of living at the whim of one man that it spurred them to press for some form of representative government. Kieft's War is fairly named, for in pursuing it Kieft overrode the vast majority of the residents; and what is striking is that both his hard line and their instincts towards moderation reflected the moods of the times. The Dutch were constructing an empire – by definition an ugly business. Over the course of the seventeenth century the Dutch trading companies, their directors and soldiers, proved themselves as bloody and inexorable as their English, Spanish and Portuguese counterparts. Kieft was not very different from contemporary Dutch administrators in Malacca or Macassar, the Portuguese rulers of Goa, or the eighteenth-century English East India Company directors in Calcutta and Madras.

But the colonists who opposed bloodshed were also acting true to type. It was no innate goodness that motivated them, but a practical wisdom won through decades of strife in the Dutch provinces. In both De Vries's journal and the anti-Kieft pamphlet, the passage describing the horrors of the Pavonia attack is followed by a sentence that must have echoed in the minds of many of the colonists: 'Did the Duke of Alva in the Netherlands ever do anything more cruel?' Seventy years before, with rebellion against Spanish rule simmering in the

Low Countries, the Spanish regent had sent Fernando Álvarez de Toledo, the notorious Duke of Alva, to quell it and reform heretics – that is to say, Protestants. The duke went on an inquisitional rampage of torture and murder that became known as the Council of Blood, which involved decapitating rebellious nobles and slaughtering commoners in the hundreds.

The Council of Blood became ingrained in the national psyche; it helped vault the Dutch states towards an open war of rebellion. It also reinforced the notion of tolerance as a part of what it meant to be Dutch. This had been building for some time, and would continue to do so throughout the seventeenth century, as more and more people from other parts of Europe came to live in the Dutch provinces – in fact, it is something of a mistake to think of 'Dutch' in this era as an ethnic signifier. To the Dutch provinces in the seventeenth century came English, French, German, Swedish and Jewish immigrants; they settled, adopted the language, 'Batavianized' their names (so that, for example, Bridges became Van Brugge) and, in time, adopted a common basic framework for looking at the world, one of the main features of which was the need to accommodate others. As the 'Dutch' emigrated to their New World colony, then, they brought with them not only a ready-made mix of cultures but a tolerance of differences, the prescription for a multicultural society. In its very seeding, Manhattan was a melting pot.

We should be clear, however, about the contemporary meaning of tolerance, which had nothing to do with 'celebrating' diversity – a concept that would have provoked only uncomprehending laughter in the seventeenth century. 'Putting up with' was probably closer to the mark. If that sounds wan, consider that in Germany an estimated 40 per cent of the population died as a result of the unholy enmeshment of religious intolerance and politics that gave rise to the Thirty Years War (in the city of Magdeburg alone, thirty thousand were killed in a single day). In the United Provinces, meanwhile, tolerance had developed into a cultural trait. Dutch writers openly acknowledged that knowing how to get along, fit in, accommodate, was good for business. Foreign tourists in the provinces constantly noted the phenomenon, and usually found it odd, seeing it as a destabilizing force, a symptom of moral laxity. As they moved into their empire, the Dutch put their strange approach to use, and it revealed itself in the most mundane ways. The ruthlessness of Kieft and other merchant warriors masks the fact that the farmers and traders who made up the colony learned Indian languages, adopted Indian farming techniques, not only embraced the wampum trade but made it their own, and, for a time and in a great many ways, tried to co-exist with the native population. Kieft's own council of blood thus led to a reaction on the part of the Manhattanites that came straight from their experiences in Europe. Colonists bemoaned the war on the most practical grounds: they were vastly outnumbered by the Indians, and what was more, the Dutch were not trappers; the fur trade, their whole reason for being here, depended on the Indians. It made better sense to get along than to fight.

Even as the attacks, counterattacks and colonists' complaints escalated, the settlers tried to maintain their way of life. Thomas Chambers signed a contract to build a house for Jan Schepmoes. Skipper Willem Dircksen agreed to ship cargo for John Turner and Willem Holmers and deliver it safely 'on the beach beyond high water, at the island of St. Christopher, in the Caribbees'. Isaac Allerton filed a complaint against Anthony 'The Turk' van Salee. John and Richard Ogden, of Stamford, Connecticut, contracted to build a stone church for the company within the walls of Fort Amsterdam. The company finished building a stone tavern and inn at the spot along Pearl Street where arriving sailors and passengers disembarked. Jeuriaen Hendricksz filed a complaint against Anthony 'The Turk' van Salee. Jan Haes called Nicolaes Tenner 'a rogue and a double rogue', and Tenner took him to court for slander. Harmen van den Bogaert, who had made the daring winter journey into Mohawk country several years earlier, received the unfortunate Claes Swits's property, having been named in the old man's will, and in turn sold it to James Smith and William Brown. Van den Bogaert later testified, along with Claes's son Adriaen and another man, that they had been served beer at the tavern of Jan Snediger three times, the first time it was 'one pint short in hardly three pints, the second time it was found to be scarcely wine measure, the third time it was found to be a gill short in three pints'. Andries Hudde filed a complaint against Anthony 'The Turk' van Salee. Catalina Trico and her daughter Sara testified in a custody case that the promiscuous Nanne Beech had told them that 'Mr. Smith' had fathered the child she was carrying. Hendrick Jansen sold Willem Adriaensen his 'garden dwelling and brewhouse'. Pierre Pia and Jean St Germain testified, in the case of a shot hog, that they had seen an Englishman with a gun in the vicinity a short time before. Cornelis Hooglandt sold to Willem Tomassen his house across the river on Long Island, together with the right to operate the ferry that had recently gone into regular service to bring Manhattanites to their farmland in what was already being called Breuckelen.

But the trouble would not go away. Kieft's action had brought about something that previously had been unachievable: the unification of area tribes into a confederation. And it was one aimed at slaughtering Europeans. Attacks came without warning, in the deep of night, with a whispering hail of arrows and explosions from the muskets sold to the Indians by traders in the area around Rensselaerswyck. The plantation at Achter Col (today Newark, New Jersey) was reduced to burning heaps. Budding communities on Long Island were decimated. Small groups of Indians made sudden strikes on the outlying farms on Manhattan, hacking cattle, burning crops, killing anyone with a white face, sometimes dragging women and children away into captivity, and forcing residents to seek the safety of the fort.

In a matter of months over the course of 1642 and 1643, years of brutally hard labour – clearing and tilling fields, building by hand the mills that would saw the timber with which they then constructed successively more comfortable homes – were erased. Families huddled in hastily constructed straw huts inside the walls of the fort. Fort Amsterdam occupied approximately the position where the Old Customs House stands today. Standing outside that fortress-like building, it is surprisingly easy to summon the image of those men, women and children, through the relentless winter months of 1643 and on into the cold spring, gathered inside the walls, here at the extreme southern rim of the island that had been their home, which had, for a time, seemed to offer itself to them, to beckon them to stay, prosper, root their families, but which now seemed ready to tip them into the bay. Refugees in their own homeland now, they huddled in the open courtyard, exposed, at the mercy of their several Gods, wondering what would happen to them, but not wondering whom to blame.

7
The Cause

FAR TO THE NORTH, MEANWHILE, THE AIR STILL HAD ITS glorious native sweetness, complicated by pine needles and grape blossoms and lacking the dark pungency of burned homesteads. Adriaen van der Donck, the young man from Breda who had lived all of his 22-odd years within a few dozen square miles of flat country that had long since been divided, channelled, poldered and tamed by humans, spent his first months in his new land entranced by the rawness and bigness of its nature, and blissfully cut off from the horrors further south. The mountains to the north of the colony of Rensselaerswyck loomed like a dreamscape. To one coming from a place where wood was precious, the forest beggared the imagination – 'so much so,' Van der Donck wrote, 'that practically the whole country is covered with it, and in a manner of speaking, there is too much of it for us, and it's in our way.' The river on which his small house sat was a quarter of a mile wide, and yet the winters were of such ferocity that the entire expanse typically froze over every December, leaving the subjects of diamond merchant Kiliaen van Rensselaer cut off from Manhattan and points south, alone with the mountains and the snow-smothered pines until spring.

Van der Donck decided that April and May were the finest months to explore the countryside. 'The trees are then in bloom,' he wrote, 'and the woods are full of sweet smells. By mid-May, without fail, we have ripe strawberries, not in the gardens, because they are not planted there, but in the fields, where they grow naturally.' But he found he loved autumn best in this new world: 'Above the highlands, advancing northerly, the weather is colder, the fresh waters freeze, the stock is sheltered, the kitchens are provided, and all things are put in order for the winter. The fat oxen and swine are slaughtered. The wild geese, turkeys, and deer are at their best in this season, and easiest obtained.' He observed the bears, 'none like the gray and pale-haired bears of Muscovy and Greenland' but rather 'of a shiny pitch black color', and with such an acute sense of smell that 'the Indians when setting out to hunt bears . . . impart Esau's odor to their bodies and clothing, that is, they apply the scent of field and forest so that they will not be betrayed by a contrasting scent.' He marvelled at the 'incredibly numerous' deer; he studied eagles, observed that they 'soar very high in the air, beyond the vision of man' and can 'strike a fish, and jerk it living from the waters'. He stalked turkeys in the woods, shot quail by the dozen, admired thick populations of 'woodcocks, birch-cocks, heath-fowls, pheasants, wood and water snipes'. Like a good Dutchman, he made a special study of the winds of the New World – 'the swift and fostering messengers of commerce'. He noted the contours of the land, the character of the soil in different regions, the native trees and fruits: 'The mulberries are better and sweeter than ours, and ripen earlier.' He counted 'several kinds of plums, wild or small cherries, juniper, small kinds of apples, many hazelnuts, blackcurrants, gooseberries, blue India figs, and strawberries in abundance all over the country, some of which ripen at half May, and we have them until July; blueberries, raspberries, black-caps, etc., with artichokes, ground-acorns, ground beans, wild onions, and leeks like ours.' He was intrigued by a local fruit he called 'cicerullen, or water-lemons' (i.e. watermelon), which grew 'the size of the stoutest Leyden cabbages', and had 'a light-textured pulp like a wet sponge in which the pips are embedded. When really ripe and sound, it melts away to a juice as soon as it enters the mouth, and nothing remains to spit out but the pips . . . they are so refreshing and often served as a beverage.' He canvassed the gardeners, European and Indian, and, with a seventeenth-century intellectual's passion for the new scientific fad of analysing and classifying, made an inventory of the wild herbs and edible plants for which European taxonomy had a name:

> The plants which are known to us are the following, *viz*: Capilli veneris, scholopendria, angelica, polypodium, verbascum, album, calteus sacerdotis, atriplex hortensis and marina, chortium, turrites, calamus aromaticus, sassafras, rois Virginianum, ranunculus, plantago, bursa pastoris, malva, origaenum, geranicum, althea, cinoroton pseudo, daphine, viola, ireas, indigo silvestris, sigillum, salamonis, sanguis draconum, consolidae, millefolium, noli me tangere, cardo benedictus, agrimonium, serpentariae, coriander, leeks, wild leeks, Spanish figs, elatine, camperfolie, petum male and female, and many other plants.

Over the course of the next fourteen years, Van der Donck would create an impressively wide-ranging body of writing, nearly all of it on the topic of his new home, its inhabitants (European and Indian) and its need for proper government. But on one level what is even more striking in his writing than his political skills or legal reasoning is the sheer exuberance that rises from the pages. The man simply fell in love with America. He saw its promise and its grandeur. He revelled in its rawness, and the opportunity it provided. Within a short time of his arrival his mind had skimmed far beyond the plodding mercantile thoughts of the West India Company officials who ran the New Netherland colony; he saw the continent not just as a source of exploitable materials but as a new home, a virgin base for the expansion of the civilization that had nurtured him. He understood that this was a land of incomprehensible vastness (even the Indians 'know of no limits to the country' westwards, he wrote, and 'deem such enquiries to be strange and singular') into which a new society, an extension of Europe, could grow. He understood that it would need a framework of laws, a system of justice, and he was brazen enough to think he could help carve out such a system. That is not to say he could have foreseen the New World colonies one day breaking free of their motherlands. He was a product of the seventeenth century, not the eighteenth. But he was, as his writings make plain, one of the first genuine Americans. He was so not because of where he came to live, but because of the expanse of opportunity that opened inside his breast once he arrived – opportunity he imagined not for himself alone but for others.

It is hard to say when that feeling took control of him. Probably in those first months, when he wasn't revelling in the landscape he was focused on the practical execution of his work. For he had a job to do, and he threw himself into it with what his employer soon found to be inordinate zeal. From the moment he touched the soil of what he called 'the New American World', Van der Donck seems to have been in constant motion. The first issue he faced was that of freelance, off-the-books trading taking place between Rensselaerswyck colonists and those of New Netherland and New England. Within days of his arrival in Rensselaerswyck, he stood in full Rembrandtesque costume before the collected farmers and tradesmen of the colony and delivered his first ordinance, which must have stirred up the lot:

> We, Adriaen van der Donck, chief officer, with the commissioners and councilors of the colony of Rensselaerswyck, to all who shall see these or hear them read, greeting. As we see and notice daily the great strife, uproar, quarreling, yes what is more, mutual discord, all of which are causes that generally bring about the ruin of a well ordered community,

> springing solely from the trade which our inhabitants carry on with the foreign residents . . . have seen fit to order, enjoin, and command, as we do by these, all the inhabitants of the colony . . . that they shall not undertake to buy from or exchange with the residents any goods, or in any manner let them have any beavers, otters or other furs, directly or indirectly, upon fine and forfeiture for the first offense of three times the value of the goods first bought . . . But, if any shallops or vessels of the Company or any one else come up the river and the inhabitants want to buy anything of which they are in great need, they shall ask permission of the Officer.

Whether or not Van der Donck realized it before leaving Amsterdam, it soon became clear that his duties were less concerned with administering justice for the welfare of a new society than with serving the profit interests of the patroon. Van Rensselaer may have been an ocean away, but through his voluminous instructions he showed himself an inexorable taskmaster unwaveringly focused on efficiency. Van der Donck was to devote himself to cracking down on a black-market grain trade, hunting down those who had ventured away from the colony before doing their contracted time, and prosecuting residents who bought and sold beaver pelts on the sly. Van der Donck rode the valleys of the colony on horseback and sailed up and down the North River between Rensselaerswyck and Manhattan on Van Rensselaer's business. In November 1642 he was in New Amsterdam searching for a young woman who had skipped out on her service contract at Rensselaerswyck. When he found her, he discovered that she was pregnant, indeed nearly ready to give birth. In court at Fort Amsterdam, he did his duty by 'demanding' that she return to fulfil her obligation, but then struck a deal allowing the woman to stay put until she had delivered and her baby was old enough to travel. The old patroon didn't care to see flexibility in his lawman's personality. 'It is your duty to seek my advantage and protect me against loss,' he barked in a letter.

Already, even from faraway Amsterdam, Van Rensselaer could detect, through reports from various quarters, a dangerous wilfulness on the part of his law officer, and he began to regret choosing Van der Donck. 'What pleases me now in you is the zeal and diligence which I notice in your honor in expediting several matters,' Van Rensselaer wrote early on, but these same qualities came with a downside. The young man took affairs into his own hands – settling disputes as he saw fit, deciding the colony needed a brickyard, working out improvements to the sawmill and gristmill, without consulting Van Rensselaer or Arent van Curler, the commercial officer of the colony and Van Rensselaer's grandnephew. When the patroon demanded that his law officer collect late payments from tenants, Van der Donck visited their shacks, saw that they had no money and, rather than inform the patroon that he had not carried out his wishes, simply ignored the matter. Van Rensselaer's letters soon began to nag: 'Your principal fault has been that you have wanted to prevail over Corler and that you have gone ahead too independently.'

Van der Donck offended the patroon's business principles when he formally protested at a direct order from Van Rensselaer that forced farmers in the colony to swear an oath of loyalty to him not only for themselves but on behalf of their servants. Van der Donck seems to have taken the position that the middle ages were over and that servants should be held responsible for their own behaviour – a notion that Van Rensselaer considered 'outrageous'. From this point in his career, Van der Donck's personality rings out from the centuries-old pages of letters, court records and other surviving documents of the period. It is a personality well suited to tackling a raw continent and helping to forge a viable new community: self-willed, righteous, insistent, arrogant, hot-tempered. It comes through in his private dealings: at one point someone takes him to court to accuse him of slander (the parties arranged an 'amicable and a friendly' settlement); another time an argument with a Rensselaerswyck functionary escalated until the two men, as Van Curler later gossiped to the patroon, 'pursued each other with swords', and ended with Van der Donck buffeting the man. Most of all, Van der Donck's headstrong nature is apparent in his relationship with his superior. It seems remarkable that, still in his early twenties, having travelled an ocean away from the only world he had known, he immediately set about defying his employer and patron, a man universally feared and respected as a kind of latter-day medieval prince. 'Most honorable, wise, powerful, and right discreet Lord' is how people addressed letters to Van Rensselaer. Van der Donck, by contrast, in his first act on arrival at Rensselaerswyck, angered Van Rensselaer by rejecting the farm set aside for him and taking another, at the far end of the colony. He then chose one of the patroon's prized black stallions as his personal mount.

And he persisted in his defiance, as evidenced in the exasperated references to him that peppered Van Rensselaer's letters to other officials of his colony (in which he tended to underline names): 'I take it very ill that Officer <u>vanderdonck</u> . . .', 'And as to <u>vanderdonck</u> . . .', 'These young people, like . . . <u>vanderdonck</u>, do not think at all of my interests . . .', 'write me especially how <u>vanderdonck</u> behaves in the matter . . .' The relationship that Van der Donck developed with Van Rensselaer – at first insinuating himself as an upright, model-son figure with the older man, then proceeding, stridently, almost flamboyantly, to go against him – would replay itself, first with Willem Kieft in New Amsterdam, then again a few years later with another father figure, this time with historic consequences. One can only wonder what his relationship with his real father was like.

At times Van Rensselaer seemed to suspect that his law officer accorded the interests of the colonists greater weight than his own. At other times he feared the young man would attempt something like a *coup d'état*. 'From the beginning you have acted not as officer but as director,' he complained at one point, adding sourly that if and when the time for a promotion came he wished 'to have the honor of the advancement myself'. Van Rensselaer's fear of the young man somehow trumping him seemed to be vindicated by a tale-telling report that Arent van Curler sent him in June 1643. Van der Donck had been spending a great deal of time in the Catskill mountains to the west of the patroon's lands, and Van Curler informed his uncle that 'Your Honor may be assured he intends to look for partners to plant a colonie there.'

Van der Donck had indeed been roaming the mountains. His all-consuming fascination with the New World had a focal point: the native inhabitants. The pitched battles and terrorist warfare taking place to the south was between the Europeans and the tribes of the Lower Hudson valley, which were distinct from the Mohawks and Mahicans in the area around Rensselaerswyck. The mayhem did not reach this far north. Indians remained a constant presence at the trading post and among the homes and farms of the patroon's domain, and soon after his arrival Van der Donck took up with some of them and began venturing into their lands. In Europe by this time a sizeable literature had built up about the American natives, and the Dutch in particular, who were eager to develop any arguments that showed their Spanish oppressors in a bad light, had focused on the plight of the Indians at the hands of the conquistadores. At universities such as Leiden, young men read descriptions in flowing Latin of natives who 'go naked' and have no knowledge of 'that source of all misfortunes, money'. Thus certain educated Europeans formed an idealistic image of these New World inhabitants, an image that wouldn't seem out of place in, say, the 1970s. It was perhaps with this in his mind that Van der Donck was drawn to Indian society.

He thus cracks the stereotype of a European of the time as culturally unable to see indigenous peoples as anything other than savages. Through the finely detailed observations of Indian society he later put in writing we can see him, during this period, immersing himself in the culture of the Mohawks and Mahicans, roving the wooded slopes and valleys with them, sitting in their homes, canvassing the women on their cooking methods, observing rituals, fishing and planting techniques, sexual and marriage customs, and 'the sucking of their children'. These two dominant tribal groups spoke different languages and had very different cultures – the Mohawks were more settled, living in palisaded villages organized around agriculture, while the Mahicans tended to move with the hunting season – a contrast which to Van der Donck helped explain why they were so often at war with one another. He would later describe these natives, for the benefit of curious European readers, as 'equal to the average and well-proportioned here in the Netherlands'. He characterized their houses: built snugly so that they 'repel rain and wind, and are also fairly warm, but they know nothing about fitting them out with rooms, salons, halls, closets or cabinets'. He learned some of their languages, classified the Indians of the region as falling into four different language groups, and analysed these carefully ('Declension and conjugation resemble those in Greek, for they, like the Greeks, have duals in their nouns and even augments in their verbs'). He observed their medicine men at first hand and marvelled that 'fresh wounds and dangerous injuries they know how to heal wonderfully with virtually nothing,' and that 'they can treat gonorrhoea and other venereal diseases so easily as to put many an Italian physician to shame.' However, he questioned the 'devil-hunting' methods used for the very ill, which 'make noise enough to frighten a person in extremity to death'. He studied their religious practices, and, in answer to the question of whether they could be converted to Christianity, frankly doubted it, but, in a remarkable passage, urged his country to institute a plan of social welfare among the Indians of the colony:

> Public authority ought to become involved and provide for sound teaching of our language and the elements of the Christian religion to their youth in good schools established in suitable locations in that country, so that in due course

> they could and would teach each other further and take pleasure in doing so. It would take a deal of effort and preparation, but without such measures not much good can be achieved among them. The neglect of it is a very bad thing, since the Indians themselves say they would be happy to have their children instructed in our language and religion.

Van der Donck's major work, *A Description of New Netherland*, from which these quotations are taken, is considered a classic of early American literature, but it has been forgotten by history thanks to the fact that it was written in the language not of the eventual masters of the American colonies but of their bitter rival. (The historian Thomas O'Donnell called the book 'one of America's oldest literary treasures', and said of Van der Donck, 'Had he written in English rather than Dutch, his *Description* would certainly have won from posterity the same kind, if not the same amount, of veneration that has been bestowed on Bradford's *Of Plymouth Plantation*.') The neglect of Van der Donck's book mirrors the treatment American history has given to the whole corpus of records of the Dutch colony centred on Manhattan, and for that matter the colony itself. There has been only one published English translation of the *Description*; it first appeared in print in 1841 (the translator, Jeremiah Johnson, was not only a former mayor of Brooklyn but counted himself a descendant of Catalina Trico and Joris Rapalje), and historians have relied on it ever since for the wealth of information the book contains about the colony, the American wilderness that the first Europeans found, and the Indians. But those generations of historians were apparently ignorant of the fact that the translation from which they were working was badly flawed. In places it is accurate, and indeed captures the poetry and zeal of the original; but in other places Johnson completely distorts what Van der Donck has to say.

The main flaw in this translation, however, which was reproduced most recently in a 1968 edition of the *Description*, is that it simply omits whole portions of Van der Donck's text. A major section that did not appear in print until 1990, when Dutch scholar Ada Louise van Gastel published it in translation in an academic journal, and of which historians have thus been ignorant, shows the young Van der Donck making a serious study of the Indians' treaties, contracts, and 'government and public policy'. It is fascinating reading in the light of Van der Donck's recently completed legal training and the work he would soon undertake on behalf of the Manhattan-based colony.* Looking at it in that context we see a young man fresh out of law school and filled with new, practical ideas about the law and how governments might function when those ideas were put into practice in an alien society, in a kind of scientific study outside the laboratory.

Like a good student of Grotius who also had a practical interest in how Europeans might better deal with the natives, Van der Donck, in this 'lost' section of his book, dispassionately analysed their ideas of right and wrong. He found in force among them none of the 'rights, laws, and maxims' common in European countries, but instead a general 'law of nature or of nations'. He shows that at least some of the Dutch colonists were aware of the nuances in the Indians' understanding of property rights, noting that to the natives 'wind, stream, bush, field, sea, beach, and riverside are open and free to everyone of every nation with which the Indians are not embroiled in open conflict. All those are free to enjoy and move about such places as

* I am deeply indebted to Diederik Willem Goedhuys for the new translation he made of the *Description* in 1991, a vast improvement on the Johnson translation that unfortunately remains unpublished; to Ada Louise van Gastel, whose 1985 doctoral dissertation, 'Adriaen van der Donck, New Netherland, and America', outlined for me many of the problems with the earlier translation; and to Hanny Veenendaal of the Netherlands Center in New York City, who helped me to translate afresh some passages of the *Description*.

though they were born there.' He identified their respect for certain principles of war that Europeans also held, such as giving safe conduct to 'state envoys' and honouring pacts. He noted, for the sake of future emissaries, that when making an offer such as a land treaty, the protocol was to state the request orally and at the same time give a suitable gift. 'The offering is hung up, the request is put, and those to whom it is addressed examine and deliberate the proposition seriously. If they take the offering, the request as made is accepted and consented to, but if it remains where it hangs for over three days the matter is held in abeyance and the petitioner has to alter the conditions or augment the offering or both.'

He seemed to admire the Indians for having government 'of the popular kind', but found that it had its problems. While a whole village would gather to debate matters of importance, and a chief would work like a politician to sway the people to his preferred course of action, democracy went only so far – and it had an abrupt end point. If an opponent remained obstinate, eventually 'one of the younger chiefs will jump up and in one fell swoop smash the man's skull with an axe in full view of everyone.' Van der Donck was forced to conclude that this species of popular government was 'defective and lame'.

So yes, Arent van Curler was right – Adriaen van der Donck had been spending time among the Indian villages in the Catskill mountains in 1643. And while he was up in the highlands, he began negotiations with tribes to buy a vast tract of land. Two years into what was probably a three-year contract with Van Rensselaer, Van der Donck was chafing, and planning for the future. He saw how things stood at Rensselaerswyck, saw that the old man proposed, against common sense, to run his colony as a medieval fief, with serfs and himself as the law personified, and to do it all from the other end of the ocean. By now Van der Donck had undergone a change in this new world; as with Peter Minuit, what had started as a raw adventure had matured in him into something deeper. He wanted to make something here, something that would last; and as with Minuit, it was almost inevitable that he would think to found his own colony.

Immediately on receiving news of this development from his nephew, Van Rensselaer despatched a man to the colony charged with purchasing the tract called Catskill from the Indians. He wrote Van Curler a letter filled with invective towards Van der Donck. The man had 'dishonestly designed' to deny his patron his rights, which as far as he was concerned included the right to obtain any properties adjacent to his colony. The man was to be 'constrained', and if he 'should prove obstinate, he shall be degraded from his office'.

The old man got his way: his agent outmanoeuvred Van der Donck, purchased Catskill and extended his colony by several thousand acres. But Van Rensselaer didn't live to enjoy it. It is tempting, but probably not warranted, to infer that Van der Donck's impudence gave him a literal fit; whatever the causes, Kiliaen van Rensselaer, diamond merchant and patroon of Rensselaerswyck, died shortly after the Catskill purchase, leaving the estate to his sons. The odd medieval fief would live on, existing in its own universe through the period of the English colony of New York and well into the history of the United States (the city of Albany, later the capital of New York State, would eventually be forced to file papers clarifying that its territory was distinct from that of the duchy that entirely surrounded it). In fact, Rensselaerswyck would prosper under the on-site stewardship of Kiliaen's son Jeremias and later managers, eventually sprawling to include upward of a million acres of land and a hundred thousand tenant farmers.

For Van der Donck, the failure of his plans to found his own colony near Rensselaerswyck brought about a change of thinking. He turned his attention southwards. His term in office probably had another year to run, but he had given up on the northern reaches of New Netherland, and began spending more and more of his time at what was now undeniably the nerve centre of Dutch holdings in North America.

*

By 1644 events on Manhattan were moving into a new phase. The opposition to Kieft and his disastrous Indian war had begun to coalesce and was being led by Cornelis Melyn, the farmer who had been Van der Donck's shipmate on his voyage to New Amsterdam in 1641. Melyn was in his early forties, an upright Fleming from around Antwerp and a tanner by trade, who had also brought with him on that voyage his wife, children, some farmhands and some animals, with the intention of farming a vast tract on Staten Island. His timing was dreadful. Indians destroyed his plantation, and Melyn and his family were forced to cross the North River and seek refuge, along with almost everyone else, near the fort on lower Manhattan. He bought land at the spot where the 'canal', or ditch, drained into the East River, and built a two-storey house on it. Soon he had a neighbour – and a fellow sufferer. Jochem Kuyter was a German who, having served in the Danish navy in the East Indies, decided to search for a peaceful corner of the world in which to settle down and arrived in Manhattan in 1639. He took up tobacco farming on the north of the island, across the river from the plantation of his friend Jonas Bronck (who would give his name to a New York City borough). Kuyter had had success with his first crops, and was hoping to turn a profit, when a Wickquasgeck assault destroyed his plans too, forcing him to move south. Having compared notes on the ordeals they had been through Melyn and Kuyter decided to launch an offensive against Kieft and the West India Company.

With the huddled masses in the fort close to anarchy, Kieft, in an effort to restore order, proposed naming a new council of representatives to assist him. This mollified people somewhat, and they didn't make a fuss when he hand-picked the eight members. Naturally, he chose men who he believed would support him. He picked Melyn as leader, figuring that the leather-worker turned plantation-owner ought to be grateful to the company for giving him such an opportunity for advancement. He also chose two Englishmen, acknowledging the fact that by now 20 per cent of the province's population was English; one of these, Isaac Allerton, was a wily trader who had sailed with the Pilgrims on the *Mayflower*, then, feeling constricted in their society, had moved from New England to the freer atmosphere of New Amsterdam.

Kieft assembled the board on 18 June. With him, probably, were Cornelis van Tienhoven, his secretary and henchman, and, as a reminder of his authority, a contingent of soldiers. Adriaen van der Donck was not yet one of the board, but he was probably present at the meeting; he had recently arrived in New Amsterdam on one of his frequent river journeys from Rensselaerswyck. Also likely to have been on hand was the town's minister, Everardus Bogardus, a stout, hard-drinking Calvinist who had begun denouncing Kieft from his pulpit.

The colony, Kieft told the men, was out of cash. The treasury had been emptied fighting the war. He now proposed to raise money by taxing beavers and beer. A cry went up from the board members. The population he proposed to tax had lost their homes, property and family members thanks to this war. People were living in makeshift dens and wearing rags. They couldn't pay, and wouldn't even if they had the money. And anyway, the men argued, such a tax, without authorization from the company in Amsterdam, was unlawful. Kieft flushed with anger. 'I have more power here than the company!' he roared at the men, and announced he would do whatever he felt was necessary. At this point Kuyter, the ex-sailor, rose menacingly, pointed a heavy finger at the director and vowed that some day, when Kieft no longer wore the protective mantle of office,

Kuyter would 'certainly have him'. The meeting broke up in chaos, and several days later Kieft's soldiers were seen hammering placards around the fort informing the residents of the new taxes.

A tax on beavers might possibly have been tolerated, but adding one stuiver to every tankard of beer sold was beyond endurance; a popular uprising ensued. The people refused to pay it, and tavern keepers refused to charge it. Kieft retaliated by sending soldiers down the road to the City Tavern, where they arrested Philip Gerritsen, its proprietor.

The board members had previously written letters to the West India Company directors in Amsterdam and to the leaders of the Dutch government at The Hague, complaining of their plight, but they were disorganized and anaemic protests. These men were farmers and traders, not lawyers; their initial letters were probably written by the Revd Bogardus, who was as bitter towards Kieft as anyone. 'Almighty God finally, through his righteous judgment, hath in this current year kindled around us the fire of an Indian war,' the first letter had lamented. The tone was pious and grovelling, with refrains of 'we poor inhabitants of New Netherland' and 'Your Honors can easily conceive how wretchedly it fares with us, distressed people.'

At the time that letter was written, Van der Donck had been sitting around camp fires far to the north, playing card games with the Mohawks and Mahicans. At this point, however, the character of the opposition changes. Up to now the colonists had been fumbling, convinced that they were subject to an injustice but without a sense of direction or an understanding of the mechanisms for redress of grievances – mechanisms that were of long standing in the Dutch Republic, and in which Van der Donck – the only jurist in the colony – had recently trained.

Van der Donck may have returned north after the meeting with Kieft in June, but his term as law officer of Rensselaerswyck apparently expired in August, and he was back in New Amsterdam by early October, when the Manhattan activists met again, this time in secrecy. The scent of heated political activity would have been unavoidable, and irresistible to the young lawyer. He had journeyed from Leiden to Rensselaerswyck in search of adventure and with a young man's dreams of great achievement – of helping to found a new society in a brave new world – only to find that his dreams didn't square with Van Rensselaer's business plan. But here, in the capital of the Dutch province, was a genuine cause in the making, a political struggle at the cutting edge of legal thought. What rights did individuals have in an overseas outpost? Were they entitled to the same representation as citizens in the home country? Never before had an outpost of a Dutch trading company demanded political status. Here, Van der Donck must have thought, was his chance to make his mark.

From the fort, where Van der Donck was appearing at this time in a court case related to his duties at Rensselaerswyck, to Cornelis Melyn's house – the centre of the populist opposition to Kieft and the West India Company – it was a three-minute walk along Pearl Street (one can still take it today), with the river on his right and the church and a little row of brick homes on his left. And here they all were, the merchants and traders of the colony, grieving over their dead children, wives and comrades, bitter at the burning of the homes and acreage in which they had invested their savings, wanting to express their outrage but not quite sure how to go about it. Van der Donck knew how. He must have offered himself at about this time as their lawyer, listened to their complaints, and begun to write.

From this point onwards, the archives of the colony contain an increasingly more elaborate and strident series of legal petitions and arguments, documents sent by colonists either to the West India Company or to the States General in The Hague, aimed at securing the political foundations of the colony. Many of these writings have Adriaen van der Donck's name on them. There are also many others that were written either anonymously or in the name of one or another of the colonists, people who were illiterate or whose level of education doesn't match the prose. Building on an argument put forward by Professor Willem Frijhoff, a prominent Dutch historian at the Free University of Amsterdam and an authority on the Dutch language and history of the seventeenth century, especially as related to the New Netherland colony, I have culled from the whole corpus of this correspondence what I believe to be Van der Donck's work or work in which he was involved. As Dr Frijhoff put it to me, these writings, put alongside those that we know to have come from Van der Donck's pen, constitute 'a coherent vision of a new society, sprung up from an Old World-trained academic'. Charles Gehring, the translator of the official records of the colony and a man who knows both the language and the personalities of the colonists better than anyone else now living, agrees that Van der Donck is the only likely author of these documents. 'The only other candidate is Van Tienhoven,' he told me, but while Cornelis van Tienhoven was educated, intelligent and shrewd, as Kieft's right-hand man he would hardly have been the person to craft a series of documents defying the current administration.

Dr Frijhoff finds it remarkable that no historian before him has realized that Van der Donck must have been the force behind these writings, but the neglect of a fairly obvious point is simply another instance of the way that American history has ignored the Dutch colony. This body of writing dovetails with the actions Van der Donck would soon take on behalf of the colony; put together, the actions and the writings fill out a picture of Van der Donck as the pivotal figure in the history of the colony, the man who, more than any other, and in ways that have gone quite unnoticed, mortared together the foundation stones of a great city. It would probably be overly dramatic to call him the unheralded father of

New York City; at the very least, he is an important figure whom history has forgotten.*

By 28 October 1644 the new petition was complete, and the difference in tone from the earlier ones is striking. Instead of circuitous abasement before an all-powerful authority, it begins by crisply laying out a history of the colony's troubles, with the finger pointed directly:

* My method of determining Van der Donck's involvement in those documents that have not previously been associated with him is fairly straightforward. The population of the colony was small. As both Dr Gehring and Dr Frijhoff argue, Van der Donck was the only jurist, and thus the only person capable of framing his arguments with Latin legalisms and of constructing elaborate 'interrogatories'. I simply took out of the archives all documents from this period that had such features. I then took a step that I hoped would serve as a check on my surmises. I had noted in some of the documents known to have been written by Van der Donck the repeated use of an unusual word: *American*. In the 1600s, the noun, applied to a person, was very rare. European colonists didn't use it in reference to themselves: the Dutch colonists considered themselves 'New Netherlanders', the English to the north were 'New Englanders', and those to the south thought of themselves as 'Virginians'. Only very occasionally does one see 'American' used in the period, and then it refers to Indians. The first recorded usage in English is in 1578, in a report about Martin Frobisher's voyage to Canada: 'the Americans . . . which dwell under the equinoctiall line'. The usage is even rarer in Dutch writing of the period. The word typically employed by the Dutch to refer to the Indians was *wilden*, meaning natives or, as Van der Donck himself wrote, people who 'seemed to be wild and strangers to the Christian religion'. Van der Donck used that word, or else *naturellen*, people of nature; but he also, in a few places, referred to the Indians as Americans. Having noticed the word also used in a few instances in the legal documents I suspected were written by Van der Donck, I then did a search of the entire corpus of political documents related to the Manhattan-based colony retrieved from the Netherlands in the nineteenth century. I found nine occurrences of the term 'American', all referring to Indians, and all nine in documents that either have Van der Donck's name attached as the author or had already been separately identified by Dr Frijhoff or myself as the work of Van der Donck. With uncanny appropriateness, then, 'American' turns out to be a clue to the identity of Adriaen van der Donck.

> For the sake of appearances, Twelve men were called together here, in November 1641, on the subject of the murder of Claes, the wheelwright; the Director submitted to them whether the blood of the aforesaid wheelwright should not be avenged? Whereupon divers debates arose on the one side and the other ... [but] a hankering after war had wholly seized on the Director ... the aforesaid 12 men could not continue to meet any longer ... for such was forbidden on pain of corporal punishment. Shortly after, [the director] commenced the war against those of Wesquecqueck, on his own mere motion ...

The letter goes on to describe how Kieft had appointed the new board, but only after his disastrous war was well under way, and only for the purpose of rubber-stamping his plan for new taxes to pay for it – a case, it in effect argues, of taxation without representation. Then it states its complaint clearly: 'That one man ... should dispose here of our lives and properties at his will and pleasure, in a manner so arbitrary that a King dare not legally do the like.' It goes on to take the bold step of asking that Kieft be recalled and a new governor installed, and continues prophetically, 'For it is impossible ever to settle this country until a different system be introduced here,' in which villagers will 'elect from among themselves a Bailiff or Schout and Schepens, who will be empowered to send their deputies and give their votes on public affairs with the Director and Council; so that the entire country may not be hereafter, at the whim of one man, again reduced to similar danger.'

The colonists smuggled the petition out of Manhattan on the person of the trader Govert Loockermans, who was about to leave on one of his voyages to Amsterdam on behalf of his patrons, the Verbrugge family. In Amsterdam, the letter, coming in the wake of the plaintive ones sent earlier by the colonists, certainly made an impact – but not the one the activists were hoping for. The West India Company was at that moment in disarray; losses were mounting, for which the various regional chambers blamed one another. The nation – and therefore the company – was still at war with Spain, and in Brazil company soldiers had just lost a major battle against the Spanish, with whom they were locked in a struggle for control of the sugar market. Their North American outpost had foundered for too long. Memos were flying back and forth between the company offices in Amsterdam and the government offices in the courtyard complex in The Hague known as the Binnenhof. For both the merchants and the government officials this letter sharpened the focus. It was dawning on them that this North American outpost was an oddity – different from the Dutch colonies in Brazil, Batavia, Taiwan, the Spice Islands and indeed everywhere else. Others may have caused trouble from time to time – in incidents such as the messy massacre of Englishmen at Amboyna – but there was no question of their doing other than remain military and trading posts, firmly under company control. Following receipt of this letter, the directors came to the conclusion that they had to treat Manhattan differently – not by acknowledging it as a settlement in its own right, but by cracking down. They agreed with the upstart colonists that Kieft had to go, but not for the reasons the colonists outlined. In the thirty-five years since Henry Hudson had claimed the place for the Dutch, there had never been a strong, capable leader on the ground. The directors had been appalled, earlier, to discover that after launching a war, Kieft had been unwilling to take the field – in fact, had rarely left the safety of the fort. They ignored the letter's novel assertion of rights, its talk of representative government for the province. They felt the colonists' pain, but concluded that their plight was due not to the lack of popular representation but to a governor who didn't understand the use of force.

So they began a search for a new director, and this time they didn't want an incompetent nepotist. They needed a committed company man who was also a true leader. Someone to keep the colonists in line. An administrator, yes, and a skilful diplomat – but also something more. They needed a man of nerve and grit and guile, someone unafraid of pain. They needed a boss.

8
The One-Legged Man

He was a serious young man, thick-necked, with a piggish face and hard eyes offset by voluptuous lips. As he stood on the high poop-deck of a West India Company frigate, staring out into the humid air of the Caribbean Sea, three hundred soldiers awaited his command on the deck below and on the surrounding ships. He was an administrative agent with little military experience, but West India Company officials, if they had ambitions, expected to see action. It was March 1644; he had left Amsterdam nine years earlier, and had served doggedly through the sticky malarial seasons, first in Brazil and recently on the Dutch-controlled island of Curaçao. The company was a major means of advancement for a Dutchman. Not long before this the young man had been a clerk; now he commanded a fleet bearing down on the enemy.

The island of St Martin appeared on the horizon of emerald water and azure sky. With Spanish empire in a weakened condition, its Caribbean and South American holdings were in play. This little island – strategically located at what the Dutch called the *hoek*, or corner, of the Antilles chain – had gone back and forth between the two European powers. Currently the Spanish held it; the West India Company wanted it back, and the official was determined to get it for them. His intelligence had told him that the Spaniards had only lightly manned the fort on the island, and indeed his men hit the beach without incident, dug in and set up a siege cannon. Then the big guns from the fort exploded. The intelligence was wrong. The fort had recently been re-garrisoned; the Spaniards were armed to the teeth. But there was an upside for the Dutch commander: this would be his first opportunity to show his mettle. He ordered his men to return fire, then, with the tang of gunpowder perfuming the air, he grabbed a Dutch flag and leaped onto the mounded earth that formed their defensive wall. Apparently, in his zeal, he had moved too close, bringing himself into range of the enemy guns. He was about to plant the flag when the Spaniards unleashed their second volley. The man collapsed, his right leg shattered by a direct hit – probably a stone ball fired as a projectile. Before losing consciousness, he ordered the siege to continue.

Thanks to the abundance of wars and the rising tide of scientific inquiry, the seventeenth century saw a large increase in the amount of space medical treatises devoted to amputation. There were many techniques, all of them hideous. Typically, the patient, fully awake, was placed in a chair with two men holding him down. The doctor would use his hands to 'pluck up the skinn and muscles' of the limb in question, then, as one wrote, 'we cut the flesh with a rasor or incising knife . . . to the bone, the said bone must be diligently rubbed and scraped with the back of the sayd knife, which back must be made purposely for that effect, to the end the periost which covereth the bone, may be lesse painfull in cutting of the bone. Otherwise it teareth and riveth with the same, so causeth great dolour . . . This being done, you must saw the bone with a sharpe saw . . .' Without anaesthetic or sedative, the horror was often enough to kill the patient before the saw finished its work. One surgeon's handbook frankly instructed doctors how to advise a man about to go under the knife: 'Let him prepare his soul as a ready sacrifice to the Lord by earnest prayers . . . For it is no small presumption to dismember the image of God.'

But though he suffered through weeks of delirium following the amputation of his own leg, Peter Stuyvesant, the 34-year-old son of a Calvinist minister, would not die, and, after the siege of St Martin had failed, was apologetic in his correspondence with the 'Honorable, Wise, Provident, and Most Prudent Lords' of the company in Amsterdam, explaining drily that the attack on the island 'did not succeed so well as I had hoped, no small impediment having been the loss of my right leg, it being removed by a rough ball'. With herculean exercise of will he ignored the pain and pus flowing from the angry stump and recommenced his ferocious micro-management of the company's affairs in the Caribbean: monitoring the salt pans that were the reason for its presence in this palmscaped wilderness, formulating strategy and tactics to keep the Dutch possessions from the lurking English, French and Spanish vessels and from pirates, even fussing about how to get freshly baked bread out to ships on manoeuvres. The pain increased, the wound festered in the heavy air, but the sheafs of instructions and resolutions kept coming. Even in a century and an arena in which guts were a necessary part of everyday life, he must have stood out.

He came from plain country. The village of Scherpenzeel in the region of Weststellingwerf in the province of Friesland in the far northern reaches of the Netherlands was known for nothing because no-one knew of it. It was flat farmland, incised by hedges, the horizon unencumbered by castles, fortresses, cathedrals or any other sizeable manifestations of civilization. It was sparsely populated. The villagers were grim, pious, stalwart and self-reliant, and he was one of them. Frisians believed in a natural, unchanging order to things. A peasant gave birth to little peasants. If you were a minister's son, your career path was pre-ordained. Strangely, however – and this is perhaps a key to understanding his personality, the place at which it twisted away from conformity – Peter Stuyvesant did not follow his father Balthasar, the minister of the Frisian Reformed Church of Scherpenzeel. One possible explanation may be that in 1627, shortly after his mother's death, his pious father remarried, and immediately and zestfully set to work siring a new family with his bride. Teenage sons tend to react strongly to such things; one of a proud and stubborn disposition especially so, perhaps. At about the time of the remarriage, Peter seems to have left home. He studied at the Latin school in the larger town of Dokkum, whose harbour also happened to be a way-station for West India Company ships bound for the New World. Growing up, his literal horizon had been as low as they come; to a youth shaped by God and flat land, these vessels, jutting a hundred feet into the air, taller than anything he had seen, natural or man-made, great cathedrals of wood with spires promising real-world deliverance, must have made an impression.

He went on to attend the university at Franeker, his father's alma mater, but he enrolled as a student of philosophy rather than theology – another signal that he intended to veer away from the expected path. Whatever career notions Stuyvesant may have had on entering university changed when he left abruptly after two years. According to a story later told by his enemies, he was kicked out after abusing his landlord's hospitality by having sex with his daughter. Whether there was any truth in that, he was proud of his university association: ever after, he signed himself Petrus, the latinized (and thus scholarly) form of Pieter.

And so the college dropout found a position with one of the going concerns of the day, signing on at the lowest administrative level. Company officers were soon impressed with his devotion to work, and gave him a rather dubious reward: a posting to the remote island of Fernando de Noronha, two hundred miles off the Brazilian coast, renowned in company ranks for its vigorous rat population. From there he was promoted swiftly to a position in the coastal colony of Pernambuco, and then to Curaçao. Like natural leaders before and since, he gathered lieutenants as he went, men who were attracted to his energy and who saw opportunity for themselves in serving alongside him.

Unlikely as it may seem, given how his career would end, he had a certain fondness for the English which would persist throughout his life, and there were at least two Englishmen in this posse of his. The man who appears in the Dutch records as Carel van Brugge was born Charles Bridges in Canterbury; Brian Newton had been in the company's service for twenty years. These men would follow Peter Stuyvesant all the way to Manhattan, and play their own parts in its struggle to survive.

But the most revealing of these friendships was with a young man who did not accompany Stuyvesant to Manhattan. John Farret had been born in Amsterdam to English parents. Like Stuyvesant, he was posted by the West India Company to Curaçao; the two may have met there, or perhaps earlier in Amsterdam. They formed a fast friendship that mirrored others Stuyvesant would have – with Stuyvesant in the more powerful role, and Farret almost fawning before him. But Farret had some things Stuyvesant lacked: he had completed his time at university and received a degree in law, and was a poet and painter. Stuyvesant envied all of these indications of culture, and their relationship built itself around his envy and Farret's ingratiating efforts to please. In a development that suggests depths of personality beneath the wooden image of Stuyvesant that history has fashioned, he and Farret kept up a long-distance correspondence . . . in verse. A lengthy catalogue of poems detailing their changing fortunes exists in the Netherlands Maritime Museum in Amsterdam; as far as I have been able to determine, it has never been translated or published, except for a few snippets.

The existence of this cache of poetry – which was discovered in a Dutch archive in the 1920s – in itself sheds light on the relationship between the two men. It was Farret who, back in Amsterdam, preserved the poems and bound them in vellum together with his own illustrations, apparently proud of his association with the man who had by then become renowned for his leadership of the Manhattan-based colony. Throughout, Farret addresses Stuyvesant as 'Excellency' and 'My Stuyvesant'.

'Never a greater honor would befall me or greater reward / than that you should order me around as a servant,' he asserts, and declares that 'My will is tied to your will, my heart to your heart.' At times the correspondence cries out for a reading in terms of latent homosexuality (as, for example, when Stuyvesant writes of receiving 'such pleasure' from the 'skilled hand' of the other); it's probably more profitable, though, to see the poems as little portals onto the kind of relationship that existed between seventeenth-century Dutch merchant–soldiers, in which there was a frank deference to the one's greater power and in which friendship was expressed in language as baroque as the pink-cheeked characters in a Frans Hals portrait. Throughout the collection, Farret's verse is sprightly; Stuyvesant's ungainly. Stuyvesant admits to an inability to express himself in 'rich Latin or fancy French', but Farret, in his response, insists that Stuyvesant could write poetry in those languages if he wanted to, and shamelessly refers to Stuyvesant's verse as 'goddlijck' – divine.

Stuyvesant served three years as supplies officer on Curaçao, working hard at his job and at positioning himself for advancement, and in the process making enemies, among them the commander of Dutch political and military operations in the Caribbean, Jan Claeszoon van Campen. This could have made things difficult for Stuyvesant, but he was lucky twice over in 1642 when Van Campen died, and Stuyvesant got his job. His friends toasted him; Farret wrote a poem for the occasion, praising 'Brave Stuyvesant' who was now poised for greatness, and filled with vitriol for Stuyvesant's detractors – which suggests that Stuyvesant never had qualms about making enemies.

Stuyvesant himself had to be pleased with his success. A proud, stiff Frisian, raised on a diet of gloomy skies and thick soup, he now ruled a tropical-paradise-cum-malarial-swamp that lay in the no-man's-land of the Spanish war, from which he lorded it over Dutch operations in the entire Caribbean arena. This was the scene of vivid, hot, bloody warfare between the decaying Spanish empire and its breakaway rival. Sugar, salt, dyewood, tobacco, horses, copper – the ways to exploit the Caribbean and coastal South America were intoxicating in their variety, and while the Dutch were eager to capitalize on the weakness of Spain's grip on the region, the Spanish would not easily give up such a stream of wealth. Besides opening a new window onto the birth of Manhattan, the massive trove of Dutch documents being translated by Charles Gehring in the New York State Library contains hundreds of pages detailing Stuyvesant's time in the Caribbean and opens other windows onto the unrelentingly grim business of wringing profits out of slaves, Indians and the land, while simultaneously battling other European colonizers. More than anything else, the documents tie together the pieces of the Dutch empire in the Americas, showing Stuyvesant overseeing with militaristic efficiency an army of suppliers, privateers, traders and couriers passing between Manhattan and Curaçao as the Dutch sought to solidify their New World holdings. They make clear that Manhattan began its rise as an international port not in the eighteenth century, as the Port of New York, but in the 1630s, as a cog in the mechanism that kept trade circling from the Netherlands to western Africa to Brazil and the Caribbean, then to New Amsterdam, and so back to Europe.

In his Caribbean post, Stuyvesant became one of the movers of that trading circle. He was plugged into the communications network that ran through all its nodes, and in this way began to involve himself in the affairs of the Manhattan-based colony. He got word of Kieft's troubles there, and tried to help, in what would become an extended comedy. While returning to Curaçao from the disaster at St Martin, his ship apparently passed in the night another heading in the opposite direction. It contained 450 Dutch soldiers who had fled from an outpost in Brazil that the Spanish had overrun, and turned up on Curaçao, seeking food and orders. They were told there that they could assist in the action on St Martin, but arrived late, to receive only a second wave of shelling from the Spanish guns. Eventually they made it back to Curaçao, where the ailing Stuyvesant must have been fairly sickened by their presence: first because had they shown up earlier they might have turned the tide on St Martin; second because food rations were desperately low on Curaçao, and he couldn't afford to feed them. He decided to solve two problems at one go by ordering them to New Amsterdam, where, he hoped, they could assist Kieft with his Indian troubles. He thought he had seen the last of them.

Despite the endless attempts by Adriaen van der Donck and others to point out the strategic importance of Manhattan to the directors of the West India Company, it was always an afterthought for them. Brazil, with its more manageable and profitable sugar fields, was the jewel of the company's operations, and therefore the scene of the bloodiest conflicts with Spain. Complicating the situation was the fact that in coastal Brazil the Dutch were engaged in battle not directly with Spain but with the Portuguese, who were under the vassalage of Spain and who were themselves in the process of declaring independence. Like heavyweight boxers, the two empires took turns in gathering momentum, unleashing a savage blow on the opponent, then bracing themselves for the response. In one such effort, Portugal sent eighty-six ships and twelve thousand fighting men across the Atlantic from Lisbon to pummel the Dutch ships laying siege to the province of Bahia in eastern Brazil. As grim as Kieft's war against the Indians surrounding Manhattan was, it barely registered compared with the scope of battle in the Caribbean, and especially along the Brazilian coast, where hundreds of engagements took place over three decades, great ugly mix-ups of European tactics involving musket battalions and infantry pike charges thrown in with Indian bow-and-arrow warfare, the terrain scarred by siege cannon fire, the European soldiers on both sides stifling in their laughably heavy clothing and often fighting while riddled with yaws, dysentery and intestinal parasites. Each encounter was punctuated by the ritual of old soldiers on both sides streaming silently out from the ranks to seek out their half-dead comrades amid the corpses and help them along with a swift slit of the throat. The savagery of the battles and the grimness of the besieged settlements – 'leather, dogs, cats, and rats' was the diet in one town withering under a Dutch siege – speak to the stakes involved, and also to the pitiless environment that helped shape the man whom Manhattanites would come to call 'the General'.

Shortly after leaving the Brazilian sphere for Curaçao, and no doubt in part to test his mettle, Stuyvesant had led a successful attack on a Spanish outpost on the Venezuelan coast. Then he settled into the role of administrator, determined to bring Dutch order to a world of tropical chaos and laxity. He had relished the opportunity to retake St Martin, and his fury at the failure of that expedition helped feed his commitment to his administrative duties. In the midst of his work and while struggling with the pain of his wound, he took time to pen a letter to Farret, who was now back in the Netherlands, giving him the news of his misfortune. Farret responded with a poem entitled 'On the Off-Shot Leg of the Noble, Brave Heer Stuyvesant, Before the Island of St Marten':

What mad thunder ball comes roaring towards your leg
My dear Stuyvesant, and causes your collapse?
The right pillar that used to support your body
Is that crushed and stricken off this way in one blow . . .
You presented too fair a mark – O! much too cruel chance!
My Stuyvesant, who falls and tumbles on his bulwark,
Where, like a dutiful soldier, he taunted the enemy,
To lure him into the field, on the Island of St Marten.
The bullet hits his leg; the rebound touches my heart . . .

But ignoring the pain wouldn't do. Doctors told Stuyvesant the stump where his leg had been amputated wouldn't heal in the climate; if he remained, it would fester. He resisted – he had served only eighteen months as head of Dutch operations in the Caribbean – then finally gave in to the idea of recuperating at home.

A sea crossing with such an affliction would have been a brutal affair in the best of circumstances. As it happened, the voyage was horrific. *The Milkmaid* left Curaçao in August 1644, and didn't put into Dutch port until December. By ship, canal barge and horse-drawn cart, then, past gabled façades and through a pleasant wintry swirl of peat smoke and stewed vegetables, Peter Stuyvesant was hauled to the home of his sister Anna, who lived near Leiden. Life was instantly transformed; the pestilential tropical endurance test of the past nine years vanished. In the civilized Dutch countryside he was plied with boiled meat and smoked fish, his stump salved and ministered. It was a classic scenario: the wounded soldier returning home to be cared for; and, completing it, he fell in love with his nurse. Judith Bayard was the sister of Anna Stuyvesant's husband, and was living with the couple when the invalid arrived. She was no gay young thing but a decided spinster – at thirty-seven, three years older than Stuyvesant – who had previously been living with her father (a minister, which no doubt gave the two something to talk about). When her father died she had joined her brother's household, and it was natural enough that she should take charge of the patient. Judith came from Breda in the south, the same town from which Adriaen van der Donck hailed. She was a Huguenot, a Calvinist whose family had fled Catholic persecution in France.

During the long weeks of his voyage, Stuyvesant might have spent some time mulling over an incidental benefit of his enforced trip home: that at least he would have an opportunity to get himself a Dutch bride. It must have seemed a stroke of providence that one would all but fall into his lap, or what remained of it. But courtship didn't come easily to him. His sister's husband, Judith's brother, actually seems to have bet Stuyvesant a quantity of French wine that he wouldn't have the nerve to propose marriage, and even his staunch friend John

Farret was dubious, writing in yet another poem that Stuyvesant would never consummate the relationship because 'Priapus has died in him.' That got Stuyvesant's dander up. He tore off a response, in verse more purple and heated than usual, accusing his friend of trying to 'make sure I will lose the bet of the wine' and declaring that – manly creature that he was – he fully desired the lady to 'occupy this bed'. Less than a year later, they were married.*

The wound healed at last, and Stuyvesant declared himself fit for duty. And so one day he came wobbling into the courtyard of the company headquarters in Amsterdam (the building still exists, and is occupied by a catering company whose waiters flit across the same courtyard, paying no attention to the bronze statue of Stuyvesant in the centre), sporting a new wooden leg and a reputation for grit and efficiency. At nearly the same time, a certain letter arrived in these offices. It came from Manhattan. It presented, in unusually strident and lawyerly terms, the ruined state of affairs in the North American colony. It demanded the removal of Kieft and the installation of a new governor, one who would usher in a representative government, 'so that the entire country may not be hereafter, at the whim of one man, again reduced to similar danger'. The directors' eyes must have swivelled up and down, from the letter to the hardened young man recently arrived from the New World and eager to get back to his Caribbean post, and back again. The directors didn't like this talk of representative government coming from Manhattan any more than they liked Kieft's blundering management style. Clearly the tough young Frisian before them couldn't give a damn for Grotius or Descartes; for

* The couple travelled south to Breda to be married. The record in the Walloon (French-speaking) church for 13 August 1645 reads: 'Mons. Pierre Stuyvesant, J. H. directeur de la part de la Compagni de Oestinde en Nieu Nederland et Judith Bayard jeune fille de Mons. Bayard, en sa vie pasteur de l'Eglise Franc, a Breda.'

him, the company's law was the only 'natural law'. He was no newfangled thinker, but a stout minister's son who understood duty and station. Altogether, an excellent young man. And soon, no doubt, he would learn to manage the peg leg.

*

Meanwhile, in Scotland, on a summer day in 1637 a woman named Jenny Geddes set in motion another chain of events. According to the story that has ossified into myth in Scotland, she was an Edinburgh 'kail wife', or cabbage monger. If you subscribe to the application of chaos theory to history, then her act that day – hurling a stool – was the flapping of the butterfly's wings that led to the hurricane.

Her target on the Sunday in question was the head of one of the most learned and respected men in Scotland, Dr Hanna, dean of St Giles' Cathedral. The dean stood in his pulpit, stately and berobed, in his hand a slender volume, fresh off the press, the title-page of which, in red and black ink and with a sober but elegant border, laid out its purpose: 'The Book of Common Prayer, And Administration Of The Sacraments, And other parts of divine service for the use of the Church of Scotland, Printed by Robert Young, Printer to the Kings most Excellent Majestie, M.D.C.XXXVII.' The cathedral was packed with lairds and peasants alike. Everyone, apparently, knew trouble was in the air, and many of them had come spoiling for a fight. Obliging them, the dean opened the book and began reading from it. Whereupon a piercing voice interrupted him – Jenny Geddes, crying out lustily, 'Dost thou say mass at my lug [ear]?' She then picked up the stool she had brought (pews were for men – women were required to bring their own stools if they wanted to sit), took aim, and flung it at the dean's head. The place erupted.

That thrown stool was the seventeenth-century equivalent of Emerson's 'shot heard round the world'; the event that would trip the English Civil Wars. In the years ahead, King Charles would be forced to give up the role of stately monarch and take on that of general, commanding armies loyal to him against those marshalled by Parliament. Events surrounding the conflict would have a multilayered impact on American beginnings, on Manhattan as well as in the English colonies.

Perhaps more than anything else, the English Civil Wars were a religious conflict. If the seventeenth century was outlined by the struggle for global empire, the outlines were filled in by warfare brought on by the clash of religious world-views as societies endured the aftershocks of the Reformation. Since coming into being after the rift with the Roman Catholic Church under Henry VIII, and having eventually survived the attempt of his elder daughter, Queen Mary, to restore the Pope's authority in her realm, the Church of England had adopted a moderate form of Protestantism, maintaining a hierarchy of church officials and a Rome-influenced taste for elaborate vestments and complex liturgy. Most English people were content with this, but others chafed. Puritanism was not originally an English movement but an ideological implant from the European continent, a kind of Reformation II, a call to keep the revolution going. The English Puritans looked at events in the wider world through a theological lens. They saw the religious strife sweeping the continent – the Thirty Years War of 1618–48 was essentially a series of attempts by Catholic powers to reverse the breakaway momentum, both religious and political, in Protestant countries – and developed, along with their minimalist fashion statement, a belief that England was the New Israel, the place God had anointed as the great bulwark against the Pope and his swaggering red-robed henchmen. Puritanism rolled through English society during the years of Charles's reign, winning over peasants and aristocrats alike. It provided a how-to manual for improving your personal life and a focal point for national pride.

Puritanism also represented a fundamental challenge to church – and state – authority. Following first Martin Luther and then John Calvin, the Puritans aimed their wrath at the Catholic idea of a church-appointed hierarchy that thrust itself between ordinary Christians and their God. By extension, Catholic paraphernalia – the gorgeous priests' garb, the gaudy paintings, the candles and incense – interfered with the profound central activity of Christian life, namely studying and following the Bible, and were thus to be banned. Inevitably, in a period where monarchs claimed to rule by divine right, suspicion of churchly power had political implications. The Puritans came to oppose any authority that might interfere with what they saw as their divine mission of church reform, even if that authority was their own king. Those who crossed the ocean to settle in North America may have given up on England as the New Israel, but they brought their sense of chosenness along with them. The New World would be the 'New Jerusalem'. The democratic seed that planted itself in the revolt against Charles would come to flower in the colonies thirteen decades later with the American Revolution. It was this combination of plain-spoken religious zeal tied to political reform that would be the Puritans' great contribution to shaping American destiny; this is why American historians and leaders, down to Ronald Reagan and his 'shining city on a hill', have sung the country's Puritan beginnings. The argument in this book doesn't deny that influence, but adds to it another that played a genuine role in shaping the American personality.

What made civil war inevitable in England was Charles. Cocooned in luxury in his palaces and country houses, their great halls draped with Van Dycks and Rubenses, surrounded by compliant courtiers and accompanied by his Catholic wife, he existed in his own universe, and his distance from the society he governed grew with every year. At his encouragement, the clergy introduced additional finery into their dress and adornments to their churches – steps that led Puritans to believe the king was edging closer to Roman ways. (One Puritan leader characterized Charles's project to embellish St Paul's Cathedral as 'making a seat for a Priest's arse to sit in'.) Charles himself considered the Puritans just as superstitious in their way as the relic-adoring Catholics they despised. He was happy to enforce a ban on the printing of their religious tracts – which sent them off to the printers of Leiden and Amsterdam.

The Puritan reform movement was strongest in Scotland, and so Charles decided, with an impressive lack of political horse sense, to bring the Scots into line by introducing in their churches a new prayer book and liturgy, one that was decisively more Catholic in ritual and language. The result was Jenny Geddes lobbing her stool and, eventually, the Scots breaking out in open rebellion. Raising money to put down the Scottish uprising required Charles to call Parliament into session in 1640 – for the first time in eleven years. Once it had assembled, Puritan leaders had a power base from which to carry out their campaign against the king.

The Dutch authorities followed every wrinkle in the growing crisis. Beginning in July 1642, Albert Joachimi, the Dutch ambassador in London – who a decade before had pleaded with Charles to release the *Unity*, which had been carrying Peter Minuit back from Manhattan when the English impounded it – wrote a series of vivid and increasingly strident dispatches to his superiors at The Hague: 'Some more cavalry have made their appearance here; and infantry are continued to be enlisted by beat of drum.' 'News is received here of the siege of Sherborne Castle . . . those besieged have slain between two and three hundred of the Parliamentarians . . . The French Ambassador hath taken his leave of the King, and calculates to depart this week . . . A Parliamentman of quality told me, on Saturday last, that the Earl of Essex was with the army within twelve miles of Shrewsbury; that place has been fortified by the King, who keeps his main force there.' The old diplomat had a sense of what was coming, and he advised his government to take advantage of Charles's embattled state; the States General, he wrote, 'should write to the King and request his Majesty to be pleased to order the English in New England to leave the Dutch undisturbed in New Netherland'.

Joachimi felt the need to act because in the Dutch colony the pressure from the north was growing. Thanks to the turmoil in England, the population of New England had swelled to ten times that of New Netherland. What had been in Minuit's time a pair of small settlements (Plymouth and Massachusetts Bay), struggling to survive and thankful for the odd care package the Dutch representatives on Manhattan might send their way, was now four fully functioning colonies. Connecticut and New Haven had been carved out of territory the Dutch considered their own. Each of these colonies had its own administration, and all of them, with king and parliament at home busy with each other, were free to act more or less without interference from England. In 1643, in order to strengthen themselves, principally against the Dutch province, they formed a league: the United Colonies of New England.

However, even as it was feeling the weight of the growing population to its north, the Manhattan-based colony also benefited significantly from the stream of refugees moving from England to New England. The Puritan revolt in England was, for all its breadth among the populace, wondrously narrow in ideology. It wasn't enough that you were a fire-breathing Protestant – you had to be the right kind of fire-breathing Protestant, otherwise the very brightness of your flame marked you as in need of theological cleansing. As far as the established church was concerned, all the radical Protestant groupings were anathema, and all their members were consequently in the same danger. 'Thou shalt not suffer a witch to live,' declared Exodus as translated under the direction of Charles's father, and Baptists, Anabaptists, Familists and Mennonites were all considered little better than witches. It is easy enough now to shake one's head at the folly, but in an age awash in incantations and potions, deciding whom to make fuel for the pyre was a serious matter.

So people left England in waves. But members of despised sects who chose to follow the Pilgrims' lead and emigrate to America found, to their annoyance after enduring the horrors of the open ocean, that the Puritan majority in New England had followed the same hard-line trajectory as its counterpart in the old country. In fact, there was even less theological flexibility in the open spaces of New England. The hysteria over accusations of witchcraft wouldn't reach its height for some time, but communities moved swiftly to excommunicate alternative religionists and turn them out. So there was a double-rebound effect during the early 1640s, with a stream of English sectarians fleeing from Old England to New, then, recalling in their desperation the vaunted tolerance of the Dutch, moving south to seek sanctuary on Manhattan. Here they came straggling through the lattice-worked gatehouse of Fort Amsterdam – and Willem Kieft was pleased to have them. By this point he was seriously embattled and recognized that the colony had to increase its population if it were to survive. And – here is the inscrutability of seventeenth-century Dutchness – in addition to giving them land to settle (having required them to swear an oath of allegiance to the States General), he also granted them liberty to practise their religion as they saw fit, a genuine rarity in the era. Forbidding his own countrymen even marginal political representation while at the same time practically insisting on covering newcomers with the blanket of religious liberty that was part of his proud cultural inheritance – these stances were apparently not hard to reconcile. It is worth noting, too, that the colonists themselves were fully aware of New Netherland's status as a haven, and proud of it. Van der Donck, writing of one of these English refugees, summed up the situation with as much of a sense of perspective as a historian from the far future might: '[He] came to New England at the commencement of the troubles in England, in order to escape them, and found that he had got out of the frying pan into the fire. He betook himself, in consequence, under the protection of the Netherlanders, in order that he may, according to the Dutch reformation, enjoy freedom of conscience, which he unexpectedly missed in New England.'

Thus welcomed, the English arrivals went about helping to build the foundation of what would become New York City. Several of these were remarkable individuals. Lady Deborah Moody, a self-possessed London aristocrat, had converted to Anabaptism and declared herself ready to die for the outlandish notion that baptism must be withheld until the recipient was old enough to understand its meaning. Londoners were shocked; she was in her dignified fifties when she crammed into a stench-riddled wooden ship cheek by jowl with peasants and worse, and fled to the Massachusetts Bay colony. There, the court of Salem threatened to banish her unless she renounced her mad ways, Puritan chieftain John Endecott famously declaring 'Shee is a dangerous woeman.' Kieft gave her and her followers title to the south-western tip of Long Island. The redoubtable Lady Deborah herself sketched the plan of her community, to be called Gravesend (the skeleton of her original plan can still be seen in the intersection of McDonald Avenue and Gravesend Neck Road). She then set about tending to her flock and thus established, in the corner of Brooklyn that now includes Bensonhurst, Coney Island, Brighton Beach and Sheepshead Bay, the first New World settlement founded by a woman.

Anne Hutchinson also travelled from England to Massachusetts to Manhattan, in search of freedom to follow her belief that individuals could commune with the divine without any help from organized religion. New England's leaders looked on her as the seventeenth-century equivalent of an anarchist, threatening the very basis on which they maintained law and order. Among other things, Hutchinson wanted to do away with the doctrine of original sin, a moral cudgel that Puritan leaders believed not only theologically but politically indispensable. Particularly alarming was the fact that she had rapidly gathered supporters in Boston. Kieft didn't mind – or maybe he sensed she wouldn't be around long enough to cause trouble: when she showed up in his domain, he placed her in a no-man's-land at the height of the Indian troubles. Less than a year after she and her small band of followers had settled on the land he offered (on Pelham Bay in the Bronx, on the shore of the river that now bears her name), Hutchinson, six of her children and nine others were massacred in an Indian attack.

The Revd Francis Doughty, the third of the semi-legendary leaders of English refugees to the Dutch colony, had been forced from his vicarage in Gloucestershire for 'nonconformity', shocked the crowd in Massachusetts by preaching 'that Abraham's children should have been baptized', then headed for Manhattan. He too received a generous grant of land from Kieft, and had begun to plant what would be the first European settlement in the future borough of Queens when a vicious Indian attack set him on a different path. The Revd Doughty survived but gave up on the wilds of Long Island, and, seeing another opportunity, ensconced himself as minister to the growing English-speaking population of Manhattan. Kieft didn't approve; he envisioned a buffer zone of communities surrounding New Amsterdam, and he insisted that Doughty take the remains of his English flock back to his Long Island tract. Doughty, yet another strong-willed creature, rebuffed the director, more or less arguing that if Kieft thought these were safe times to camp out in the wilds he could try it himself. Kieft rescinded the land grant and, for good measure, threw Doughty in the fort's gaol cell for twenty-four hours.

Doughty was thus a natural addition to the colony's burgeoning anti-Kieft movement. He was also naturally litigious, and in June 1645 found himself in court, accusing another Englishman, William Gerritson, of singing a slanderous song about him and his daughter Mary. It may have been here that he caught the eye of a certain young lawyer – or, more to the point, that his eighteen-year-old daughter did. We don't know where Adriaen van der Donck and Mary Doughty first met, but it appears Van der Donck was in court at this time. If there was an initial language difficulty between the patrician Dutchman and the young Englishwoman, daughter of a strident and independent-minded father and herself in time a resourceful pioneer, it was soon got over. They were married before the year was out.

For the time being, however, the romance was put on hold as Van der Donck headed north again. Shortly before the couple met, the nineteen directors of the West India Company had gathered in Amsterdam to review their affairs in various outposts. They pronounced themselves pleased with the synergy between Angola and Brazil: what had been at first only a tentative notion of moving slaves from west Africa across the ocean to do work in the company's fields in South America was now a going concern. 'Every thing is, by God's blessing, in a good condition,' they reported to government ministers in The Hague, sounding freakishly cheerful about their part in what would become one of humanity's saddest and ugliest endeavours, 'and in consequence of the employment of the negroes, which were from time to time introduced from Angola into Brazil, in planting grain, flour is produced in such quantity that what used to always cost 8 to 10 guilders, still continues to be sold at the low rate of six stivers.'

Regarding Manhattan, while they were quietly arranging for Kieft to be replaced, the directors decided to order him to work out a peace treaty that would end the disastrous Indian war. Kieft received these instructions in midsummer and, perhaps sensing that his term might be coming to an end, took vigorous steps to carry them out. He knew the centre of power among the tribes was to the north. The Mohawks and Mahicans kept the Munsee-speaking tribes of the lower river valley within their thrall, regularly sending representatives among them demanding tribute payments. So even though the hostilities were with the more southerly Indians, Kieft determined that the wisest course would be to secure a formal peace treaty with the stronger tribes first, to ensure that the Raritans, Tappans and other groups closer to Manhattan would fall into line. This, however, meant penetrating the heart of darkness to the north, exposing himself to the savages. Kieft still had rarely set foot outside the boundary of New Amsterdam. He needed someone who knew the Indians of the north, who spoke their languages, someone whom they knew and trusted. He turned to Adriaen van der Donck.

Kieft as yet had no knowledge of the letter written the previous autumn demanding his removal. He certainly didn't know that Van der Donck had been meeting with the disgruntled colonists. Van der Donck seems to have been playing the role of model son again, keeping himself in the director's good graces, just as he had done with Kiliaen van Rensselaer before he began defying the old man. He agreed to help.

Kieft also took with him on the 150-mile journey upriver Johannes la Montagne, the second member of his original two-man council, and, no doubt, a contingent of soldiers. The Indians agreed to meet the Dutch embassy within the confines of Fort Orange; the officials of Rensselaerswyck also took part. One man with an official role was a Mohawk named Agheroense, who knew all the languages of the Iroquois confederation as well as Mahican and would assist Van der Donck as interpreter. Agheroense – and, presumably, Van der Donck and Kieft – had spent the night at the 'patroon's house', where the director of Rensselaerswyck lived. He came downstairs that morning, greeted Van der Donck, who introduced him to Kieft, and the three men sat and chatted at the breakfast table while Agheroense applied his ceremonial face paint. Kieft became visibly excited as he sat watching, for the man was painting his face with a glittering golden substance. He asked Van der Donck to enquire about it; in his mind the dormant hope first lit in all Europeans by the Spanish discoveries of gold in South America had reawakened. Could it be that here was the answer to the colony's financial problems? If so, wouldn't it also save his own career? Agheroense handed the pot to Van der Donck, who handed it to Kieft, who asked if he could buy it to study more closely.

There had to have been a note of irony playing in Van der Donck's mind during the peace talks. The student of law and intergovernmental relations had a unique opportunity to observe. On one side of him was the 'alien', the 'enemy': Indians with whom he had lived, whose society he had studied and whom in many ways he admired; on the other was the representative of his own people – a man he despised for his lack of integrity. In the course of the treaty discussions, it became clear to Van der Donck that Kieft had not come prepared. We have already noted where, in his later writings about the Indians of the region, Van der Donck described treaty rituals, noting that the protocol was to state one's proposition orally and at the same time offer a suitable gift. The gift was to be hung up as deliberations commenced; the other side had three days to accept the offering and thus signal that an agreement had been reached. Kieft had brought no offering to be hung up. A treaty of this magnitude, with both the Mohawks and the Mahicans, would require something significant, or the chiefs would be insulted. Kieft asked Van der Donck for a loan, and promised to repay him handsomely for his service to the colony.

Van der Donck supplied what was necessary – apparently, a large cache of sewant or wampum – and the treaty was signed; a period of peace between Dutch and Mohawk ensued. Back in New Amsterdam in late July 1645, Kieft fulfilled his promise. He gave Van der Donck what he most wanted: his own domain, the patent to a vast tract of land. It was ideally situated, not in the far hinterlands to the north, but adjacent to Manhattan. Van der Donck's grant began on the mainland directly to the north of the island, continued along the river for 12 miles, and extended eastwards as far as the Bronx River – a total of twenty-four thousand acres. For his services, then, and for keeping his feelings about Kieft in check, he became lord of much of what is today the Bronx and southern Westchester County. He moved at once to purchase the land from the Indians, and over the next year he and Mary got to work, hiring tenant farmers to clear land and carpenters to build a house and a sawmill. (The sawmill became so vital to the community that later grew up in the area that the river on which it stood – and, later, a parkway that ran along it – would be named after it.) With such a vast tract came a kind of unofficial title. In the Netherlands, a Jonker (later Yonkheer) was a young squire or gentleman of property. From this time on, the Dutch records refer to Van der Donck as 'the Jonker'. Long after his death the title would remain informally associated with the property – 'the Jonker's land', people would say. In the English period, this was shortened to Yonkers, and so it is that a city in lower Westchester County has embedded in its name the only wan tribute American history has ever paid to Adriaen van der Donck.

On his return to Manhattan, Kieft immediately plunged into arrangements for a peace treaty with the Indians of the region. On 30 August 1645, under 'the blue canopy of heaven', the whole town assembled in front of the fort. A stately array of chiefs had gathered – Oratany of the Hackinsack, Sesekemu of the Tappan, Willem of the Rechgawawanck, Mayauwetinnemin for the Nyack and Aepjen of the Wickquasgeck – either on behalf of their own tribes or in some cases 'in the capacity of attorneys of the neighboring chiefs'. Both sides agreed to 'a firm and inviolable peace', and agreed that future disputes would be settled not by violence but discussions. Twenty men on both sides made their marks or signatures at the bottom of the treaty. Adriaen van der Donck was not present, but his soon-to-be father-in-law, the Revd Doughty, was among the signatories. The next day Kieft issued two proclamations: one ordering a day of general thanksgiving, the second ordering an investigation of the mine from which the Mohawk's intriguing gold material had come. He believed he had pulled off a triple coup: saved his job, stopped the war and – if preliminary tests on the gold substance were correct – found something that would bring prosperity to the colony and, maybe, an end to the residents' grievances.

He was right about the end of the Indian war, but wrong

about everything else. All around him the situation was going downhill fast. The civil war in England had reached a climax on a June morning in the grassy Northamptonshire uplands, when a massive conflict between the pikestaffed forces of Parliament and the king's cavaliers ended with the Puritan cavalry wing under Oliver Cromwell – crying 'God is our strength!' – cracking the royalist army in half, resulting in the surrender of four thousand of its troops. The English turmoil had the effect of further emboldening the Puritan New Englanders. Not content with taking possession of Connecticut and New Haven, they were continuing to push, shiploads of them crossing the sound from the mainland to the easternmost tip of Long Island and setting up bivouac communities on Dutch soil. To the south, Kieft's failure to pursue the Swedish incursion that Peter Minuit had started on the South River was proving disastrous. The colony of New Sweden now had three forts and maybe three hundred settlers; its capable military commander had outflanked the Dutch trading post on the river and convinced the Indians of the region that they should trade exclusively with Swedish agents. As for the gold substance, it was found to be pyrite – fool's gold.

Regarding the colonists and their grievances, Melyn and Kuyter had only begun to mount their opposition to the West India Company and its feudal treatment of them. They now had an ally, a man of property who had a vested interest in the community, who had precisely the skills they needed, who recognized that the colony's problems, external and internal, could only be solved by a dramatic change of status, and who had secretly committed himself to carrying the fight as far as it would go – to the very inner court of the halls of government at The Hague. Van der Donck was poised to strike. He had reached the moment in life when a man moves from the role of student and observer to that of actor. By 1647 he had a wife and the estate he had longed for; but ironically, he would now have little time for either. The struggle was to be all-consuming, a cause, a chance to apply the principles of justice in an unprecedented way.

The day of Kieft's replacement came at last. In a way, Kieft must have been ready for it, no doubt remembering that he had been ousted as a failure once before, when he was forced out of the French port of La Rochelle. He was a man burdened by the deaths he had brought about, and as he stood on the waterfront on 11 May 1647, watching a skiff approach from four ships newly arrived at anchor, the strain and darkness doubtless showed in his eyes and face, in grim contrast with the cerulean spring day. Like characters at the end of a play, all the residents of the community were gathered alongside him, stars and bit-players alike: Joris Rapalje and Catalina Trico, along with their children and grandchildren; Anthony 'The Turk' van Salee and his wife Griet Reyniers – both respectable now but still cantankerous – and their four daughters; Anna van Angola, a widowed African woman who had just received a patent for a farm on Manhattan, as well as Antony Congo, Jan Negro and other black residents, slaves and free; assorted Danes, Bavarians and Italians, and a handful of Indians from round about; Cornelis Swits, son of the murdered Claes Swits; the English refugee leaders Lady Deborah Moody and the Revd Francis Doughty; Everardus Bogardus, the beer-swilling minister who had assisted the colonists' effort against Kieft by excoriating him from the pulpit; the activists Kuyter and Melyn; the company henchman, Cornelis van Tienhoven, who had slaughtered and tortured Indians while in Kieft's service and was hoping to be kept on in the new administration. And there too on the cobbled quayside stood Adriaen van der Donck and his English wife Mary (it is from Van der Donck that we have one of the extant descriptions of this scene). The mood was festive. Shouts went up; celebratory cannon blasts were fired. The day of deliverance had come.

Then, slowly, like grey rain, the silence fell upon them. From a distance they would have seen first the hardness and smallness of the eyes, like sharp pebbles set in the broad plate of the face.

Then the flash of the sun on his breastplate must have caught their attention, and the sword at his waist: the efficient, meticulous, militaristic parcel of him. Finally they would have watched him unpacking himself from the boat, and noted at once, as people do such irregularities, that curious movement of his, an unnatural stiffness, and no accompanying grimace or flinch, as if in defiance of pain itself. And all eyes then naturally moving down, and seeing it – the leg that wasn't there.

9
The General and the *Princess*

HE CAME WITH A RETINUE: FOUR SHIPS OF SOLDIERS, HIS posse of 'councillors' and a wife. He impressed the colonists gathered on the quayside with his grim decorum, his soldier–statesman demeanour. 'Peacock like, with great state and pomposity' was how Van der Donck summed up the manner of their new leader's arrival. The people had likewise turned out in their best: we can imagine, on this spring day in 1647, lots of floppy-brimmed hats, lace collars, tight trousers or hose ribboned at the knees, and wide-topped boots – a scene out of Rembrandt on lower Manhattan.

A formal ceremony took place – the passing of the torch of leadership – beneath the sails of the windmill and the dilapidated walls of the fort and against the stupendous backdrop of the harbour. In his remarks, Stuyvesant vowed to act 'like a father over his children'. His signals of power were clear-cut: while the men of the community had removed their hats in his honour, he kept his on. While the colonists remained standing, he took a chair.

Kieft spoke, thanking the colonists for their loyalty and faithfulness to him. It was pure cant, the empty verbiage employed by politicians everywhere, and in a normal Dutch outpost it would have been swallowed in silence. But he made the mistake of pausing to give the community the chance to thank him in return, as protocol suggested. Jochem Kuyter filled the pause, giving vent to a sailor's lungful of taunts, the effect of which was that what Kieft deserved was something other than thanks. Cornelis Melyn added a few loud comments of his own. Others began to chime in; the ceremony was about to disintegrate into a familiar chaos.

Then, somehow, everyone was looking at Stuyvesant. He had presence; people felt it, followed his cues. They fell silent. Stuyvesant had of course been apprised of the entire situation; in fact, having seen the file in Amsterdam, which contained the colonists' complaints, he knew more about it than Kieft. He must have had for Kieft the withering disdain that a military officer holds for another who has failed to earn the respect of his subordinates. On the other hand, it would have gone against his every instinct to side with the rabble against authority. He knew at least some of the leaders of the activist camp, knew the names Melyn and Kuyter. He assured the community that under his administration justice would be applied equally and swiftly. Then he brought the occasion to a quick conclusion.

He must have been shocked by this indication of the level of chaos and insubordination prevailing in the colony. Curaçao he had run as a military dictatorship, which had worked out in everyone's best interest; he had witnessed the same approach in Brazil. These outposts were wild lands, in which people were bound to lose all sense of civilization, apt to decline into syphilitic delirium tremens and allow themselves to be picked off by savages, disease and lurking European foes, unless strict order were maintained. Anyone who had come to live in such a place understood that it operated under martial law – they were in no position to demand a voice or express outrage at the management of affairs. It would be necessary for him to remind them of that. And once he did, and they saw the benefits of it, the harmonious society that was possible under a Calvinist corporation, they would quickly fall into line. There would be no honeymoon with his subjects (for that was how he referred to them).

From this, the moment of his arrival, he was immersed in the unique political currents at work in the colony. With the welcome ceremony unceremoniously ended, he and his wife turned and made hastily for their sanctum, their new home, which lay just behind them. Fort Amsterdam was a four-sided structure with bastioned guard towers at its corners. Passing through the front gate and by the secretary's office, the Stuyvesants would have entered the central courtyard. The place was like a refugee camp. All along the right side of the courtyard were the barracks of the company's soldiers, the backbone of the director-general's power in the colony. But soldiers spilled out of the barracks; they were bivouacked around the courtyard and elsewhere in the town. Stuyvesant would have recognized among them some familiar faces, for it was because of him that the town was overrun. The shipload of soldiers who had fled from Brazil to Curaçao, whom Stuyvesant had sent to aid Kieft in New Netherland, were still here. They had arrived at the end of the Indian war, and Kieft hadn't known what to do with them. They were languishing now, underfed, demanding back pay, roaming drunkenly through the streets, causing fights and destroying property – another problem for Stuyvesant to deal with.

On the left side of the courtyard was the church and, beside it, the gabled brick house reserved for the director-general. Here the newly arrived couple took a few moments to settle in. Stuyvesant rested his aching stump. Judith began the process of recovering from the ordeal of the voyage. She had to have been her husband's equal in grit, considering that she had arrived four months pregnant, meaning that she had spent most of the first trimester of her pregnancy being tossed around by the Atlantic.

And then the regime began. The change from the old order was immediately apparent. Gone was the leisurely schedule of Thursday council sessions. The new director would be active on every front every day. Cornelis van Tienhoven got his wish in that Stuyvesant kept him on as secretary, but he may have regretted being so keen to stay on: the volume of paperwork in the secretary's hand – proclamations, propositions, resolutions, judgments, commissions, summonses – increased dramatically and at once.

Stuyvesant had known what the place needed even before coming, and his first few hours on the ground had only confirmed him in his conviction that order – the kind he could bring, a mix of military structure and corporate efficiency, all shot through with a heartfelt Calvinist focus on sinners abasing themselves before a stern God – was the cure. A drunken knife-fight broke out the Sunday afternoon after his arrival; on learning that such were regular occurrences, he issued a pair of commandments: the first forbidding tavern-keepers from selling alcohol on Sunday before two in the afternoon, the second decreeing that anyone who drew a knife 'in passion or anger' could face six months' imprisonment on bread and water; if he wounded someone with the knife, the sentence jumped to eighteen months.

His justice was blind when it came to distinguishing between colonists and West India Company sailors and soldiers. No-one could accuse him – as they had accused Kieft – of favouring company employees. When two of the sailors from his voyage over were caught in violation of the ordinance forbidding sailors to go ashore without permission, he sentenced them 'to be chained for three consecutive months to a wheelbarrow or a handbarrow and put to the hardest labour, strictly on bread and water'.

But all this was window dressing – straightforward 'quality of life' directives that would play fairly well with the populace. The real issue to be dealt with was the semi-organized mutiny that was festering. As he marched around the little town those first few days, he had with him a piece of paper that fairly burned a hole in his pocket: a copy of the October 1644 letter sent by the colonists, in the names of Jochem Kuyter and Cornelis Melyn, demanding Kieft's recall. Ironically, the letter had achieved its purpose, but in so doing had brought to the colony a man who looked on such acts as treason. The documents of the Manhattan-based colony give an idea of the complexity of Stuyvesant's mind. On the one hand, and in contrast to the standard view of him, he had a genuine appreciation of nuance, a politician's ability to play opponents off against one another, a capacity to weigh alternatives. For instance, historians have been mystified as to why Stuyvesant chose to retain Kieft's secretary; Cornelis van Tienhoven was greedy, dishonest and famed for lechery, all traits that the prim Stuyvesant – the man history remembers – would have abhorred. But Van Tienhoven was also one of the most intelligent men in the colony, a tenacious debater who was doggedly loyal to the West India Company, a man capable by turns of carrying out negotiations with Indian tribes in their own languages and leading pitiless military assaults on the very same people in their villages. Clearly, Stuyvesant was able to weigh up the man's various traits and make his decision on the basis of how he – and 'his' colony – would benefit. At other times, however, the more elemental Stuyvesant, who saw the world in the black and white of orthodox Calvinism, would predominate. This letter he had carried with him from Amsterdam struck him deeply. Its authors had violated the principles upon which the Dutch empire was founded, principles of order that had a theological underpinning and had resulted in the creation of a successful and civilized society; the very clarity of the transgression in itself must have been satisfying. He would handle it with the decisiveness it deserved.

Meanwhile, a few steps away down the dusty riverfront streets of the town, clandestine meetings were taking place. The new director had promised a formal review of the case of Kieft versus the citizens of New Netherland, and Kuyter, Melyn, the jurist Adriaen van der Donck, trader Govert Loockermans, Englishman Thomas Hall, a brilliant and multi-talented Bohemian from Prague named Augustin Herman and several other residents of New Amsterdam had taken Stuyvesant at his word and were preparing their case. Stuyvesant had no idea of the scale of their intentions, the depth of their commitment. Someone making a casual study of this portion of the records would be confused by the masses of pages, filled with impassioned invective and arguments, devoted to what ought to have been by this date – 1647 – a stale issue. They had complained about the director and had succeeded in getting him ousted; the war was over. Couldn't they all get on with their lives?

They were getting on with their lives. With the threat of Indian attacks removed, prosperity was returning. The ring of hammers on nailheads was constantly in the air; more and more new housing was going up; fields were being cleared and ploughed for planting; the harbour's shipping lanes were busier than they had ever been. And these men didn't want it to happen again – the sudden immersion in chaos that war and mismanagement brought. Once again they were building something; now they wanted a voice in the decision-making. It hasn't been given much attention in the history books, but the little community on Manhattan represented one of the earliest expressions of modern political impulses: an insistence by the members of the community that they play a role in their own government.

There were two major forces at work in the Dutch Republic, and this face-off pitted them squarely against one another. First was that of the empire-builders, the merchant princes and their military–trading captains, the slavers and slaughterers, the builders of outposts whose stone skeletons today form curious weed-strewn tourist attractions in places as far apart as Ghana, Brazil and Sri Lanka. The other force was intellectual and political; its roots lay in the Renaissance; it expressed itself in the philosophy of Erasmus, Spinoza, Grotius and the country's adopted son Descartes. It had taken root in the trade-oriented, outward-looking cities of Amsterdam, Rotterdam, Antwerp and Leiden; and through individuals such as Kuyter, Melyn and especially Van der Donck, it had exported itself to American soil. These men in turn examined their situation from two perspectives. First, they had families to think of. But beyond the simple human impulse to protect and provide, they had these ideas in their heads, having to do with being in charge of their own destiny – ideas still fuzzy and immature relative to how they would develop in the next century, but also fresh and vital. They had passion.

Stuyvesant, for his part, had spent most of his years in an isolated farming province or in military outposts where life was a series of orders given and orders obeyed. He was smart, deep, honest and narrow. He had little knowledge of intellectual currents in the wider Dutch world, let alone the wider European world. The situation had the makings of a showdown.

Through the days of early June, then, in private homes or the 'clandestine groggeries' of which Stuyvesant would later complain, drinking ale from thick green glass goblets, while those around them held to more innocuous games like backgammon and cribbage the activists laid out a legal case against their former leader, which they believed would become a vehicle for winning a form of representative government for the colony. It's clear that Van der Donck held the pen, and shaped their anger into argument. He laid out, first of all, a long and highly legalistic series of 'interrogatories' to be proposed to various men who had played parts in the crisis surrounding the Indian war. The slate of questions to be posed under oath to Hendrick van Dyck, a West India Company soldier who had led attacks on the Indians, cut directly to the core of the conflict and Kieft's responsibility for it:

1. Is he not well aware that the late Director General Kieft, did, on the night between the 24th and 25th February, in the year 1643, send a party of Soldiers over to Pavonia by the bouwery of Jan Evertzoon, and behind Curler's plantation on the Island of Manhatans and cause them to kill a party of Indians, with women and children, who lay there?
2. Did Mr. Kieft previously propose this expedition to the Council, and subsequently communicate it to him as

Officer of the Soldiers, which he then was; and did he vote for it?

3. Were not the Indians much embittered by this act; and did not the general war between our Christians and these Americans* follow the next day, and date its commencement from that time?
4. Is it not also true, that all those Indians had fled to the above described place some days before, through dread of the Maicanders†; in the hope of being protected by our people from their enemies?
5. Did not we, the Dutch, in this country, live in peace with these Indians before and until this cruel deed had been wrought on them over at Pavonia and on the Island Manhatans?

The questions for Van Tienhoven, Kieft's secretary and enforcer, began with the disastrous effort to force local tribes to pay a tax to the company for their protection, and grew, in perfect trial lawyer fashion, into a web of damning accusation:

1. Can he, the Secretary, not fluently speak the Manhatans language, which was used by the Indians hereabout?
2. Did he not, therefore, act as interpreter to the late Director General Kieft, with those Indians?
3. In what year was he sent to those Natives to collect the contribution of maize from them; if he was not employed, who then was?
4. To how many tribes was this done; and how are they named?
5. Did those Indians willingly consent to this contribution; or did they then protest against it; and what were their debates about it?

* Note the use of 'Americans' in reference to the Indians – see note to p. 159.
† I.e. the Mahicans.

6. Can he report in writing – if not, verbally – the result of this mission, which Mr. Kieft entrusted to him?
7. In what terms did he endeavor to persuade the Indians to consent to the contribution?
8. In what year was he, deponent, sent by Mr. Kieft to the Raritanus; and did he not go there with a party of armed soldiers and sailors under the command of Heindrich, captain of the Neptunus?
9. What order did the Director give him, the Secretary, particularly in this case; and how did he execute it?
10. Did Mr. Kieft give any different orders to the soldiers generally, when they stood in front of the director's house, previous to setting out?
11. Were not similar expeditions sent out in the same year against the Raritans; and does he know what was the reason and object of them; and what was then accomplished?
12. Did not the Raritans revenge themselves the next year; killing four Christians, on Staten Island; and did they not afterwards destroy the houses of David Pietersen*?

In mid-June 1647, Stuyvesant gathered the parties – Kieft on one side, Melyn and Kuyter on the other – for a meeting he intended to be swift and decisive, at which the adversaries would sit quietly and listen to him lay out the situation and render his judgment. He was stunned to receive these long lists of questions, together with demands that they be posed to the parties indicated and a call for the reorganization of the colony. He was known for his temper, and – his soldier's training winning out over his Calvinist upbringing – salty language, and this was a perfect time to unleash some of it. He ordered a hasty end to the session, read through the documents that evening and, the next day, reconvened his council (which consisted of

* I.e. David de Vries.

supporters of the former government, including Kieft himself, and men he had brought with him from Curaçao) to help him judge the matter. He had, however, already made up his mind – the pages of interrogatories only sharpened his conviction – and he gave his councillors a list of helpful questions to consider as they read over the material. These questions offer an exquisite glimpse into his mind, and onto what might be called the Dutch empire mindset, when it came to the matter of popular government:

> 1. Was it ever heard or seen in any republic that vassals and subjects did without authority from their superiors, conceive, draft and submit to their magistrates self-devised interrogatives to have them examined thereon?
> 2. Whether it will not be a matter of very bad consequence and prepare the way for worse things to have two malignant private subjects arrogate to themselves the right and presume to subscribe for the entire council interrogatory articles on which to examine the former board, without being authorized thereto by their superiors or orders of the commonalty? I say malignant subjects, in view of the animosity between them and the late director and council, by whom they were held and proved to be disturbers of the public peace . . .
> 3. Whether, if this right be granted to these cunning fellows, they will on account thereof hereafter not assume and arrogate to themselves greater authority against us and the appointed councilors, to usurp similar, yes, greater power in opposition to us, should our administration not suit their whims?

Stuyvesant's yes-men said yes – they agreed with him wholeheartedly that, in the words of the Englishman Brian Newton, 'evil consequences' would ensue if these colonists were allowed to proceed in framing a full-blown legal argument against the lawful administration of the colony. Stuyvesant rejected out of hand the notion that Kuyter, Melyn and the others were acting as representatives of the colonists via the original board of eight men that Kieft had called together. These men represented no-one but themselves.

Several things now happened virtually simultaneously. Kuyter and Melyn complained that Stuyvesant and his council were prejudiced in favour of Kieft and the West India Company (they might have noted that Kieft, while awaiting passage to Holland, now sat as a member of the council), and that therefore any verdict they rendered would be tainted. Stuyvesant, meanwhile, apparently showed Kieft the letter in which, three years earlier, this same handful of men, acting as they said on behalf of their constituents in the colony, had demanded his removal. The directors in Amsterdam had never shown the document to Kieft. He studied the letter in a growing rage, the realization dawning that those he had to thank for his career's ignoble end were not his employers in Amsterdam but his own colonists.

Stuyvesant had banked on this reaction: acting more or less in line with Stuyvesant's wishes, Kieft then wrote a formal complaint, declaring that these men had endeavoured 'with false and bitter poison, to calumniate their magistrates and to bring them into difficulty', complaining that they had 'dispatched in an irregular manner and clandestinely sent off, that libellous letter', and demanding that they be prosecuted and his name cleared.

This was what Stuyvesant needed to move forward. He sent a messenger running down Pearl Street to Melyn's and Kuyter's houses with a copy of Kieft's letter and an order that they submit a response within forty-eight hours. The leaders of what was rapidly becoming a political party then assembled to prepare their answer. It had to be done with some secrecy: Cornelis van Tienhoven's house stood right next to Kuyter's and Melyn's along the East River shore, and Stuyvesant was keen for information about other conspirators. If there was a time to back down, to respond gingerly and throw themselves on the mercy of the new director-general, it was now. They chose the opposite tack. The letter they crafted on 22 June is long, legalistic, courtly, precise and unflinching. It is pure Van der Donck.

The man had been steadily enmeshing himself in the affairs of New Amsterdam for three years now, and especially since his recent marriage and move to his estate to the north of the island. As an attorney, he had appeared before Stuyvesant and his council. And, as he had with Kiliaen van Rensselaer and Willem Kieft, he had begun insinuating himself into Stuyvesant's good graces from the moment of the new director's arrival. Stuyvesant evinces a fondness for him early in their relationship, and it's not hard to imagine the Stuyvesants inviting Van der Donck and his English wife Mary Doughty (by Dutch custom women often kept their maiden names) into the director-general's home. Van der Donck and Stuyvesant's wife, Judith Bayard, must surely have reminisced and talked of mutual acquaintances in their common home town of Breda. As Stuyvesant spent time with Van der Donck – who at twenty-nine was eight years younger than him – he found him capable and ambitious, a man he could develop into a West India Company official, a man who could help him in managing the colony. And Van der Donck, as he had with other father figures, took pains to present his model-son visage to Stuyvesant. The week before the preparation of the response to Kieft, he magnanimously offered to put on his own account with Rensselaerswyck farmers a shipment of 350 bushels of wheat and oats that the new director-general would need for the coming year for his family and animals. Stuyvesant accepted the offer.

At the same time Van der Donck was involving himself in the affairs of the wider community, representing sailors, merchants, widows and farmers in court, and associating himself with the colony's ministers of religion, who were naturally men of influence in the community. Van der Donck comes across in the records from this period as a budding politician, a man working hard to make friends in both high and low places. While making himself useful to the director, he was also assisting his friend

Melyn – whom he had known since their crossing together six years earlier – and his co-conspirators. And it is clear where his sympathies lay; indeed, it would soon become evident that his whole reason for building a political base was to provide himself with a platform from which to fight the cause that by now burned inside him.

The letter crafted in response to Kieft's is channelled into the firm banks of legal protocol, but a river of emotion flows through it. It is addressed to Stuyvesant and his council, and begins with a flourish and a bracing succinctness:

> Honorable Gentlemen!
>
> The written demand of the late Director General Kieft was sent to us by the Court messenger about 9 o'clock on the 19th June of this year, 1647, with express orders to answer thereunto within twice 24 hours. Coming then to the point—

Item by item, then, it rebuts Kieft's charge that in their earlier letter to the directors in Amsterdam they had libelled him in representing the state of affairs. In some instances emotion shows through in biting irony:

> The piles of ashes from the burnt houses, barns, barracks and other buildings, and the bones of the cattle, more than sufficiently demonstrate the ordinary care that was bestowed on the country, God help it, during the war.

At other times, such as when disputing Kieft's charge that the council had agreed with his plan to tax the Indians, it is all business:

> The agreeing to the Excise is seen by 3 letters, E., F., G.; by the Acts of the 18, 21, 22 June, 1644, and therefore no further declaration is necessary.

Raw emotion is allowed to emerge once again on the subject of the slaughter in neighbouring Indian villages:

> It is chiefly manifest from their own act, that the Indians conducted themselves like lambs, before the melancholy spectacle of which they were the victims in the year 1643 over at Pavonia and on the Island Manhatas. Be it remarked, that they allowed themselves, their wives and children to be slaughtered at that time like sheep, and came (so to speak) like lambs to lie in our arms. We appeal in this case to the entire Commonality and to each member of it individually, who hath survived that time, to say how murderously the Indians were then treated. Would to God we may be found to be liars on this point.

Rather than sidestep the issue of whether the colonists have a right to involvement in their government, the letter takes the matter on directly. The late director-general took on 'princely power', the council of eight was the closest thing to a representative body in the colony, and in the face of the outrageous decision to launch a war against the Indians the council acted properly in protesting. In the manner of the 'elegant law' that Van der Donck studied at Leiden, the letter lines up ancient authorities to speak on the matter: Diogenes, Ambrose, Aristides and Xenophon all weigh in on the rights and limitations of rulers in making the decision to go to war. Before Stuyvesant and his council, Kieft had demanded that Melyn and Kuyter be sent to Amsterdam and tried there 'as pests and seditious persons'. The letter now demands the right to go there, not as Kieft styled the two men but 'as good patriots and proprietors of New Netherland'. The case should be put to the highest governing body in the nation; the issue was not this particular war, this particular colonial administrator, but the rights of citizens in a far-flung outpost. It was a landmark issue; a test case. 'Let us then once see what the law of nations thinks of it,' the letter demands, calling on Grotius' recently minted principles of law.

Stuyvesant responded in kind – and at, for him, unusual length – with an extended legal analysis of the situation, which suggests that he too saw the matter as a showdown between two competing views of the law. He called on his own ancient authorities, including biblical ones, which reveal his views of governance: 'Thou shalt not revile the gods, nor Curse the ruler of thy people' (Exod. 22: 28); 'curse not the king, no not even in thy thought' (Eccles. 10: 20); 'Be subject unto the higher powers' (Rom. 13: 1). Finally, military man that he was, he called on the Articles of War set down by the Dutch government: 'To utter words tending to mutiny and rebellion demands capital punishment.' Technically, after all, the Dutch Republic was still at war with Spain, and Manhattan was an outpost of that war. As much to make an example for the colonists to note as to enforce the law as he saw it, he expressed his view that Cornelis Melyn, as avowed leader of a treasonous party, should be put to death, while Jochem Kuyter should be banished and his property confiscated. Melyn expressed his intention to appeal against the sentence in Holland, and Stuyvesant (as quoted by Van der Donck) shot back with black wit: 'People may think of appealing during my time – should any one do so, I would have him made a foot shorter, pack the pieces off to Holland and let him appeal in that way.'

Nevertheless, at the urging of his council, Stuyvesant amended the sentences of both men to banishment from the colony – effectively giving them an opportunity to appeal – and ordered them to depart by the first available ship.

A remarkable number of vectors then came to bear on a single object: the ship *Princess Amelia*, 600 tons, crenellated with 38 guns, riding at anchor out in the harbour, her hull neatly packed with 200,000 pounds of red dyewood she had picked up in Curaçao. It was the same ship that had brought Stuyvesant here; she was now ready for her return to Amsterdam. Her commander, a 28-year-old named Jan Claesen Bol, was, like

John Farret, one of Stuyvesant's admirers: during his three-month stopover on Manhattan, he had sat on Stuyvesant's council as it oversaw the matter of Kieft *v.* Melyn and Kuyter. By mid-September, additional cargo – about 14,000 beaver pelts – had been stowed away, and she was ready for passengers.

And so they embarked: Kieft, eager – now that he had, in Stuyvesant, a powerful ally – to return home and defend himself, to clear his name and see his accusers punished; Kuyter and Melyn, armed with sheafs of documents, ready to contest Stuyvesant's verdict before the States General in The Hague; the Revd Everardus Bogardus, with whom Kieft had also tangled – and a good many of the lost contingent of soldiers who had bounced from Brazil to Curaçao to Manhattan, raggedly and repeatedly crossing Stuyvesant's path, the director having ordered them home in hopes of finally getting them off his back.

They set sail on 16 August. The Atlantic crossing was uneventful. And then, in a bizarre climax to the whole affair, Captain Bol made a classic mariner's error, mistaking the Bristol Channel (also known as the False Channel) for the English Channel. The ship ran aground off the coast of Wales. Heavy surf heaved it up and down in three titanic hammerings, dashing it to pieces against the rocky bottom. For days after, Welsh farmers combed the beach for beaver pelts and other items of value: once-cherished pieces of lives transformed into flotsam.

*

The initial news of the wreck of the *Princess* must have stunned the residents of New Amsterdam. The general view, once the initial shock wore off, was that God had been unusually straightforward in punishing Kieft for his many sins, and that the other passengers had had the misfortune of being too near the lightning bolt. The house of the director-general was probably not decked out in mourning either. Stuyvesant had tolerated Kieft because of his position; he had supported not the man but the office. As for Melyn and Kuyter, they had been misguided followers of an incoherent new line of thinking that was dangerous and immoral. He must have seen the wreck, in its totality, as an instance of the pure and terrible justice of the Almighty. There had been ugliness on both sides; as with Sodom and Gomorrah, and in the time of the Great Flood, the Lord had chosen to wipe the slate clean. But even in the direst of times He had kept faith with His people, by preserving a leader. Noah had been spared from the Flood; Moses chosen to lead His people from waywardness. Now Stuyvesant could lead. He could turn his attention to matters of genuine importance.

And so he did, moving with ferocious competence. Had a lesser man been given the commission to strengthen the Dutch hold on their North American territory, the English would have swept in decades sooner than they did, and the Dutch imprint on Manhattan Island would have been too faint to make a difference to history. The problems that literally surrounded the colony were considerable and they had been allowed to fester. Stuyvesant had stepped into a chess game in which his predecessor had been an inferior player who had committed his resources into one ill-conceived strike while ignoring attacks from other areas. Stuyvesant assessed the threats, ranked them in order of priority and went to work. He saw at once what historians later failed to recognize: that New England was not monolithic; that there were four separate colonies, each with its own agenda, and they had a hard time getting along. The two southern colonies, Connecticut and New Haven, were aggressive towards the Dutch; the other two, Stuyvesant sensed, wanted to find a way to live with their neighbour. New Plymouth, after all, had been founded by English Pilgrims who had spent long years as guests of the Dutch, and so were predisposed in their favour. Massachusetts was likewise amenable; it was the largest and most powerful of the New England colonies, and John Winthrop, its elderly governor, who had devoted nearly two decades to fashioning a Puritan utopia in the New World (it was he who coined the phrase 'Citty upon a Hill' to describe it), was, despite age and ill-health, still the most influential man in New England. (It was largely because he had chosen to live there that Boston, rather than any of the other villages founded about the same time, became the capital.)

So Stuyvesant targeted Winthrop. 'Honored Sr,' began the letter he dictated to Winthrop (at the other end of the pen, translating into English, was one of Stuyvesant's English hangers-on, George Baxter), 'I shall be boulde to propose to your wise Consideration, that your selfe, with other indifferent men of yor Countriemen ... may be pleased to appoint the tyme & place, where & when yourselfe & they will bee pleased to give me a meeting.'

Stuyvesant knew that while powerful forces in England wanted to wrest control of his colony from him, in the chaos caused by the Civil War the New England colonies had largely been free to govern themselves as they saw fit. If he could cement a treaty with the leaders of the four in which they bound themselves to respect one another's borders, it would be a great step towards putting his colony, as well as theirs, on a permanent footing. As it happened, Baxter, who delivered the letter in person, arrived in Boston while leaders of the four New England colonies were gathered there for a meeting, so Winthrop showed it to them. He then wrote back that while his illness had left him with a 'Crazines of my head,' he was still fit enough to agree with his fellow New Englanders that all wanted likewise to live in peace with the Dutch colony and all 'doe readilie embrace yor friendlie motion concerning a meeting'. The leaders also jointly sent a similar letter to Stuyvesant, welcoming him to America, 'hoping all the English Colonies shall enjoy within your limits all the fruites of a neighbourly and friendly correspondency in a free concourse', and laying out a number of items that needed to be hashed out, including illegal trading activities and a high tariff being charged at Manhattan for shipping. Stuyvesant knew that the Civil War in England had increased the New Englanders' reliance on Manhattan as a shipping hub. It must have pleased him that they raised the issue at once – he could use it as a bargaining chit in working out an agreement on borders. The New Englanders signed themselves 'Your lovinge Friends the Commissioners of the vnited Colonies'.

Next, Stuyvesant turned southward. He commissioned a detailed report on events that had taken place in the region the Dutch called the South River. It was now ten years since Peter Minuit had led a Swedish expedition up this waterway that the Dutch considered a vital part of their North American territory. It would be no accident that the future cities of Philadelphia, Trenton, Camden and Wilmington would spring up in this region. Stuyvesant could see, as Minuit had before him and William Penn would after, that water power, water transport, ocean access and hundreds of square miles of rich and hitherto unexploited land could be translated directly into industry and commerce.

Kieft had ignored the foreign presence in this southern territory, and the Swedes had used that time to dig in. The leader of New Sweden now was Johan Printz, a great hog of a man whose 28-stone body, as it lumbered within the palisades of his central fort, was less dressed than sided in the armour of the Swedish military. Printz had served as an officer in the Thirty Years War, leading troops into battle in Germany and Poland before being discharged for surrendering the town of Chemnitz to a Saxon army. His New World posting was a chance to redeem himself by turning this wilderness into a functioning, profit-making colony. The Indians of the region gave him the nickname Big Belly, and he was as formidable in military guile as he was in size.

The Dutch had constructed their original military–trading post on the river in what must now have seemed the distant past: 1624, when they were still considering making this region the capital of their colony. They had built Fort Nassau at the confluence of the South River and what they called the

7 November ao 1626

Hooghe Moghende Heeren

Hier is gisteren 't Schip het Wapen van Amsterdam aengecomen ende is den 23 septemb. uyt Nieu Nederlant gezeylt uyt de Rivier Mauritius. rapporteren dat ons volck daer kloeck is en vredich leven. haere vrouwen hebben oock kinderen aldaer gebaert hebben 't eylant Manhattes van de wilde gekocht, voor de waerde van 60. guld. is groot 11000 morgen. hebben alle koren half mey gezayt, ende half augusto gemaeyt. daer van senden monsterkens van somer koren, als tarwe, rogge, garst, haver, boeckweyt, kanarizaet, boontjes en vlas.

Het Cargasoen van 't voorsz schip is

7246 bever vellen
178½ otter vellen
675 otter vellen
48 mincke vellen
36 catlosse vellen
33 mincken
34 ratte vellekens

Veel eycken balcken en noten-hout.

Hiermede

Hooghe Moghende Heeren, zyt den Almoghende in genade bevolen.

In Amsterdam den 5 novem ao 1626

Uwe Hoo: Moo: Dienstwillighe

P. Schaghen

In 1626 Pieter Schaghen, a Dutch government official, wrote to his superiors that colonists had 'purchased the Island Manhattes from the Indians for the value of 60 guilders'.

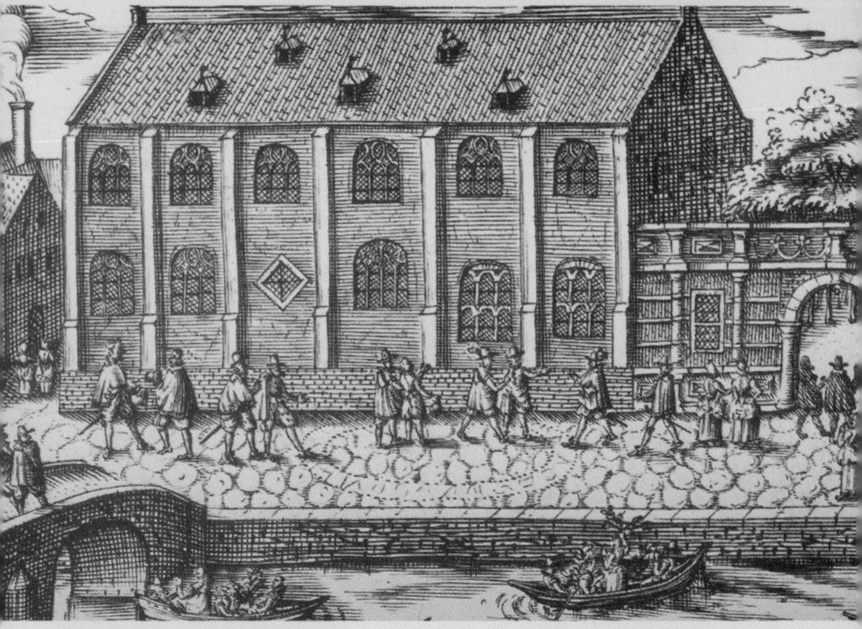

THIS PAGE

Above: Leiden University in the seventeenth century.

Left: René Descartes, the founder of modern philosophy, was the dominant intellectual during Van der Donck's time at Leiden.

Below left: Hugo de Groot, a.k.a. Grotius, the father of international law and the guiding light of Adriaen van der Donck's generation of legal scholars.

OPPOSITE PAGE

Top left: In 1630, the West India Company advertised for settlers in the New Netherland colony, depicting it as a grand and lucrative adventure.

Top right: David de Vries, a Dutch adventurer, tried to talk Willem Kieft out of his disastrous plan to make war on the Indians around Manhattan.

Bottom left: Ironically appropriate for a man obscured by history, this portrait of Adriaen van der Donck is now considered of uncertain authenticity.

Bottom right: Peter Stuyvesant.

VRYHEDEN

By de Vergaderinghe van de Negenthiene vande Geoctroyeerde West-Indische Compagnie vergunt aen allen den ghenen / die eenighe Colonien in Nieuw-Nederlandt sullen planten.

In het licht ghegheven.

Om bekent te maken wat Profijten ende Voordeelen aldaer in Nieu-Nederlandt, voor de Coloniers ende der selver Patroonen ende Meesters, midtsgaders de Participanten, die de Colonien aldaer planten, zijn bekomen.

Westindjen Kan syn Nederlands groot gewin.
Verkleynt 'svyands Macht brengt silver-platen in.

T'AMSTELREDAM,

Voor Marten Jansz Brandt Boeckverkooper/ woonende by de nieuwe Kerck/ in de Gereformeerde Catechismus. Anno 1630.

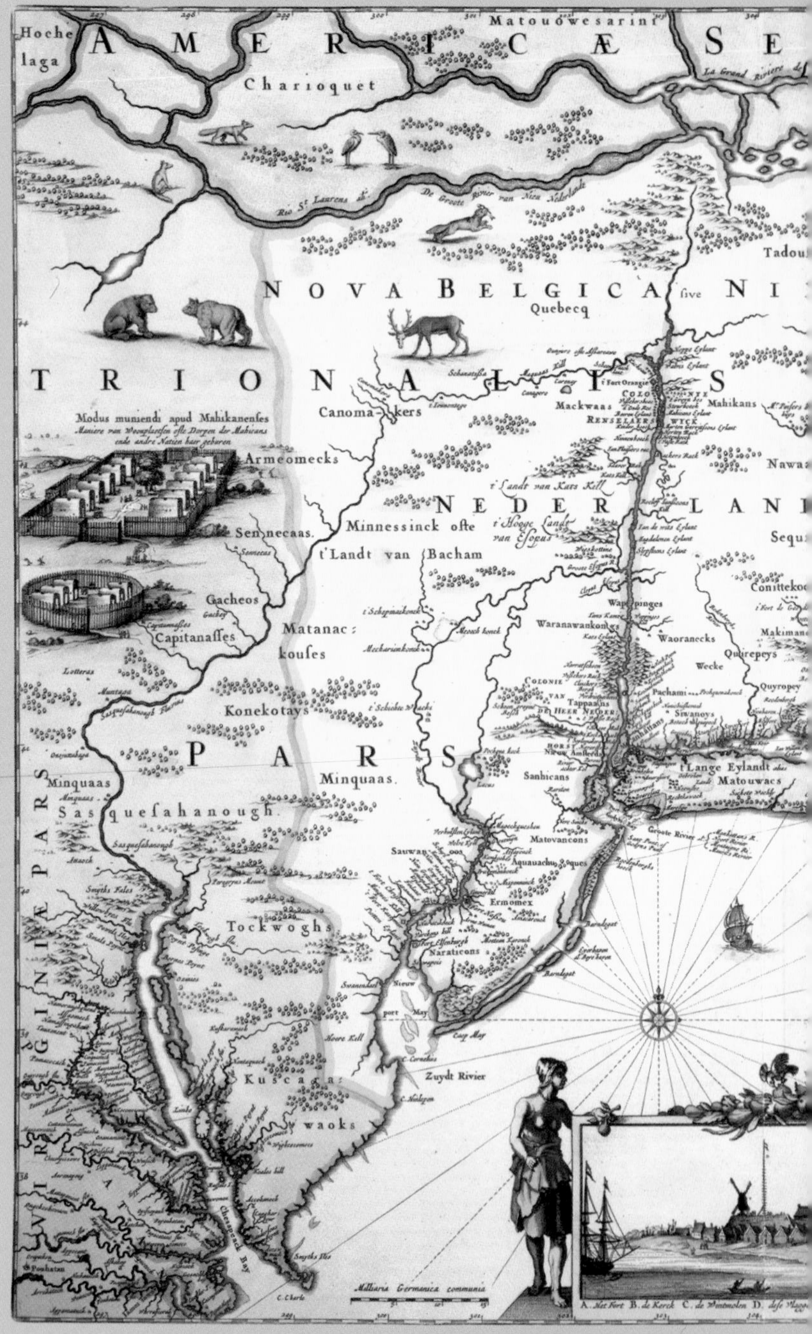

AMERICÆ SE
Matouowesarini
Hoche laga
Charioquet
Rio St. Laurens
De Groote Rivier van Nieu Nederlandt
NOVA BELGICA sive NI
Quebecq
TRIONALIS
Canomakers
Mackwaas
Mahikans
Modus muniendi apud Mahikanenses
Armeomecks
NEDER LAND
Minnessinck ofte
t'Landt van Bacham
Sennecaas.
Gacheos
Capitanasses
Matanac: kouses
Konekotays
PARS
Minquaas.
Minquaas
Sasquesahanough
Sanhicans
t'Lange Eylandt
Matouwacs
Wappinges
Waoranecks
Matovancons
Ermomex
Naraticons
Tockwoghs
Kuscaga waoks
Zuydt Rivier
Tappaans
Pachami
Siwanoys
VIRGINIÆ PARS
Chesepeack Bay
Millaria Germanica communia
A. Het Fort B. de Kerck C. de Wintmolen

The so-called Jansson-Visscher map, which Van der Donck had printed in the Dutch Republic about 1651, became the definitive map of the American north-east for more than a century and helped imprint Dutch names on many American places.

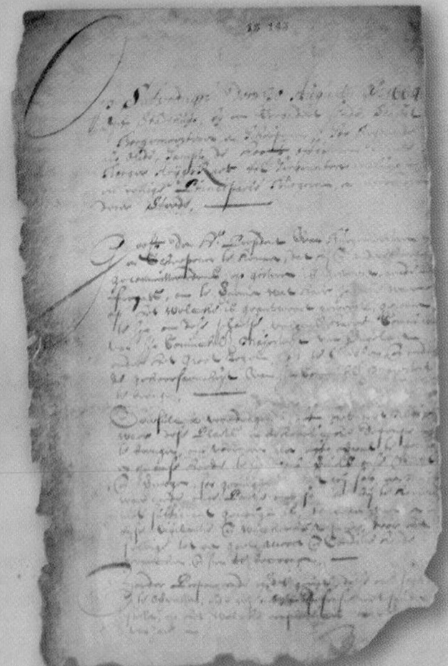

BESCHRYVINGE
Van
NIEUVV-NEDERLANT.
(Ghelijck het tegenwoordigh in Staet is)
Begrijpende de Nature, Aert, gelegentheyt en vrucht-baerheyt van het selve Lant; mitsgaders de proffijtelijcke ende gewenste toevallen, die aldaer tot onderhout der Menschen, (soo uyt haer selven als van buyten ingebracht) gevonden worden.
ALS MEDE
De maniere en onghemeyne eygenschappen vande Wilden ofte Naturellen vanden Lande.
Ende
Een bysonder verhael vanden wonderlijcken Aert ende het Weesen der BEVERS,
DAER NOCH BY GEVOEGHT IS
Een Discours over de gelegentheyt van Nieuw Nederlandt, tusschen een Nederlandts Patriot, ende een Nieuw Nederlander.
Beschreven door
ADRIAEN vander DONCK,
Beyder Rechten Doctoor, die teghenwoordigh noch in Nieuw Nederlant is.

t'AEMSTELDAM,
By Evert Nieuwenhof, Boeck-verkooper, woonende op 't Rusland in 't Schrijf-boeck, Anno 1655.

Above: Adriaen van der Donck presented this rather sombre view of New Amsterdam at The Hague in his effort to convince the Dutch government to take control of the colony of New Netherland from the West India Company. Despite the drawing's ephemeral appearance, features in it can be matched with features of Manhattan's financial district today.

Opposite left: One of the 12,000 pages of manuscript records of the Dutch colony based on Manhattan.

Opposite right: The title page of Adriaen van der Donck's *Description of New Netherland*, written in exile, into which he poured his passion for his adopted home.

Right: The 1660 plan of New Amsterdam shows the impact of Van der Donck's mission to the Dutch government. Seven years later the town has regular streets, fortifications and a canal. The wall along the northern (right) edge gave Wall Street its name and the broad street heading northward from the fort became Broadway.

Below: New York in 1673 at the moment when Dutch forces retook it from the English: there are soldiers on the street and a cannon is firing from the fort.

Above: Slaves, tobacco and sugar processing: this Dutch image promoting New Amsterdam fancifully copied elements from a similar one for Barbados, giving Manhattan the appearance of a tropical port.

Below: Memories of the killing of English traders by Dutch soldiers in the East Indies in 1623 were rekindled whenever tensions between the two nations mounted. This pamphlet was reissued in 1665, during the Second Anglo-Dutch War.

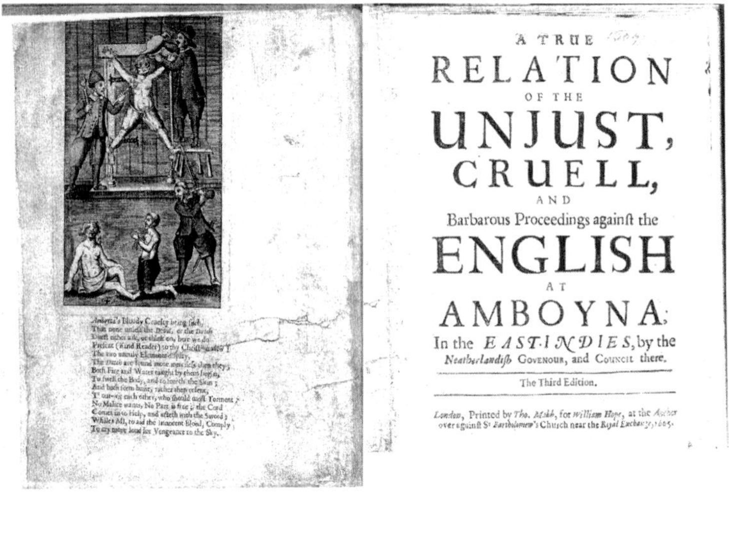

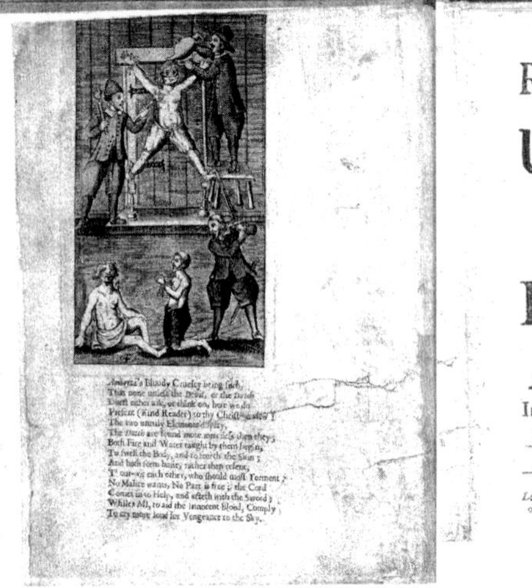

A TRUE
RELATION
OF THE
UNJUST,
CRUELL,
AND
Barbarous Proceedings againſt the
ENGLISH
AT
AMBOYNA,
In the *EAST-INDIES*, by the *Neatherlandiſh* GOVENOUR, and COUNCIL there.

The Third Edition.

London, Printed by *Tho. Mabb*, for *William Hope*, at the *Anchor* over againſt St *Bartholomew's* Church near the *Royal Exchange*, 1665.

Schuyl Kill* or Hidden River – convenient, they believed, for the Indians bringing furs downriver from the west. But there was a flaw in this placement. The trading post was on the eastern side of the river, so that the Indians had to ford it to reach them. Peter Minuit had seen this problem from the beginning; so when he made his dramatic return to America to found New Sweden, he erected Fort Christina on the west, outflanking the Dutch and making the Swedes instantly more attractive to the Minquas (Susquehannocks), the tribe that dominated the fur trade in the valley. When Johan Printz took over the Swedish colony, his first move was to further stymie the Dutch by constructing another fort further downriver, nearer the bay, thus giving the Swedes effective control of the South River. Kieft did nothing to counter this, but the Dutch got help from an unexpected ally: the mosquito. The Swedes had built on a swamp. Soon the fair-skinned soldiers looked, one commander wrote, 'as if they had been affected with some horrible disease'. The soldiers called the place Fort Myggenborgh – Fort Mosquito; the bugs won, and it was soon abandoned.

But Printz was far from finished. He began an elaborate rumour campaign among the Indians to the effect that the Dutch were planning to slaughter them; at the same time, he sweetened the deals Swedish traders were making with them. Then complaints started streaming into Stuyvesant's Manhattan headquarters from soldiers and company officials stationed on the South River. The Dutch had recently built another trading post there, but even before it was finished Printz erected a Swedish fort so close to it that the structures nearly touched. The massive Swede was as snide as he was wily, and the Dutch knew he was rubbing their noses in it. The Swedish fort, one officer whined in his report to Stuyvesant, 'is the greatest insult in the world . . . for they have located the house about 12 or 13 feet from

* Technically, its modern name Schuylkill river is a redundancy since 'kill' means river or waterway.

our palisades, depriving us thereby of our view of the stream.' 'My lord,' another official wrote, 'I firmly believe that he [Printz] had it built there more to mock our lords than to expect that it could realize any profit for him, since there is room enough beside our fort to build twenty such houses.' Sitting in his office on Manhattan, Stuyvesant was now able to summon a clear mental picture of his southern territory: the flat landscape; its placid river; warships whose masts were surmounted not with the orange, white and blue flag of the United Provinces* but the blue and yellow cross of Sweden; the hidden inlets echoing with the cadences of the Swedish tongue as the golden-haired Nordics bartered with the Indians, struggling to comprehend their allegiances and business tactics.

Stuyvesant knew from the start that the real threat was not from the Swedes but from the English. Dutch forces had already chased out English settlers who had sneaked south from the New Haven colony and tried to stake a claim on the Schuyl Kill. Stopping English activity in the region was paramount, for the Dutch, with their focus on waterways, knew what the English as yet did not: that the South or Delaware River began not in the south but far to the north of Manhattan, and wound its way three hundred miles southwards (it would serve as the border between the future states of New Jersey and Pennsylvania) before emptying into Delaware Bay. Thus, if the English ever got control of it, they would have a stranglehold on Manhattan, and the Dutch colony would vanish.

But Stuyvesant also understood the need to deal with the Swedish problem before it sapped his colony's strength. He must have had a dossier on his rotund opposite in New Sweden, as he

* The colours of the seventeenth-century Dutch flag were adopted in 1915 by the city of New York in recognition of its origins. There is thus a bizarrely direct connection between the colours flown by Dutch privateers cruising for booty on the Spanish Main 350 years ago and the jerseys worn today by the New York Mets and the New York Knicks.

did on John Winthrop in Massachusetts. The three men had quite a bit in common. All were autocratic, moralistic Protestants. Printz, like Stuyvesant, was a minister's son who had been groomed for the ministry but shifted at the last minute into military service. Stuyvesant may have known of Printz's failure on the battlefield; at any rate, he began laying out a course of action to consign New Sweden to history's dustbin. Eventually, he would have to journey to the region personally. For now, however, he issued sheaves of instructions. He ordered his representatives to buy up more land from the Delaware and Minquas Indians. He wanted the Dutch forts on the river repaired. He wanted them stocked with goods, since the Minquas had complained about travelling long distances with their furs only to find the Dutch traders out of supplies. This was especially important, he wrote, because Printz had not been receiving regular shipments from Sweden. Another issue: Minquas Indians had complained to him that New Amsterdam's dominant trader, Govert Loockermans, while on a foray on the South River, had killed their chief. Loockermans denied it, claiming he had only roughed the chief up a bit. In a clear example of Stuyvesant's political instincts winning out over his Calvinist upbringing, he instructed his official on the river to 'inquire diligently into the circumstances and truth of the matter, and should you find Govert Loockermans to be at fault, conceal it so that on our part the Indians are given no occasion for new discontent.' Then he added brightly, 'I thank you very much for the eel which you sent.'

*

Matters right outside his front door were equally pressing. The fort itself was tumbling down and had to be rebuilt from the ground up. Besides that, Stuyvesant informed his council, the place needed 'a school, church, sheet piling, pier and similar highly necessary public works and common buildings'. It all had to get started more or less at once, as far as he was concerned. He had a duty to the place, and beyond that, it was his home; he cared about it. If it was to survive against the threats that loomed on all sides, then 'this our capital' had to be made strong. He had kept Johannes la Montagne, the Walloon medical doctor who had been the second member of Kieft's government, as a member of his own council, and La Montagne argued that the funds necessary for these projects could be raised only if the director had the colonists on his side; and the only way to do this was to allow the residents to elect a board of representatives to advise him. Stuyvesant agreed. Following the custom in Dutch towns, the residents would select 'a double number of nine persons' from among 'the most notable, most reasonable, most honorable and most prominent' of them, and out of this group he, Stuyvesant, would then choose 'a single number of nine' to serve. The first board included the Bohemian Augustin Herman, Dutch trader Govert Loockermans, English tobacco farmer Thomas Hall, and Michael Janszen, a close friend of Adriaen van der Donck, at whose home Van der Donck stayed when he remained in New Amsterdam overnight.

Van der Donck himself was not among the first 'double number of nine', but the method of its selection helps explain his vigorous networking during this time. The board was to be the vehicle for political change in the colony, and becoming a member required winning the support both of the residents and of Stuyvesant himself. It's hard to avoid seeing a strong element of calculation in the determined, almost fawning way Van der Donck assists Stuyvesant in this period. Thanks to his marriage, he was by now proficient in English, and in September 1647 he volunteered for a novel assignment when New Netherland had an odd and less than welcome visitor. A Scotsman named Andrew Forrester made his way through the Dutch towns of Long Island – Vlissingen (later Flushing), Heemsteede, Gravesend and New Amersfoort – waving a large square of parchment, covered in writing and seals, which, he declared to the startled residents, made him governor of the entire region by virtue of a grant from the English crown. He arrived finally in New Amsterdam and, before a snickering crowd, demanded that Stuyvesant surrender to him. 'Wherefore I had him taken into custody and on the next day placed under arrest at the City Tavern at the Company's expense,' Stuyvesant later explained to his council.

It was a pretty bewildering turn of events. 'What shall be done with said pretended governor?' Stuyvesant wondered aloud to the council. Was the man insane, or was this an organized tactic on the part of the English that needed to be treated with proper diplomatic niceties? Stuyvesant accepted the proffered help of Van der Donck, and of two other English-speaking men, in investigating. They studied the commission, interrogated Forrester and concluded that the man was the somewhat potty agent of the estate of an English lord who claimed title to Long Island and surrounding lands. With the assent of Van der Donck and the others, Stuyvesant decided to put the man in irons and ship him to Amsterdam, where government officials could deal with him and his claims.

The Forrester case was bizarre, but by no means unique. The settling of the North American continent had gone on long enough to be firing the imaginations of a fair number of European eccentrics. One sort particularly intrigued was the English nobleman of modest circumstances. Such individuals had seen with their own eyes the piece of paper King Charles bestowed on Lord Baltimore, by which he became master of his own private realm in the New World. The dream that took shape in some such minds was of a return to the middle ages – America in its virgin freshness they saw as a land of opportunity where dreams could come true; but, in a quixotic reversal of the direction that history would take, their dreams were all about the past, the halcyon days of knights and damsels, when their ancestors were still men of real power and substance. Sir

Ferdinando Gorges was one such nobleman who actually did receive title, back in the days of King James, to a huge chunk of North America, which he hoped to divide into medieval estates that he would distribute among his closest associates, who would build castles, gather squires and courts, drink mead, and belabour one another in pageants. Gorges died without ever setting foot in the New World, his dream died in the chaos of the Civil War, and his tract eventually became the state of Maine. (Two hundred years later, when the US government, during its own civil war, constructed a military installation on an island in Portland Harbor, somebody had the inspiration to name it after the odd dreamer who inadvertently founded the state, and so it remains Fort Gorges.)

Shortly after Forrester's appearance, yet another eccentric from the British Isles pitched up on the New Amsterdam waterfront with a similar claim. It was, in fact, the second visit from Sir Edmund Plowden, who had also shown up during Kieft's tenure, brandishing a document signed by the deputy general of Ireland, which, he said, gave him title to the area extending from Long Island westwards beyond the Hudson River and including all of present-day New Jersey and parts of Delaware and Maryland. Plowden had it all worked out. The kingdom would be called New Albion, and he, its lord, would be styled the Earl Palatine of New Albion. Long Island would henceforth be known as the Isle of Plowden. There was apparently another arraignment at the fort in New Amsterdam, at which Van der Donck seems again to have served. Plowden declared that prior to his arrival in New Amsterdam he had been to New Sweden to inform its governor of his title, and was very much annoyed at the way he had been treated. Stuyvesant, who was perhaps getting used to the drill by now, and who must for once have sympathized with Johan Printz, simply told Plowden to leave the colony. Returning to England, Plowden published a little book called *A Description of the Province of New Albion*, in which, under the dazzling pseudonym of Beauchamp

Plantagenet, he extolled the virtues of the new realm and especially of the Earl Palatine himself. He eventually wound up in an English debtors' prison.*

There occurred another bizarre and ultimately tragic piece of business at the time of the Forrester episode – late 1647 – with which Van der Donck may have assisted Stuyvesant. Harmen van den Bogaert, the one-time barber-surgeon who thirteen years earlier had made the first daring journey westwards deep into Iroquois country, had been an active member of the colony ever since. He had married and fathered four children, had purchased an interest in a privateer called *La Garce*, which he then accompanied on a raiding voyage to the Caribbean, and had subsequently served as supply master to the West India Company, first in New Amsterdam and then at Fort Orange. He had also been involved in the affairs of the murdered wheelwright Claes Swits, to whom he had apparently been related.

In addition to all of this Van den Bogaert had a secret, which he kept as quiet as possible since its discovery would almost certainly lead to a sentence of death. He had a fondness for men.

In the Calvinist Dutch colony, as in the Puritan English colonies, homosexual activity was a crime on a par with murder. Van den Bogaert thought he had found a discreet outlet in the

* The Plowden affair would not end here, but would go on and on, as a kind of Pythonesque subplot to American colonial history. In 1784, amid the confusion at the end of the Revolutionary War, an Englishman named Charles Varlo appeared in the new country brandishing Plowden's charter, which he had somehow purchased. Varlo distributed handbills to various Americans detailing his rights to a significant portion of their newly won land, and apparently delivered an address in several places 'to the people of New Albion'. We can only imagine his surprise when he reached St Mary's, Maryland, which was held to be the seat of New Albion, and found there a man named Edmund Plowden – a descendant of the original, who had kept his ancestor's dream alive and travelled to the New World to claim his palatinate. This Plowden settled at an estate in Maryland called Bushwood, and Plowdens continued to live there for many generations. Charles Varlo returned to England and published his memoirs, which he called *Floating Ideas of Nature*.

person of his young black servant, Tobias; we have no idea how Tobias felt about the relationship, but somehow the two men were caught in flagrante. Van den Bogaert fled. In 1647 New Netherland, however, there were few places to hide. You couldn't exactly lose yourself in a crowd; everyone knew everyone else. He might have tried to stow away on a ship, if one were departing, but upon discovery he would have been shipped back for punishment. Instead, he went back to the one place he knew of where few other Europeans had been – into Mohawk country, retracing his journey of years earlier. It was autumn now, not winter, so the going would have been less difficult, but this time he was alone, travelling across dozens of miles of virgin woodland without a guide.

He made it to one of the villages that had befriended him years before, and presumably was welcomed by the inhabitants. Meanwhile, Nicolaes Coorn, who had taken over from Van der Donck as the lawman of the independent fiefdom of Rensselaerswyck, did a bit of Sherlock Holmes-style reasoning and sent a woodsman named Hans Vos off westwards through the same forests on what may have been America's first bounty-hunting expedition.* In a sequence foreshadowing the Wild West of two hundred years later, Vos cornered Van den Bogaert in an Iroquois longhouse used to store grain, and a shootout commenced. Van den Bogaert, once the hero of the colony, now laid low by his sexual proclivities, attempted a distraction by setting fire to the place. Vos caught his man anyway, and brought him back to Fort Orange. Coorn then wrote to Stuyvesant, informing him of the event and asking what should be done with the man.

Stuyvesant wrote back that he himself would stand in judgment at Van den Bogaert's trial, but not until spring, when the ice on the northern stretches of the river had broken and ships

* Vos would later require legal services, and would hire Adriaen van der Donck to represent him. The Dutch colony was a small world.

could get through. Before that, however, Van den Bogaert, certain what Stuyvesant's judgment would be and desperate beyond reckoning, escaped from the prison in the fort. As he ran across the frozen expanse of the river, he fell through a hole in the ice and drowned.

So ended the life of the barber-surgeon turned explorer; but not the controversy he stirred up. Shortly thereafter, the Mohawks – in a turn of events that suggests the depth of their understanding of European ways by this time – sent a delegation to Manhattan to sue the West India Company for damages resulting from the loss of their building and its stores of supplies. In deciding the matter, Stuyvesant may well have taken counsel from Adriaen van der Donck, who knew the Mohawks and their methods of resolving grievances better than anyone in the colony. Stuyvesant concluded that the Indians were in the right, and ordered the sale of Van den Bogaert's Manhattan property, the proceeds from which would pay what he acknowledged was the company's debt to the Indians.

Van der Donck seems to have assisted Stuyvesant with yet another matter at about this same time – this one crucial to Stuyvesant's leadership and to the colony as a whole. Besides the threats from the English, Swedes and Indians, there remained the persistent problem of insubordination from the semi-private domain of Rensselaerswyck. Since the death of Kiliaen van Rensselaer the estate had been under the ownership of the diamond merchant's son, and in March 1648 a new director arrived to run the place. Unluckily for Stuyvesant, Brant van Slichtenhorst, a bluff 59-year-old with vast experience as an administrator in the Dutch Republic, was virtually his equal in grit and resolve. He understood the language of the charter that old Van Rensselaer had won from the Dutch government, which, in a throwback to the glory days of the middle ages for which men like Edmund Plowden pined, gave him almost autocratic powers. Stuyvesant read things differently; his own commission obliged him to rule the entire colony of New

Netherland, which included the manor of Rensselaerswyck. It was a dispute over political jurisdiction, and Van Slichtenhorst brought it to the surface just weeks after he started work.

Stuyvesant had sent to Rensselaerswyck a seemingly innocuous proclamation declaring the first Wednesday of May a day of public fasting and thanksgiving throughout the colony. It was common for leaders in all Dutch communities, following storms, fires, invasions or harsh winters, to set aside a formal day of thanks to the Almighty for seeing the inhabitants through the ordeal. But when the proclamation was handed round during church service in Rensselaerswyck, Van Slichtenhorst saw the symbolism in it, which he considered an infringement of his office. He stomped back to his headquarters and fired off a defiant protest.

Stuyvesant too understood the importance of symbols of power and the need to back them up. Almost immediately he set sail from New Amsterdam with a full military escort. When, some days later, the company sloop put in before Rensselaerswyck, Van Slichtenhorst extended him the courtesy of firing a welcoming salvo from the estate's cannons, but when the two men met and Stuyvesant ordered the other to stand down and obey the greater authority of the Dutch colony, Van Slichtenhorst replied sharply, 'Your complaints are unjust. I have more reason to complain, on behalf of my Patroon, against you.'

This was only the beginning of a strident territorial battle between the two men, which would result, among other things, in the founding of the city of Albany. Of more immediate significance, we can see here another step in the dance between Stuyvesant and Van der Donck, who seems to have accompanied Stuyvesant on this trip. It would have been natural for Stuyvesant to call on his experience: Van der Donck had spent his first three years working as the legal enforcer at Rensselaerswyck; he knew the politics and personalities of the fiefdom and of the West India Company's Fort Orange. And, indeed, the court records of Rensselaerswyck show that, after a long absence, Adriaen van der Donck appears again in the fiefdom's court in July 1648 – exactly when Peter Stuyvesant made his trip northwards.

So we have a nice picture coming into focus, of the correct, zealous, militaristic 38-year-old leader of the colony working energetically and with considerable creativity to establish control over his domain and secure its position. And as he assesses the men around him, he comes to rely increasingly on the younger lawyer who knows so much of the law, the land and the natives, and who goes out of his way to be of service.

December came. As the last day of the year approached and the ever-present winds off the harbour turned icy, the residents of New Amsterdam met to choose the first replacements to the board of nine representatives. Van der Donck's careful politicking in the community paid off – he was chosen as one of a pool of potential representatives. It was then a foregone conclusion that Stuyvesant, in selecting half of the men from this group, would pick the young man who had been of such service to him. And from the new board's first meeting, Van der Donck, who had already done much behind-the-scenes work with several of these men, stood out, in the eyes of both his fellow representatives and the director. The others named him their leader and gave him a title: 'President of the Commonalty'. For a short time – a period of days, really – Stuyvesant was well pleased. Together, he must have thought, they could do great things.

10

The People's Champion

THE SUN ROSE ON 28 SEPTEMBER 1647 TO REVEAL, BOBBING IN the steel-coloured waters off the gnarled limestone headland on the Welsh coast called Mumbles Point, a lone human figure, nearly lifeless, clinging to a spar of wood. All morning and well into the afternoon the man rode the waves, until at last they tossed him onto a sandbar two miles from the shore. Along with the sputtering realization that he was alive came more information: there were other people here, similarly storm-tossed and stranded. Working together, they constructed a makeshift raft out of pieces of debris, and so made their way to the shore.

There, Cornelis Melyn found that his friend and fellow prisoner from the court of Peter Stuyvesant, Jochem Kuyter, was also alive. When the *Princess* broke up, Kuyter had been towards the aft of the ship, which cracked off in one large piece and floated, with him aboard, towards the scavenging Welshmen onshore. In all, 21 of the 107 passengers and crew members survived the wreck. Kieft died, the minister Bogardus died, and so too did most of the West India Company soldiers Stuyvesant had sent back to the Netherlands.

But surviving drowning was only the first stage of what would be an epic escape from fate's grasp. The two Dutchmen managed to cadge a few beaver pelts from the flotsam, sell them in a nearby town (possibly Swansea) and, using these funds, make their way through the rutted, civil-war-scarred countryside to Bristol, and then to London, which they reached about three weeks later.

From our vantage point, the seventeenth century seems an odd combination of the archaic and the modern. On the one hand, there was no infrastructure to assist shipwreck victims; you had to fight for survival, on land as much as against the waves. On the other, institutions that would feel instantly familiar today had a way of kicking into gear. As the various survivors of the wreck of the *Princess* staggered into London, insurance companies lined up to handle claims, lawsuits were filed, and public examiners picked up their quill pens, dipped them in pots of black iron-gall ink, and took testimony from survivors and eye witnesses. The tangle of suits and claims took years to settle.

Melyn and Kuyter had hoped to find in London the long-serving Dutch ambassador Albert Joachimi, who would help them to get home, but he was in Holland. Diplomatic relations were complicated by the war: King Charles was in prison, and no state in Europe yet recognized the government that Parliament had installed. The two disaffected citizens of the New World languished for months in England before finally winning passage to Holland, where they arrived around the end of the year. But the calamity had eroded none of their resolve; if anything, the shipwreck and its result – Kieft drowning and both of them surviving – reinforced their belief in the justness of their cause. They would even tell the story, in later years, that one of them had encountered Kieft on the waves just as he was about to go under, and that the former leader, in extremis, had admitted he had been wrong in his management of the colony and wrong to oppose them, and asked their forgiveness. Not the sort of confession a judge would be likely to accept, but a good indication of how thoroughly vindicated, how righteous and flush with new life and purpose, the two Manhattanites felt after the wreck of the *Princess*.

*

The walk from the City Tavern on the waterfront in New Amsterdam to the fort at the southern tip of the island was a matter of two minutes or so. It was pleasant enough: stepping out of the tavern – so common a place for transacting business that it was now a semi-official headquarters for many merchants and traders – you found yourself smack on the shore of the East River, looking out on the ships at anchor and across to the farmsteads in the village of Breuckelen. You turned right and walked south, with the river to your left and a row of gabled houses on your right, crossed the little bridge over the canal, continued down the narrow lane extending from it called, sensibly enough, Bridge Street – and there stood the fort, the ragged heart of town. Someone made this simple journey in the first days of January 1649, and delivered a letter to Director-General Stuyvesant. It was from the new assembly that represented the people of the colony and from now on would stand apart from Stuyvesant's council, which represented the company. The people in New Amsterdam and surrounding towns were calling this assembly the board of nine.* The letter informed the director that the board would like leave to send one or more representatives to The Hague in order to appeal for the Dutch government to take over management of the colony.

The petition – in effect a request to be allowed to emasculate him – infuriated Stuyvesant. It must have confused him as well. He had actually lauded many of the activities the board had undertaken in its first year in existence. The members had taken seriously their duties as representatives of the people and served a useful role. When residents brought them complaints about merchants fixing their prices on bread and wine, the board

* Officially, the board represented the residents of the villages of New Amsterdam, Breuckelen (later Brooklyn), New Amersfoort (the future Flatlands section of Brooklyn) and Pavonia (Jersey City, New Jersey).

appealed to Stuyvesant to stop it, and he did. Then, getting bolder, they laid before him a list of measures they said would improve the economy. He fulminated a bit at their effrontery, then, on second thought, decided to take 'more closely into consideration and deliberation the petition and written remonstrance of the nine elected selectmen, our good and dear subjects', and made the suggested changes. But now, suddenly, the arrogance of these men had shot off the scale. It must have seemed especially strange given that his dutiful protégé, Van der Donck, was now in charge of the board.

At the time, however, there wasn't much leisure to dwell on the matter. Another issue was pending, which at first blush seems quite removed. Stuyvesant had to arrange a celebration in honour of something that had happened in Europe the previous year. In 1648, in the German city of Münster, negotiations involving representatives from across Europe had culminated in the signing of a peace treaty between Spain and the Dutch Republic. Eighty years of war were officially at an end. The echoes of this great event would reverberate even to the island of Manhattan. The West India Company colony had been founded, after all, as a base for carrying out the war. Manhattan, in the eyes of strategists in the Netherlands all those years ago, had been considered a staging area for launching raids on Spanish vessels coming to and from South America and the Caribbean, such as those carried out by the privateer Willem Blauvelt. All that was now in the past. The West India Company directors in Amsterdam would have to rethink the status and future of their North American possession.

In fact, the Münster peace treaty and the petition from the board of nine were related. Both were shoves from the forces of history between the shoulderblades of Peter Stuyvesant, urging him towards the future, towards a new vision for the colony. But while he would have to accommodate the peace treaty, he chose to ignore the petition, saying he would first have to inform the inhabitants of the several English villages that had come into being under Kieft and continued as loyal components of the Dutch colony. Then he put the matter aside.

But the board did not. From the City Tavern, Adriaen van der Donck was busy greeting and machinating with everyone from ship's captains to fur traders to bakers and distillers, all of whom had an interest in the future of the colony, and all of whom had something to say. Businessmen in the Netherlands had renewed their involvement in Manhattan since the end of Kieft's war with the Indians. Traders in New Amsterdam, with their ties to the world's greatest commercial power, were among the most sophisticated on earth. Van der Donck and his fellow board members met them and listened as they described the conditions necessary to maintain a stable trade. He catalogued their output, and calculated that eighty thousand beaver pelts were passing through Manhattan every year on their way to the fur market in Europe. Because the beaver was so important to the colony, he himself had become an authority on the creatures; he had raised them, studied their life-cycle, read everything that the ancient Roman authorities had written about them. (Later he would make it his business to disabuse Europeans of some erroneous beliefs that had originated with Pliny and others, notably about the miraculous powers of beaver testicles. 'None of these', he concluded confidently about the Latin writers, 'had ever seen a beaver.')

At the same time, Van der Donck was aware that the beaver trade was only, as he put it, 'the means for the initial settlement of this fine country by Europeans'. Tobacco was just as important a product, and one with a future. Amsterdam was already the tobacco capital of Europe; that fact, combined with the artfully cost-cutting shipping and trading practices of the Dutch (they pioneered the concept of buying in bulk), led English tobacco farmers in Virginia to rely on Manhattan as a shipping centre. The world tobacco trade was in the first stage of its centuries-long surge, and even at this early point the Dutch had developed a marketing flair that a Philip Morris or a Procter & Gamble might admire. They created a variety of blends, mixing premium Virginia leaf with lower-grade Manhattan product as well as Dutch-grown to suit a range of tastes and pockets, added flavourings (lavender, nutmeg, rosemary, coriander, dill, vinegar) and paid careful attention to packaging. There was even a kind of advertising in the form of popular still-life paintings involving tobacco motifs.*

The civil unrest in England had only increased Virginia's dependence on Manhattan as a shipping centre. In 1648, when it looked as though England would block its colonies in North America from using foreign shippers, the governing body of Virginia had derided its own shippers for their high prices and declared that Manhattan was vital to Virginia's economic survival. The recent excavation of the Jamestown settlement has uncovered Delft pottery, Dutch coins and pipes, and Chinese ceramics that came via Dutch shippers – all indications of the Virginians' reliance on Manhattan, and of the power of the Dutch Republic, which by now was not only the leading shipper in the world but the largest maker of manufactured goods.

All of which is to make the point that, whereas American history has always portrayed Manhattan succeeding as a commercial centre only after the English takeover, in fact it was in the late 1640s that the city of New Amsterdam began its rise to become the hub of North American shipping. And now – starting on 1 January 1649, when he took his place on the board of nine – Van der Donck began in earnest to organize the businessmen who made the port function.

At the same time, he and his wife were beginning the task of developing their gargantuan estate along the river, just a stone's

* The Netherlands is still renowned for its tobacco connoisseurship, and, not entirely coincidentally, one of the major Dutch cigarette brands is called Peter Stuyvesant.

throw from the northern shore of the island. In keeping with the grandeur of his dream, Van der Donck had given his estate a name: Colen Donck, a contraction of 'Van der Donck's Colony'. He had building plans; he knew what crops he wanted to plant; he had made lists of the jobs that needed to be filled and the numbers and kinds of workers he wanted to recruit from the home country. Archaeological evidence suggests that he and Mary may have chosen a site for their home at the southern end of a long, flat expanse that would have been ideal for large-scale farming. In 1910, New York City workers digging a sewer trench in this area of the present-day Bronx came across what proved to be the foundation of a seventeenth-century farmhouse. A 1667 map of the district shows a house labelled 'Van Dunks'. No proper excavation of the site was done until 1990, and while the archaeologists found that the integrity of the site had been destroyed by the sewer trench, so that they could not obtain any further information from it, the sewer diggers had found Dutch bricks (slimmer than standard American or English bricks and of a yellow colour), Delft ware pottery fragments, combs, mirrors, lead window frames, pipe stems, even wampum beads. Taken together with the early map of the area, these remnants support the idea that this was the spot where Adriaen van der Donck decided to pursue his American dream. If this was indeed the location of the Van der Donck home, there is a pleasant appropriateness: today the area is Van Cortlandt Park in the Bronx, a vast, weedy stretch of grass informally subdivided into fields and pitches used by Bangladeshi and Guyanese cricketers, Irish hurlers and Japanese softball players – none of whom is likely ever to have heard of the man who once lorded it over the area and who helped make New York City a multicultural enclave.

The location had a lot going for it. The soil was rich, which Van der Donck could have discovered from the Wickquasgeck Indians from whom he had obtained title to the land – they kept a village here, which may have remained through Van der

Donck's time.* A long, lazy stream ran through this stretch of farmland, skirted the house and snaked down into the creek that separated Manhattan from the mainland, which the Dutch had named Spuyten Duyvil, or devil's spout, after the dangerous eddies caused by the tide. By following this in a light sloop, or even in a canoe bought from the Indians,† the leader of the board of nine, in anticipation of the millions who would commute into Manhattan, could have made his way into the Harlem River, and then, riding with the tide, headed southwards along the coast of the island, and come to dock at the small pier in front of the City Tavern.

The agitating residents of the town would have grouped themselves around that same shoreline one day in January 1649 to see an amazing sight: a ghost being rowed to the dock. It wasn't a total shock – Cornelis Melyn had written to his compatriots from Bristol, telling them about his and Kuyter's survival – but seeing the man in the flesh had to have reinforced what they had felt on getting word of their fellows' survival and Kieft's death: that they had a genuine cause, and that it was just.

As soon as Melyn could get into a secure space, free from eavesdroppers (his own house, perhaps – there, just a few steps up the shore to the right of the pier) with Van der Donck, Govert Loockermans, Augustin Herman, Jacob van Couwenhoven, Thomas Hall, Jan Evertsen Bout, Michael Janszen and others who considered themselves a part of this new political party, he opened his satchel and spread before them the fruits of his time in the homeland: documents. Papers dramatically inscribed with

* The site of the supposed Van der Donck house is just behind the gardens of the Van Cortlandt House; the Indian village, which was called Mosholu or Keskeskick, was located at what is now the Parade Ground.

† There are several references in the records to settlers using Indian-made canoes, and someone who had spent much time among them would have recognized their convenience.

the flourishes of government business and tied with ribbons bearing heavy official seals.

From the moment they had landed in the United Provinces, Melyn and Kuyter set about making their case, trying to undo Stuyvesant's sentence against them and in the process to make men of power in the home country appreciate the value of their North American colony. They found national politics in a state of flux in the aftermath of the peace treaty with Spain; old alliances were shifting. Before, supporting the West India Company, which had been organized as a profit-making venture to raid Spanish shipping, had been the patriotic thing to do. Now people were free to consider other visions for the North American colony. It took months, but Melyn and Kuyter won from the governing body a remarkable concession, which now lay on the table: a mandamus, an order from the government of the Dutch Republic to the director-general of the colony of New Netherland. The members of the board of nine must have gasped as they read the document, for in its tone and language it was an utter vindication of their position. It decried 'the war that Director Kieft illegally and contrary to all public Law, had commenced against the Indians' and the atrocities 'which must startle the Christian heart that hears of them'. It approved of the fact that popular representatives had been chosen to ensure that such calamities didn't happen again; it noted that Kieft, and after him Stuyvesant, had hampered these representatives. Stuyvesant's sentences against the two men were revoked, pending appeal, and Stuyvesant himself, or a representative, was to return to the home country to explain his conduct.

And there was more. Willem, the Prince of Orange – leader of the army and symbolic head of the Dutch state – had felt strongly enough about the matter to make a personal intervention on top of the official decree. So he had written a letter, which Melyn had with him:

To Petrus Stuyvesant, Director of New Netherland, the 19th of May 1648
Honorable, prudent, and discreet, specially dear.

You will receive by the bearers hereof, Joachim Pietersen Kuyter and Cornelis Melyn, the commands which the High and Mighty Lords States General have resolved to communicate to you, to the end that you allow these people to enjoy their property free and unmolested there . . . we are disposed earnestly to admonish you hereby, in addition, expressly notifying that you shall have to allow said petitioners, peaceably and without objection to enjoy the effect of their High Mightinesses aforesaid resolution.

And herewith,
Honorable, &c.
Willem,
Prince d'Orange

All of this was riveting to the board of nine and their supporters. For the first time they understood that there was a new era taking shape in the home country; and the new climate there gave them an opportunity to state their case for a government that would put the colony on a secure footing.

In one of his responses to requests from the board to be allowed to send delegates to The Hague, Stuyvesant had stalled by suggesting that, as representatives of the people, the board should be sure that what they were proposing was indeed the will of the people. Now, emboldened by the support from Holland, the board members decided to follow up his suggestion. They would ask the people – one by one – whether they felt there was a need for a reform in government. In a remarkably direct approach to democracy, Van der Donck, Loockermans, Janszen, Herman and the other members of the board walked out the front door of the tavern, divided the streets of New Amsterdam among themselves, and began knocking on doors. People must have had a lot to say, because once the canvassing was finished the board decided to compile a dossier. Van der Donck took on the task of collating the comments and distilling the thoughts of the entire community into a single document.

Stuyvesant watched the canvassers marching through the town and, as far as he was concerned, openly instigating revolt. For a time, he sat on his fury; then it erupted. At some point during the months of January and February 1649, while Van der Donck was putting together his brief, there was a confrontation between the leader and his one-time disciple, in which Stuyvesant tried to comprehend how the younger man could turn on him, perhaps even gave him an opportunity to back down, and then finally severed personal ties. Unfortunately, Van der Donck does not record the details of the meeting, saying only that 'the General' had, from the time of the door-to-door canvassing, 'burned with rage'. This was the moment when Van der Donck finally showed his hand. Three times now he had gone through the same trajectory of relationship with men in power – ingratiating himself as he worked into a position of some authority, then suddenly turning brash, defiant, self-willed. Now he let his true feelings, his patriotic fervour, show. Stuyvesant would surely have countered that it was he who was acting in the best interests of the colony, pointed out that they were beset on all sides and made plain that any effort to undermine him in such circumstances was tantamount to treason. Both men had strong points. Stuyvesant was indeed holding the colony together. But at the same time he was blind to what Van der Donck saw: that military and diplomatic manoeuvring *vis-à-vis* the English, Swedes and Indians would yield results only for a short while; that without a revamp of its entire structure the colony would die from within.

No compromise was possible for either man. As a last attempt at coming to an understanding, Stuyvesant apparently offered a method of joint working: the board would share with him the information it had gathered, and he would take their advice into consideration. But this would defeat the whole purpose of the board's endeavour, which was to be independent of the West India Company. Van der Donck informed the director, as he later wrote, that the board 'would not communicate with him or follow his directions in anything pertaining to the matter'.

That was it. The confrontation ended with Stuyvesant exhibiting what Van der Donck called 'a bitter and unconquerable hatred' for the members of the board, 'but principally against those whom he supposed to be the chief authors' of the move to undermine him. As Van der Donck describes this encounter for the benefit of officials in the Netherlands and characterizes Stuyvesant's change of feelings towards certain once-trusted comrades, the formality of the prose actually seems to heighten the emotions involved, leading one to believe that there really had been warm feelings between the two men: 'these persons had been good and dear friends with him always, and he, shortly before, had regarded them as the most honorable, able, intelligent and pious men of the country, yet as soon as they did not follow the General's wishes they were this and that, some of them rascals, liars, rebels, usurers and spendthrifts, in a word, hanging was almost too good for them.'

Stuyvesant had reached his limit; and, as always, when he decided to move, he did it forcefully. One day at the beginning of March, probably accompanied by a contingent of West India Company soldiers, he marched around the corner from the fort to the home of Michael Janszen – the board member with whom Van der Donck had been friends since the time both had lived at Rensselaerswyck. Van der Donck had, as usual, been staying here, but at that moment no-one was home. The party searched the place and found the sheaf of papers that contained the lists of residents' complaints and laments about the colony and its management, and also the draft document Van der Donck had been preparing. Stuyvesant took the papers and what he found in them confirmed him in his next step. The next day he had Van der Donck arrested and imprisoned. Then he hastily sent Philip de Truy, his 'court messenger', to the members of his council and to some of the board of nine, demanding their presence at an emergency 'supreme council'.

The men – fifteen in all – assembled in an atmosphere of great tension. Stuyvesant's face, even in light moments, had a jowly grimness to it, and it cannot have looked anything but black as they waited for him to announce the reason for the unusual gathering. Then he told them that Van der Donck had been arrested and charged with *crimen laesae majestatis* – high treason. The documents found in his possession 'grossly slandered' the director-general and contained 'great calumnies' against the government leaders in The Hague.

At this moment Stuyvesant's deputy-director, Lubbert van Dinklagen, the only lawyer in the colony besides Van der Donck, stunned his superior by interrupting him with a formal protest, charging that 'the honorable director . . . has heretofore done and still does many things' on his own, without informing his council, 'also because he has caused Adriaen van der Donck to be placed under arrest' without consulting them. It was an electric moment. That Stuyvesant now faced insubordination from his own council of hand-picked members – indeed, from his second-in-command – must have shaken him and given new hope to the board members present, all of whom had to have been fearing for their own lives as well as Van der Donck's.

Stuyvesant collected himself, and, changing tactics, turned on Van Dinklagen. He read out a passage from the confiscated writings in which Van Dinklagen supposedly defamed the government in Holland. Van Dinklagen, indignant now, denied he had ever said such things, and demanded to see the pages where they were written. Stuyvesant refused. Then he asked each man present to state for the record his opinion on what should be done with Van der Donck. Van Dinklagen spoke up first, insisting that, in accordance with Dutch law, Van der Donck be examined on the matter and then released on bail. But Brian Newton, who had served Stuyvesant loyally since

Curaçao, who had been at his side when he lost his leg, declared that the man should remain in prison and be interrogated there. Most of the others agreed. Augustin Herman, in an act of defiance against the entire proceeding, refused to give an opinion.

Stuyvesant had summoned only six of the board members to this special council – seemingly out of fear that the whole group of them would vote against him. With six of them and eight of his trusted advisers, plus himself, he could be more sure of a favourable outcome. Now, however, it looked as though Van Dinklagen and one or two others would swing the other way; so he adjourned the session without calling a vote. Two days later, he assembled his ordinary council, without the board members, and 'by a plurality of votes' it decided to keep Van der Donck in custody until a committee had investigated the case. Two days following that, on 8 March, with Van der Donck still in confinement, people from all the villages in the area around Manhattan gathered in the church at Stuyvesant's bidding to debate a matter that would have serious import for the colony. Shortly before this public meeting, Stuyvesant had gathered with his council and declared that he would read a 'writing' to the populace. Presumably it contained an account of Van der Donck's treasonous behaviour and Stuyvesant's decision on his punishment.

But he never got to read it. After Van der Donck's arrest and the abortive special council, his supporters had gathered with Cornelis Melyn and plotted a bold countermove. Now, in the church, before nearly the entire population of New Amsterdam and the surrounding villages, just as Stuyvesant was getting ready to speak, Melyn rushed to the podium. The States General had given him the task of carrying their mandamus to New Amsterdam and serving it on the director-general himself, or naming some other officer or officers to do so. It was a legal technicality – the serving of a summons – but Melyn, who had a flair for the theatrical, wanted to make the most of it. He now declared in a loud voice his intention to fulfil the wishes of the

States General by having the board of nine serve the mandamus on Stuyvesant. Then he handed it to Arnold van Hardenbergh, a member of the board, and asked him to read it.

Stuyvesant knew what the document contained, and had no wish to have its chastising language, ordering him back to Europe like a misbehaving child, aired in front of his constituency. He declared there was no need to read the document, as he was ready to receive it. 'I must have the copy,' he roared, and reached out to grab the thing. In the scuffle, the document was torn and the heavy wax seal that marked it as an official order of the Dutch government came loose. Everyone watched in amazement as the disc of wax fell towards the ground and then hung at the end of a strand of parchment. The symbolism was blatant: here these men stood in the holiest building in the colony, defaming it with their raised voices, while the seal of government dangled between them. In the gasp of silence that followed, Melyn informed Stuyvesant that, if he wanted a copy of the document, there was one for him as well as one to be read to the populace.

The crowd erupted at that point. Stuyvesant must have had soldiers on hand, and things were starting to look ugly. He was a born leader; never had he endured such a breakdown of authority. His impulse was to crack down hard, but he also saw that the place was on the verge of chaos; the event, he later wrote to the States General, was 'so shaped that massacre and bloodshed might have been the result, had we not converted ourselves from the highest to the lowest, and permitted the indecent service of the summons'. Recognizing that his enemies had trapped him, he brought the assembly to order, and directed the man to read the scolding document.

When it was done, with all eyes on him, Stuyvesant spoke with wrathful brevity:

'I honor the States and their Commission, and will obey their Commands, and send an Agent to maintain the judgment, as it was well and legally pronounced.'

And then he left.

It was surely the most humiliating moment of Stuyvesant's life. 'Mutinous and insulting' he would later call the spectacle. His soldier's pride, his simple, country-bred dignity, had been trampled. He believed steadfastly in his commission, his devotion to the colony was real, and already he was achieving results in relations with the English to the north; but none of this mattered to these men, who seemed bent on self-destruction.

Melyn was undoubtedly impassioned, but he tended to be too histrionic even for his fellow agitators; Stuyvesant was right to complain about how the man, even before reaching Manhattan, had disembarked in Boston and bragged to the English that he had a commission to send Stuyvesant back to Holland as a prisoner. Such behaviour was no help to the director-general in his dealings with the New England governors. Then again, Stuyvesant had provoked the men. It's hard to imagine that the board would have gone along with the spectacle in the church had Stuyvesant not taken Van der Donck into custody. The crime of high treason was, of course, punishable by death. All their necks were on the block. He had raised the stakes, and forced them to do the same.

At this moment, with his popularity at a low ebb, Stuyvesant walked into a political scandal. It happened that a case of muskets arrived in port at this time. When people found out that it was Stuyvesant himself who had ordered them, and that he intended to sell them to the Indians, in order to maintain goodwill, it became the talk of the town. The residents were barred from selling firearms to the Indians; here was the director himself doing just that, apparently for his own personal gain, and at a time when firearms were in short supply even among the colonists. Stuyvesant was forced to explain his behaviour before his own council, but whether or not he had committed a crime he was guilty of violating the politician's first rule: never to give the appearance of wrongdoing. He was thrown on the defensive.

So it was while he was under this cloud that Stuyvesant had to decide what to do with Van der Donck. If he had had the support of his council and the people, he might have executed the man. As it was, however, his once loyal lieutenant, Van Dinklagen, was now firmly against him, watching his every move to see that he acted in accordance with Dutch law. It was probably at his insistence that Stuyvesant accepted that he could not try and punish the man on the basis solely of the sheets of papers confiscated from him – especially as Van der Donck had, from confinement, agreed that it was possible some of what was contained in the pages was in error, since it consisted of raw data that he had compiled from interviews with residents. So Stuyvesant ordered Van der Donck to 'prove and establish or to revoke what he has injuriously written'. For the time being, Van der Donck was released. He was, however, banned from serving on the board of nine.

Van der Donck stepped outside into the late winter daylight a new man. By imprisoning him, Stuyvesant had anointed him as the people's champion. If Stuyvesant was now on the defensive, Van der Donck, the one under criminal charge, was flush with momentum. And by ordering him to prove the truth of what he had written, Stuyvesant in effect had given him a licence to pursue the business of governmental reform.

And so he did. Walking the gabled streets of the young, rude, vibrant town, with the rough winds of early spring at his back and the inhabitants greeting him and congratulating him in their unique mix of accents and languages, he must have felt that everything he had done – from his university days at Leiden to his stint out in the wilds as the lawman of Rensselaerswyck to his diligent politicking among the Manhattanites – had led to this moment. People knew him as an estate owner – 'Jonker' (young squire) is what everybody called him on the street. And that role sharpened his profile as activist: he had the stature of a landowner, and yet he was clearly not following the path of a man like Kiliaen van Rensselaer, who had set about milking the New World of profits from the comfort of his Dutch home.

Van der Donck was invested in the colony personally, in its people and its future.

Everything now went into preparations for a delegation to the Dutch Republic. Legally, all the principal players should be involved; so, beginning the day after he was released from prison, Van der Donck fired off a series of summonses – to Van Dinklagen, La Montagne, Brian Newton, and other councillors and officials – requesting each man 'to appear by the first opportunity at the Hague, before their High Mightinesses'. He delivered these, received their answers (mostly variations on 'Of course I won't go'), and recorded the whole thing in a flurry of paperwork. He can't have expected the entire government of the colony to up and sail to Holland to defend itself, but getting these things down on paper was, to him, a necessary step.

Van der Donck's busyness annoyed Stuyvesant no end – so much so that, on 8 May, he issued a new ordinance:

> Whereas it is daily observed that . . . great abuses are committed in the writing and procuring of depositions by private persons who are neither pledged thereto by oath nor qualified thereto by official authority, whereby frequently many things are written to the advantage of those who have the papers drawn up, interspersed with sinister, obscure and dubious words . . . to the great prejudice and damage of the parties; therefore, in order to prevent this result, dangerous in a republic . . . we annul and declare invalid . . . all affidavits, interrogatories, or other instruments serving as evidence, which are written by private individuals.

Undeterred, through May and June, writing like a man possessed, Van der Donck pulled together all the information he and his colleagues had collected from residents, and constructed what would become perhaps the most famous document to come out of the colony: the *Remonstrance of New Netherland*, an 83-page formal complaint, which he intended to present to the States General in The Hague.

The *Remonstrance* would in time root the Manhattan colony's structure in Dutch law; eventually, it would help give New York City its unique shape and character. Its opening words carry the full measure of Van der Donck's thoughts and emotions. He managed to bundle together in a few lines his exuberant pride in Dutch exploration and discovery and his passion for his adopted homeland, even his familiarity with the local Indians. At the same time, for the benefit of government officials who had little knowledge of the colony, he put the matter of its future development in a concise and accurate historical context, going straight back to the beginning:

> Among all the enterprising people in the world, who search for foreign countries, navigable waters and trade, those who bear the name of Netherlanders will very easily be able to hold their rank among the foremost, as is sufficiently known to all those who have in any wise saluted the threshold of history. It will, in like manner, be also confirmed by our following Relation, for in the year of Christ 1609, was the Country of which we now propose to speak, first found and discovered at the expense of the General East India Company – though directing their aim and design elsewhere – by the ship *Half Moon*, whereof Henry Hudson was master and factor. It was afterwards named New Netherland by our people, and that very justly, for it was first discovered, and taken possession of, by Netherlanders and at their expense, so that even at the present day, the natives of the country (who are so old as to remember the event) testify, that on seeing the Dutch ships on their first coming here, they knew not what to make of them . . . We have heard the Indians also frequently say, that they knew of no other world or people previous to the arrival of the Netherlanders here. For these reasons, therefore, and on account of the similarity of Climate, Situation and fertility, this place is rightly called New Netherland. It is situate along the North Coast of

> America, in the latitude of 38, 39, 40, 41, 42 degrees, or thereabouts ... The land of itself is fertile, and capable of being entirely cultivated by an abundance of people.

Many other supporting documents were necessary – a formal petition asking the States General to take charge of the colony, and dozens of pages of heavily annotated 'additional observations' on the state of affairs, the West India Company's 'tyranny' and the need for 'suitable municipal government'. It was a major legal undertaking, appropriate to the gravity of the situation and the potential that Van der Donck and his colleagues saw in the island of Manhattan, the river in which it lay, and the continent to which it formed the gateway.

Stuyvesant, meanwhile, had decided he couldn't stop the board from sending its delegation, but that he could and would counter them. It was unthinkable that he would go himself in response to the mandamus; he was in the midst of delicate diplomacy with the New England governors and with chiefs of the Raritan, Nyack and other local tribes. Travel personally, he explained to the States General, 'we cannot do consistently with honor and oath.' He would send Cornelis van Tienhoven both to represent him against Melyn's charges and to represent his government in the battle for control of the colony. But while Stuyvesant remained busy managing the affairs of what he still saw as his domain, an instance of how remarkably strongly he could bear a grudge occurred on 14 June when a trader named Jacob Loper appeared before him asking for a licence to trade on the South River. 'Whereas the said Loper married the daughter of Cornelis Melyn,' Stuyvesant's decision was recorded, for all to see, 'the honorable director general is of the opinion that the request cannot be granted.'

The board of nine, meanwhile, chose a delegation consisting of two of its members – trader Jacob van Couwenhoven and farmer Jan Evertsen Bout – and its former leader, Van der Donck. If Stuyvesant protested that he had released Van der Donck from prison with the express order that he not engage in official business, there is no record of it. Van der Donck would certainly have countered that he was only following the order to 'prove and establish or ... revoke what he has injuriously written'.

The men prepared to leave. Van der Donck spent time with his wife on their estate, making lists of supplies needed and skilled workers he should hire in Europe. He agreed to represent a woman named Annetie van Beyeren, who lived in the Long Island village of Vlissingen, in the settling of her affairs in the home country. And he took on one other piece of legal work in the last days before departure. Willem Blauvelt, the sometime pirate, had been a swaggering presence on the island for many years, and his frigate, *La Garce*, had been a financial interest for many of the prominent men of New Amsterdam, including Augustin Herman, Jacob van Couwenhoven, who was about to accompany Van der Donck to Holland, and the former director Willem Kieft. With the full backing and support of the colonial government, the frigate had, for a considerable period of years, repeatedly set off for the West Indies and returned bearing Spanish prizes: ships laden with tobacco, sugar, ebony wood and wine. All the partners in the venture received profits from these raids; indeed, this sort of activity had been the centrepiece of the West India Company's business in the New World.

With peace, privateering had become illegal; but Captain Blauvelt had had a hard time coming to terms with the news. Recently, as so often before, an eager crowd had gathered on the waterfront at the cheery sight of *La Garce*, the Dutch flag snapping at the mast, approaching with a fine prize in tow. The problem was that Blauvelt had caught the Spanish bark 'in the river of Tobasco in Campeachy Bay' (on the west coast of the Yucatan peninsula) five months after the peace treaty was signed, setting off a series of lawsuits. Van der Donck had been hired by one of the owners of Blauvelt's vessel, and took part in untangling the mess until the day before he sailed for Europe. It was a fitting last piece of business, for it signalled the end of the old order on Manhattan.

There was a final encounter between Van der Donck and Judith Bayard, Stuyvesant's wife. He met her on the street on 29 July. Whether they talked – whether they had somehow maintained cordial relations – we don't know. She may have been preoccupied: the Stuyvesants' first son, Balthazar, was now twenty-one months old, and the second, Nicholas, a baby of seven months. At any rate, Van der Donck handed her a letter from Melyn to Stuyvesant – which he himself had surely helped write. Stuyvesant still had not allowed Melyn use of his land and property, as the mandamus had ordered. The letter demanded that he do so, and also that he make available to the delegates such documents as they required to present their case, and to do it soon since 'time is short and the vessels are making ready'.

Judith handed the letter to Stuyvesant, who slashed out a reply, which he titled 'Answer to Cornelis Melyn's disrespectful Protest handed to my Wife, as she says, by Adriaen van der Donck and A. Hardenbergh', and in which, through clenched teeth, as it were, he granted the man use of his property, and declared, 'Who the delinquent is, God and the law have to decide.'

From this letter we have the information that Stuyvesant planned to send his representative Van Tienhoven on the readying vessel; so the diligent, forward-looking lawyer Van der Donck and the sweaty, corpulent, wily defender of Stuyvesant and the West India Company Van Tienhoven must have stood on the deck of the same ship as the low spread of the little town, with its windmill and fort prominent, receded into mist. Ahead of Van der Donck lay the distant continent of his birth.

11

An American in Europe

IN JANUARY 1646 A COACH, DRAWN BY SIX HORSES, LABOURED through the frozen ruts of a road in the German countryside. With gilded woodwork and attendants tricked out in scarlet capes and hats, it made a vivid impression against the dead landscape. Two rows of retainers rode ahead, swords at their sides. Peasants by the roadside couldn't help but gawk as the entourage passed.

Inside the coach sat a 61-year-old man, his sedate attire in contrast to the grandeur of the vehicle. He had a tapered beard and sharp eyes, an expression of sad, solemn decency. Sharing the cabin with him were his wife and their granddaughter. All three of them must have been weary as they neared the end of their 120-mile journey; just now, as they rounded this bend, the steepled skyline of the city of Münster came into view.

The man's name was Adriaen Pauw. He had long been one of the most important men in the Dutch Republic, and now he was about to attempt something that, should it come to pass, would transform European history. He was quite conscious of this – so much so that he would commission the painting just described, depicting the moment of his arrival, to document his role in history. He believed that he and his like-minded colleagues had an opportunity to redraft the rules by which nations had governed themselves for centuries, to lay a new course for politics and for human affairs.

As Pauw's carriage rumbled along, nearly every state in Europe was at war and had been for the entire lifetime of most of its inhabitants. Going back into the middle ages, it had been generally accepted that war was the natural state of nations; that a country defined itself in large part by its clashes with enemies and alliances with friends. In the early 1640s, however, one of those epochal changes of thinking began to occur in the minds of men from different nations and traditions. The new mindset had its intellectual origins, most notably, in the Dutch jurist Hugo Grotius, the man who was the guiding light to Adriaen van der Donck and other law students of the era. Twenty years before, Grotius had put forward the idiosyncratic proposition that peace was the natural state of mature, civilized nations, that war ought to be considered only as a last resort, and should even then be governed by rules to which all parties subscribed. Remarkably, monarchs paused in the midst of flinging their armies at one another to read Grotius' book. King Gustavus Adolphus of Sweden supposedly kept *De Jure Belli et Pacis* on his person as he led his troops into battle.

Grotius' radical concept had gained momentum in the intervening years and was now a prominent element in the political climate. The peace negotiations at Münster would be unlike anything that had come before in world history. Each envoy, in expression of his government's awareness of the magnitude of the undertaking, arrived with an entourage of knights, halberdiers, trumpeters, archers, foot soldiers and an army of retainers; the French delegation numbered one thousand people. As it became clear that a treaty would be reached, each envoy commissioned a suite of portraits of all the dignitaries – the collection in Gripsholm Castle near Stockholm, still intact, runs to seventy-four paintings.

Negotiations actually went on in two places at once – Münster and Osnabrück – and linked together the eight decades of combat between Spain and the Dutch provinces on the one hand and the three decades of brute slaughter that had occupied much of the rest of Europe on the other. Needless to say, Thirty Years War and Eighty Years War were names given after the fact; at the time it was simply endless strife.

The proceedings were all self-consciously monumental because, as the participants were well aware, it was the first time emissaries of European nations had come together as representatives of separate political entities, rather than of units under the umbrella of the Vatican or the Holy Roman Empire, acknowledged one another as sovereign and tried to work things out on this basis. It was the birth of secular politics, the forerunner of Versailles, Paris, Camp David and the United Nations, the creation of a political map of Europe that would hold into the twenty-first century. It was, in a political sense, the launch of what historians would one day call the modern era.

Adriaen Pauw cut an unusual figure in Münster. The term 'baroque', so fitting to the age, applied as much to personal fashion as to art; an ambassador considered himself a diplomatic peacock, whose personal finery informed others of his nation's magnificence. As a representative of the anomalous Dutch Republic, Pauw was one of the few non-nobles in attendance, and his drab Calvinist dress – a study in grey, black and white – was a signal of what, as far as the Dutch were concerned, the negotiations were all about.* For them, the central purpose of the gathering was to get Spain – with the most determinedly regal court in Europe – to acknowledge the independence not only of a long-rebelling protectorate but of a nation that proposed to exist without a monarchy. Virtually all the titled envoys to the peace negotiations – the Duke of Longueville, the Count of Peñaranda, Papal Nuncio Fabio Chigi, Count Hugo Eberhard Kratz von Scharfenstein, Johan Ludwig, Count of

* There was also a linguistic irony in Pauw's drab appearance, since his surname meant 'peacock'.

Nassau-Hadamar, Count Palatine Charles Gustav – had trouble swallowing this; the very word 'ambassador' had always had as its referent a royal court. Pauw was no spartan – he lived in a castle with a moat, surrounded by fields of red-and-white striped tulips that were his own personal hybrid – but there was a point to be made.

In the end, peace prevailed at Münster and Osnabrück. The marathon negotiations were followed by appropriately baroque treaty preparations, then, in 1648, by the signings themselves (history has linked the two treaties by referring to them jointly as the Peace of Westphalia, after the region in which both towns were located). And then the parties started. They went on for years, criss-crossing central Europe like brush fires. For most of Europe, the celebration was of the end of decades of slaughter. In the United Provinces of the Netherlands, the feelings were even more acute. Independence, recognition, vindication – the results of the treaty amounted to, on a societal level, a catalogue of psychological power terms. When Pauw, his fellow Dutch envoys and the Spanish representatives put their signatures and seals to a single piece of paper, it signalled the Moment, the ignition of the golden age. Publishers ran off copies of the treaty, which became a bestseller. Celebrations flared through every city and village in the seven provinces. The euphoria built steadily over the months following the signing. Plays, poems, salutes, parades, porcelain tiles, sermons, drinking bouts, brothel binges, painting commissions, public works projects – in every possible human manifestation, the Dutch proclaimed the new age.

It was into this atmosphere – of a society conscious of a future laden with prosperity, peace and power, and alive to the possibilities of secular politics – that Adriaen van der Donck sailed in the beginning of October 1649. He found his homeland reborn, the cause for which his grandfather had fought and become a hero vindicated. The war into which he himself had been born and raised was over. It was a new world, a new country.

But it was not Adriaen van der Donck's country – not any

more. Whatever joy he experienced and celebrations he took part in, he seems not to have wavered in his commitment to his adopted land. He was a prototype of a species that would number in the millions in the coming centuries: the European who crossed the ocean and found, in the vast continent at the other end, a new home and purpose. He was an American.

Into the harbour at Texel, the grassy, windswept North Sea island from which Henry Hudson had set out forty years earlier, the ship sailed. From there Van der Donck and his colleagues, Jacob van Couwenhoven and Jan Evertsen Bout, would have boarded a public transport boat, and so sailed southwards, into the famed forest of masts that was the harbourfront of Amsterdam, the most vital city on earth.

Of course, the city had not waited for the signing of a document to begin its golden era. Prosperity had been building for decades now, and so had Amsterdam. The city had more than doubled in size since Henry Hudson's time, and it was thirty years since its merchant rulers – with impressive confidence in the city's future growth – had conceived of a staggering urban development project, now nearing completion: a series of concentric canal rings. The canals of Amsterdam are so iconic that many people assume they have always been there, but they were dug, by hand, hundreds of tons of earth moved out and sand brought in, forests' worth of pilings driven into the banks: a truly massive feat of engineering and city planning. The result was the creation of some of the first suburbs, for the idea was to encircle the core of the city – with its dens of commerce, sex and drink – with neighbourhoods of elegant housing for the army of newly rich, each home backed by ample gardens and provided with access, right outside the front door, onto the state of the art in urban transit systems. Here, aside from the incessant thrum of construction, all was serenity and gentility. In a foreshadowing of modern property marketing, the canals themselves were named in blatant appeal to their upwardly mobile clientele: you had the option, depending on the precise altitude of your pretensions, of living on the Herengracht (Gentleman's Canal), the Prinsengracht (Prince's Canal) or the Keizersgracht (Emperor's Canal).

Van der Donck had been away for nearly a decade. As for his comrades, Jacob van Couwenhoven, now in his thirties, had followed his father to Manhattan as a teenager, and Jan Evertsen Bout had been in the New World since 1634. For all three, roaming into the heart of the city, following the waterway called the Damrak to the central plaza of the Dam, would have been a frontal assault on the senses.

It was also a premonition of the society they were in the process of helping to create an ocean away. In the Dam, the city's main square, the results of Amsterdam's years of accepting foreigners were on vigorous display. Turbans, saris and skullcaps mingled in with musketeerish ensembles; the confused remark of a visiting Frenchman – 'It appears at first not to be the city of any particular people but to be common to all as the centre of their commerce' – was one that would be echoed in coming centuries by visitors to Amsterdam's offspring across the Atlantic, New York City. The hawkers – Cantonese, Franconians, Gujaratis, Livonians, Lorrainese, Ashkenazim – contributed as much to the visual cacophony as the pyramids of goods each had laid out at the bases of columns ranged around the place. The whole parade of exotic outlanders, Dutch guardsmen and stout, aproned housewives was set to music by itinerant lutists, fiddlers, bagpipers and hurdy-gurdy boys; and everyone was fuelled by street-corner pancake sellers. René Descartes, back in Amsterdam after his years in Leiden, found comfort in the anonymity: 'I can walk out each day in the bustle of the crowds with as much freedom and ease as you have in your paths,' he wrote to a country friend, 'and I pay no more attention to the people I meet than I would to the trees in your woods or the animals that graze there.' (Then again, the frenetic atmosphere may have got to him in the end: in the wake of peace, just as Van der Donck was arriving in Amsterdam, he left for the court of Queen Christina of Sweden, never to return.)

The availability of goods and services was stupefying to newcomers: sacks of pepper still giving off the perfumes of south-east Asia, bricks of sugar from the humid deltas of Brazil, hogsheads of Virginia tobacco, Turkish carpets, not to mention berths to Genoa, Smyrna and Sumatra and prospectuses for homes going up at the as yet unfinished south end of the canal ring, or in the new Jordaan area to the west. You could buy scientific measuring devices, tools for dissecting corpses or, if you were foolish enough, a pair of spectacles, which were associated with a weak intellect ('to sell someone eyeglasses' was Dutch slang for 'to deceive'). Sex, of course, was another product arrayed in plenitude – tourists could obtain a map of the city's red-light districts, which featured women whose whispered sighs came with French, Swedish and German accents. If they weren't put off by the charming nicknames of some of the girls (e.g. Krentecut: Currant Cunt), the new arrivals might have found the sheer variety hard to pass up.

Art and printing were among the goods on offer. There were stalls in which art brokers sold paintings created for the home market, with an emphasis on those two iconic Dutch genres – landscape and still life – that in their very nature spoke of a society broken loose from religious dominance of its mental life and satisfied a secular consumer urge for evocative scenes and a precise, almost eastern fascination with ordinary objects in the here-and-now (the terms themselves came into English via the Dutch *landschap* and *stilleven*). Prints were common as well: at this moment those depicting the signing of the Treaty of Münster were everywhere, though, if you preferred, you could also find copies of the papal brief denouncing the treaties (much Vatican property had been 'secularized' in the agreements). There were also engraved portraits of the signatories of the treaty, pictures of various Dutch towns reacting to news of the treaty, and pictures of companies of soldiers drinking quantities of beer in celebration of the treaty.

In addition to the increase in intensity – of population and activity – there had been a big change in Amsterdam's central square since Van der Donck had left for the colony of Rensselaerswyck in 1641. One whole side of it, formerly a sprawling neighbourhood, had been levelled, and in its place now stood the pilings and foundations of what would become the city's monument to itself in its ascendancy: a new town hall, built on classical lines, filled with art and slogans aligning the Dutch Republic with Rome and Greece. It was dedicated not only to the peace of '48 but to Peace itself, for, in the first waves of idealism following the diplomatic language about 'eternal peace', people really did seem to believe that they had just lived through the war to end all wars. As the tourist Van der Donck stood observing the first courses of stones being laid, that idea was still credible.*

But the Manhattanites didn't linger in the big city. Their business was pressing; as soon as they had rested themselves, they left, heading south-west.

Three centuries earlier, the corner of Holland that was their ultimate destination had been the country property of Willem, Count of Holland. Over time, it became useful as a commodious and convenient spot at which the medieval warlords of the region could meet and thrash out their differences. It was surrounded by a hedgerow that must have been a stunning feature of the landscape because people of the area took to calling the property itself 's-Gravenhage – the Count's Hedge. Even after the meeting spot became formalized into a court and a town grew up around it, the name stayed, though it was often shortened to Den Haag, which English emissaries transliterated as The Hague. From a provincial court, it grew into a national capital with the start of the war for independence.

* The finished building remains a tourist site, but it ceased to function as a town hall when it was converted into a palace in the nineteenth century, so that it is now known as the Royal Palace.

The city that Van der Donck and his colleagues entered in October of 1649 was small and stately – 'the largest village in Europe', people liked to call it – with meadows on one side, an oak forest on another and the dunes of the coast a short distance away. Planned government town that it was, it had its broad, tree-lined avenues where, of an evening, men of standing would promenade or ride in carriages with their families. Everything was clustered around the central government plaza called the Binnenhof, a four-sided fortress-like complex featuring government offices around the sides and, in the centre, the thirteenth-century Knights' Hall, the original meeting place of the medieval nobles.

It was a clunky, byzantine style of governing the Dutch had devised. Each of the seven provinces sent a delegation to the States General of whatever size they chose, though each province had only one vote. The few dozen men sat together around a single table, the title of president passing weekly from one province's leading delegate to the next. The tricky part was that all decisions required a unanimous vote, which made for intense politicking and few resolutions, something the Dutch seem not to have minded terribly, taking the view on the whole that the less the government actually did the better.

On 13 October, not more than a few days after their arrival, Van der Donck and his comrades won a spot on the States General's daily calendar of business and took the opportunity to present the document Van der Donck had crafted on Manhattan, the 'Remonstrance of New Netherland, and the Occurrences There, Addressed to the High and Mighty Lords States General of the United Netherlands, by the People of New Netherland'. Van der Donck the jurist, a bit over thirty years of age, took the lead. He had earned it; it had taken years of struggle, against Kieft and then Stuyvesant – winning a seat on the representative body, canvassing Manhattanites, being imprisoned and released – and finally a long journey back across the ocean to get to this point. In addition to the Remonstrance, he laid before the governing body several supporting documents, including a letter from the board of nine introducing him and his colleagues and, as a coup, a letter of reference he had coaxed out of Van Dinklagen, Stuyvesant's disgruntled vice-director. 'These persons are thoroughly conversant with the situation of the country,' he had written of Van der Donck and his colleagues. 'I hope your High Mightinesses will be pleased thereby and extend them a favorable audience.'

It was a ripe moment for the Manhattan delegation to present its petition. The nation was still in the throes of its independence celebrations, and the speed with which the rulers took up the matter suggested that they were disposed to look favourably on the colonists. They knew the name Manhattan well by now, knew of the West India Company's mismanagement of the colony and were ready to do something about it. The delegation presented itself with clarity and a distinct élan. Above all else, they called for 'suitable municipal government' for New Amsterdam. Van der Donck first painted for them an idyllic word picture, asking them to imagine this island, 'Manhathans ... the Capital of New Netherland', with its glorious geographical placement, 'very well adapted on account of the convenience of the river', and an ideal base from which 'we may pursue our country's trade ... from Terra Nova to Cape Florida ... to the West Indies and to Europe, wherever the Lord our God shall be pleased to permit'. Then came the looming threat: the New Englanders, he added, were 'fully aware that our country is better than theirs'; so the States General had to move swiftly to increase trade and settlement. Otherwise, the English would surely take over, and 'It will lose even the name of New Netherland, and no Dutchman will have anything to say there.'

Van der Donck's personal style is apparent not just in the individual elements of the presentation but in its exhaustiveness. He could not be content with the lengthy Remonstrance on its own, but had added to it a 'Petition of the Commonalty of New Netherland to the States General'. Then, for the benefit of the committee members who would study the matter in detail, he added a long section of 'Additional Observations on the Preceding Petition'. This, in turn, he footnoted to within an inch of its life, so that every aspect of the delegates' case – the limitless potential of the colony, the legality of the Dutch claim to the territory, the rights of the people who inhabited it – was covered, documented, supported, cross-referenced. The man's exuberance comes through in the utter mania of his documentation, which reads in parts like the output of a law clerk on amphetamines. A single sentence of what are already 'Additional Observations' might have eight footnotes. At one point, in a sentence in which Van der Donck says that he and his colleagues presume to know the reasons for the colony's mismanagement, which he then goes on to enumerate, he footnotes the word 'presume' in order to add: 'Not that there is any doubt of it; for it is as clear and notorious as that the sun emits light.'

Then came the props – supporting materials to give the rulers graphic reminders of the fat promise of their overseas province. Beaver pelts were laid before the high and mighty gentlemen: still reeking of the American forests, they seemed almost illicit, in this civilized setting, in their bushy fecundity. And there were samples of unspecified 'fruits' of the land, which, given the season and timing of the journey, might have meant tobacco, pumpkins, squash, beets, apples, nuts or corn, and certainly sacks of grain, of which the colonists were proud ('I have seen rye', Van der Donck himself would write elsewhere, 'which grew so tall that a man of common size would bind the ears together above his head').

Realizing that, like as not, these rulers had no clear idea of the geography of the area in question, Van der Donck also produced a meticulous hand-drawn map – probably created by Augustin Herman, who was a skilled cartographer – showing the province in its entirety, covering the coast from Maine to Virginia and extending as far west as central Pennsylvania.

There was perhaps one further piece of documentation. In

1992, a researcher at the Austrian National Library came across two pieces of a coloured pen-and-ink townscape that had for decades been shelved separately. Fitting them together, he realized he had an early view of New Amsterdam – one that fits into the history of the Dutch colony at precisely this moment. This delicately coloured illustration shows a motley spread of dwellings – some of wood, some gabled brick – hugging the shoreline, and a crude fort sporting the Dutch flag. There are no people in the scene. There is reason – which will be discussed below – to believe that Van der Donck brought this almost haunting portrait of his colony's capital to cap his presentation.

All of this work – the delegates' own efforts and those of others on Manhattan who were supporting them – was done, Van der Donck declared, with a touch of feeling surely unusual in an official communication, 'for the love of New Netherland'. Then, having spread these layers of details and baskets of bounty before the men of government, he brought his presentation to a graceful end, expressing the hope that the mighty rulers would 'interpret most favorably this our presumption'.

Presumption was the right word. The context into which the Manhattan activists dropped their proposals requires a bit of unpacking if we are to appreciate their nerve to the full. The Dutch system in the seventeenth century was one in which power ran through well-worn channels. The States General was a fairly weak national body, rather like the original confederation that existed for the first eight years of American independence (the customary title of 'High and Mighty Gentlemen' being something in the nature of a compensation); it had sway in overseas matters, such as overseeing colonial affairs, but most power was held by the provinces, and by the great overseas trading companies, which functioned almost as branches of government. The maintaining of overseas trading posts by these companies – and their right to make money from them – was deeply embedded in the system. Yet Van der Donck was quite explicit in what he asked of the leaders: 'In our opinion this country will never flourish under the Honorable Company's government . . . It would, therefore, be better and more advantageous for the country and themselves were they rid of it and the remnant of their property transported hence.' Remove the niceties and the request is: 'Get them out of here, and their belongings too.' It was a call to change the system, to strip West India Company shareholders of a property into which they had put enormous amounts of money and to have the central government take over that property and give it political status within the Dutch system.

For Van der Donck, Melyn, Loockermans, Herman and their colleagues to expect the States General to undercut the entire political and economic system of the newly independent country for the sake of a few merchants and settlers clustered on a distant island was certainly bold. So bold, in fact, that some historians have seen their mission as a freak, a pipe-dream – very forward-looking, perhaps, and in a way anticipating the political demands made during the American Revolution, but basically out of step with the times.

It was no such thing. As an illustration of how Van der Donck's undertaking meshed with other events, shortly before the delegates had set sail from Manhattan, news of the beheading of King Charles in London that January reached the colony. By the time Van der Donck arrived in Holland, a debate was being waged via pamphlets – which, in the era before the coming of newspapers, were the national soapboxes – on the rights of the people and the limits of monarchs. It was sparked by the presence in the Dutch Republic – to be precise, at the Honselaardijk Palace near The Hague, where he had been living in splendour and taking as full advantage of Dutch haven as had waves of humbler refugees from across Europe – of none other than Charles's son and would-be successor, the future Charles II. One prominent intellectual took the line of the traditionalists and argued that even if King Charles had been guilty of crimes that warranted execution, the law of primogeniture, by which power was transferred in a hereditary monarchy, demanded that his son, who had not participated in the crimes, should become the new king, and thus that it was right for the country to harbour him until the Cromwellian madness had passed. But other people felt uncomfortable about harbouring a fugitive royal. In the freewheeling public forum of the Dutch Republic a law student from the University of Utrecht, a young Dutchman very much of Van der Donck's ilk, fired off a responding pamphlet, which was printed and read everywhere, proclaiming that, in the new Europe, and in a newly independent republic, such attachment to royalty was out of step with the times. Monarchs, he declared, derived their power not from God but from the people. Van der Donck's cause was not king-versus-people, of course. But this debate about the limits of a king's power shows that what it was about – the right of a people to have a voice in their government – was a subject very much in the public mind at the time the Manhattan delegates presented their case.

There was also outright political activism in the air. As Van der Donck was beginning his mission in The Hague on behalf of the colony, a former Jesuit named Franciscus van den Enden was organizing a kind of Socratic academy in Amsterdam, encouraging young men to experiment freely with ideas of democracy and social equality. The most famous student to emerge from Van den Enden's coterie was Baruch Spinoza, the Amsterdam Jew who would become notorious in his lifetime, and legendary beyond, for continuing to develop the principles of modern philosophy laid down by Descartes. Some of the ideas that would emerge from this circle – democratic government, communal living, joint ownership of property, questioning the literal truth of the Bible, a state school system – sound almost freakishly modern, which makes the point that the roots of the modern world go back further than is often thought.

Van den Enden's circle would have had a natural sympathy with Van der Donck and his idealistic scheme for his colony. It's possible that Van der Donck got to know them during his time in

Holland. Certainly they eventually came to know of the Dutch colony, perhaps as a result of his efforts, and would come to make it the focus for one of their schemes, a bizarre, proto-communist experiment in utopian living. A decade after Van der Donck's mission, Van den Enden would write a draft constitution for such a community, to be based in the American colony. The group actually won a charter for the venture, and in 1663 forty-one latter-day Pilgrims, led by Pieter Plockhoy (who has become known as a father of socialism), settled on Delaware Bay, on land Stuyvesant had won back from the Swedes. But the timing was bad. Just months later, the English took over the whole Dutch colony of New Netherland, and when they did they destroyed the utopian settlement. Plockhoy himself would survive and live the last thirty years of his life in the New World, ending his days upriver, a resident of the new city of Philadelphia.

Like Van der Donck's mission, these projects were probably overly idealistic, products of the first wave of thinkers to come along in the wake of men like Descartes and Grotius, who had aspired to shift the centre of human effort from the church to the human mind. But if, in the end, Van der Donck and his colleagues did not get all they wanted, they did nevertheless change the system and pave the way for a new society. Why American history has overlooked their accomplishment has to do in part with anglocentrism and also probably with something as mundane as the way colonial studies have traditionally been divided in American universities: English departments focusing on the English colonies, the Spanish colonies covered in the Spanish departments, and so on. This meant both that the Dutch colony was relegated to the margins (few American universities have Dutch departments) and that colonial studies as a whole were approached narrowly. The discipline of history has broken down some of those walls in recent years, as it has become clear that educated Europeans of the seventeenth century were aware of the world and their place in it, and were affected by distant events. To understand events in one region therefore requires an appreciation of what was going on elsewhere. The fact that one volume of primary source material crucial to understanding what the Dutch did on Manhattan Island is entitled *Curaçao Papers* illustrates the point. There were global networks even then.

Give Van der Donck's mission its context, therefore, and it pops into relief. The records of the colony, still being translated and published, show a churning settlement inhabited by a mix of tough individuals who see the possibilities of the place and want to explore them. It was a society – something worth fighting for. Then, too, the colonists were quite connected to the wider world. What fuelled Van der Donck and his colleagues, what drove them in their idealism, was the spirit of the age. Extraordinary things were happening in Europe, and they knew it. They wrestled with the implications of the Treaty of Münster, and the broader Peace of Westphalia. Like the delegates to the treaty talks, like the members of Van den Enden's circle, they were following in the footsteps of Hugo Grotius, applying his principles of law to their New World colony.

It is also noteworthy that, as radical as the colonists' petition may have been, it was treated seriously in the halls of government. Following the initial presentation, the high mightinesses shuffled in their chairs, flipped through pages, discussed the matter and appointed a committee to explore it in depth. It had been a nagging issue; now was the time to deal with it.

There must have been some revelling that night in The Hague. The three Americans had to have been delighted with their first appearance before the governing body. But if they hoped for a speedy resolution of their case, they were soon disappointed. Within a matter of days the States General found itself in the middle of a royalist crisis of its own, which had been building for some time and which now swept all lesser matters aside. The Dutch government was based not on a written constitution, but on a patchwork of institutions and laws, some quite forward-thinking, others relics of the feudal past. It was a republic, but it also had its noble families, and it had a first family, the House of Orange and Nassau. By long tradition, the Prince of Orange was elected as stadtholder – an office akin to president, but one whose duties were ambiguous. The ambiguity had been a source of irritation to the previous Prince of Orange, Frederik Hendrik, who had served as stadtholder since 1625, had led the armies to victory in the war on Spain, and had steadily and astutely increased his power during his life. His ultimate objective was to convert his family to the status of monarchs, but his big step in that direction had been fantastically ill-timed: in 1641 he had married his fifteen-year-old son, Willem, to Mary Stuart, the nine-year-old daughter of Charles I of England. At virtually the same moment the first English Civil War began, and by the last year of the decade Charles, to whom Frederik Hendrik had linked his fortunes, was headless.

From the beginning, the Dutch were annoyed that their premier noble family had hitched itself to royalty, and to doomed royalty at that. Frederik Hendrik's second major blunder was to try to waylay the peace talks at Münster. The Eighty Years War had been very good for his family; it had made his father, William the Silent, into an icon, the 'father of the nation'. Beyond that, the stadtholder was the head of the army; peace with Spain would mean a shrivelling of his significance. But the merchant rulers of the province of Holland, and especially of the city of Amsterdam, had determined that peace was in their interest, and history moved in their direction. The peace treaty was signed, and, just as it became clear that he had lost, Frederik Hendrik died.

The matter was far from over, however. The new stadtholder, Willem II, was now twenty-one, volatile, arrogant, and as indifferent towards his advisers as he was towards his English child-wife. He was clever but wild, and soon proved a more dangerous force than his father. Only days after the Manhattan delegates had presented their petition, the States of Holland – the regional assembly of the province of Holland, which also met at The Hague – voted to decommission many of the soldiers in its pay. It ought to have been an ordinary postwar measure; the world over, when wars are concluded, armies downsize. But every soldier lost was a lessening of the stadtholder's power, and Willem reacted as if stung. He sent out orders of his own to the army officers, instructing them to maintain their troops. The officers obeyed the prince. The joyous atmosphere of The Hague instantly clouded. The States General hastily arranged to talk things over with the prince. He agreed to a reduction in troop totals, but only if those let go were Dutch. This sent a chill through the nation's chattering classes; all knew that a sizeable portion of the army consisted of mercenaries, and that, in the event of a schism between the prince and the States General, these foreign hirelings would be more inclined to stay at his side, less likely to succumb to patriotism. It was suddenly clear that Willem, feeling his power threatened, was actively considering a military move against his own newly independent nation. In fact, Willem was even more intent than his father had been on exchanging the title of stadtholder for a crown. In secret meetings with the French ambassador, he had already accepted French offers to help him achieve what the ambassador referred to in a report as 'a grandeur far beyond that of his predecessors'.

With the government facing a crisis of this magnitude, all lesser business came to a halt. Van der Donck refused to sit still, however, and used the time to strike out in another direction. The colony wasn't merely a political cause; it also needed settlers, traders, shippers. Maybe most of all, it needed publicity. So he switched from politician to public relations agent, and went off in search of a printer who would publish his 'Remonstrance'. It wouldn't be easy; the document was a sustained attack on one of the most powerful companies in the country. It would have to be a publisher unafraid of controversy.

He found his man. Michiel Stael was a 24-year-old baker's son who, in the wake of the peace treaty, had left his hometown of Delft to come to the capital and set up as a printer of books and pamphlets. He had chosen his time well; Europe was churning with political and intellectual activity in the aftermath of Westphalia, and the Dutch Republic was the publishing capital of the continent. At the turn of the century there had been four publishers in The Hague; now there were thirty-nine. Stael was eager to make a name for himself. At the time Van der Donck found him, he had just begun, publishing a few pamphlets for the French market. The work he was soon to do reveals a sharp taste for controversy. Nearly all his output for the years 1649 and 1650 would be political, and the titles suggest both the international nature of his business and the hot-off-the-press currency of their contents: *Two Letters of General Cromwell, Telling the Particulars of the Battle Between the English and Scottish Armies at Dunbar*, *Propositions of the Ambassador of Spain to the Lords States General*, *Letter of a Private Individual to the Parliament of Paris on the Detention of Princes Condé, de Conty and Longueville*. He had a penchant for radical politics; in 1650 he would get into trouble with the law for producing publications critical of some of the leading men in Holland – proving that even in the most liberal of publishing climates there were limits. At one point he would be put in the stocks. His career in The Hague would reach its climax with his being chased by law officers through the streets of the city and into an inn (the 'Bend of Guinea'), whence he would escape through a window. He turned up in Rotterdam a few years later and continued publishing.

Van der Donck found Stael in the cramped apartment he shared with his wife, their child and his business partner. The print shop was also on the premises, and, appropriately for a man drawn to danger, the place looked out across the outer court of The Hague onto the Gevangenpoort, a squat brick building with an arched gateway that gave entrance into the government complex and also served as the town prison.* With his penchant

* The Gevangenpoort still stands, and is today a museum of torture and punishment.

for goading men in power, Stael must have been delighted by Van der Donck's document and its radical proposal to divest the West India Company of one of its own provinces. As a businessman, he must also have sensed a market for the work – the West India Company was widely seen as a failure now (its share price, once as high as 206 guilders, had fallen to 14) and a ripe target for ridicule. He agreed to publish the 'Remonstrance'.

Stael apparently introduced Van der Donck to an engraver named Hendrik Hondius, who lived a few doors away on the Buitenhof. Van der Donck wanted his map of New Netherland to be published alongside the 'Remonstrance', and it seems that Hondius put him in touch with his brother-in-law in Amsterdam, Johannes Jansson, to engrave it. If Van der Donck had done nothing else, publishing this map would have merited him a place in history. The so-called Jansson–Visscher map (Claes Visscher produced a corrected edition) would be reprinted thirty-one times between 1650 and the mid-1700s, would become the definitive map not only for the Dutch but for the English as well, and is still reproduced today as the most accurate rendering of north-eastern North America in the colonial period and one of the most beautiful examples of early mapmaking. It would show up in drawing rooms, shipping offices and libraries across Europe, and thus help permanently affix Dutch names – from Cape May to Lange Eylandt to Roode Eylandt (Rhode Island) – to much of north-eastern America. It also represents a fine example of the little-studied genre of cartographic propaganda: the conscious use of maps, especially by the Dutch and English, to imprint the imperial nations' mastery of the globe onto European minds. The Jansson–Visscher map purports to show north-eastern North America dispassionately, but in fact the Dutch colony is given central position, and, more to the point, the map associates the name of New Netherland with a distinct portion of the globe, an arc of the continent from Cape Cod to Delaware. This followed Van der Donck's dogged insistence on adhering to the broad boundaries originally established by

Henry Hudson and the explorer who followed him, Adriaen Block.

There was one other item of propaganda embedded in the map. The little pen-and-ink view of New Amsterdam, which Van der Donck had apparently brought with him to illustrate the mournful countenance of the colony to the States General, was to serve a second function. Just as he would use the 'Remonstrance' twice – once to impress the rulers with the woeful condition of the colony, and again as a public relations tool to entice settlers – Van der Donck seems to have taken the piece of art to the engraver Johannes Blaeu and asked him to create something from it suitable for publication. The finished coloured engraving, labelled 'NIEUW AMSTERDAM op 't Eylant Manhattans', would appear both in stand-alone editions and as an inset view on later editions of the map; it follows the pen-and-ink illustration in every detail, except that where the original artwork shows a tumbledown village devoid of humans, the Manhattan town in Blaeu's engraved view is pert and orderly – chimneyed, gabled, weather-vaned, and bristling with life. Van der Donck's personality as an unflagging partisan for his New World colony, and his willingness to flex the truth to suit his audience, is stamped on these items, which are now housed in museums and libraries around the world.

About this time, with the States General preoccupied and Stael getting the 'Remonstrance' ready for publication, Van der Donck journeyed south to his native city of Breda to visit his family. Of his two sisters and three brothers, with their spouses and children, most seem to have been living in Breda at this time. His sister Agatha had gone off to Amboyna with her husband, an official in the East India Company, but had returned after he died there; his sister Johanna was soon to marry a local merchant. So we can imagine a boisterous homecoming, there in the (comparatively) sunny southern city, with its buildings clustered in medieval fashion around the gothic church. A year before, however, Van der Donck's parents had done something unusual for the times even in what was the most progressive society in Europe: obtained a legal separation. Even more remarkable, it was his mother, Agatha van Bergen, who agreed to pay alimony to her husband. Little is known about Adriaen's father, Cornelis; clearly, what money and prestige the family had came from the Van Bergen side. It was Adriaen van Bergen, namesake and grandfather of Adriaen van der Donck, who had become legendary for his role in the liberation of Breda from the Spanish, and the fact that Agatha van Bergen was willing and able to pay her husband 100 guilders per year suggests that the money was hers by inheritance.*

The family greeted the long-gone son. It was a different human being who had returned to them; the bookish boy had become a man, with a wider gait and firmer grip. He had tramped over purple mountains, slept on forest floors, shared meals in native longhouses. For nine years he had breathed a different air. It was in his eyes and voice; Van der Donck arrived in Breda irradiated with enthusiasm, and not even whatever feelings he had over his parents' separation could quell it. To all his relations, he talked up the American colony that was his home and his cause as a land of opportunity. The only thing that was missing from this potential paradise he himself was in the process of arranging: good government. His passion, coupled with the admiration they must have felt for him – he who had gone into the wilderness as a boyish adventurer and returned a leader of men, a statesman, presenting his case before the national government – swept his family members off their feet. Over the next two years, both of his parents – separately – would liquidate their holdings, pack up everything and board ships for Manhattan. The same journey was made by one of his brothers, his wife, their son and several servants. Van

* Whereas in Britain, and the British colonies, property was passed down to the eldest son, in the Dutch system it was divided among all children, regardless of gender.

der Donck's zeal seems to have engulfed everyone in its path.

In The Hague, meanwhile, after a hiatus of some months, the colony's petition had been put back on the government calendar. Cornelis van Tienhoven – who had been working behind the scenes to undermine the Manhattan delegation – appeared several times and regaled the high and mighty leaders with information intended to show that the colony was not so badly off. Taxes levied at Manhattan, he argued, were favourable compared with what New Englanders paid. There was good farmland available to settlers. And in what is perhaps the earliest record of Manhattan's high cost of living, he produced a comparison chart of the going rates for farm animals in New Netherland and New England: a farmer on Manhattan could sell a year-old sow for twenty guilders, where in Boston it would fetch only twelve.

There is an irony in the contrasting views of the colony presented by the bitter rivals Van der Donck and Van Tienhoven. Van der Donck, in his effort to win support for an overseas province that he believed could in time out-earn the entire home country, stressed the bleak state of affairs there, at every turn skewing things towards the desperate, in many cases depicting as current the situation that had existed a few years earlier, in the aftermath of the Indian war. Van Tienhoven's brighter picture, designed to bolster the position of the existing regime, may have more accurately reflected the actual state of affairs. The irony is that Van der Donck's more forceful and elegant presentation, which after all was intended ultimately to bolster the colony, has over the long term swayed historians and contributed to the image of the Dutch-led settlement as inherently defective.

Despite Van Tienhoven's presentation before the committee, as Van der Donck returned to The Hague the real excitement was taking place outside the government chamber. Michiel Stael's pamphlet version of the 'Remonstrance' – dramatically retitled *Remonstrance of New Netherland, Concerning Its Location, Fruitfulness, and Sorry Condition* – had hit the streets, and it was making a stir not only in The Hague but in Amsterdam, Haarlem and elsewhere. The *Remonstrance* gave a grim picture of recent events and the colonists' struggle, but Van der Donck's descriptions of a vast, fertile land, 'capable of being entirely cultivated by an abundance of people . . . many very fine flats and maize lands' and 'very good meadows' that 'could with little labor be converted into good tillage land', of rich soil that bears crops 'with less labor and tilling than in the Netherlands', made an impression. His trademark tangents of poetic cataloguing (the trees of the colony: 'post-oak . . . butter oak . . . oil nut . . . hickory . . . water-beech . . . hedge beech, axhandle wood, two sorts of canoe wood, ash, birch, pine, lathwood, Imberen or wild cedar, linden, alder, willow, thorn, elder') added to the allure, inflaming the imaginations of people who had lived all their lives on forestless plains and polders.

The response to the publication – and to the accompanying map and illustration of New Amsterdam – was immediate. Perhaps through Stael (whose address was given on the title-page), people contacted the delegates and pronounced themselves ready to go, to pull up stakes and seek their fortunes on Manhattan. The directors of the West India Company were flabbergasted. 'Formerly New Netherland was never spoken of,' they wrote to Stuyvesant, 'and now heaven and earth seem to be stirred up by it and every one tries to be the first in selecting the best pieces [of land] there.' Van der Donck and his colleagues acted quickly. They found a ship's captain in Amsterdam willing to convey settlers to Manhattan. People streamed to the harbour; in a short time, 140 settlers, all paying their own way, had been accepted, and the skipper, Willem Thomassen, pronounced the ship full to capacity. He turned away hundreds more.

Van der Donck then moved to capitalize on this outpouring of interest in the colony. He composed a breathless petition to the committee of the States General – addressing in particular its chairman, Alexander van der Cappellen, whom Van der Donck knew to be an enemy of the West India Company – in which he described the turn of events: the ship now lay ready to sail, and its skipper and owners attested that had they six more such ships they would be able to fill them. '[I]n the hope of better government,' Van der Donck wanted the States General to see, 'more passengers begin to set their faces toward New Netherland, according as the passage and opportunity offer.' With his customary attention to detail, he then got the ship's captain to attest as much before a notary.

It seems to have been a classic case of popular will exerting sudden pressure on politicians. The same day that Van der Donck presented them with the evidence of popular interest in the colony, the States General fired off a series of letters to the various chambers of the West India Company, asking them to send representatives to The Hague to appear two weeks hence in a joint meeting with the delegates from Manhattan, to confer 'on the whole subject of New Netherland', and concluding: 'Wherein fail not.' A week later, Van der Donck got the Amsterdam chamber of the company to sign a contract with him and the other delegates to charter a ship capable of conveying an additional two hundred settlers to Manhattan. The company would foot the cost, and the delegates would arrange the details. The ship would set sail before 1 June.

He was the consummate promoter now, working on all fronts, and getting results. By now he had a close working relationship with the members of the committee of the States General who had been assigned to deal with the colony, and they were showing distinct signs of favouring the cause, each of which elicited a protest from Van Tienhoven. On the committee's recommendation, the States General decided to send a notary from The Hague to the colony; this in particular aroused Van Tienhoven's anger, for in doing so the leaders were taking certain political powers away from Stuyvesant and his council – away from the West India Company – and investing them in an official of the government. From Van der Donck's perspective, it was a step in the right direction.

Then, in April 1650, came the decisive ruling. With nearly all the principals gathered in the chamber – Van der Donck and his colleagues as well as representatives from most of the regional chambers of the West India Company – the committee issued a 'Provisional Order respecting the Government, Preservation and Peopling of New Netherland'. No doubt all leaned forward in their chairs as a member of the committee laboured through swathes of boilerplate text before declaring that the committee, 'having inquired into the system of government hitherto maintained in New Netherland', had concluded that the members of the States General 'cannot, and ought not any longer approve of the perverse administration of the privileges and benefits granted by charter to the stockholders of the West India Company [while] neglecting or opposing the good plans and offers submitted for the security of the boundaries and the increase of the population of that country'. There it was – the clear signal of the committee's verdict.

Then came specific orders to be put into effect. First and most importantly, 'within the city of New Amsterdam a municipal government' should be instituted. Until such a government came into being, the board of nine would continue to sit 'and have jurisdiction over small cases arising between Man and Man'. The committee also referred to the sudden popular interest in emigrating to the colony: 'Private vessels proceeding to the north parts of America and the islands thereabouts, shall be obliged to convey over all passengers who will present themselves to be taken to New Netherland'. And there was a recommendation that a sum of 15,000 guilders be put into an account for the benefit of would-be settlers who could not afford the passage.

Off on its own, unadorned by editorializing commentary, was a separate order: 'Petrus Stuyvesant, the present Director, shall be instructed to return home and report.'

That was it; the government had given its unequivocal support to the cause of the delegates. The company representatives were outraged; the Amsterdam chamber quickly prepared a rebuttal. Van der Donck, meanwhile, moved in for the kill. Not content even with this ringing endorsement of his presentation – for the orders still left the West India Company in charge of the colony – he addressed the committee. He was no longer a tentative outlander; six months of appearing at The Hague had given him confidence.

'Noble, Mighty Lords,' he began, flourishes of exultation empurpling his prose, 'The very laudable zeal which their High Mightinesses and you, Noble Mighty, have been pleased to evince as well for the preservation of whatever yet remains by God's especial blessing in ruined New Netherland as for the restoration of the sad and prostrate affairs there, supplies me with confidence and courage to lay before you, Noble Mighty, some means which will be highly necessary, and, according to all human calculation, advantageous and profitable to their High Mightinesses' design herein.'

He didn't want the States General to forget that the suffering of the settlers of the Manhattan-based colony was due to the disastrous actions of certain West India Company officials – 'how much innocent blood, as well of heathens as of Christians and even of sucklings, hath been unnecessarily and barbarously shed'. He asked the committee to accept into the record the list of interrogatories to be put to Van Tienhoven that he had drawn up on Manhattan. Van Tienhoven and others responsible for the Indian war, he declared, should be prosecuted.

Van der Donck had noted that Van Tienhoven was disliked in The Hague, and hoped to build on that antipathy to broaden the provisional orders into an outright removal of the West India Company from the colony. But the committee took no action on that front. It did, however, approve of a plan to send two of the delegates – Bout and Van Couwenhoven – back to Manhattan, at the head of a party of settlers, both to convey to Stuyvesant the rulings and to deliver a shipment of guns for the defence of the colony. They headed off at once, exchanging exultant farewells with Van der Donck, who would stay to see that the committee's order was adopted by the States General.

Before they left, Van der Donck penned a secret letter they were to deliver. It was addressed to Dr La Montagne, who had served under both Kieft and Stuyvesant and whom Van der Donck now pinpointed as vital to the power politics being played. This letter was discovered as recently as 1997 – by Dr Jaap Jacobs, one of the pre-eminent Dutch historians working on the New Netherland colony – in the Amsterdam Municipal Archives; like a flashlight piercing a centuries-darkened room, it shows Adriaen van der Donck, at this most critical moment of his embassy to The Hague, alive to the wider currents of the era, playing the game of politics with zest and cunning. It also shows that he considered himself the leader of the activists' cause. 'The old friendship and familiarity bids me to write you these few lines in haste, in order that you may remain assured of our good will towards you,' Van der Donck begins, addressing the man who had sat in judgment on him when Stuyvesant had imprisoned him, but who seems to have taken pains to remain neutral in that and other debates. 'I have verbally charged and pressed upon Jacob van Couwenhoven many things to tell you from me, to which I refer.' Then Van der Donck begins massaging in the classic manner of politicians of every era. Certain of triumph, he assures La Montagne that 'you will be included in a good position' in 'the next government, which we expect shortly'. Then he comes to the point: 'It will be very good if you join ranks with the complainants. And it is my request that you will assist the Nine men as much as possible with advice and action.' Then he switches tacks to let La Montagne know that the winds of favour have changed direction, and that it would not be wise to remain in the ambit of the West India Company representatives: 'It is well known here that the authors of the war are not punished as they should have been . . . Tienhoven is not in much esteem here and . . . his actions and those of director Kieft regarding the war are damned here by the whole world. The directors try to do their best to defend Stuyvesant, his secretary and their supporters, but they themselves, except for a few, are not in much esteem but are regarded with suspicion.'

Clearly, Van der Donck foresaw a time in the very near future when New Amsterdam, and the entire Dutch colony, would be taken over by the government, given normal political status and made an integral part of the republic. In one of his petitions to the States General, he stresses the vital role he sees the colony playing in the future of the newly independent nation: 'this State . . . alone is of greater extent than the Seventeen Dutch Provinces*, and . . . in the hour of need, will be found a strong arm, by the assistance it will render in people and provisions; for after the population shall have increased, your High Mightinesses will carry on a very large trade from the one to the other of your own countries – hinc inde et inde hinc – without any save your High Mightinesses having control or authority over it.' Such an arrangement would have been unprecedented – almost as if New Netherland were an eighth province in the Dutch republic, a non-contiguous state along the lines of an Alaska or Hawaii. Had it happened, of course, history – American, English and Dutch – would have turned out very differently. In the spring of 1650, at least in Van der Donck's mind, it was a real possibility. The government was on the side of the colonists, Stuyvesant had been recalled and Van der Donck, an ocean away from Manhattan, was laying out a new administration.

* Here he is referring to all the provinces traditionally considered by the Dutch as part of their domain, including those that did not become part of the republic but would one day form the state of Belgium.

12
A Dangerous Man

AFTER ALL, PETER STUYVESANT WAS A COUNTRY BOY. BESIDES, a military compound was no place for toddlers to toddle, no place for a woman. So, some time around 1650, he must have loaded his wife and their two young sons into a wagon and headed north up the Highway. Within five minutes they were in open country, meadows and pastureland punctuated by stands of forest. The road turned sharply to the right to skirt the bouwerie of his secretary, Van Tienhoven, then cut northwards, elbowing through wilderness, before opening, on the left, onto an expanse of lots that were being farmed by freed slaves. Soon this area would form a village in its own right, which for a time would be called Noortwyck, or North District, before a settler from the Long Island village of Greenwyck (Pine District) would relocate here and give his property that name. (It would seem to be from this, not from English sources, that Greenwich Village would receive its name.) Turning right off the Bouwerie Road, as this stretch of the trail was known, Stuyvesant brought his family down a lane and into the patch of the island he was in the process of taming as his own. In its marshy serenity – snipes and widgeons alighting on swampy ponds, stiff winds coming off the river bending the grasses, cows gathering in groups under bruised skies – it may have reminded him of home. It was

2 miles from the pit of troubles that was the capital city of his domain, and it must have seemed an ocean away. From the beginning, the West India Company had set aside this stretch of acreage for the use of the director of the colony, to be farmed by his workers, and Kieft and his predecessors had used it so. Stuyvesant had other ideas. He was a family man now, and he wanted to put down his roots. Within the year he would arrange to buy the farm, called Bouwerie Number One, outright from the company, and then purchase acreage on both sides of it, giving him a plantation stretching from the East River to the centre of the island and covering approximately 300 acres. Here he built a manor and a chapel. Here he would live out his life and be buried, and here, over the parade of centuries, flappers, shtetl refugees, hippies and punks – an aggregate of local residents running from Trotsky to Auden to Charlie Parker to Joey Ramone – would shuffle past his tomb.*

Leaving Judith with the young armfuls of Balthazar and Nicholas, he rode daily from this retreat into the maelstrom, greeting, as he passed the company orchard and cemetery and approached the cluster of streets of the town, the matrons, Indians, tapsters, smugglers, sailors and Africans, the toughs and urchins, the refugees and erect citizens and the slope-shouldered, eye-patched miscreants that formed his populace. And they in turn, at the unmistakable sight of him, with his cuirass and sword, a military princeling on his steed, offered lusty hellos or muttered curses depending on their political views. And then he disappeared into the fort, stiff as oak and ready to work. He was forty years old, beset by troubles on all sides, but possessed of a personality that fed on adversity.

The wounds kept coming, and many were still being inflicted by Van der Donck, even from an ocean away. Every time the

* As a nice metaphor for the way history has muddled Manhattan's Dutch period, Stuyvesant's tombstone, embedded in the foundation of the Church of St Mark's-in-the-Bowery, manages to get both his age and his title wrong.

Dutch flag appeared in the harbour these days, the sheaf of news that came with it was stippled with his doings. These 'seditious persons, like Cornelis Melyn, Adrian van der Donck and some others . . . seem to leave nothing untried, to upset every kind of government,' the company directors wrote to him in February 1650. By April they had apparently learned of Stuyvesant's former friendliness towards Van der Donck and were exasperated that he had given the man an intimacy that he had then exploited for political purposes. 'We suppose that you have trusted too much in some of these ringleaders or become too familiar with them,' they wrote, 'now that their ingratitude and treachery have come to light, you must still act with the cunning of a fox.'

It was annoying to be scolded in this way, and infuriating that Van der Donck seemed to have charmed the States General into siding with him and his cronies. Stuyvesant had by now heard of the provisional orders for the reorganization of the colony, but no-one had yet sent him a command to enforce them. Far from preparing to do so, he reacted to the threat posed by Van der Donck's mission by becoming not more conciliatory but more summary. He decided that he had had enough insubordination from his deputy director, Van Dinklagen, and had the man thrown into prison. He placed spies among the board of nine and their associates. He virtually gave up on the quaint idea of allowing the people a voice in their government, and more and more took to deciding matters on his own. Augustin Herman and the other leaders of the opposition sent Van der Donck a stream of correspondence, keeping him updated on these turns of events. 'We live like sheep among wolves, one friend not being able to speak to another without suspicion,' one despatch read. 'He proceeds no longer by words or writings,' went another, 'but by arrests and stripes.' Reading the pages of complaints against Stuyvesant, you feel in his harshness the uncorking of a long-bottled fury the sources of which are at least guessable. There was the dutiful son of a minister who had watched his godly and upright father remarry and lustily devote himself to his new young bride. There was the would-be wooer so embarrassingly pent up that the brother of the woman he wished to marry bet that he would be unable to ask for her hand. Finally, there was the administrator who put his trust in a protégé only to see the favoured youngster turn on him and up-end heaven and hell to have him ousted.

And he was already having to deal with the practical repercussions of Van der Donck's activities: the incoming ships were packed with new arrivals, seasickened and unwashed but ready to stake a claim, and this too was a result of the delegation. 'Many free people are coming over in this ship . . . Many free people have taken passage on these two ships . . . It looks as if many people will come over by every ship.' There was a hint of annoyance in the directors' letters – 'people here encourage each other with the prospect of becoming mighty lords there, if inclined to work' – but they had to admit that 'it may have a good result'.

Ironically, while Van der Donck was devoting a large part of his zeal to getting Peter Stuyvesant ejected from his post as director of New Netherland, Stuyvesant himself was executing some brilliant diplomacy, working hard to ensure the stability of the colony in the face of its steadily encroaching neighbours to the north. Indeed, it is owing to the successes of both of these bitter rivals that New York City would develop as it did. Had either failed, the English would probably have swept in before Dutch institutions were established, New York would have become another English New World port town like Boston and American culture would never have developed as it did.

In his three years on Manhattan, Stuyvesant had nudged and nagged the New England governors in repeated attempts to get them to settle the boundaries between the English and Dutch territories. They had declared their desire to meet, but then had prevaricated and stalled. And when the aged John Winthrop, on whom Stuyvesant had depended as his best ally among the Puritan leaders, died in 1649, that put another spanner in the works. But Stuyvesant was a soldier as well as a diplomat; he knew the maxim that force can help bring the other side to negotiate, and now he put it to work. It happened that a Dutch trading vessel owned by an Italian businessman based in Amsterdam had put into harbour at New Haven. Stuyvesant had determined that the vessel – the *St Beninio* – was engaged in smuggling. According to Dutch claims, the entire New Haven colony lay in Dutch territory. By now there were so many English settlers there that the point was academic, but Stuyvesant saw the ship's presence as the pretext for an attention-grabbing act. He had previously sold one of the West India Company's ships to the deputy governor of New Haven, with a promise to deliver it. Now – with utter audacity, considering that he was at the same time sending polite diplomatic letters to the governor – he undertook a bit of derring-do generally reserved for wartime, known as cutting a ship out of harbour. He had the vessel to be delivered to New Haven stuffed, Trojan-Horse-like, with soldiers. As her skipper brought her into the harbour at New Haven, he came in alongside the *St Beninio*; his soldiers leaped aboard, cut the ship's lines, took command, and piloted her out to sea and back to New Amsterdam.

As expected, Theophilus Eaton, the rigid Puritan governor of New Haven, fired off a letter, practically tripping over his clauses in his outrage,* declaring that Stuyvesant had violated his colony's territory and absconded with a ship doing peaceable business there. Stuyvesant replied with mock innocence ('For what have I either written or done, that may seeme offensive . . .') while at the same time asserting that the vessel in question was a Dutch ship, that it had violated Dutch laws, and – the *coup de grâce* – that the Dutch regarded the territory in

* 'And now latelie in a ship belonging to Newhauen, as bought by Mr. Goodyeare, yow haue sent armed men, & (without lycence, not soe-much as first acquainting any of the magistrates of this Jurisdiction with the cause or grownds thereof) ceised a shipp within our harbour . . .'

question as theirs by right of first discovery. In subsequent letters he politely reminded the New England governors of the overwhelming might of the Dutch navy, without bothering to mention that virtually none of that might was under his control.

At the same time, he turned on the charm to John Endecott, Winthrop's replacement as governor of Massachusetts (we 'Congratulate and reioyce that our neighbours there have Chosen soe worthy & prudent a successour'), in hopes that Endecott would continue Winthrop's tack of treating with the Manhattanites. It worked – the two forged a relationship. Indeed, one of the curiosities of Stuyvesant's term in office was his tendency to impress and even befriend potential enemies – English ones in particular – while treating his own colonists more or less like dirt. Eaton of New Haven and Edward Hopkins of Connecticut remained moody about the Dutch, but the combination of Stuyvesant's wooing of Endecott and his brinkmanship with the southern New Englanders – stealing a ship, resurrecting the Dutch claim to their lands and brandishing the bogeyman of the Dutch navy – got results. Endecott and the other leaders of Massachusetts wanted peace; they forced the other New Englanders to agree to Stuyvesant's offer to meet and sort out their boundaries, and instructed their delegates to 'doe your utmost endeavor to make up an Agreement between [the Dutch] and Newhaven & Conecticott least if a warre or broiles arise betweene them wee be chardged and encoragged in it'.

The governors wanted to meet in Boston; Stuyvesant suggested Manhattan. The compromise was Hartford, some miles up what the Dutch called the Fresh River. It was a humming little community of pious breakaways from the other New England territories, but right in its midst sat a squat and forlorn outpost manned by a handful of Dutch soldiers. Twenty-seven years earlier traders from Manhattan had been the first Europeans to establish themselves here, but the population of the Dutch colony was too thin to enable them to cover the region, and they had been forced to watch the English muscle in.

Here Stuyvesant alighted from his ship in September 1650, pegged up the quay, no doubt greeted Gysbert op Dyck, the commander of the Dutch fort, and moved on to meet his four fellow statesmen. With him as secretaries and interpreters were two Englishmen, George Baxter and Thomas Willett; had things gone differently, this no doubt would have been an occasion where he would have relied on Van der Donck.

The negotiations were intense but cordial. The New Englanders pulled out their best wines and otherwise treated Stuyvesant like a visiting head of state. Eaton and Hopkins did not want to give quarter, but Stuyvesant and Endecott had stacked the deck in their favour by ensuring that all of New England's negotiators were from the less anti-Dutch colonies of Massachusetts or New Plymouth. In the final agreement, Stuyvesant gave up only what was already lost: the territory now indisputably occupied by New Haven and Connecticut. In exchange, he won acknowledgement by the English of a 'permanent' boundary between them and the Dutch colony. The negotiators drew a north–south line that ran through Long Island and the mainland, and gave the eastern two-thirds of the island and territory on the mainland east of present-day Greenwich, Connecticut, to New England, and western Long Island and lands west of the same point on the mainland to the Dutch. Today, the division of Long Island into counties with distinctly Dutch and English names – Nassau and Suffolk – reflects this agreement, though the county line runs about 10 miles east of the Hartford Treaty line. The Dutch were also allowed to keep their meagre trading post, bravely named the 'House of Hope', in Hartford.*

It was a remarkable achievement for Stuyvesant. He had used diplomacy and bluff to leverage what little military power he had to advantage; he had given up only what had already been

* The fort lives on – sort of – in the name of Huyshope Avenue in downtown Hartford.

lost, and in exchange had won from his English neighbours recognition of his colony's sovereignty. The two southern New England colonies were disgruntled, but the line held: throughout the lifetime of the Dutch colony, there would be no invasion from the north.

*

In The Hague, meanwhile, the Prince of Orange was once again upsetting things. On 5 June 1650 regular business in the States General chamber was disrupted when the hot-blooded Willem, still incensed over the attempt by the province of Holland to reduce the size of his army, appeared in person and announced that he intended to lead a contingent of soldiers to all the cities of Holland to explain to the military commanders of each that the only valid orders regarding disbanding would come from him. Van der Donck, his ceaseless political activity suddenly baulked by this new crisis, was no doubt in the crowd that gathered in the centre of The Hague three days later to observe the grim spectacle of four hundred soldiers, Willem flamboyantly at their head, assembling and riding off in the direction of Dordrecht.

The mission failed. In the face of this major power struggle between the prince and the strongest province in the republic, the towns of Holland closed ranks behind their provincial leaders; some even refused the prince entry. He returned to The Hague in a rage, stalked into the chamber where the States of Holland met and demanded that the members from the city of Amsterdam withdraw their call for troop reductions. The Amsterdammers, feeling confident in their base of support, were in a position to respond with legalities. Technically, they informed Willem in an icy reply, it was the stadtholder who served at the pleasure of the provincial assembly, not the other way around. If anyone was in a position to give orders, it was the States. There was no possible rationale for keeping troop numbers at wartime levels. In their inactivity, the soldiers would soon start getting into trouble. It was time they went to their homes.

Willem's response was unprecedented: he ordered the arrest of several members of the provincial assembly. They were taken to nearby Loevestein Castle and held prisoner.

The news of this shocking breach of authority swept through The Hague. Crowds gathered spontaneously on the streets and plazas around the Binnenhof, and even as they gossiped they were further alarmed by the spectacle of mounted mercenaries gathering on the perimeter. Van der Donck's hot-blooded printer, Michiel Stael, seems to have put out a pamphlet on the affair, for which he was rewarded with a libel charge.

Then came the decisive stroke. At the end of July Willem Frederik, cousin of the Prince of Orange, led ten thousand troops on an all-night march across Holland. Their mission was to take Amsterdam by force. All of Holland was in shock: Willem was restaging the play that had just run in England, at terrible cost to all. A *coup d'état* was in progress.

But Willem's power play was foiled by the weather. Travelling across the province by night and in a lashing storm, the army arrived at the gates of Amsterdam well past daybreak, by which time the city magistrates had had warning and prepared their defences. Having lost the element of surprise, Willem Frederik paused. A delegation from the States General hurried to the scene to negotiate a settlement. A messenger brought the Prince of Orange the news of the army's blunder while he was at the dinner table. Seeing the end of his dream of royalty, he stormed into his private apartment, where, in the words of one writer, he 'was heard stamping his feet and throwing his hat upon the floor'. Soon thereafter the prince and the city reached a compromise on troop reductions. The crisis had passed.

Then Willem obliged history by dying immediately on the heels of his failed power grab. In an effort to wind down from the affair, he went on a hunting trip with his cousin and fell ill from what was apparently smallpox. On the night of 6 November the States General gathered for an emergency session to hear the startling news that the 24-year-old prince was dead.

Willem's coltish lunges for power kept the case of the Manhattan-based colony shelved for months. All the parties concerned stood on the sidelines and waited to see the outcome of the larger battle between the nation's leading nobleman and its most powerful city. In the course of the mad summer of 1650, it must have struck Van der Donck that his far-off colony, for all its seeming lawlessness, was hardly more chaotic or fragile than the civilized and supposedly stable home country. Far from trying to seize anything by force, he and his colleagues were following the rules – indeed, they were among the first Americans to exercise a right that would achieve near-hallowed status in the colonies and later in the nation, the right to petition the government for redress of grievances.

When the alarming interlude came to an end, however, the government could return to something like normal, and the cause of the colonists did not seem to have been hurt by the delay. Less than two weeks after Willem's death, Van der Donck was again before the States General, as was Van Tienhoven. All through the following winter and into the spring of 1651 the two men alternated in presenting their cases as Van der Donck tried to have the provisional orders for the reorganization of his colony put into force and Van Tienhoven tried to block them. Van der Donck had his foe repeatedly on the ropes, as the States General asked Van Tienhoven several times to submit answers to Van der Donck's interrogatories concerning his conduct during the Indian war. Each time, however, Van Tienhoven managed to dodge the issue.

Then, astonishingly, in the middle of this high-level politicking that was surely the most important work of his life, Van Tienhoven vanished. The States General had got word that the man might attempt to flee the country, and the governing body took the unusual step of issuing a decree forbidding him to leave. As information about his disappearance began to trickle out, the facts proved to be not only a blow to Stuyvesant and the West

India Company, but an embarrassment as well. Despite being grossly overweight, 'of red and bloated visage', and sporting a prominently juicy cyst – not to mention having a wife and children in New Amsterdam – Van Tienhoven fancied himself a ladies' man, and his flight had at its root, in addition to growing doubts over the chances of his mission at The Hague, in sex. The girl, Lysbeth Croon, was the daughter of an Amsterdam basketmaker, and Van Tienhoven had assured her that he was single and wanted to marry her on Manhattan. The matter blossomed into a fully fledged scandal, with witnesses dragged before notaries to give prurient testimony of lustful behaviour observed. (An undertaker's wife testified that Van Tienhoven had paid her 3 guilders to find a room for him and his young miss, which she did, 'at the house of a grocer . . . at the sign of the Universal Friend'. A tavernkeeper's wife reported that he 'evinced great friendship and love, calling her always, Dearest, and conversing with her as man and wife are wont to do, sleeping in one bed'.) Van Tienhoven was collared by the sheriff of The Hague and fined, and shortly afterwards, in defiance of the States General, he and the girl left the country, boarding a ship bound for Manhattan.

So it was with some exuberance that Van der Donck appeared before the entire governing body of the country on 10 February 1652 to make the final argument on behalf of his colony. His adversary had literally fled the field, and in the room were some of the most distinguished men in the country. Adriaen Pauw, who had hoped to retire after successfully concluding the Treaty of Münster, had been called back into service in the aftermath of Prince Willem's abortive coup, and now led the Holland delegation. Pauw would have had some personal interest in the American colony; two decades earlier, his brother, one of the directors of the West India Company, had founded one of the early patroonships on the Hudson River, to which he had given the latinized form of his surname, Pavonia. (He soon abandoned the project and sold the land back to the company, but it was the first permanent settlement in what would become New Jersey, and eventually became the cities of Hoboken and Jersey City.) Also present was Jan de Witt, who would soon rise to become leader of the nation and one of the great European statesmen of the age.

To these assembled worthies Van der Donck made an elaborate presentation energized by his and his colleagues' convictions: that Manhattan and its surrounding territory represented a vital foothold on the unexplored world of the North American continent; and that while the West India Company had squandered this opportunity, it was not too late to reverse the trend. What was needed was new thinking. The leaders of the republic should abandon the old ways that allowed the company's bureaucracy to treat it as a feudal possession, and instead take this land across the ocean into the bosom of Dutch law, give its people the rights of Dutch citizens, and give its capital the status of a Dutch city, with all the rights and protections that that entailed. Then they would see it flourish, and the Dutch Republic would reap the rewards.

Sensing victory, Van der Donck struck hard on the negative tack, summarizing the case against the West India Company and Stuyvesant, and, in typical fashion, methodically supporting his case with letters, journal entries, resolutions from the board of nine and sworn statements that his colleagues in New Amsterdam had sent him over the previous months, all of which showed that Stuyvesant had not only failed to carry out any of the reforms the committee had stipulated but had taken to ruling by fiat. His justice had become summary and brutal, especially against members of the board (he had confiscated property and threatened them with imprisonment or banishment unless they swore that they knew 'nothing of the Director and his government, but what is honest and honorable'). He had even blocked the notary sent over by the States General, forbidding him to do his job; this man had then joined the opposition, and his letters were included in the sheaf of complaints Van der Donck exhibited.

Nevertheless, the letters revealed that there was still great hope on Manhattan that Van der Donck's mission would achieve results. 'The people here are somewhat solaced on learning from the despatch that the affairs of New Netherland are beginning to be thoroughly and truly considered by their High Mightinesses, but they anxiously expect absolute Redress,' one letter read. 'Whatever you have done there for the public interest, I, for my part, do especially approve,' Augustin Herman wrote to Van der Donck. 'We are anxiously expecting the approval of the redress and a change.'

These updates on the situation in the colony had an effect on the assembly. Among other things, they drove home the point that the community on Manhattan could no longer be considered an ad hoc collection of soldiers, fur traders and whores, for whom martial law could suffice. The core of this society were men of standing, who had risked everything on the promise of North America, and their government had a responsibility towards them.

Van der Donck went on to discuss the Hartford Treaty, which he found particularly appalling. Not being in Stuyvesant's position on the front line, it was easy for him to denigrate the agreement for giving up land to the English. As Van der Donck saw it, the New England governors had 'pulled the wool over the Director's eyes', and he rued the loss of 'many fine bays, kills, rivers and islands . . . and the beautiful Fresh River [i.e. the Connecticut river], where full fifty Colonies or more might be planted.'

The presentation was thorough, and Stuyvesant had no-one there to offer any counterarguments. The chambers of the West India Company, asked by the government to respond, began to split into factions. The Manhattan-based colony had been 'monopolized' by the chamber from Amsterdam, declared the Zeeland representatives, and its mismanagement was Amsterdam's fault. The members from Dordrecht agreed, and suggested a reorganization of the colony's government. Sitting in their pretty little canalside offices just down the road from the house where Jan Vermeer was beginning his quiet career of creating quiet masterpieces, the members from Delft concurred that something had to be done 'in order that so magnificent a country may not go to ruin by bad government and management'.

The States General were wholly won over, and at last took the first steps towards a massive reorganization of the colony. Under pressure from the government, the Amsterdam directors sent Stuyvesant a grudging directive: 'in order to silence everyone', he was to establish a municipal government in New Amsterdam with 'a bench of justice formed as much as possible on the laws of this city'. The order was nearly lost in the shuffle of circumstances, but it would be enacted, and would change history.

There was some question whether Stuyvesant would have time to charter a city government, however, because in late April the States General drafted the letter Van der Donck had worked and waited for. It was telegraphically blunt:

> To Petrus Stuyvesant, Director General in New Netherland
>
> Honorable, etc. We have, in view of the public service, considered it necessary to require you, on sight hereof, to repair hither, in order to furnish us circumstantial and pertinent information, as to the true and actual condition of the country and affairs; also, of the boundary line between the English and Dutch there. Done 27 April, 1652.

The letter demanding Stuyvesant's recall was handed to Van der Donck to deliver in person. Holding it, stepping out of the chamber into the courtyard of the Binnenhof, he must have felt light-headed, drunk on his achievement. And crossing the colonnaded plaza – the same public square in which, seven decades earlier, the leaders of seven separate Dutch states had signed a declaration of independence from Spanish rule – can only have underscored the historic significance of it.

Had Van der Donck been a diarist of the likes of his younger contemporary Samuel Pepys, the page for this day would have been starred, and we might have had from it a follow-up scene of revelry at a 'Haagse' taphouse, with a throng of bureaucrats, in black hats and flowing capes, high boots perhaps topped with lace cuffs, suddenly conscious of their routine lives and routine government jobs as they gathered around the victorious representative from a far-off land, expressing keen interest, between pinches of snuff and swallows of Rhenish wine, in his holding forth on every aspect of his country, from its mythical-sounding flora and fauna, to the island capital so enticingly positioned to exploit the continent, to the intriguing sexual forthrightness of the native women ('They make light of their virtue,' Van der Donck would write, and while they scorn 'kissing, romping', and other sexual play, 'at the right time they will decline no proposition and almost all of them are available and ready to carry on with abandon.') There is little doubt that the men of government were taken with Van der Donck. The day before his victory, the States General voted a resolution granting him the right to pass his New Netherland estate on to his heirs – a power reserved for fiefholders such as Kiliaen van Rensselaer, and an indication both that Van der Donck was looking forward to returning home (and siring heirs) and that the officials had been won over as much by the man as by his vision for Manhattan.

It was with this vision in particular that he would have regaled listeners. The new government would definitively establish Manhattan Island as the free-trading hub of the Atlantic and would guarantee its status as gateway to the North American continent for generations of Europeans. It would be modelled on 'the laudable government' of the home country, with personal guarantees of freedom of conscience deriving directly from the Union of Utrecht ('each person shall remain free, especially in his religion'), the de facto Dutch constitution, which dated from the beginning of the war for independence and codified the nation's adherence to ideas of tolerance. And it would be based too on certain inherent rights of the people – even to overthrow their rulers should they become oppressive – which stemmed from the so-called Act of Abjuration, the Dutch declaration of independence from Spain.

Van der Donck was exultant, of course, believing that his work in Europe was at an end, and went through a blizzard of errands preparatory to departing for home. He had been away two and a half years, and his property was suffering in his absence. He hired several employees who would serve six-year contracts at Colen Donck. His wife had come to join him in the Netherlands sometime in the preceding year, and together they now purchased supplies and had them loaded for passage.* He had recently helped his mother sell some of her property, and now she, his brother and sister-in-law, and their servants were preparing to emigrate to Manhattan also. It was springtime: renewal was in the freshening winds, and the victorious emissary would soon be at sea, sailing homewards.

In May, Van der Donck appeared before a government committee formally asking to be allowed to return to Manhattan and resume his previous political role – 'to hold peaceably the office of President of the Commonalty in New Amsterdam'. He not only planned to be in the colony for the change of administration, not only to deliver personally Stuyvesant's walking papers – he planned to lead the new government.

*

It never happened, of course. The shot that sank Van der Donck's mission – robbing him of a major historical

* The ship's manifest listing Van der Donck's supplies still exists, and gives a nice snapshot of a settler's needs: whetstones, millstones, baskets of nails, 'farmer's stockings', shoes, linen, 'coarse woolen cloth', hats and caps, kettles, ribbons, thread, books and paper, '2 boxes and 2 barrels of steel', '8 casks of bird lime', '10 ankers of brandy', '32 cakes of soap' and a whopping '300 lbs. of pepper and 20 lb. cinnamon', suggesting Van der Donck hoped to do some trading in spices on Manhattan.

achievement, leaving him instead a spectral presence in history, author of a still remarkable but shadowy contribution – came from a thoroughly unexpected quarter. It wasn't Stuyvesant who upset things; his plans too would be waylaid by events. The disruption didn't come from the New England colonies or the Indians of New Netherland, or even from the Swedes camped out along the Delaware river to the south. Its origin was a grim and tempestuous creature who had burst to life, fifty-three years earlier, in the swampy fens of eastern England. As historical figures go, Oliver Cromwell, like Peter Stuyvesant, remains a deeply unlovable sort: complicated and vigorous, but somehow enduringly repellent – in Churchill's phrase, 'that smokey soul'. Soon after assuming power in the wake of the king's execution, he took actions that would help root America's myth of origin by viewing the New World through his religious lens. His Puritanism, sown in a strongly Calvinist upbringing and entrenched by personal spiritual conversion in his thirties, was virile and practical. He was all for the settling of North America, and, like John Winthrop, he considered New England a shining city on a hill, a potential promised land. At one point he had considered emigrating himself. While that didn't happen, he helped seed the American idea of manifest destiny: of a people preordained first to conquer the continent and then to lead the world.

His zeal knew no bounds; out of the ruins of civil war, he plotted a course to global dominance. With the backing of the nation's businessmen, he raised taxes and ordered the building of a new fleet of warships; under him, the modern English navy came into being – and the balance in the century's great rivalry began to shift from the Dutch to the English. Cromwell's 'Western Design' had several components. In North America, he would aid New England and try to dislodge the Dutch from Manhattan Island, which by now English traders were beginning to see as crucial to control of the continent. In the Caribbean, Cromwell had his eye on another key island:

Jamaica, which English troops would capture from the Spanish in 1655, would become a slave-trading base. He wouldn't get Manhattan, but English 'success' with the Jamaica project would of course yield centuries of profits and misery, from the cane fields of the Caribbean to the cotton fields of the American South.

During the Civil Wars, trade between England and its North American colonies had collapsed, and Manhattan had grown in consequence. Now Cromwell hoped to break the overweening Dutch dominance in trade – in Europe and Asia as well as North America – by means of legislation. The problem with this tactic, so often employed throughout history, is that one cannot expect a rival nation to abide by one's own laws, and the Dutch didn't.

It happened that the first action in Cromwell's assault on the Dutch trading empire occurred at virtually the moment Van der Donck won his case in the States General. While Van der Donck was drawing breath from his victory and petitioning the States General to let him return to Manhattan, in the straits of Dover, 150 miles south-west of The Hague, portions of the English and Dutch fleets encountered one another. The weather was brewing and there was a strong north-eastern wind; the system of communicating by means of flags and sail position had yet to be developed, and each side was confused about the other's intentions. Foremost in the minds of both commanders was the so-called Navigation Act, the piece of hard-core protectionism that Parliament had recently passed, which was aimed directly at the Dutch. With it, England had declared that only English ships would be permitted to deliver products into English ports. An impertinent clause in the bill called for foreign vessels sailing in the Channel to lower their flags in salute. When this information made its way to the continent, Dutch commanders expressly ordered their vessels not to do any such thing.

The two men who stood with feet firmly planted on the swaying decks of their respective men-of-war, eyeing the foreign sails and assessing what to do, were both destined to become legendary figures, and together form a tableau that encapsulates the odd cross-currents of the times. Robert Blake, head of the English fleet, was a flowing-haired, Oxford-educated son of wealth who had taken to sea only recently, at the age of fifty. Maarten Tromp, the leathery, pug-like Dutch commander, had gone to sea at age nine, serving under his father's command; when he was twelve, the ship was taken by English pirates, his father killed, and the youth pressed into service as a pirate's slave. He had risen through the ranks of the Dutch navy, and was now admiral of the fleet and the greatest seaman alive. The twist – so characteristic of the times – was that Tromp, of humble origins, was a firm supporter of the House of Orange and of the English Stuarts (he had actually been knighted by Charles I for assisting in his struggle against Parliament), while Blake the dandy was an anti-royal Parliamentarian.

Accounts of what happened off Dover differed, but all agreed that the battle was sparked by Tromp's failure to lower his flag in recognition of English sovereignty. From four o'clock in the afternoon until nine in the evening, forty-two Dutch vessels and twelve larger, more heavily armed English ships emptied their cannon at one another, sometimes from point-blank range, in an encounter that surprised both sides in its savagery. But decades of tensions had been building up to this, and at least some among the Dutch had seen it coming. Months earlier a courier pouch had arrived at The Hague bearing a curious document. It was printed in English, but even those who couldn't read that language could make out the word AMBOYNA in large red letters across the title-page. A London publisher had reprinted the inflammatory pamphlet of twenty-eight years earlier, describing atrocities committed by the Dutch on Englishmen in the East Indies. Of the two great statesmen in the Dutch government, the 27-year-old Jan de Witt preferred to believe that this bit of resuscitated jingoism represented only a random stirring among the English rabble, but as wise old Adriaen Pauw glanced over the pamphlet he knew it meant the country's leaders were whipping up the populace, preparing them for war.

It was not long in coming. Pauw left for London to take part in emergency talks with Cromwell's Council of State (where, incidentally, the man he would have dealt with as Cromwell's translator and speech-writer in foreign languages was no less a figure than the poet and pamphleteer John Milton). In The Hague, the mood of magnanimity and optimism that had spread through the republic since the 'eternal' peace of '48 had vanished. The government was placed on a war footing. Orders went out to ships at sea and to outposts across the globe to strengthen their defences.

The impact of all of this on Adriaen van der Donck was spectacular. The West India Company's fortunes had fallen steadily in recent years, and Van der Donck's assault had further crippled it. But with the first rumours of a war with England, the company, which after all had originally been conceived as a quasi-military entity, came roaring back to life. Its once-powerful directors were once again flush with influence. Under pressure from them, and fearing that this was the wrong time to institute liberal reforms, the States General reversed their rulings on the Manhattan-based colony. They rescinded the recall of Stuyvesant, and ordered Van der Donck personally to hand back the letter of recall they had given him. On top of that, Van der Donck's activism, which only weeks before had been lauded as the full flowering of Dutch legal progressivism being applied, in a test case, to the nation's overseas province, suddenly looked positively dangerous. He was detained and refused permission to return to America. The ship bearing his family members and belongings left for Manhattan without him. Overnight, things had turned upside-down. He was no longer a patriot but a radical, someone to be kept under surveillance.

*

The Dutch Republic's declaration of war against England in July 1652 was a kind of rite of passage for both nations. Their recent histories had been so intertwined that they often seemed like siblings, shifting endlessly from argument to co-operation to vindictiveness. The gunboat salvoes in the Channel signalled that in the struggle for control of the indescribably lucrative international trade in this first era of globalization, each saw the other as the only real adversary. Their rivalry would dominate the century and give shape and substance to America's beginnings.

The First Anglo-Dutch War, as history has titled it, was a true and literal trade war. A peasant in either country could have been forgiven for feeling detached from it: no homes were burned, no villages sacked. The entire thing took place at sea, with England going after the Dutch herring fleet and spice- and fur-laden merchantmen, and the Dutch forced to defend their trading empire. ('The English are about to attack a mountain of gold,' Pauw wryly remarked at the outset; 'we are about to attack a mountain of iron.')

This is not to say that the war lacked ferocity. The pent-up grudges on both sides came out in a series of savage exchanges that rewrote the books on naval warfare and began the build-up of tactics, rules and technological innovations that reached a peak more than a century later in the age of Horatio Nelson. The clashes in the Channel and the North Sea that murderous summer marked the debut of 'line of battle' fighting, with ships of each fleet arrayed stem to stern so that their side-mounted guns could form a long, deadly chain. In the culminating sea battle, the largest in world history to date, more than two hundred ships formed opposing ribbons along a 16-mile corridor, hulls screeching against one another and cannon unleashing inhuman mayhem (this era before the exploding shell featured such low-tech innovations as the broadside of chains, which sliced through rigging and scissored bodies to pieces). The ships caught up in the encounters were reduced to floating wrecks literally caked in gore, 'their masts and tackles', one correspondent aboard an English vessel reported, 'being moiled with brains, hair, pieces of skull'.

Cromwell had caught the Dutch leaders off guard. While he had been building a new generation of larger warships, the States General, after nearly coming to civil war with the Prince of Orange over their insistence on decommissioning the military, had been laboriously downsizing since the peace of 1648. As a result, the States General and the regional chambers of the East and West India Companies were now forced to drop all other concerns as they focused on the task of defending trade routes and rigging more ships for battle.

Van der Donck, his cause shelved, himself an exile in his home country, prowled angrily like a caged animal. For months he roamed restlessly back and forth between The Hague, Amsterdam, Leiden and Breda. In Leiden, he returned to the university and received his *Supremus in jure* degree, which allowed him to practise as an attorney before the Dutch supreme court. In Amsterdam, he went again to the States General asking to be released, but learned that, at the instigation of the company, word had gone out to every ship's captain departing for the Americas that anyone who received him on board would face punishment. In the same city he organized a group of influential friends and went with them to the stately West India Company headquarters to meet with company officials. But this only gave the company men a chance to loose their pent-up invective over this man's efforts to rob them of their colony. He was a dangerous man, a 'notorious ringleader', illegitimate representative of a 'lawless and mutinous rabble'. He reported this encounter to the States General and used every argument he could rustle up to appeal to them, pleading that his farm in America was 'going fast to ruin', that he was personally being subjected to 'an extraordinary civil banishment', even reminding them that he was a descendant of the great patriot responsible for liberating Breda during the war for independence. It got him nowhere. The bureaucratic wall had gone up.

Then, indefatigable still, he hit upon another idea for promoting his colony. His embassy was at a standstill, his family had gone on to Manhattan. He was alone and rudderless. In this abrupt hiatus, images gathered. Wild raw mountains, and the river with its majestically broad belly reigning over the landscape. An autumn afternoon in which, following days of rain, a sudden burst of sun ignited the world, cows in a primordial meadow lit to glowing by it, the grass iridescent. Himself, ten or twelve years younger, sitting before the fire in a Mohawk longhouse with its hundred or so inhabitants, discussing – of all things – theology: agreeing with the dark-eyed chiefs in their belief that God was almighty and good, but arguing against their notion that God was too preoccupied with his eternally enticing female companion deity to pay notice to the affairs of men, thus leaving the devil to hold sway over the Indians in their smoke-filled dwellings, the Europeans on their island stronghold, and people across the waters of every hue and language, all of whom, in the Indians' cosmology, wallowed in wickedness.

His mind filled with these images, Van der Donck spent the next months, while at sea the war raged and at home the doors to influence were shut against him, closeted away with pen and paper, and emerged with a manuscript entitled 'A Description of New Netherland' – a work which brought a humanistic, scientific sensibility to bear on the colony he had come to love. The *Description*, from which I have quoted throughout this book, was unabashedly a paean to the America that Van der Donck knew. He arranged it thematically, devoting sections to the waters, woodlands, wild vines, minerals, winds, seasons and, of course, the Indians, each of which received the doting attention of one who had been too long absent. At the end of the book, in order to make a direct appeal to his audience, he broke out of his anatomical dissection of the colony to deploy a favoured convention of contemporary writers, the dialogue. In this case, the exchange was between a 'Dutch patriot' and a New Netherlander, the former, having read all that came before, standing in for the reader and posing questions. Van der Donck doesn't much trouble to disguise himself in the cloak of the anonymous New Netherlander, but launches into opinions that, as before, in the *Remonstrance* and elsewhere, show an almost eerie foresight. Manhattan and its surrounding region will grow exponentially, he assures his listener, and not so much because the Dutch people themselves will leave their homes for it but because the Netherlands has had a long tradition of welcoming refugees from elsewhere in Europe. It is these masses – 'from eastern Europe, Germany, Westphalia, Scandinavia, Wallonia, etc.' – who, having steeped themselves in the Dutch tradition of tolerance, will populate the colony, entrenching its multi-ethnic character and increasing its strength and vigour. In this reverie of his, Van der Donck seems practically to summon the vast sweep of the coming centuries' migrations, the huddled arrivals being processed at Ellis Island, the barrios and ghettos coming into being. Aiding this future mass migration, making it happen and making it stick, he sees a unique cultural glue: 'the Dutch have compassionate natures and regard foreigners virtually as native citizens,' with the result that, in their system, whoever is 'prepared to adapt' can make a go of it. This freakish burst of historic clairvoyance is tempered somewhat by his assured statement that the colony would remain Dutch, that would-be emigrants had no need to fear an English takeover any time 'in the next fifty years'.

Van der Donck was granted a licence to publish his work, but publication was withheld because, with the war raging, the government didn't want to draw attention to the colony, which it now feared the English might invade.

At last, late in 1653, four years after his arrival, Van der Donck received permission to leave for Manhattan. But it came at a price. The forces that had branded him a danger had not relaxed their grip. The heads of the Amsterdam chamber of the West India Company took particular delight in assuring him that his cause was shattered. Finally he understood what he had been up against all these years – that the power he had been attempting to thwart was rooted in the vastness of the Dutch empire. He had been too far ahead of his time, and now he understood it. For the first time in his life, he described himself as 'wholly disheartened and cast down'. The petition he now penned was different in tone from anything he had ever written:

> The undersigned, van der Donck, humbly requests consent and passport of the Board to go to New Netherland, offering to resign the commission previously given him as President of the community, or otherwise as its deputy, and promising upon arrival in New Netherland and taking up residence there, to accept no office whatever it may be, but rather to live in private peacefully and quietly as a common inhabitant, submitting to the orders and commands of the Company or those enacted by its director.

His request was granted. He was forbidden from engaging in public life and forbidden to practise law in the colony, on the extraordinary grounds that there was no other lawyer in the colony, and thus no-one with the knowledge to stand up to him in court. (Actually, Lubbert van Dinklagen, Stuyvesant's former deputy-director who was also a trained lawyer, was still in the colony; but he had been silenced by Stuyvesant following his backing of Van der Donck's mission, and had gone into retirement on Staten Island.)

Over a period of several weeks prior to his voyage, Van der Donck turned up repeatedly at the office of an Amsterdam notary public named Jacob de Winter, each time with one or more men and women. Together they sat while the notary carefully inscribed the terms and conditions of a contract, and then each signed or made his or her mark on the paper:

> June 4, 1653. Adriaen van der Donck, patroon of his colony in New Netherland, takes Hendrik Cornelisz Broeck into his

> service as carpenter for a period of three years. He will sail to New Netherland with his own tools. The passage will be paid by Van der Donck . . .
>
> June 13, 1653. Adriaen van der Donck, patroon of his colony in New Netherland, takes Jan Mewesz. and Evert Jansz., both from Steenwijk, into his service as carpenters . . .
>
> June 16, 1653. Adriaen van der Donck . . . engages Helena Wand for a period of six years . . . Helena Wand is obliged to do the household and such as a maid-servant and to assist his family. She will receive as annual wages f36 besides board and lodging.
>
> July 26, 1653. Adriaen van der Donck, living in New Netherland, engages for his colony Henrik Claasz., pottery-maker from Rotterdam . . .
>
> July 28, 1653. Adriaen van der Donck, free man in New Netherland, engages as gardener for a period of three years: Gommaart Paulusz., from Antwerp . . . Paulusz. shall be obliged to keep the garden of Van der Donck, to set, to plant, to clip and do similar jobs . . .

Van der Donck had apparently succumbed: he would give up his political pretensions. But he hadn't abandoned his home, or the idea of America. And even in defeat he left evidence for the persistence of his vision: records that foreshadow the course of the coming centuries, momentarily shining the light of history onto a handful of individuals who became caught up in the idea of a land of opportunity across the ocean, and followed him there.

Part III
The Inheritance

13
Booming

ON A THURSDAY MORNING IN FEBRUARY 1653, IN THE THICK of winter, seven men left their narrow, low-ceilinged homes and the warmth of their Delft-tiled hearths, stamped through the streets of lower Manhattan and entered the gates of the fort. Assembled in the council room there, they swore an oath of service to the States General, then bowed their heads as a minister intoned a prayer – 'Thou hast received us in Christ . . . make us fit through Thy grace, that we may do the duties imposed upon us' – that signals, among other things, that we are well before the era of the separation of church and state.

Adriaen van der Donck was still in the Netherlands, struggling against the political fiat that was preventing him from returning to America, when their honours, the magistrates of the newly incorporated city of New Amsterdam, transacted their first, brief piece of business, putting their signatures to a statement 'herewith [to] inform everybody that they shall hold their regular meetings in the house hitherto called the City Tavern, henceforth the City Hall, on Monday mornings from 9 o'clock, to hear there all questions of difference between litigants and decide them as best they can'. Two and a half weeks later, in a physical break from the government of Peter Stuyvesant and the West India Company that was visible to all, they convened at the three-storey building on the waterfront that had long been the centre of the town's activities. In case anyone missed the significance, the bell in the front courtyard sounded the change of government.

It was very modest. But it meant something to those involved. For years the settlers of Manhattan Island had insisted that their community was more than a military or trading outpost, that they were not serfs forced to toil for a distant master but citizens of a modern republic entitled to protection under its laws. This little gathering transported them into a new era. Officially, they were a city. The magistrates were well aware of the heritage of the political offices and legal traditions they were taking on. The government they formed had a structure – there were two co-mayors and a panel of judges, which, when combined, formed the legislative body – copied from Amsterdam and based on Roman–Dutch law, the Roman part of which had come to Holland by way of the Holy Roman Empire, and before that traced itself all the way back to the caesars and the Code of Justinian. When, in February 2003, the speaker of New York's city council cut into a birthday cake and gave a champagne toast in honour of the 350th anniversary of the city's charter, it was to these gatherings in the former tavern that he paid homage.* The city dates its political foundation not to the English takeover, when it was named New York, but to this moment.

But then – so what? Aside from the bit of arcana that New York is perhaps unique in the United States in that its legal roots go back to ancient Rome, does it mean anything? The political founding of a city may be a matter of consuming interest to a narrow clique of historians but of justifiable indifference to the rest of the world. For that matter, it's also worth noting that

* The festivities were held in the Museum of the American Indian, on the site of the fort. A sort of flattened tribute to the original city hall exists in the form of a brick outline of its location on the sidewalk at the corner of Pearl Street and Coenties Slip.

Stuyvesant blunted the power of the city government by initially refusing to allow popular election: he himself appointed its first officers.

What matters is where the founding of city government on Manhattan led. The idea posed at the beginning of this book was that New York City is different in its origins from Boston, Hartford and other early east coast cities. It was different because a sulky but dogged English explorer named Hudson happened to chart the area for the Dutch. But it would only matter in the long term – its difference would only stick – once it had a real structure. Municipal incorporation provided that structure, one born of long experience of containing and maintaining peace among a dozen cultures. The proclamation that Stuyvesant's superiors forced on him as a result of Van der Donck's efforts granted 'to this growing town of New Amsterdam' a government 'to be framed, as far as possible and as the situation of the country permits, after the laudable customs of the city of Amsterdam, which gave her name to this first commenced town'. Thus the achievement of Adriaen van der Donck. This was the foundation on which New York City was built, and, seeping outward in every direction, it would colour and mould the American continent and the American character.

The two matters that occupied the new government in its first weeks form a diptych of the settlement's concerns, which always seemed to veer between the historic and the ridiculous. Into the newly outfitted council chamber, on its first full day in business, burst a raucous knot of locals, near to blows. Joost Goderis was a harried man: he was married to a woman with a wayward eye; the fact was well known in the town, and he was fed up. He'd recently been out oystering on Oyster (now Ellis) Island, and as he canoed back to Manhattan he encountered his supposed friend Gulyam d'Wys loitering on shore with a gang of young toughs. D'Wys wanted to give the boys something to laugh at, and so he told Goderis (as the court recorded it) 'that Joost should give him, defendant, a better opportunity to have sexual connection with his, plaintiff's, wife'. When Goderis tried to maintain his dignity by feigning confusion, d'Wys helpfully explained that 'Allard Anthony has had your wife down on her back.' The boys with him laughed and called the man a cuckold who 'ought to wear horns, like the cattle in the woods'. Goderis hoped the new municipal board was the sort of body to help a man in emotional distress, and gravely brought the matter before the magistrates.

At the same time, on a darker front, the magistrates were grappling with daily reports of fallout from the war between England and the Dutch Republic. Stuyvesant – who had fought against the forming of a town government but who now, at least for the time being, seemed to welcome the opportunity to share the burden – regularly stumped over from the fort with three-month-old news from Holland. As in all wars, the reports conveyed a mix of paranoia, rumour and inscrutable behaviour. 'The government in England is at present very odd,' one letter informed Stuyvesant; according to informed sources, the English were demanding 'that all apprentices shall again wear blue caps'. While the Dutch leaders pondered that one, it had also become apparent that the American colonies of both countries were in play in the conflict. The West India Company was to begin gearing up once again for privateering work, as it had against Spain. The company proposed that '5 or 6 ordinary, but well manned, frigates' should use Manhattan as a base for attacking English colonies. At the same time, the States General was afraid of a surprise attack; reporting that they were 'certainly informed that New Netherland is in great danger and imminently exposed to invasion', they ordered Stuyvesant and the magistrates to reinforce the fledgling city's defences.

The magistrates, with Stuyvesant sitting in on their session, took action. The first decision was 'to surround the greater part of the City with a high stockade and a small breastwork'. To fund it, the magistrates raised money from the town's wealthiest residents, Stuyvesant matching the top figure of 150 guilders.

Then they plunged into the details. The palisade along the northern perimeter of the town would be composed of 12-foot oak logs, each 18 inches in circumference and 'sharpened at the upper end'. These would be sunk 3 feet into the earth and be fortified by a 4-foot-high breastwork. Payment to the builder, the government declared, 'will be made weekly in good wampum'. A crier was sent out, declaring that the town council was asking for bids to carry out the work. Englishman Thomas Baxter signed on to provide the wood, and the thing was built by early July. In the long term, what is notable about this first public works project orchestrated by the town government is not the wall itself but the street that ran along it. It's a safe bet that no matter how wildly they tended to dream, the magistrates could not have imagined that this rough pathway would replace the gleaming, colonnaded bourse of Amsterdam as the epicentre of global finance. It is also worth noting that the wall along Wall Street was built not to keep the Indians out, as folklore has it, but to keep the English out.

While the Manhattanites were fearing an attack from New England, the residents of Connecticut, New Haven, Massachusetts and Plymouth were likewise feeding on a steady diet of rumours that the Dutch were about to move northwards against them. One of these rumours – that the Dutch had hired Indians to massacre New England families while they were at church – made it to London, and was packaged by an enterprising printer in the most explosive way. The memory of the killing of ten English traders by Dutch soldiers on the far-off south-east Asian island of Ambon or Amboyna three decades earlier hadn't died in England, and had been rekindled the year before by republication of the inflammatory pamphlet reporting the event. Now someone in the English colonies, possibly associated with the government of either Connecticut or New Haven, had the genius to use Amboyna specifically to stir the New Englanders against the multi-ethnic, Dutch-run colony to their south. The new pamphlet that swept through England and was shipped to America was entitled *The Second Part of the Tragedy of Amboyna: Or, a True Relation of a Most Bloody, Treacherous, and Cruel Design of the Dutch in the New Netherlands in America. For the total Ruining and Murthering of the English Colonies in New-England.* It was a double-barrelled shot of ethnic hatred, decrying the Indians as 'bloody people, fit instruments for so horrid a design', and lauding an English colonist who had 'in one night cut off fourteen hundred of them', while also seeing the plot as an instance of the genetic wickedness of the Dutch, 'Amboyna's treacherous Cruelty extending its self from the East to the West Indiaes, running in its proper channel of Dutch blood'.

The pamphlet was a model of wartime disinformation, forcing the Dutch government to carry out an investigation and deny the accusation while keeping the flame of English public opinion fuelled. Months earlier, several New England leaders had disembarked at New Amsterdam to discuss the allegations with Stuyvesant. He had assured them that his people had no designs on the English colonies. While on Manhattan, however, the Puritans got an eyeful of the rude, boisterous, growing port city, through which, they well knew, much of their own region's trade passed. If England was going to make a play for the Dutch colony and so gain a lock on the interior of the continent and the shipping centre of the entire coast, it had better be soon. The trade war was as good a pretext as any – and anyway, the story was too good not to use. In addition to supplying the material for the 'second Amboyna' pamphlet, the New England governors wrote to Cromwell personally and put the case that his so-called Western Design, by which England would weave the lands of the Atlantic Rim into the beginnings of an empire, would be perfectly served by conquering the island at the mouth of the Hudson River. Cromwell, who had just assumed the title Lord Protector and with it many of the trappings of the king he had helped behead, liked the ambition of the plan, agreed it was time to carry it out, and wrote back to say he was sending a four-frigate flotilla and a company of soldiers to Boston, whose 'utmost assistance may be given for gaining the Manhattoes'.

At this juncture, Adriaen van der Donck finally sailed back to Manhattan. It's frustrating, but not surprising, that we have no record of his homecoming. People viewed him as a hero; residents had followed every action he undertook in The Hague on their behalf. The new magistrates had him to thank for their jobs, and must still have considered him the leader of the reform party. But there was no public display – no-one wanted to incur the wrath of Stuyvesant. It is especially frustrating that we are forced to imagine the encounter between Van der Donck and Stuyvesant, which had to have been freighted with emotion. When last they had met, Stuyvesant had imprisoned Van der Donck for treason. Since that time, the director's former protégé had spent four years in the Dutch Republic hectoring the government for Stuyvesant's removal, and had actually succeeded, only to have the decision reversed. Now, having gambled everything and lost, he was returning and putting himself at Stuyvesant's mercy. The only document we have directly concerning Van der Donck at this time shows him, shortly after his arrival, asking Stuyvesant for access to the records of the colony, so that he can add to the book he had written, which was still awaiting publication in Amsterdam. Stuyvesant turned him down, citing the advice of the company directors, who warned of 'new troubles' from 'Meester Adriaen van der Donck', and feared he would turn 'the Company's own weapons . . . upon itself'. Stuyvesant could be a dangerous enemy. Van der Donck had to proceed with extreme caution, and the fact that he drops from the official records at this point suggests that he did.

But that doesn't mean he stayed out of politics. Certainly on his arrival he was busy with domestic matters, reacquainting himself with his property and helping his newly arrived relatives adjust to America. His mother moved into a house on Pearl Street looking out across the East River to the Breuckelen meadows, and his sister-in-law needed help dealing with her teenage son, who was a bit of a handful (Gysbert van der Donck, along with his friend, the son of Cornelis Melyn, was a member of the gang who had taunted Joost Goderis as a cuckold). But Adriaen van der Donck was not the kind of character who would be content with domesticity alone for long.

In fact, he seems to have picked up right where he left off in The Hague, only now working behind the scenes. Within weeks of his return, there was a new political uprising against Stuyvesant. With the colony thriving and growing, towns in the vicinity of Manhattan (which would later be incorporated into the boroughs of Brooklyn and Queens) were expanding, and the leaders of several of these – Gravesende (later Gravesend), Vlissingen (Flushing), Middelburgh (Newtown), Heemsteede (Hempstead), New Amersfoort (Flatlands), Breuckelen (Brooklyn) and Midwout or Vlackebos (Flatbush) – began clamouring for their rights. The controversy was sparked by piracy, which was still commonplace in the colony; a recurring problem stemmed from locals who, having failed to make a go of things through legitimate business, turned pirate. The most recent villain was well known to all: Thomas Baxter, who had supplied the oak posts for the 'wall', was marauding along Long Island Sound, stealing horses. The residents of outlying towns assembled to declare that if the company couldn't protect them they would stop paying taxes.

Some historians have explained this breach between Stuyvesant and the Long Island towns as a Dutch–English encounter. There were many English residents in these towns, and there was a war on between the Dutch and the English; therefore, according to the reasoning, the agitation amounted to an internal revolt, a way of assisting England in the war. The episode has also been used to support the long-accepted notion that any yearning for political rights that existed in the Dutch colony could only have come from its English residents. This is a misreading of events. The confusion seems to stem from the fact that the petition presented to Stuyvesant in December was written in English and then translated into Dutch. But the 'Remonstrance and Petition of the Colonies and Villages in this New Netherland Province', in which colonists complained of the 'arbitrary government' Stuyvesant exercised, follows Dutch legal forms. John Brodhead, the nineteenth-century historian who gathered together the records of Van der Donck's doings in The Hague and who was intimately familiar with Van der Donck's writing, noticed a similarity in tone between Van der Donck's *Remonstrance of New Netherland* and this current remonstrance, with its spirited rejection of Stuyvesant's continued rule by fiat. Another early historian of the period noted the similarity in style of this complaint to the earlier complaints written during Kieft's time – in which, as detailed in Chapters 7 and 9, there is ample evidence that Van der Donck was involved.

In demanding a voice in their affairs, the residents of the Long Island towns – Dutch and English alike – were reacting not to the war but to the founding of the municipality of New Amsterdam. In fact, the magistrates of the New Amsterdam government not only supported their petition to the West India Company; they called on these leaders to travel out of their wooded plains and valleys, cross over on the Breuckelen Ferry, and join with them in the capital to craft a formal complaint. In other words, this mini-revolt that Stuyvesant found himself facing at the end of 1653, within weeks of Van der Donck's return, was a direct result of the young lawyer's achievement in The Hague, and it was also a direct continuation of that work, an attempt to push Stuyvesant and the company further towards political reform. Van der Donck was uniquely suited to act as intermediary between the Dutch and English leaders: his wife was English, and his father-in-law, the firebrand English preacher Francis Doughty, was now minister of Flushing, one of the towns that was party to the complaint. Van der Donck also knew well the Englishman who penned the remonstrance. George Baxter had been around since Kieft's time, like Van der Donck had assisted Stuyvesant as an English translator, and had even served on Stuyvesant's council during Van der Donck's trial – and therefore, like Van der Donck, had split with Stuyvesant after once being close to him. Stuyvesant himself seems to have complained to his superiors about the possibility of Van der Donck being behind this latest insurgency. In response to a letter of his that is now lost, the directors write: 'We do not know, whether you have sufficient reason to be so suspicious of Adriaen van der Donck, as all the charges against him are based upon nothing but suspicion and presumptions, however, we shall not take his part, and only say that as we have heretofore recommended him to you on condition of his good behavior, we intend also that he be reprimanded and punished, if contrary to his promise he should misdemean himself.'

The picture that emerges, then, is not one in which English interlopers come into the colony, lie in wait for several years, and then, Trojan-Horse-like, emerge at time of war to add to the Dutch troubles. Indeed, there is no indication in this encounter of the English residents expressing a longing for English government. As they point out in their complaint, they had fled to these parts to escape it, and hoped to put down roots in the area surrounding Manhattan to take advantage of the more liberal justice of the Dutch Republic, the government of which, they noted, was 'made up of various nations from divers quarters of the globe'. What they wanted was exactly what Van der Donck had striven for all these years: an end to the West India Company's rule, and a spread of political rights through the rapidly growing towns of the colony. Such rights, the remonstrance declared, in a phrase out of Grotius that Van der Donck liked, were based on 'natural law'.

So the movement Van der Donck had launched was still animating the people of the colony, and in fact had spread. It was the continuation of a long, sustained, well-reasoned appeal for political reform that came not from England but from the early modern heart of the European continent.

It did little good, however. Stuyvesant was nothing if not

consistent, and he reacted to the remonstrance in trademark fashion. The directors of the West India Company, he declared, were 'absolute and general lords and masters of this province'. The petition was denied.

Then again, Stuyvesant himself was in danger of being trumped: violent change was bearing down on the colony while this debate still echoed. Unknown to everyone in New Netherland, Cromwell's invasion squadron left England in February of 1654. New Amsterdam would have been quickly subdued – the West India Company's soldiers were spread thinly around the colony, and hundreds of New Englanders, alarmed by the rumours of a threatened Dutch invasion, had declared themselves ready to follow an English military leader in a pre-emptive strike.

But fate – i.e. the weather – intervened. The storm-tossed squadron didn't arrive in Boston harbour until June; and then, as Major Robert Sedgwicke, commander of the fleet, wrote to Cromwell, the very day he was about to embark from Boston with 'nyne hundred foote' and 'one troope of horse' for the assault on Manhattan, 'there arrived a shipp from London, bringing with her diverse printed proclemations of peace between the English and the Dutch.' Jan de Witt had hammered out a treaty with Cromwell, yielding England control of the Channel while retaining Dutch trading supremacy in the Mediterranean and in Asia. The First Anglo-Dutch War ended with the North American sphere unchanged. The invasion squadron was called back home.

*

One might say that this is the point in history when Manhattan became Manhattan. With a rudimentary representative government in place, the island rapidly came into its own. Stuyvesant and the West India Company still officially ran the place, but, whether they were Dutch, English or any of the other nationalities represented in the colony, the businessmen – the fur traders and the tobacco farmers, the shippers of French wines, Delft tiles, salt, horses, dyewood and a hundred other products – increasingly got their way. As the business leaders won positions in the city government and became political leaders, others – bakers, tavernkeepers, schoolteachers, ministers – came to them for support. These alliances strengthened New Amsterdam's municipal government, which, in its turn, set a flurry of development in motion. Roads were paved with cobbles. Brick houses replaced wooden ones; tiled roofs proliferated (mostly red and black, giving the town a crisp finish), and the old thatched ones were banned as a fire hazard. A proper wharf was built off Pearl Street. A street survey of New Amsterdam was commissioned. As the town picked itself up, it took on that defining Dutch characteristic: tidiness. Its streets and stoops were swept clean. Trees were aesthetically pruned; gardens took neat diamond, oval and square shapes. An order went out forcing farmers to tear down pigsties and chicken coops that occupied prominent roadside positions. Owners of vacant lots on the main streets were charged with an extra tax to encourage them to develop their property. The ditch that had been chopped through the centre of the town was widened into a proper canal, with banks reinforced with pilings and crossed by pretty stone bridges, which, together with the gabled buildings, gave the town a strong echo of its namesake. Taverns were even more numerous than before, but staggering, puking drunkenness had abated somewhat. The inns now functioned as clubs where traders and businessmen could meet, places where news was exchanged, and maybe as dens for sampling that wanton new elixir, coffee.

It was still a port town, with tentacles that stretched across the globe, so piracy and whoring, syphilitic scabs and cutlass scars, remained fixtures. But you get glimpses, too, of the well of ordinary life that fills any society, even though, in its quiet, pious normality, it rarely seeps beyond the margins of the official records. A family gathers in the evening around the hearth, the father reading the Bible and carefully recording special events inside its front cover. A minister, writing home to Europe, recounts his weekly circuit on the Breuckelen Ferry between the churches of Long Island, New Amsterdam, and 'Stuyvesant's Bouwerie'. An 'orphanmaster' describes the progress of his charges.

The colony was maturing, thanks largely to the municipal leadership on Manhattan. It gave people a sense that this island on the edge of the wilderness, which had always veered sharply between lawlessness and tyranny, had become a place where families could let their dreams take root.

In what might have been seen as a good omen, one of the colony's dodgiest residents, Kieft's and Stuyvesant's long-time henchman Cornelis van Tienhoven, disappeared for good at this time, with appropriate flamboyance. His flight from The Hague, where he had been opposing Van der Donck, and later arrival on Manhattan with a young mistress, had made him a laughing stock: we can only guess how his wife greeted him. Stuyvesant had kept him on for a time, but he soon became too much of a liability. He had bullied the colonists for years, and there was a growing suspicion that he was involved in cooking the company's books. As the trouble surrounding him reached a climax, he vanished one day in 1656. His hat and cane were found floating near the shore. Stuyvesant wanted badly to cover the matter up, declare a death by drowning and have his association with the man forgotten. Other people felt they knew better – for one thing, Van Tienhoven's brother, who had also become entangled in financial irregularities, vanished at about the same time, and later turned up on Barbados. Whatever happened to Cornelis van Tienhoven remains one of the unsolved mysteries of New Netherland.

But Manhattan wasn't the only eventful part of the colony; it wasn't just the island capital that took off after 1653. Only a year before the municipal government came into being, in an effort to resolve his dispute with the upriver duchy of Rensselaerswyck,

Stuyvesant had created by decree the town of Beverwyck on territory staked out around Fort Orange. The beaver trade for which it was named was still flourishing, and the community came into being seemingly overnight. Mills, brick yards and tile yards were laid out and produced the materials for creating a town whose citizens were self-consciously urban enough to construct a poorhouse as one of their first community projects. By 1660, it was the colony's second city, with a thousand residents – though compared with New Amsterdam, it kept its remote, Wild West feel. Through the records we get fleeting views of Indians as ordinary participants in town life. They are boarders in residents' homes, sitting by the fireside of an evening with pewter mugs of beer. One shows up, purse in hand, at the baker's house to buy cakes. In 1659, two Mohawk chiefs ask for – and receive – an extraordinary session of court in which to present grievances against Dutchmen who have been abusing their people. For the twelve years in which it existed, before being turned into the English town of Albany, Beverwyck was a tough, no-frills place, poised between the looming mountains and the vast river, the thunk of beaver skins on countertops the characteristic sound of its commerce. But it was also a well-ordered community, with a court of justice that functioned identically to the one in New Amsterdam and those in Holland. In makeup it was more Dutch than New Amsterdam, but still a quarter of its residents came from outside the United Provinces, and with Germans, Swedes, French, English, Irish, Norwegians and Africans among its inhabitants, it had a far more mixed population than the New England towns.

In Amsterdam, meanwhile, men like Seth Verbrugge and Dirck de Wolff – the coiffed and groomed merchant princes who ran Europe's trade from their red leather chairs and ornately carved desks, their walls hung with framed maps showing their global sway, their wives collared in lace and studded with diamonds – took advantage of the new-found stability on Manhattan. They gave their agents there greater sway and purchasing power, and the agents used their contacts with English and Dutch merchants from Canada to Virginia and from Jamaica to Brazil to make their island port the hub of Atlantic trade. The products first appearing in New Amsterdam's shops at this time speak of a more refined life for its inhabitants – medicine, measuring equipment, damask, fine writing paper, oranges and lemons, parakeets and parrots, saffron, sassafras and sarsaparilla.

With municipal government on Manhattan came an innovation whose effect would long outlive the colony itself, and would help to impress the island's legacy into the American character. Going back into the middle ages, cities throughout Europe had offered a form of local citizenship to inhabitants: English cities had their freemen, Dutch towns their burghers. Amsterdam had recently installed a new, two-tiered system, and the local government on Manhattan promptly copied it. The so-called 'great burgher' was a powerful trader who contributed sizeable sums for civic improvements, and in exchange got the right to trade and had a voice in setting policy. What was different was the offering of small burgher status. Nearly every resident of New Amsterdam applied for it, and it gave even the humblest – shoemakers, chimney sweeps, tailors, blacksmiths, hatters, coopers, millers, masons – a stake in the community, a kind of minority shareholder status. The system encouraged inhabitants to support one another and largely did away with the itinerant traders who used to sweep in, make a quick profit and then leave. It also made for a more egalitarian place than New England, where the number of freemen, or town citizens, never exceeded 20 per cent of the population. In New Amsterdam, nearly everyone – rich and poor, the coiffed and the scabby – was a member of the same club. And when shipping increased in the port, all benefited from the boost to the local economy.

A further significant feature was that workers in the colony never organized themselves into the guilds that had held sway in European economic life since the middle ages. This was probably because the West India Company did its best to prevent the guilds from becoming established, fearing their power. But this form of union-busting turned out to have an advantage. It meant that artisans could branch out into areas beyond their original crafts: a baker might own land, invest in a shipment of tobacco and earn extra income as a soldier. Young men who entered the colony's rolls as humble artisans rose to considerable heights, and a muscular strain of American upward mobility was born. Frederick Flipsen (Philipse) travelled to Manhattan from Friesland and signed himself a lowly carpenter when he became a small burgher in 1657; at the time of his death in 1702, after a long career of multi-faceted wheeling and dealing, he was one of the wealthiest men in America, his upriver estate, the famous Philipsburg Manor, encompassing 92,000 acres of what would become Westchester County (including, incidentally, all of Adriaen van der Donck's former holdings).

There is a linguistic inheritance that would come along with this new relationship to work. Frederick Flipsen's workers, and the assistants to the colony's smiths, wheelwrights, bakers and gunstock-makers, had a looser relationship to their superiors than did workers in traditional guilds; a wheelwright's apprentice might also serve beer in the tavern or help bake bread. In time the typical Dutch word for master – *baas* – would take on a different connotation in the New World, and an Americanism came into being. And no Americanism is more American, and at the same time more New York, than 'boss'. From Tweed to Corleone to Springsteen, the ur-bosses are all-American and utterly New York.* As New Amsterdam gave way to New York, the word would have a natural attraction for English colonists too, because in its adapted usage it frankly

* Yes, Springsteen is a New Jersey icon; but New Jersey was, after all, part of the Dutch colony, and from that time to now at the centre of Manhattan's sphere of influence. And, while we're at it, Springsteens were among the original Dutch settlers of New Netherland.

distinguished itself from the power system that held sway in Old England; it spelled out a different kind of power relationship. 'No,' it says, 'we have no class system in place here, but there is someone in charge. I'm not your master, lord or sovereign, but I am your boss. Now get to work.'

In this period of growth and activity, we see the emergence of other customs and usages that would influence American culture – little things, meaningless in themselves, but indications that the Dutch colony never really died out, but became part of something larger. In October 1661 there was a grain shortage in the city, and the municipal government issued an order to the bakers of the town to restrict themselves to baking bread and not 'to bake any more *koeckjes*, jumbles or sweet cake'. It's the tiniest of things, but note the Dutch word. It is pronounced 'cook-yehs' – literally, 'little cakes'. More than a century later, with the publication of *American Cookery*, the first American cookbook, in 1796, Amelia Simmons would lock in print what had by then become a standard usage. It's because the first Manhattanites called them this that Americans would never eat biscuits, but cookies.

While they were waiting (or not) for the bakers to produce their sweets, the women of New Amsterdam were inclined to pick up a head of cabbage, chop it finely, slather it with vinegar and melted butter, and serve it alongside, maybe, a platter of pike with smoked bacon, or veal meatballs. *Koolsla* – cabbage salad – was their straightforward name for the dish. Again, jump forward a century. In 1751 a Swedish traveller in the Hudson valley, in describing a meal his Dutch landlady had served him, fused into the written language a term that was still given the original Dutch pronunciation but now had a phonetic American spelling: cole slaw.

As the town expanded and developed its seasonal routines and rituals, those of the dominant culture tended to prevail. We can imagine how the colony's most iconic legacy got established: every year in early December, children of non-Dutch families in

New Amsterdam had to have pouted at being left out of something good. As in the home country, the Dutch children would break out in song:

Saint Nicholas, good holy man,
Put on your best coat,
Then gallop to Amsterdam . . .

And on the sixth of the month, the saint's feast day, they would wake to find that he had left treats for them. This, surely, was unbearable; among the English, the French, the German, the Swedish families of Manhattan, pressure was brought to bear on parents; the Dutch tradition was adopted, and, later, pushed forward a couple of weeks to align with the more generally observed festival of Christmas. So 'Sinterklaas' began his American odyssey.

All of this activity – children clamouring, bakers baking, tradesmen muscling their way to the top – intensified as Manhattan matured in its last decade under the Dutch. How New Amsterdam flourished in the years following the establishment of the municipal government is an area that has only recently been studied in depth, thanks largely to Charles Gehring's translation work. Ironically, however, the very intensity of activity in this period of the colony's life has slowed the translating of its records. 'In the late 1650s, I'm dealing with much more complicated legalese,' Dr Gehring told me one day in 2002 as I sat observing him at work in his office in the New York State Library. His desk was stacked with volumes of an eighteenth-century guide to Dutch, Latin, and French legal terms; the shelves behind him were lined with the forty massive volumes of *Het Woordenboek der Nederlandsche Taal*, the definitive historical dictionary of the Dutch language from the year 1500, and the ten-volume *Middelnederlandsch Woordenboek*, which focuses on the sixteenth century. 'There's more legal activity now because there are more people,' he said.

'And there are more arguments. In the early days the land grants were vague because there was plenty of land. By now people are more packed in, and they are fighting about where property lines are. So you find Stuyvesant having to employ surveyors. And then you see the municipal government order a street plan with all the building lots indicated.'

All of this paints a picture of Manhattan in its Dutch phase very different from the haggard, inept settlement we get in traditional histories. But while trade and shipping details suggest that the region was thriving, they aren't what mattered most about the place. Who was there, how they got along, how they mixed – that is the colony's unheralded legacy. From the French Atlantic coast, the pine forests of Denmark, the streets of London, hopeful emigrants made their way to this island, and, thanks to a far-sighted programme started by the city leaders, found someone waiting to offer them 'burgher' status as they came off the ship. If they couldn't afford citizenship dues ('twenty guilders in beavers'), they could pay it in instalments. Eventually, maybe, they found a way to make enough guilders, beavers or hands of wampum to convince them that it was worth staying.

The village of Harlem ('Nieuw Haarlem', after the city in Holland), founded at this time at the northern end of Manhattan, was a kind of microcosm of this microcosm of the future American society. The initial bloc of thirty-two families who staked out lots along its two lanes came from six different parts of Europe – Denmark, Sweden, Germany, France, the Netherlands and what is now southern Belgium – and spoke five different languages. Perched alongside one another on the edge of a wilderness continent, families that would have gravitated to their respective ethnic ghettos in Europe instead had to come together, and learned a common language.

Nothing better shows the kind of mixing that took place in this setting than a phenomenon that was unprecedented elsewhere in the colonies: intermarriage. Scan the marriage records of the Dutch Reformed Church of New Amsterdam and you find a degree of culture-mixing that is remarkable for the time in such a small place. A German man marries a Danish woman. A man from Venice marries a woman from Amsterdam. Isaac Bethloo from 'Calis in Vranckryck' (i.e. Calais in France) weds Lysbeth Potters, from 'Batavia in the East Indies'. Samuel Edsall, reared in the English countryside around Reading, finds himself on Manhattan, where he somehow manages to woo a girl named Jannetje Wessels who spent her early years in the wild heath country of Gelderland near the German border. A Norwegian marries a German. Swedish–English; Danish–Swedish; Prussian–German; German–Danish; French–Dutch – in all, a quarter of the marriages performed in the New Amsterdam church were mixed. Intermarriage also appears among the Africans of the population, as when a man from the island of St Thomas marries a woman from West Africa, and there are instances of marriage between whites and blacks.

It's easy to imagine Van der Donck, newly returned from Europe and strolling through New Amsterdam, comparing the rush of cultures in its streets to the mix he found on the Dam square in Amsterdam. He had come back to witness something that he himself had helped bring about: the forging of America's first melting pot. It so happened that in this melting pot the common language to which everyone defaulted was Dutch. And it was a seventeenth-century Dutch sensibility – a mix of frankness, piety, a keen business sense, an eye on the wider world and a willingness to put up with people's differences – that formed the social glue. Already, a type was forming, which visitors were beginning to remark on: worldly, brash, confident, hustling.

Of course, equality was not part of the fabric of this pluralistic society. It wasn't even an ideal. Tolerance – call it grudging acceptance – was the major leap forward in human civilization that had recently occurred, helping to form the societies of both the Dutch Republic and the Manhattan colony. But in the seventeenth century no-one believed that blacks and whites, men and women, Catholics and Protestants, were equals, or should be treated as such. Last among the unequals were the Africans. The slaves in the colony were the human workhorses. In trying to get a sense of what life was for the African Manhattanites, however, it is necessary to erase from your mind the idea of the fully formed institution of slavery as it existed in, say, the American South in the early 1800s. The institution was in its early days and there was a strong belief in the Netherlands that it was morally wrong to buy and sell human beings, so that in the records of the colony you see a queer range of perspectives on Africans and their condition. There is the pious Revd Michaelius referring to the black women who have worked in his house as 'thievish, lazy, and useless trash', and there is Stuyvesant, sounding the classic slaver, accusing a woman slave of theft, denouncing a man for his 'laziness and unwillingness', and decreeing that both be sold 'for the maximum profit of the Company'. But there are also more than a few cases of owners freeing slaves after a number of years, in the belief that they had served their time, and there are even a few occasions when Europeans are recorded as working for freed Africans. A number of Africans owned property, and Stuyvesant himself declared, in a document as yet unpublished, that their ownership was to be looked on as 'true and free ownership with such privileges as all tracts of land are bestowed on the inhabitants [of this] province'. Slaves also had some legal rights: repeatedly, slaves appear in court, filing lawsuits against Europeans.

It is also necessary to keep in mind the scale of slavery in the colony. Manhattan was far removed from the sugar fields of Brazil and the Caribbean, where slave labour was a prominent factor in the economy. In its first decades there were no more than a few dozen slaves scattered across the colony at any one time; by the time of the English takeover there were about three hundred. What stands out in the records is less the presence of slaves on Manhattan than the development of the West India Company's slave trade. At first the company had refused to sully itself with the business, but after failing in its other ventures and seeing the money to be made from the trans-shipment of humans, it reversed course and became a significant player in one of history's ugliest episodes. The island of Curaçao was transformed into a processing station for tens of thousands of chained, disease-riddled and seasickened west Africans, and the records show Stuyvesant – whose title was, after all, director-general of New Netherland, Curaçao, Bonaire and Aruba – managing from afar, in the midst of running the North American colony, his vice-director on Curaçao, Matthais Beck. In reading their correspondence one is repeatedly jarred by the appearances of humans in the humdrum, helter-skelter inventories of goods being moved around the Atlantic, as in a ship that arrives at Curaçao in August 1660 carrying '724 pine planks ... 1245 pounds of English hardbread ... 2 barrels of bacon ... 75 skipples of peas ...' and '10 Negroes' valued at '130 pieces of eight'.

Africans were not the only group to receive less than equal status. Cultural diversity management was about the last item on Peter Stuyvesant's list of job skills, and it's safe to say he was less than thrilled to see Manhattan's streets becoming an ethnic kaleidoscope. Religion was at the root of it: Stuyvesant despised Jews, loathed Catholics, recoiled at Quakers and reserved a special hatred for Lutherans – which is to say he was the very model of a well-bred mid-seventeenth-century European. Religious bigotry was a mainstay of society. The four New England colonies to the north were founded on it. Across Europe it was universally held that diversity weakened a nation. Of course, the United Provinces of the Netherlands were supposed to be the exception to this rule, but the blanket of tolerance got a bit tattered on the transatlantic voyage. It's strange that the one nod that history has given to the Manhattan-based colony – as a cradle of religious liberty in the early America – is misdirected. Not that it is wrong exactly, but it needs to be combed out.

Dutch tolerance was indeed renowned throughout Europe,

but it continued to be debated in the country, and every decade or so brought a shift in the prevailing cultural wind. One such shift had occurred in 1651. When the stadtholder Willem II died following his attempted *coup d'état*, leaders of all the Dutch provinces headed towards The Hague for a Great Assembly, the first such gathering since 1579, when the separate provinces had met to hash out a common nation. The main topic was supposed to be what to do about the lack of a stadtholder, but the assembly turned into a debate on tolerance. The orthodox Calvinist faction took the opportunity to push the line that the whole tolerance business had got out of hand – that, in effect, before you knew it the streets of Amsterdam would be filled with drug dens and legalized prostitution. A wave of hardline sentiment rippled outwards, and it became fashionable for a time to crack down, in particular, on Catholics, Lutherans and Jews.

It was in this atmosphere that Stuyvesant, whose feelings were strongly anti-diversity anyway, moved against the religious groups that had proliferated as the colony had grown. When the Dutch Reformed ministers asked him to block Lutherans from worshipping in public on the grounds that it 'would pave the way for other sects', so that eventually the place 'would become a receptacle for all sorts of heretics and fanatics', he did so with gusto. In 1654 twenty-three Jews, some of whom had fled the fall of Dutch Brazil to the Portuguese, showed up seeking asylum. You can almost see Stuyvesant shaking his head at being told that, on top of the usual list of problems he had to deal with, he now had a Jewish population. His reaction was matter-of-fact, and perfectly in character: the Jews were 'a deceitful race' that would 'infect' the colony if he didn't stop them. He barred one from buying land, 'for important reasons'. He even refused to allow them to take turns standing guard with the citizens' militia, citing 'the aversion and disaffection of this militia to be fellow soldiers of the aforesaid [Jewish] nation'. If they didn't like it, he told Jacob Barsimon and Asser Levy in a terse decree, 'consent is hereby given to them to depart whenever and wherever it may please them.' But Abraham de Lucena and Salvador Dandrada, leaders of the Jews, knew their rights in the Dutch system, and appealed to the Dutch Republic. The Jewish community of Amsterdam applied political pressure in the time-honoured manner, and won. Stuyvesant's superiors reminded him loftily of the law that 'each person shall remain free in his religion' (and added that certain influential Jews had invested a 'large amount of capital' in the West India Company), and ordered him to back off.

But it was English Quakers who pushed tolerance to the limit. They had followed other sects in fleeing from Old England to New, and then southwards into Dutch territory. There they began proselytizing in the largely English towns of Long Island. With their sermonizing and taunting and the jiggling fits of spiritual frenzy for which they were named, they all but invited Stuyvesant's disdain. They were, in his estimation, a threat to the peace and stability of the colony, and probably out of their minds as well. He thought he was being magnanimous when, instead of banishing them, he sent them an English preacher – none other than Adriaen van der Donck's father-in-law, Francis Doughty – but they rejected him, and continued holding their own avant-garde services. When Stuyvesant forbade the town of Vlissingen to abet them, thirty-one of the villagers, all English, followed the Dutch form of complaint by signing a remonstrance to Stuyvesant. The law of 'love peace and libertie . . . which is the glory of the Outward State of Holland', they reminded him, extends even 'to Jewes Turkes and Egiptians'. Therefore, they respectfully refused to obey. The so-called Flushing Remonstrance is considered one of the foundational documents of American liberty, ancestor to the first amendment in the Bill of Rights, which guarantees that the government 'shall make no laws respecting an establishment of religion, or prohibiting the free exercise thereof'. But here too, history has spun the episode as a Dutch versus English story, with the English in the role of lovers of liberty and Stuyvesant, standing in for his non-English colony, representing the forces of reaction. In fact, the currents running through the colony were more complex, the Netherlands being the source both of a legal code of tolerance and, at times, of the failure to adhere to it. If the first amendment harks back to the Flushing Remonstrance, the Flushing Remonstrance clearly bases itself on the religious freedom guaranteed in the Dutch constitutional document.

True to form, Stuyvesant responded to the English remonstrance with a series of arrests and imprisonments. His orthodox roots were showing in all of this: he was pushing hard, and against the inexorable forces of history, to make his colony, and the island he considered home, somehow, eventually, pure. If he had had his way, he would probably have picked off foreign religious elements one by one, scaring each away, until, like the New Englanders he seemed to admire, he had established a religious monoculture, a Calvinist oasis in the New World.

But the place had its own character, and it was evolving rapidly. Thirty years later one of Stuyvesant's successors, Governor Thomas Dongan, casually referenced the varieties of religious experience that had proliferated by then in the New York colony. Besides a Church of England presence, a Dutch Calvinist population, French Calvinists, Dutch Lutherans and Roman Catholics, there were 'Singing Quakers; Ranting Quakers; Sabbatarians; Antisabbatarians; Some Anabaptists some Independants; some Jews'. 'In short,' he added to sharpen the point, 'of all sorts of opinions there are some, and the most part, of none at all.' Stuyvesant must have lurched in his grave.

*

If the growth of the colony brought Stuyvesant headaches, it also brought opportunity – bursts of happiness, even – into his stormy life. One day in late summer 1655, he found himself with a good sun overhead, the feel of a swaying deck beneath him, and enough wind to fatten the sails above him and flutter the long thin strands of his hair. Once again, as in his salad days in the Caribbean, he was at sea, heading a flotilla of seven gunboats and three hundred soldiers, bearing down on the enemy. Then, he had been thirty-four, and his assault on the Spanish at St Martin came to grief in the 'rough ball' that had shot off his leg. Now forty-five and in command of a thriving province, he was determined to win the day.

Off to starboard stretched a long ribbon of forest-backed beach that looked every bit as wild as when Henry Hudson had sailed along it in the other direction five decades earlier. Rounding Cape May and advancing into the shoaly bay and then up the river that ran through the most neglected area of his domain, he anchored between the two Swedish forts on the western shore. Here he deployed with precision, dividing his men into five companies, sending a contingent of fifty marching off to occupy the only road in the region, thus cutting off communication between his enemy's forts, and setting the rest to building a 6-foot-high breastwork a stone's throw from the nearer of the two. He sent into the fort an ensign named Dirck Smith, accompanied by a drummer escort. The message he carried was a straightforward demand: unconditional surrender.

The Anglo-Dutch War was over. A wave of prosperity was washing through the colony, and, having recently lost Brazil to Portugal, the West India Company had finally – belatedly – committed itself to New Netherland, sending troops and ships. So Stuyvesant was at last able to devote his formidable attention to his southern region. The Swedes had maintained their presence here for seventeen years now, settling the region sparsely, in part by bringing in 'forest Finns'. Decades earlier, Sweden had encouraged this particular group of Finns, who lived near the Russian border, to settle in a remote area of central Sweden which the Swedish government had wanted cleared. The Finns had a way of life that revolved around 'burn-beating' to clear forest and then cultivate the land, making them the perfect subcontractors to tame dense virgin woodland. But they turned out to be too good at their task; and when they refused to curtail their way of life and stop decimating the forests, the Swedes began shipping them to America. Together with the forest Finns, the Swedes had developed settlements on the South River and cultivated a steady fur trade with the Indians of the region, which had rankled with both Kieft and Stuyvesant. They had also taken control of one of the Dutch forts on the river. Now Stuyvesant had come to demand, as he put it, 'restitution of our property'.

After a brief pause, the Swedish commander, Shuts, stepped out to survey the force arrayed against him, then asked to be allowed to communicate with his superior in the other fort. 'His request was firmly denied,' Stuyvesant later wrote with satisfaction, 'and he left discontented.' Finally the Swedish commercial agent, a man named Von Elswick, arrived on the scene to parley. He and Stuyvesant met on the edge of a marsh just below the fort. The insects of high summer roared around them. The sun glinted off Stuyvesant's armour; his self-assured body language reflected the presence of the hundreds of soldiers behind him. The men apparently spoke in a mixture of languages, falling to diplomats' Latin for precision. Both knew that Stuyvesant had gathered an overwhelming force. The matter was simple: would the Swedes fight and die needlessly, or would they surrender the Delaware river region to the Dutch?

Von Elswick had no choice; but as he surrendered he aimed a verbal kick at Stuyvesant. '*Hodie mihi, cras tibi*,' he said in prophetic Latin. *Today it's me, tomorrow it will be you*. He meant it as a vow – that the Swedes would one day return. In fact, it was prophetic in a different way: as in nine years' time another power, in the role of the bigger fish, would give Stuyvesant the same ultimatum he was now offering the Swede.

Stuyvesant parried the jibe, and took possession of the forts, consigning New Sweden to history. He took immediate steps to settle the region, without which he knew he had no hope of keeping control of it. He started with the Finns whom the

Swedes had brought in as labourers. He decided to invite them to stay, and in fact gave them incentives to continue settling the wilderness. Like so many other aspects of the Manhattan-based colony, this decision would rattle down the centuries, affecting American history in oddly resonant ways. The Finns did indeed put down roots, and over the final decade of Dutch rule more would join them, as word spread in the old country of the opportunities offered them. From the early eighteenth century into the early nineteenth their descendants would migrate down the Appalachian valley, through the South and out into the heartland of the new country. They took with them their forest-clearing skills, which literally opened the American frontier, and something more as well. Throughout northern Europe, this group was renowned for its way with wood, and as the Finns spread they brought their technology with them – and it caught on. There is a long trail of evidence – 'v-notching', roof construction and a kind of modular floor plan – to support the idea that the American log cabin, which rooted Appalachia and shaped Abraham Lincoln's Indiana boyhood, originated with the Finns of central Sweden and spread following the Latin–Dutch–Swedish parley between Stuyvesant and Von Elswick in a bee-loud glade along the Delaware river.*

Stuyvesant felt full of himself as he prepared to head back to Manhattan. His colony was thriving. (That it was so in large part owing to the semi-representative government that he had bitterly fought was another matter.) The border agreement he had thrashed out with the New Englanders was holding. And at long last he had regained control of the southern region, without

* A bit of anecdotal support: when I told my Swedish-Norwegian father-in-law – who owns a log cabin in the traditionally Scandinavian country of northern Minnesota – about the Finns as the originators of the American log cabin, his response was: 'Around here everyone knows that if you want a log cabin built, you call a Finn.'

even firing a shot. As he prepared to board his flagship, the ache in his stump must have dulled somewhat.

*

If he was experiencing a rare problem-free moment, however, it was about to end. One hundred and fifty miles to the north, canoes were in the river, moving fast through the pre-dawn darkness, paddles knifing the water. On 15 September 1655, six hundred Indians made landfall at the southernmost point of Manhattan Island, below the fort, then flowed through the streets of the town, firing arrows, swinging axes, setting off screams, shrieks, alarms. Similar raids took place to the north on the mainland and on Staten Island, where Indians burned down homes, killed several dozen Europeans and took more hostage.

Historians have thought it an odd coincidence that this brief 'war' should take place while Stuyvesant happened to be away to the south subduing the Swedes. Trying to make sense of it, some grabbed at an incident in which a Dutchman had killed an Indian woman for stealing peaches, decided that this had launched the mayhem and named it the Peach War. But the evidence for what actually sparked the raids is there, lying in the records. The European residents of New Amsterdam could distinguish among the various tribes of the region, and in reporting the events of September 1655 they noted that the attackers seemed to be from everywhere: 'Maquas, Mahikanders, the Indians of the North River from above to below,' they wrote to Stuyvesant. And, strangely, they noted the presence of a chief of the Minquas or Susquehannocks – the tribe from the South River region, precisely where Stuyvesant had sailed. Such a multicultural Indian gathering makes no sense – unless you flip your view of events around, as some recent historians have done, and see it from the Indians' point of view. We are so used to looking at encounters between whites and Indians through the prism of later centuries that it's hard to fathom that in the 1600s the

Indians saw themselves as the dominant players. As far as the Minquas of the South River were concerned, they had devoted seventeen years to cultivating a trading relationship with the Swedes, only to see Stuyvesant and his soldiers destroy it. So the Indians retaliated. In doing so, they were in effect protecting the Swedes, who brought them valuable supplies and who, being weaker than the Indians, deserved their protection. It has also become clear in recent years that east coast Indians regularly formed alliances with distant tribes. If we grant them that much sophistication, then the reports of the Manhattanites make sense: a Minquas chief orchestrated the attack, and it was a direct result of Stuyvesant's dismantling of New Sweden.

The misnamed Peach War was a mere blip in the life of New Netherland: it was over in a matter of weeks. But it plays a bigger part in this story. Here again, as in so many other places, we have to fill in gaps with guesses. We have to imagine a party of Indians who had come from afar to attack Europeans. Just north of Manhattan, in a long valley, they come across a patch of civilization: a farmhouse, a sawmill, fields under cultivation. They raid the house; a man inside rises up to defend his family. He has always maintained good relations with the Indians of the area, but these are from elsewhere and make no distinctions between whites who are friends and whites who are enemies. The man is murdered. His wife escapes, or perhaps is taken prisoner for a time. It is over quickly, the roaring, defiant cries that signal the end of a life swallowed by the wooded hillsides.

The man was Adriaen van der Donck. For some periods of his life his presence and personality are so vivid that he seems to step three-dimensionally out of the pages of historical records. But the image of him in his last years, since his return from Europe, is flat and dim, and the circumstances of his death are sketchy. The death itself isn't even recorded. We know only that Van der Donck was alive in the summer of 1655, that he was dead before January 1656, and that his house was ransacked by Indians during the multitribal attack in September. So we have to stitch the remnants together with surmise. Interestingly, it is from Stuyvesant that we first hear of Van der Donck being dead, in an indirect reference. As the Manhattanites try to make sense of the Indian attacks, Stuyvesant tells the members of his council of a Wickquasgeck Indian, from the area around Van der Donck's home, coming to discuss what he knows. This Indian, Stuyvesant mentions, 'had been a good friend of Van der Donck, and had taken care of his cows for some time'. Thus the verb tense serves as the man's death notice, and the mention of him in conjunction with the attack adds another piece of evidence as to how he died. Since Stuyvesant himself never understood the likely connection between his military actions in the South River and the attacks around Manhattan, it probably never occurred to him that he had been indirectly responsible for the death of his one-time nemesis.

Van der Donck's wife Mary survived him. Her father, the Revd Francis Doughty, had recently accepted a position at a church in Virginia, and following her husband's death she joined him there. She found regular work as a medical practitioner, purging, sweating, setting bones and delivering babies. Eventually she married an Englishman named Hugh O'Neale, but, oddly, continues to appear in the records as 'Mrs Van der Donck (alias) O'Neale'. Having given up on the vast estate for which her husband had had such plans, Mary signed it over to her brother, who sold it. And so, very quickly after his death at the age of thirty-seven, Adriaen van der Donck – with no progeny or property to recall him to the living – was a forgotten man.

But that's not quite true. In a strange twist, his book, *A Description of New Netherland* – into which he had poured his knowledge of the colony, its people, its natives, its plants, winds, insects, mountains, snows, dangers and promises – his book, which had been admitted for publication and then withheld due to the war, came out in the Netherlands at just about the time of his death. It became a bestseller, and went into a second edition the following year. Once again, this time posthumously, Van der

Donck sparked a wave of interest in a faraway place called Manhattan, an island where ordinary Europeans could throw off the ancient shackles of their castes and guilds and sects. A place to which, now, yet more mixes of peoples – Croats and Prussians, Flemings and Limburgers, Copenhageners and Dieppois – would pin their dreams.

To the front of the second edition of the book, the publisher attached a poem that hymned both the author and his subject:

So, reader, if you desire, travel there freely and full of joy.
Although named for the Netherlands, it exceeds it far.
Does such a journey not appeal? Then lend your eyes
To the book by Van der Donck, which like a bright star,
Shows the land and people, and will teach you further
That the Netherlands, through her care, can govern New Netherland.

It wasn't very good verse. But it was as close as anyone would come to memorializing the man who first saw the promise of Manhattan Island, dreamed its future, and devoted his life to making the dream real.

The passion for the New World colony that had fuelled Van der Donck outlived him. Less than a year after his death and on the heels of the publication of his book, the municipal government of Amsterdam put together an elaborate plan for a colony of its own. Three hundred settlers signed on to emigrate, and the city drew up long lists of start-up supplies – 400 pairs of shoes, '50 pairs Prussian blue stockings', '100 red Rouen caps', '8 firkins vinegar', 250 pounds of cheese, 15 hams, 30 smoked tongues – with which it furnished them. Impressed by Stuyvesant's vanquishing of the Swedes, they decided to plant the new settlement on the South River, around one of Stuyvesant's forts. And so it began all over again: a new crop of arrivals, new hopes. 'I have been full 5 or 6 hours in the interior in the woods,' wrote one of the settlers, a schoolmaster, shortly after landfall, 'and found fine oak and hickory trees, also excellent land for tillage . . . I already begin to keep school, and have 25 children.' They called the settlement New Amstel. Today it is the city of New Castle, Delaware, and on its central square a tiny, late seventeenth-century Dutch house of sturdy brick and red-shuttered windows bears testimony to the belated effort to heed Van der Donck. The inhabitants' desires were to exploit the colony's potential and to catch up with English expansion in North America. One aim would be realized, the other would not.

14
New York

IT WOULD PROBABLY BE A MISTAKE TO THINK THAT THE English takeover of Manhattan was inevitable. The fall of Rome, the defeat of the Spanish Armada, the American colonists winning their war for independence, the Allies defeating Hitler – we have a tendency to imagine that past events, especially the big ones, had to happen the way they did. But really to believe that is to believe that our acts aren't our own, that we are only cogs in a machine carrying out pre-programmed instructions.

In hindsight, however, the takeover does have a certain obviousness about it. Partly that's because history books have portrayed the event that way, giving us the image of the English population of New England as an inexorable force of nature swelling until, like a glass overflowing, it poured southwards almost unconsciously, flooding the Dutch colony. But, looking at it another way, you might say that the colony cast off its Dutch parent. The seed that Henry Hudson transported to a distant island rooted and grew, and, really, outgrew the mother plant. It was the luckiest thing in the world for Manhattan – for America – that the English wanted it so badly, because, though no-one could see it at the time, the Dutch empire was already on the wane, and the English one was just beginning its rise. Van der Donck's mission had been all about the forces of history; his appeal was for the leaders of the Dutch government to take note of them. But the system that fuelled the Dutch golden age wasn't built to last. The English, meanwhile, especially those in America, would begin experimenting ornately and obsessively with ideas of liberty, unfettered reason, the rights of man. Put elements of the two together – seventeenth-century Dutch tolerance and free trade principles, and eighteenth-century English ideas about self-government – and you have a recipe for a new kind of society. You can almost see the baton passing from the one seventeenth-century power to the other; and at the point where it changed hands was Manhattan.

But no-one in the Dutch colony – or, for that matter, in New England – saw the end that finally came. It wasn't a result of hordes of New Englanders sweeping south. What happened was more calculated; it involved a global set of players, and, like any good final act, some sudden reversals.

The figure at the centre of it all, of course, was Peter Stuyvesant. Stuyvesant's main adversary was a man he would never meet – a man whose first, brief appearance in the history books came years earlier. In 1642 Stuyvesant was still barking orders under the tropical sun of Curaçao, Kieft was in charge on Manhattan and Van der Donck was the lawman up north, roaming the vast estate of the Amsterdam diamond merchant Kiliaen van Rensselaer. Meanwhile, outside the village of Boston, nine young men stepped from a simple clapboard building onto a long sward of grass. Just beyond the surrounding cow pastures and apple trees lay endless wilderness, but they and the cluster of people gathered around them saw the event through the lens of civilization, imbued with centuries of English tradition. The nine young men were the first class of graduates of the college founded with money granted by a Puritan minister named John Harvard.

Overseeing the ceremony was John Winthrop, governor of the Massachusetts colony, with whom Peter Stuyvesant would forge a close relationship. But the man who, more than any other individual, would engineer the takeover of Manhattan was one of those nine young scholars stepping into a New England morning in early autumn. His name was George Downing. He was a grim, athletic nineteen-year-old possessed of an ambition bordering on aggression, and he happened to be Governor Winthrop's nephew.

Like most in those first generations of Harvard graduates, Downing yearned for London. Shortly after the ceremony he sailed there, saw the civil war taking shape, pronounced himself a Puritan revolutionary and fought with the Parliamentarians. As the new government came into being, Oliver Cromwell saw the intellect and bulldog ferocity in the young man and made him his ambassador to The Hague. There Downing proved himself English to the core, which meant, among other things, fostering a loyal hatred of the Dutch. Really, he was an odd choice for a diplomat, unless you are more interested in provoking the country in question than in smoothing things over. In place of the suave manners usually considered necessary in diplomacy, Downing was brusque and obstinate. Jan de Witt and the other leaders of the Dutch government found him repellent, and his colleagues in the English government didn't much care for him either. The diarist Samuel Pepys worked under him and frankly pronounced him (to his diary, anyway) a 'perfidious rogue'.

But Downing had the diplomat's knack of getting what he wanted, and nothing shows it better than his management of his own fate following Cromwell's death in 1658 and the restoration of the Stuarts, in the person of Charles II, to the throne two years later. Downing had been among the most vicious persecutors of the royalists, hunting down friends of the Stuart family, and now the same royal family had returned to power. Turning on a sixpence, he boldly asked the new monarch to excuse his waywardness in supporting Cromwell, and blamed his faulty judgement on his having come of age in the unstable climate of the New World. He then demonstrated his loyalty to the king by trapping and arresting three of his own friends, men who had sentenced Charles's father to death. Downing's shamelessness was rewarded not only by Charles reappointing him to his position as ambassador to the Dutch, and later knighting him, but also, eventually, by the naming of Downing Street in London after him. (Downing College at the University of Cambridge has his name on it too, as a result of a bequest he made.)

So Downing settled himself back in at The Hague, and recommenced loathing the Dutch and their trade hegemony and searching, as duty compelled him to do, for cracks in it. Back in New England, meanwhile, the colonies' leaders – men who were theologically even more strident than the home country Puritans – were at least as disorientated by the restoration of the Stuarts as Downing, and most were not nearly as adept at changing direction. One result of their quandary, significant for American history in a number of ways, was the struggle for power and territory among the leaders of the English colonies in the early 1660s. Massachusetts, with its longstanding royal charter, was on firmest ground. But the two southern colonies, Connecticut and New Haven, had formed in an ad hoc way, with settlers spilling southward into territory the Dutch had claimed; as yet they had no official sanction in England. It was now necessary to petition the royals they had long despised. For New Haven, where Puritanism was purest, this was galling, and the leaders baulked at the task.

One man in Connecticut, however, was prepared to be more flexible. John Winthrop, the governor of that colony, was the son of the elder John Winthrop, first governor of Massachusetts and the patriarch of all the New England Puritans, and thus the cousin of George Downing. The elder Winthrop had long since died, much to the chagrin of Peter Stuyvesant, who had relied on his pro-Dutch leanings in his own dealings with the New England leaders. Stuyvesant now – with disastrous misjudgement – looked to the son for level-headed leadership among the Puritan firebrands. The younger Winthrop has been portrayed by history as a quiet, modest achiever, forever in the shadow of his father. This small, dark knife of a man has not been given credit either for his accomplishments or for his political cunning.

In 1661, having overcome his anti-royalist impulses, Winthrop proposed to travel to London to petition Charles for a charter for his colony. His guile shows itself first in his eagerness to go, second in the manner of his leavetaking. After promising William Leete, his counterpart in New Haven, that he would also deliver the petition for a charter that that colony had belatedly cobbled together, he sailed off without it, literally leaving the man standing on shore still holding his document. Next, he chose not to leave from Boston but instead made arrangements with his friend Peter Stuyvesant to sail from Manhattan. Of course, the island was a major travel hub; but sailing on a Dutch ship meant arriving in Holland first and then having to cross to England. Stuyvesant doesn't seem to have found it odd.

Sailing into the Dutch harbour on 8 July, Winthrop was shocked by the sound of cannonfire coming from the fort. But the shock turned to delight: his friend Stuyvesant was giving him the honoured greeting accorded to a head of state. (The Dutch records inform us that no less than 27 pounds of gunpowder was consumed 'to salute Governor Winthorp [*sic*]'.) Stuyvesant liked Winthrop. He seemed to like all Englishmen. Hartford was fast-growing but unkempt, and Stuyvesant proudly showed the visitor around his trim little capital: here the fort, here the new brick home of the director himself (Stuyvesant having decided he ought to have a house outside the fort as well as his distant farm), here the newly reinforced wall along the northern perimeter, complete now with guard towers and a central gate at the Highway. Winthrop apparently kept up a stream of convivial chatter, asking lots of questions, complimenting the director on how far he had come with his town. He spent thirteen days in New Amsterdam, and by the end of it he had detailed notes on the place, its fortifications and its troop numbers.

Trying to imagine Stuyvesant's plight at this time, it is hard not to feel some sympathy for him. He knew there were English machinations going on over his colony, and must have been livid at the Dutch company's failure to provide continuing support and send soldiers for its defence. And yet, when his own people expressed similar anger at being left without protection, he had to defend the directors' decisions.

And while he was wary of the English, Stuyvesant couldn't resist comparing notes with Winthrop on their respective colonies, and expressing frank envy of the cultural homogeneity of New England while complaining how his own population was comprised of the 'scrapings' of all countries. As the pressures on him grew, he seems to have become a more and more solitary figure, and an oddly evocative image of him at this time comes into view. One of his apparent sources of pleasure was tropical birds, with which he had presumably become fascinated in his time in the Caribbean. Over the years he had instructed company officials on Curaçao to send him birds (one packing slip indicates 'To the honorable lord director-general P. Stuyvesant . . . Four parrots in two cages' and 'Twenty-four parakeets'), so he must have built up quite an aviary by this time. On his farm, alone with the bright squawking of his pets, he must have tried endlessly to parse the problem of how to deal with the English, weighing trust against suspicion.

Stuyvesant's bonhomie towards Winthrop extended right up to the latter's departure: fifty-five soldiers lined the harbour as Winthrop's ship headed for open water, and unleashed a full military salute. At the other end of his journey, Winthrop arranged a meeting with the directors of the West India Company. Here he played up the fellow-Protestant connection, and the normally reserved men of business were convinced. 'He has always shown himself a friend of our nation,' they wrote to Stuyvesant, encouraging him in his trust.

If anyone found it suspicious that Winthrop proposed next to travel from Amsterdam to The Hague, it could have been explained away as a family matter. George Downing, English diplomat in residence there, was after all his cousin. They had last seen each other in New England, and were on familiar enough terms for Winthrop later to write several times to Downing, who was famously stingy with money, to chide him for keeping his mother living in near-poverty. Secret consultations being what they are, we don't know the details of the meeting between the two cousins in September 1661, but a map that Winthrop had drawn up of New Amsterdam's fortifications was soon circulating in government channels; this, logically, was the moment at which information about the current military status of the Dutch colony was transferred to English authorities.

Then – this historically momentous journey proceeding to the next phase – it was on to London for Winthrop. Charles II's coronation had taken place just five months earlier, and the city, having thrown off the heavy drape of Puritan rule, was in the midst of its libertine Restoration party, with thundering alehouses, brothels doing a lively trade, and theatres packing in crowds to see productions of *Hamlet*, *'Tis Pity She's a Whore*, and puppet shows satirizing Puritanism. From all of these Winthrop carefully averted his eyes as he applied himself to the task of winning royal favour.

A small, drab figure in the satiny surroundings of the king's council chamber, Winthrop – a grey little man with a hooked nose and arched, sardonic-looking eyebrows – bowed low and bowed often that autumn and winter, smiling through the small indignities (being routinely confused with Josiah Winslow of the Plymouth colony, realizing midway through the discussions that the king thought 'Massachusetts' and 'New England' were one and the same), and emerged with a document that embodied all of his desires – desires he had kept secret from everyone, most of all from his New England colleagues. When the charter was finally presented to them, they were staggered. Charles had given Connecticut a grant that extended from the Massachusetts border south, including the Dutch territories, and west as far as 'the Pacific'. Winthrop's quiet, modest, understated ambition was now revealed. He wanted all the territory between Massachusetts and Virginia. He wanted his land to stretch to the Pacific Ocean – never mind that no-one had any notion how far that was. He wanted everything. And he got it.

New Haven's officials were apoplectic at the idea that Winthrop proposed to engulf their colony, but it was a *fait accompli* – he had the royal signature – and, truly, he was so nice about it, so patient in explaining why it was for the good of all, that his opposite, Governor Leete, rapidly gave in, thus ensuring that the future United States would contain no state of New Haven. The bitterest Puritans of the colony talked about picking up stakes and heading for the Dutch territory, where they knew they would be welcomed; but their leaders knew too that Winthrop had that next in his sights.

Stuyvesant, meanwhile, had got wind of Winthrop's charter. He wrote to his friend, asking him to confirm that he would respect the Hartford Treaty boundary lines they had drawn up more than a decade earlier. Winthrop's reply was a deft little evasion. The West India Company suggested to Stuyvesant that because of 'your anxiety over the patent lately obtained by Governor Winthrop', he should shore up his defences. But they didn't give him the troops or ships to do so, despite his appeals.

Stuyvesant had troubles quite aside from Winthrop. The boom that had come to New Amsterdam in the eight years since the granting of its city charter was accompanied by a draining away of confidence in Stuyvesant and the West India Company. There had been that chance, in the months following Van der Donck's return, for Stuyvesant to support the reform that people had demanded, and give the entire colony a semblance of popular representation. Then again, the company would probably not have allowed it. At any rate, that was his last opportunity to win the hearts of the people. Soon after, English colonists on Long Island and on the mainland, who had sworn allegiance to New Netherland, began repudiating that allegiance, declaring themselves residents of Connecticut. Winthrop encouraged this and in part engineered it. Stuyvesant complained to the directors that Long Island and 'West Chester' were turning English; there had been encroachments on Jonas Bronck's and Adriaen van der Donck's former estates. While the city was thriving, the colony, he wrote, was in 'a sad and perilous condition'.

Now Winthrop prepared to make his big move, to bring the entire Dutch colony within his jurisdiction. One by one, towns on the mainland were ordered to 'yield obedience' to Connecticut, and begin paying taxes to Hartford. Winthrop was no longer Stuyvesant's friend; now he and his colleagues in Connecticut were 'unrighteous, stubborn, impudent and pertinacious'. New Netherland was disintegrating, and Stuyvesant didn't have the means to stop it.

But the end didn't come that way, with an invasion from the north. Winthrop was just about the wiliest creature of all those involved in this end-game – the wiliest, that is, but one. His cousin, George Downing, had the better of him there. Downing took the information about Manhattan that Winthrop had given him and put it to other uses. From his diplomat's offices in The Hague, Downing had the wider view of things. He saw the globe scored with the crisscrossing lines of Dutch trade routes. Dutch outposts stippled the coast of India like a beard; they were scattered across the Indonesian archipelago; the Dutch were the only nation on earth with whom the closed islands of Japan would trade. They had control of the spice trade, of cotton, indigo, silk, sugar, copper, coffee and dozens of other products. And now, as they moved into west Africa, Downing saw them about to secure an advantage in the one commodity that would tip the balance in the decades ahead: human beings.

In June 1661 Downing appeared before the States General and made an expansive appeal on behalf of his nation. England and the Dutch Republic, he intoned, must 'be instruments of good and not of hurt to each other'. The matter of trade was thorny, but, he advised sagely, 'the world is large, there is trade enough for both.' This was hogwash. After negotiating a trade treaty with Jan de Witt he went to London, where he promptly directed his indomitable energy to convincing the king that now was the time to hit the Dutch hard, with soldiers, ships and cannonfire. Living as he did in the bosom of golden-age Holland, he had seen the changes brought by the waves of wealth – dour Calvinist clothes swapped for satins and swaggering French fashions, country estates tricked out with faux-Roman pillars, the children of rich merchants (as evidenced by many portraits) growing fat and pink as young sows – and he believed the Dutch had gone soft. Their Atlantic Rim possessions were ripe for picking, starting with the slaving posts in west Africa. 'Go on in Guinea,' he thundered to the king's council. 'If you bang them there, they will be very tame.'

Downing was preaching to the converted; overwhelmingly, according to Samuel Pepys, the court was 'mad for a Dutch war'. The only man who really mattered, however, wasn't so sure. The second Charles Stuart to sit on the English throne was a man of wide interests. He was obsessed with clocks, enjoyed redesigning the royal gardens and spent late nights at 'the Royal Tube' (his telescope). He loved dogs, horses, singing Italian songs, tennis (he played daily) and sex (possibly also daily – he had many mistresses and 'royal bastards' was a category of palace expenditure). His court was the epitome of licentiousness, a mirror image of the years that had preceded it. He had been a teenager when anti-royal forces had put a price on his head, and after years hiding in barns, forests and foreign palaces, he was now where he was meant to be, and ready to enjoy the experience to the full. He cared about foreign policy, but didn't seem to have an overriding philosophy to guide its direction. He wasn't especially fond of the Dutch, but he admired them, and felt some gratitude towards them for putting him up in The Hague. He wasn't sure about launching military raids.

His brother, however, was. James Stuart, at twenty-eight, was bigger and bluffer than the king, a muscular athlete and lifelong soldier, full of can-do aggression – altogether more of a man's man. He wasn't well liked by the English and some historians have branded him a stooge, but he had something his brother lacked: constancy. When he later converted to Catholicism it was after long deliberation, and he stayed with it despite the fact that it got him deposed only three years into his reign. It was James who saw the magic in Cromwell's idea of an English empire. His brother had made him head of the Admiralty, and from that position he was determined to make good on Cromwell's dream.

The plan began to take shape in 1661. As a first step, the men at the centre of power in London – the king and his brother, the politicians, the leading merchants – agreed that the American colonies, which had been left to themselves while the nation's attention was diverted by civil war, needed reorganizing. Charles and James didn't trust the Puritan leaders there, and soon after the king had sent Winthrop away with his charter it was agreed that it had been a mistake to give the New Englanders leave to take control of Manhattan and the Hudson river corridor, which meant access to the interior of the continent.

Downing then took the lead in arguing for a master plan involving the whole Atlantic Rim. Reading the letters, minutes and military instructions surrounding this evolving plan, it's remarkable to comprehend that so much history – the change in ownership of Manhattan Island, the consolidation of the American colonies, the ramping up of the slave trade into an epoch-changing institution, the transformation of west Africa, the Caribbean, South America and North America – was quite calculated and stemmed from a series of meetings among a rather small group of men in London in the years 1661 and 1662.

James backed the plan, and pushed for the king's endorsement. Warfare was a language that the prince knew and with which he felt comfortable. In his years of exile he had volunteered to serve with the French and had fought valiantly in their war against Spain, leading men in cavalry musket charges on the snowy plains of northern France and achieving the rank of general; then, when the vicissitudes of the age dictated that the banished English princes should back the Spanish, he promptly switched sides and fought with equal bravery for Spain. Having risked his life a dozen times for lesser ends, he was more than ready to commit himself now to something as big and vital as this.

The first objective was to wrest control of the slave ports of west Africa from the Dutch. The prince organized a company to fund the operation, conferring on it the flourishing title of the Company of Royal Adventurers of England Trading into Africa. (The Royal Mint commemorated James's desire to exploit the 'Guinea Coast' by striking a new coin, which, popularly known as the guinea, would long outlast the trade.) Reorganized as the Royal African Company, this enterprise would become the single greatest shipper of slaves from Africa to America. (The prosaic tone of the 1667 announcement of its public stock offering stands in stark relief against the impact the words would have down the centuries: 'the Royal Company being very sensible how necessary it is that the *English* Plantations in *America* should have a competent and a constant supply of *Negro-servants* for their own use of Planting, and that at a moderate Rate, have already sent abroad, and shall within eight days dispatch so many Ships for the Coast of *Africa* as shall by God's permission furnish the said Plantations with at least 3000 Negroes, and will proceed from time to time to provide them a constant and sufficient succession of them'.)

In the company's first mission, James picked a roguish Irishman named Robert Holmes and sent him in command of two ships to go raiding in the Cape Verde islands and down the Guinea Coast. Holmes did all that was asked of him: the initial result of James's first corporate adventure was a rout of the Dutch slaving posts. The Dutch ambassador expressed his government's outrage to King Charles (the two countries were after all officially at peace), and the king tried to brush the matter aside: 'And pray, what is Cape Verde? a stinking place; is this of such importance to make so much ado about?' Meanwhile, the ringing success encouraged both the prince and the diplomat to move to the next stage. Downing was sure he could talk his way out of anything. 'What ever injuries the Dutch doe them,' he wrote of James's warships, 'let them be sure to doe the Dutch still greater and lett me alone to mediate between them.'

Charles now had some confidence in the geopolitical gambit, and he gave Downing and his brother their next card to play. Settlement of North America had become a primary long-term objective; the slave business was intertwined with it. In March 1664 the king signed his name to an extraordinary document. In making a gift 'unto our Dearest Brother James Duke of York, his Heirs and Assigns' of a vast stretch of the North American continent ('Together with all the Lands, Islands, Soils, Rivers, Harbors, Mines, Minerals, Quarries, Woods, Marshes, Waters, Lakes, Fishings, Hawking, Hunting and Fowling and all other Royalties, Profits, Commodities and Hereditaments to the said several Islands, Lands and Premises'), he was being more than generous. Much of the land indicated – from Maine to Delaware – he had only recently granted to Winthrop for his Connecticut colony. The gift to his brother was meant to erase that mistake. The 'Duke's Charter' took care to single out the 'River called Hudsons River', and it was in this that men in London who were attuned to global economic events were particularly interested. Like an elephant in the dawn, the full girth of the continent to the edge of which the European colonies had clung for four decades was gradually becoming apparent. It was also apparent by now that the New England colonies were on a kind of shelf, landlocked, unable to access future potential. The beavers of the north-east were on their way to extinction; the future lay to the west, which meant, first, up the Hudson river. And the key to it was Manhattan. This conclusion was borne out by the fact that much of the English trade already went through Manhattan, which, the merchants now calculated, cost them ten thousand pounds per year in tobacco shipments alone. Having identified the island as the linchpin of the American colonies, a committee at Whitehall determined in January 1664 that it was necessary to take it, and soon. Further, they wanted it in the hands of one of their own men, not those of the New Englanders.

Having made its decision, the committee moved quickly. The charter was signed in March; the next month, James summoned a man named Richard Nicolls. Nicolls was forty years old, a lifelong royalist who had stayed at the prince's side throughout his exile during the Commonwealth and had fought with him in France. He was smart and capable, which was just as well; James told him he was being entrusted with North America. He would command four gunships and 450 men; they would leave within the month. Shortly after his departure, James himself took to sea, cruising the Channel in a naval exercise, smelling the future on the sea air, fully aware that his attack on Manhattan would have to be followed up by further assaults on the Dutch.

Nicolls sailed west. To start with the squadron had good conditions. Then on day sixteen they were hit by crosswinds and foul weather, and in 'very great Fogge' Nicolls, on his flagship, the 36-gun *Guinea*, lost sight of two of his vessels. Nevertheless, ten weeks after leaving Portsmouth, all four made landfall, two on Cape Cod, the other two away to the south at Piscataway. Coming ashore at Boston, Nicolls promptly despatched riders with letters from King Charles to the New England governors, informing them that steps were about to be taken for 'the welfare and advancement of those our plantations in America'.

Arguably the man in the colonies most shocked by Nicolls's arrival was not Stuyvesant but John Winthrop. Nicolls had been ordered by James to 'putt Mr Winthropp . . . in mind of the differences which were on foot here' – in other words, let him know that the king had reneged on his promise. Winthrop's dream of a continent-wide colony of Connecticut vanished in a stroke. Smart politician that he was, however, he swiftly adjusted his expectations; while the Massachusetts leaders stalled and grumbled, unhappy with the idea of relinquishing power to the crown, Winthrop offered his services in negotiations with Stuyvesant, which Nicolls accepted.

Stuyvesant, meanwhile, was 150 miles north of Manhattan, at Fort Orange, where there were problems with the Mohawks. He hadn't been caught off guard, but he had been misled. Through one of his English friends he had learned of the English squadron even before it landed, and had his capital dig in – setting watches, preparing defences, sending men out along Long Island Sound for news of the ships' arrival. Then a remarkable letter arrived from Amsterdam. Before the squadron had left, Downing had taken the unusual step of informing the Dutch government of its existence – in order, he said, to assure the Dutch that their colony had nothing to fear; England was merely sending a commander to overhaul the administration of the New England colonies.

The Dutch leaders were completely duped; the directors insisted Stuyvesant needn't be alarmed. Nicolls's mission would not affect him, and as to the English residents of the Dutch colony, they would 'not give us henceforth so much trouble' because they 'prefer to live free under us at peace with their consciences' than risk being persecuted by 'a government from which they had formerly fled'. So Stuyvesant relaxed his guard and went up the Hudson as planned – only to find, as soon as he arrived at his northern outpost, news of impending disaster following him. He sailed back to Manhattan to find the island in turmoil. The English gunboats were perched at the entrance to the lower harbour, cutting off the river and Manhattan Island. People stepping off the ferry from Breuckelen talked of inhabitants of the English towns there forming themselves into companies of foot soldiers. Sailors from a Dutch boat anchored in Gravesend Bay reported the English ships had fired on them.

Stumping into the fort, Stuyvesant dictated a letter to the colony's secretary, which was delivered to Nicolls's ship, asking his business and declaring boldly and hopefully that Stuyvesant was not 'apt to entertaine any thing of prejudice intended against us'. Nicolls's reply came the next morning, a messenger delivering a letter informing Stuyvesant that 'in his Majesties Name, I do demand the Towne, Scituate upon the Island commonly knowne by the Name of Manhatoes with all the Forts there unto belonging, to be rendered unto his Majesties obedience, and Protection into my hands.' The king did not relish 'the effusion of Christian blood', but if the Dutch did not surrender they would invite 'the miseryes of a War'.

Stuyvesant's reaction to this thunderbolt was stylishly in period: he returned the letter because it was unsigned. Whereupon Nicolls fired off another:

> These to the Honorable the Governor of the Manhatoes.
>
> Honoured Sir.
>
> The neglect of Signing this inclosed Letter, when it was first brought to your hands, by Colonell Geo: Cartwright, was an omission which is now amended, and I must attribute the neglect of it at first, to the over hasty zeale I had dispatching my Answer to the Letter I received from you dated 19/26th instant, I have nothing more to add, either in matter of Forme, then is therein expressed, only that your speedy Answer is necessary to prevent future inconveniences, and will very much obliege.
>
> Your affectionat humble Servant
>
> RI: NICOLLS.

Townspeople were rushing through the streets with news and gossip; but Stuyvesant tended to be calm in such situations. By now he had the pertinent details. There were maybe two hundred and fifty men in New Amsterdam able to bear arms. Nicolls had nearly twice that, plus forces totalling a thousand or more amassing on Long Island, plus the firepower of his ships. The fort had its cannons, but it was so low on gunpowder they were inconsequential. The situation was probably hopeless, but Stuyvesant doesn't seem to have had second thoughts: they would fight to the death. Anything else, he informed the leaders of the city government, 'would be disapproved of' at home.

At this juncture a rowing boat, with a white flag aloft, approached the shore. In it, of all people, was Winthrop, along with several other New Englanders. They asked for a meeting, and Stuyvesant led them to a tavern. Winthrop urged his 'friend' to surrender, and handed him a letter containing Nicolls's terms. They were generous terms – extravagant, almost – and yet Stuyvesant was unmoved. Later, at the City Hall, the city officials demanded to see the letter and show it to the citizens. Stuyvesant knew his people: resistance would cave in once they heard of the favourable terms. So he tore the letter to pieces. At this, the room went wild. Long-stoppered feelings came flooding out. The company, Stuyvesant himself, the colony's government – it was all a sham; it had never been anything else. For years they had lodged requests and petitions, asking for a voice in government, and he had sneeringly rejected them, declared them childish fools who didn't understand the complexities of government, and all along he had been nothing but a good soldier blindly carrying out the orders of a bankrupt bureaucracy. Now he expected them to fight and die on his orders. Why should they? Why spill their blood, and try to hold the attackers off, when they all knew the West India Company had sent no reinforcements, despite his appeals? It would have been one thing had the company denied their petitions for reform on the grounds that its way was better, but it had never had a way.

Finally, the town leaders demanded once again to see the letter. In an odd bit of comedy, Stuyvesant offered them the pieces, which Nicasius de Sille took and carefully pasted back together.

Meanwhile, with no answer from Stuyvesant, Nicolls had moved his ships forwards, within shot of the city. The English Long Islanders, with muskets and pikes, were gathered along the Breuckelen shore. Some French privateers who were in the area had got news of the events, and showed up to see what might be in it for them.

There is then an almost Shakespearean scene, in which Stuyvesant climbs heavily onto the battlements of his fort and stands there, gazing at the guns trained on his town, his long wisps of hair flailed by the wind. He seems, at this moment in which he will be forever frozen in history, almost to have achieved the status of a tragic hero, his leadership, his particular stew of character strengths and flaws, having built this impressive place but also having caused his own people to turn against him. (To add a family dimension to the betrayal, his seventeen-year-old-son Balthazar had come out on the side of the city leaders.) There was a lone gunner at his side, awaiting his command to touch light to powder. It must have been tempting. A single cannon blast at the ships riding at anchor just beyond the walls would be enough. It would unleash a rain of violence, a storm that would swallow the place, ending the torment, ending things the way they ought to end, in good, quenching blood and fire.

Then, in his direst moment, the church came to give comfort. Two ministers of the town, father and son, with the ponderous, sonorous name of Megapolensis, appeared at his side. It's hard not to think of Stuyvesant's father here, to imagine the lifelong battle inside him between stalwart devotion to the church, personified in his father's ministry, and that streak of stiff rebelliousness. Maybe it was the church that swayed him. Then too, the warships, the guns, the French privateers and the glinting line of weaponry on the opposite shore had to have added up to something in his military calculations. He knew what the pikes and the expectant leers of the foreigners meant. It was a longstanding rule of war that if a besieged fort so much as fired a shot, the forces against it were at liberty to sack and loot; the place would be laid waste. Was he really willing to subject the people he had lived among these seventeen years to such a thing?

The ministers talked to him for a while in low voices, and then the three men went down.

But he still wouldn't yield. He crafted another letter to Nicolls, referencing the history of the Dutch claim to the territory, asserting that 'we are oblieged to defend Our place,' informing him that he had had news from Holland about a treaty between the two countries, and suggesting that Nicolls check with the home base before taking this fateful step. It may have been a bluff, but Stuyvesant was right in thinking this move by England was rash. Contrary to Ambassador Downing's assurances to King Charles, the Dutch would fight to defend their interests. At this moment, the great Dutch admiral Michiel de Ruyter was preparing to launch an expedition for west Africa. When his sweep was over, all but one of the Dutch outposts taken in James's raids would be back in Dutch hands. Outright war would then begin, and, all told, the Dutch would win the Second Anglo-Dutch War, creating a pothole in England's road to empire.

But, pulling back to the broad view, the English were riding to the top of the historical wave. In these events of late summer 1664 the island was a pivot around which the age would turn – and when it was done the floppy hats, Vermeer interiors, 'merry company' portraits, and blue-and-white Delft tiles would be thrust into the past, and ahead would be the Redcoats and the Raj, Britannia ruling the waves.

In the end, Stuyvesant truly did stand alone. All of his people deserted him. The leading citizens of New Amsterdam – ninety-three of them, including his son – signed a petition asking him to avert 'misery, sorrow, conflagration, the dishonor of women, murder of children in their cradles, and, in a word, the absolute ruin and destruction of about fifteen hundred innocent souls'. Perhaps it struck him, on reading it, that it showed he had been right all along: this was what came of a mongrel society – this rapid willingness to give up, this spinelessness, this absence of patriotism. Mixing religions and races weakened a populace, and here was proof. But it would be wrong to think that the citizens of the town had no sense of loyalty; it was just that they were practical people, and in any case they had little choice. They made clear in their final petition to Stuyvesant that they were willing to support their neighbours and their colony, but they had no qualms about abandoning the company that had left them defenceless.

And so they did. The fifteen hundred residents of New Amsterdam, the ten thousand inhabitants of the colony of New Netherland, turned their backs on the company that had long ignored them. Griet Reyniers, the one-time Amsterdam barmaid who became Manhattan's first prostitute, abandoned it, together with her husband, Anthony 'the Turk' van Salee, the half-Moroccan former pirate. They were now wealthy landowners on Long Island, and their four daughters were married to some of New Amsterdam's up-and-coming businessmen. Joris Rapalje, who with his bride Catalina Trico comprised the Adam and Eve of the colony, had recently died, but Catalina was still very much alive, as were her grown children and their families, and they too preferred to acquiesce rather than die. The same went for Asser Levy, the Polish Jew who had battled Stuyvesant over the rights of his co-religionists, and now owned Manhattan's first kosher butcher's shop; and for Manuel 'the Giant' Gerrit, the African who had escaped hanging in 1641 and who for the past five years had been living as a free landowner on a small farm near Stuyvesant's bouwerie. For all of these people, living peaceably under an English prince who promised to allow them to continue in the way of life they had fashioned was patently better than fighting and dying.

And so he relented. 'I would much rather be carried out dead,' he said, and surely everyone believed him, but instead he named six men to negotiate terms with their English counterparts. They met at Stuyvesant's farm. And the next Monday, at eight in the morning, Peter Stuyvesant, fifty-four years old, thick of build, with his cuirass and his limp and his small, bold eyes, led a military procession out of the fort, with drummers drumming and flags waving.

Then, as all attention shifted to the waterfront, where Nicolls and his main body of troops were coming ashore, a small party of English soldiers entered the deserted fort. Outside, the harbour winds were swirling around the interested throng of mixed nationalities who watched as an English flag went up the flagpole and listened as Nicolls declared the place renamed for his patron, the Duke of York and Albany. Inside the fort, meanwhile, a few soldiers climbed to the office of the colonial secretary, above the gate. In any change of government, gaining possession of the records is among the first steps, for to control a society's vital documents is to control its past and future. The soldiers found what they were looking for: rows of bulky leather-bound volumes, forty-nine in all, numbered consecutively on their spines, A to Z and then AA to QQ. Wills, deeds, minutes, correspondence, complaints, petitions, confrontations, agreements – it was all here, meticulously maintained, year by year, day by day: the story of America's first mixed society.

15
Inherited Features

As Stuyvesant surrendered the Manhattan colony, America's myth of origin was already coming into being. Starting in the 1660s, a handful of New England clergymen began singing the praises of their parents' and grandparents' generations, men and women who had braved an ocean and a wilderness to start a new life. The story they wove was biblical from first to last. In their modest telling, their forebears were none other than the chosen people of God, and America (i.e. New England) was the promised land. By the time of the revolutionary generation a century later, the story had become myth. John Adams, himself a descendant of the first Puritans, revered the Pilgrims as the launchers of the American saga.

Certainly the Puritans passed down many features to the nation. They were practical, plain-spoken, businesslike, pious – all traits that Americans from Adams on have admired and tried to emulate. But, as many people have noted in recent decades, in which the Puritans have fallen out of favour, they were also self-important zealots. Their form of government was a theocracy. It was rooted in intolerance: freedom of worship, in the words of one prominent New England minister (who became president of Harvard College), was the 'first born of all abominations'. ''Tis Satan's policy to plead for an indefinite and boundless toleration,' declared another. The Puritans' systematic crackdown on alternative views was cruel, unusual and lethal. People whose crime was being members of the Baptist denomination, or Quakers, or belonging to some other Protestant sect, were beaten with a knotted whip ('to cut their flesh and to put them to suffering'), put in a 'horse lock' of irons, had ears lopped off. They were whipped and then tied to a cart and driven through deep snow, 'the white snow and crimson blood' making a vivid tapestry. They were hanged in public spectacles. Some were hanged and their naked bodies dragged through the streets. These were not mass 'lynchings' but sentences pronounced by judicial authorities, in regimes based on an official policy of intolerance. Later, in the 1680s, came the witchcraft mania, which has gone down in history as a particularly vivid example of the dangers of fusing government and religion.

Out of the Puritans' exceptionalism – their belief that the Old World had succumbed to wickedness and they had been charged by God to save humanity by founding a new society in a new world – grew the American belief that American society was similarly divinely anointed. In 1845 the journalist John O'Sullivan coined the phrase that would carry this doctrine forwards across the continent when he declared 'the right of our manifest destiny to overspread and to possess the whole continent which providence has given us for the development of the great experiment of liberty and federated self government'. In the early twentieth century, President Woodrow Wilson extended the 'manifest destiny' concept to cover the globe. In the aftermath of the Great War, he determined that the United States, because of 'the sheer genius of this people and the growth of our power' and because it had 'seen visions that other nations have not seen', had become not only 'a determining factor in the history of mankind' but 'the light of the world'. This conviction lives on today, and is directly traceable to the first Puritans.

When the sons of those first leaders – Cotton Mather, Thomas Hutchinson, Jeremy Belknap, Thomas Prince – put their beliefs into print, their story found eager readers. Of course, in this version of American beginnings, the tellers were English and the hearers were English; subsequent generations were raised on the belief that America's origins were English, and that other traditions wove themselves into the fabric later. And history shows this, does it not? The thirteen original colonies were English colonies. The supporting evidence is overwhelming: the language Americans speak, their political traditions, many of their customs. This is all so obvious that no-one questions it.

But it ought to be questioned. The original colonies were *not* all English, and the multi-ethnic makeup of the Manhattan colony is precisely the point. The fact that the Dutch once established a foothold in North America has been known all along, of course; but, after noting it, the national myth of origin promptly dismisses it as irrelevant. It was small, it was short-lived, it was inconsequential. That wasn't *us*, the subtext runs, but someone else – an alien mix of peoples, with strange customs and a different language, who appeared briefly and then vanished, leaving only traces.

This is false. In the first place, while in population the colony was quickly outpaced by New England, it was hardly small. It covered the whole middle stretch of the east coast and encompassed parts of five of what would be the original thirteen states of the union. So far as historical evidence goes – written records – we have a steadily growing mountain of it, thanks to the translation and publication work now going on. But surely the most obvious reason to see the Dutch colony as significant is that we are not talking about a settlement planted in some obscure corner, in a hidden valley or on an inaccessible slope. We are talking about Manhattan. What would be strange would be if the settlers of the most geographically vital island on the continent, which would serve as the gateway between it and Europe, had *not* made an imprint on the nation that was to come.

Moving the story beyond the English takeover requires, first, realizing that 'the Dutch' didn't go anywhere. The people from all over Europe who had built homes and raised families on Manhattan, on Long Island, away to the south along the Delaware river, and across the river from Manhattan in what the English first named Albania (*sic!*) but on second thoughts called New Jersey, had no reason to leave after Stuyvesant surrendered his colony. In fact, ships from the Dutch Republic, with their mixed loads of European settlers, kept arriving in New York harbour. (Notaries in Amsterdam, blithely ignoring the political changeover, continued writing 'New Netherland', sometimes even 'New York in New Netherland', on immigration papers well into the 1680s.) And Richard Nicolls – who became the first governor of New York after accepting Stuyvesant's surrender – and his successors actually encouraged the traffic with their long-time foe. They even made a point of appointing prominent Dutch merchants to their economic councils to keep the ties strong. That was because these first English governors quickly discovered they were in the awkward but titillating position of being even more closely bound into world trade than London itself. With the English takeover, New York instantly became a unique spot on the globe: the only port city plugged directly into both of the world's two major trading empires. To sever connections to the great trading firms of Amsterdam would have been to strangle their long-sought possession just as it was burgeoning. The traders, bakers, brewers, tavernkeepers, smugglers and rogues of the town soon came to the same realization as the governors, and felt the power of it: their island was no longer a Dutch settlement, but nor was it really English either. It had its own trajectory.

The notion of an 'English takeover' brings with it an image of starting afresh, of a house emptied of the possessions of the previous tenant and then filled with the completely different belongings of a new occupant. What happened instead was more in the nature of a cohabitation. Continuity between the Dutch and English eras was established at eight o'clock on Saturday morning, 6 September 1664. We can imagine a percussion of hooves on dry earth as twelve riders, having travelled north up the Highway and then east along the Bouwerie Road, came to a halt and dismounted before the façade of Peter Stuyvesant's farmhouse. Maybe they paused for a moment to breathe the country air: here were fields under cultivation and, just beyond, stands of forest alternating with salt marshes. (Today the same view takes in an Arab news-stand, a Yemenite Israeli restaurant, a pizza shop, a Japanese restaurant and a Jewish deli.) Following precedent for such occasions, neither Stuyvesant nor Nicolls was present for the meeting that then took place, but each had chosen a slate of commissioners to negotiate the transfer of the colony. Stuyvesant's included four Dutchmen, one Englishman and one Frenchman; Nicolls's representatives were two of his English aides and four New Englanders, including John Winthrop.

We have no details of the negotiations, which is a pity because there is the suggestion of a move on the part of Peter Stuyvesant that, if true, would amount to a kind of reversal in his long struggle with the colonists, and in particular with Adriaen van der Donck. Nicolls's private instructions from the king authorized him to inform the Dutch colonists only that 'they shall continue to enjoy all their possessions (Forts only excepted) and the same freedome in trade with our other good subjects in those parts.' But Stuyvesant seems to have instructed his men to push for specific guarantees, and that is what they got. The end result of the negotiations, the so-called Articles of Capitulation, is a remarkable document. Packaged into it – and extended later by the New York City Charter – was a guarantee of rights unparalleled in any English colony. 'The Dutch here shall enjoy the liberty of their Consciences,' it read. People would be free to come and go as they liked. Trade would be unrestricted: by all means, 'Dutch vessels may freely come hither.' Most remarkable, the political leaders of the colony would 'continue as now they are', provided they swore an oath of allegiance to the king, and in future 'the Towne of Manhatans, shall choose Deputyes, and those Deputyes, shall have free Voyces in all Publique affaires.' Prefiguring the Bill of Rights, it even stipulated that 'the Townesmen of the Manhatons shall not have any Souldier quartered upon them.'

It is possible that this unusual slate of freedoms was authorized by the Duke of York himself, who had declared that he wanted the Manhattanites to have 'immunities and privileges beyond what other parts of my territory doe enjoy'. If James was indeed the force behind these articles, then he deserves to have his title attached to the name of the place. The thinking was that the inhabitants of the island should be allowed to maintain their way of life for the very good reason that it worked. One has to keep in mind what an oddity the new city of New York was to people of the seventeenth century, with its variety of skin tones and languages and prayer styles co-existing side by side. The English leaders in Whitehall Palace were surely aware of this unusual characteristic of the island across the water, and they may have been confused by it, but at the same time they understood that it was part of what made the place function.

Then again, there is no record that the English offered the particular catalogue of guarantees that made their way into the Articles of Capitulation. It is reasonable to assume that at least some of them were included on the insistence of the Dutch representatives, following Stuyvesant's orders. If so, there is an ironic twist here. Such a list of individual rights and liberties, preserving the unique society that had come into being in the colony, was precisely what Van der Donck had fought for, and precisely what Stuyvesant had opposed during all of his seventeen years in office. Now, faced with the end of the West India Company's rule, which he had stoutly, mulishly upheld, Stuyvesant seems to have made a turnaround. If his own brand of leadership couldn't save the place, then Van der Donck's vision – government commitments to support free trade, religious liberty and a form of local political representation – afforded the best protection for its inhabitants in the uncertain future. If this is what Stuyvesant came to think in those final hours, the question is: why? Part of the answer may be that, despite the unending turmoil of his years as director of the colony, he cared about it and its people. Some of his colonists might have wondered, but he apparently had a heart. The second part of the answer is that Stuyvesant understood power. If he had to give up the colony, better to divide that power, split off a new channel and see that some of it flowed to the people of the colony, than to have the English decide what courses it would follow. The result was surely not a complete reversal of character, not a sharp break, but rather a bending that makes for a poignant end to Stuyvesant's long tussle with his colonists.

Maybe, then, Stuyvesant came away from the negotiations with some degree of satisfaction. But it cannot have been much. He had lost his colony, and the directors of the West India Company rubbed salt in the wound by demanding that he return to Amsterdam to face charges of 'criminal neglect' in surrendering. After a grim voyage on a ship the ironic appropriateness of whose name – *The Crossed Heart* – must have raised in him a low chuckle, Stuyvesant found himself in more or less the same position as Van der Donck more than a decade earlier: making his case before the States General while the company threw argument and invective at him ('neglect or treachery . . . scandalous surrender'), blocked his effort to return to America, and kept him exiled in Holland and separated from his family. As further indication that Stuyvesant had undergone something of a transformation with the loss of the colony, he included in his defence testimonials from some of the very Manhattanites who had once denounced his autocratic rule, now declaring that he had done everything in his power to keep the colony together.

The fact that Stuyvesant petitioned to be allowed to return to Manhattan cannot be overlooked. Like Van der Donck, and yet by a very different route, he too had become an American. He may have packed his son off to seek his fortune in the Caribbean in the weeks after the English takeover (upon arrival in Curaçao, Balthazar Stuyvesant wrote home, enquiring about events and asking his cousin to 'take care of the girls on the Manhatans' and 'greet them all for me with a kiss'). But America was Stuyvesant's home, and eventually the States General granted him permission to return. He finished his days as a resident of the rapidly growing settlement, a gentleman farmer, a grandfather, a man of renown always greeted by locals as 'the General', a historical curiosity to the incoming population. The crowning irony of his life was that in surrendering the colony he had finally won himself the welcome of his fellow colonists. He had joined them at long last, but not as an inhabitant of New Netherland. He died – in 1672, at the age of sixty-two – a New Yorker.

Nicolls, meanwhile, was delighted with the deal he had struck. Without firing a shot, he had gained a prize that he knew full well was of great immediate and inestimable future value; and all the English leaders seemed aware of the scope of the achievement. 'I saw ye towne upon the Manatos Iland reduced to the obedience of our Soveraigne Lord the Kinge,' John Winthrop intoned after the articles were signed, 'Wherby there is way made for the inlargment of his Maties Dominions, by filling yt vacant wildernesse, in tyme, wth plantatios of his Maties subiects.' Nicolls fired off a letter to the Duke, practically crowing at his accomplishment, declaring New York 'the best of all His Majties Townes in America', and predicting that within five years it would be the main portal for the flow of trade between England and North America.

When the news of the takeover reached King Charles, he whisked a letter to France. His sister Henrietta – the Duchess of Orleans, sister-in-law (and sometime lover) of Louis XIV – was his closest confidante. 'You will have heard of our taking of New Amsterdam, which lies just by New England,' he wrote to her chirpily. ''Tis a place of great importance to trade, and a very good town.' The Dutch had done marvels with the wilderness island, the king noted, 'but we have got the better of it, and 'tis now called New York.'

*

But the 1664 surrender would not be the end of the struggle between the two empires over the colony. The takeover of Manhattan helped ignite the Second Anglo-Dutch War, which would see Dutch warships retaliate by taking the English outpost of Surinam to the north of Brazil, valuable for its sugar plantations, and the spice island of Run in the East Indies, while others sailed up the Medway, surprising the English fleet, torching some of its finest ships and forcing Whitehall to treat for peace. But then, with a shortsightedness that would have made Van der Donck shake his head in sad recognition, in the treaty negotiations the Dutch government allowed England to have its way regarding captured territories: rather than swap them back, each nation would keep its war spoils.

Some Dutch leaders apparently thought that was a bad deal. Only five years after the peace treaty was signed in 1667, the Third Anglo-Dutch War broke out, and a Dutch fleet crossed the Atlantic and set about strafing English possessions. It attacked Caribbean ports under English control, swept into the Chesapeake and burned the tobacco fleet about to embark for England – and then, in a little-known episode, sailed into New York harbour in August 1673, precisely nine years after Stuyvesant's surrender, and retook Manhattan. Everything then happened again, but in reverse: a Dutch commander at the head of a flotilla of gunships threatened to reduce the town; inside the fort, an Englishman was in charge, agonizing over what to do. He was outgunned and outmanned. The English surrendered; a new, Dutch-led adminstration was installed. The English troops paraded out of the fort just as the Dutch under Stuyvesant had done, and the town that had been New Amsterdam and then New York was given a third name: New Orange. The whole colony changed hands: the upriver trading town that the Dutch had named Fort Orange and then Beverwyck, and which Nicolls had renamed Albany after his patron, was now called

Willemstad. The paperwork was barely complete, however, before it all reverted again. Fifteen months after retaking the colony another peace treaty was signed and the Dutch gave it back.

But even now the tug of war was not over. Its namesake, the Duke of York, having laboured for a quarter of a century in his brother's shadow, got the chance truly to impose his vision of empire in 1685, when Charles died and he ascended to the throne. But the rule of James II began to fall apart almost at once. Thanks to his conversion to Roman Catholicism some years before, many of the English from the governing elite to the population at large suspected him of being a popish puppet, and real resistance mounted when he installed Catholics in important offices. When the news came out that the queen was pregnant – meaning that a Catholic line was in the making – James's rule teetered.

English history has characterized the Glorious Revolution – in which James was ousted and replaced by Willem of Orange, stadtholder of the Netherlands, and his wife Mary – as founded on an 'invitation'. There is an element of spin in this. In fact, the Dutch leader – the son of that Willem who had attempted a *coup d'état* while Van der Donck was in The Hague – capped the century of Dutch–English rivalry by launching a full-scale invasion of the British Isles. More than twenty thousand troops hit the beach at Torbay on the Devon coast, and a month later Willem rode triumphantly into London. The Dutch army took control of Whitehall Palace and all the other power centres, and the Dutch stadtholder was crowned king of England. The so-called invitation was considered by many Englishmen of the time a thorough disgrace; but for others the facts that Mary (who was James's daughter) was in any case heir presumptive to the English throne and that in Willem they once again had a Protestant monarch outweighed the indignities of the process.

This cross-pollination of the royal leadership of two long-standing rival nations would have an echo in Manhattan when a German-born New Yorker named Jacob Leisler (who, thirty years before, had served as a West India Company soldier under Stuyvesant), under the mistaken impression that the Dutch-born king of England would approve, led a handful of radicals in a Calvinist-backed takeover of the city. But Willem wasn't interested, and Leisler's Rebellion, as history has known it, ended quietly, with Leisler and an associate being hanged for treason and, for good measure, beheaded.

Maybe the main result of this remarkable interlude – in which the island and surrounding colony changed hands five times in three decades – was that it forced the inhabitants to solidify their identity. Which European power held ultimate control became less important to the Manhattanites than the relationships among their own ethnic communities and their ties to traders, shippers and family in other parts of the world. What mattered most was that cache of rights they had won, which they noisily insisted be honoured by whoever had just won control of the place, and which enabled the separate minority communities to flourish.

So Adriaen van der Donck's dream became real in a way he never imagined. The structure he helped win for the place grounded it in Dutch tolerance and diversity, just as he hoped it would, which in turn touched off the island's rapid growth and increased the influx of settlers from around Europe, just as he predicted. What he didn't predict was that the English would appreciate this fact, and maintain the structure, and that it would support a future culture of unprecedented energy, vitality and creativity.

*

And so off it went, spiralling upward along its path through history – the colony and city of New York, the jewel in the crown of England's North American possessions. More English settlers came, naturally enough, and also – word having continued to spread about its mixed population and the opportunities for getting ahead – French, German, Scottish and Irish immigrants, so that by 1692 a newly arrived British military officer would complain to his uncle in England, 'Our chiefest unhappyness here is too great a mixture of nations, and English ye least part.'

Newcomers were fully aware of the island's Dutch roots, and noted the continued influence in everything from the gabled houses with their front stoops to the predominance of the language. But a funny thing happened. Over time the outward trappings of Dutchness became synonymous with the region's roots; and, as those features faded with time, so, in this thinking, did the Dutch colony's significance.

There is a faulty logic in this, which would be perpetuated over the centuries. Some in the past have identified the continuance of the colony by examining the Dutch subculture in the Hudson valley. They noted that Dutch was still being spoken well into the nineteenth century, and that the Dutch Reformed Church continued strong. To this day the area around Albany is crammed with towns whose names – Rotterdam, Amsterdam, Watervliet, Rensselaer (after the colony of Rensselaerswyck, where Van der Donck first worked), Colonie (also named for Rensselaerswyck, and retaining the Dutch spelling) – reinforce the connection. As late as the 1750s English officials in that area needed to find Dutch-speakers to help them treat with Indians because Dutch was still the only European language the tribes spoke. And of course there are the great families of colonial America – the Van Burens, Roosevelts, Vanderbilts – who are traceable by their Dutch ancestry to New Netherland.

But all of that is missing the point. What matters about the Dutch colony is that it set Manhattan on its course as a place of openness and free trade. A new kind of spirit hovered over the island, something utterly alien to New England and Virginia, which is directly traceable to the tolerance debates in Holland in the sixteenth and seventeenth centuries, and to the intellectual world of Descartes, Grotius and Spinoza. Yes, there were people in the Hudson valley towns who preserved Dutch traditions, but that was mostly a reaction to the English takeover: in the way of minorities everywhere, they entrenched themselves, became self-conscious, and guarded and burnished their traditions, to the point where the 'Low Dutch' spoken in the nineteenth century was incomprehensible to visitors from the Netherlands, a relic of the tongue spoken in the golden age of two centuries earlier. In fact, the irony for the descendants of the original Dutch settlers is that it would be in blending into American culture – which they eventually did – that they paid the truest homage to their heritage.

*

The idea that the Dutch colony made important contributions to America is not new. Two nineteenth-century historians of New York who were intimately familiar with the Dutch sources – E. B. O'Callaghan and John Brodhead – saw its overlooked significance, but they were ignored, in part because America was then in the throes of a nostalgia for its Puritan beginnings. After spending four years in Europe on behalf of the State of New York, during which he gathered thousands of documents in archives in Holland and England that pertained to New York's origins (it was from these that the story of Adriaen van der Donck's mission to The Hague would emerge), Brodhead delivered a series of talks to fashionable New York society in the 1840s and 1850s, in which he laid out a case for the unheralded legacy of the Dutch colony. He was excoriated in the press – ridiculed for suggesting that the nation could have had progenitors other than the Puritans of New England. In reacting to Brodhead's claim, one newspaper correspondent showed that the anti-Dutch bias America had inherited from England in the seventeenth century was still alive in the nineteenth; he found it particularly ludicrous that so great and powerful a country as the United States could have got where it had by 'following the example of the policy of the petty cheese-paring of the

Batavian provinces, with their wind-mills, and barren soil, fit only for fuel'. Brodhead wrote a valiant response, which does not seem to have been published, beginning:

> Yielding to no one in a sincere respect for Puritanism, 'wherein it was worthy,' and in a due estimate of its influence upon the destinies of the United States, I must still venture candidly to express my dissent from the opinions of those who self complacently insist, on all occasions, and 'usque ad nauseam,' upon tracing back all the admirable features in our Social and political Organization to the 'Pilgrim Fathers' and their descendants. Unmeasured eulogy of the excellent pioneers of New England colonization has become so much the fashion, that it is almost a relief to turn to the history of other American settlements and find that there are other men whose actions and influence deserve notice in the annals of our Country. To say nothing of the 'Old Dominion' of Virginia, which was permanently settled twelve years before New Plymouth, it seems to me that it is due to historical truth that the influence and the character of the Dutch who first explored and settled the coasts of New York and New Jersey should be fairly set forth.

So Brodhead's voice went unheard. Part of the difficulty of making such a case lay in the fact that the mass of documents that constituted the records of the colony remained untranslated. In the 1970s, two things changed. One was that the discipline of history came down off its pedestal. People were suddenly interested in social history and 'multiculturalism'. The other was that the translation of the records of the Dutch colony got under way. Historians began to call for a reappraisal of this piece of America's beginnings. The titles of some of the scholarly papers that emerged – 'Writing/Righting Dutch Colonial History', 'Early American History with the Dutch Put In' – suggest the change. The names of many of the historians involved in this reappraisal, on whose work I have relied, are found in the endnotes, bibliography and acknowledgements of this book. When Scribner's published its important three-volume *Encyclopedia of the North American Colonies* in 1993 and gave prominent attention not only to New Netherland but to New Sweden as well, it signalled that the academic view of the colony and of American beginnings had changed. In August 2001, in the midst of my work on this book, the *New York Times* ran an editorial on the project to translate the Dutch archives, declaring that after a long time in which scholars of the Dutch colony had been 'clamoring for scholarly affirmative action', the tide had turned and now 'a vanquished New Netherland's influence looms larger than ever.'

The idea of the colony as a birthplace of the American melting pot has been simmering for some time. In the past few decades historians have focused on the vast chunk of land between New England and Virginia and dubbed it the Middle Colonies. With the focus has come an appreciation of what this region gave the country. The Middle Colonies, as Patricia Bonomi, one of the premier American historians of these decades, has written, were both 'the birthplace of American religious pluralism' and 'a stage for the western world's most complex experience with religious pluralism'. Religious pluralism was the seventeenth-century conduit for cultural pluralism, and the coming together of people from different backgrounds resulted in something new, which began to be remarked on a century after New Netherland's demise. In 1782, when the French-born Hector St John de Crèvecœur wrote *Letters from an American Farmer*, one of the earliest descriptions of American society and culture, it was this region he had in mind as he asked:

> What then is the American, this new man? He is either an European, or the descendant of an European, hence that strange mixture of blood, which you will find in no other country. I could point out to you a family whose grandfather

> was an Englishman, whose wife was Dutch, whose son married a French woman, and whose present four sons have now four wives of different nations. *He* is an American, who, leaving behind him all his ancient prejudices and manners, receives new ones from the new mode of life he has embraced, the new government he obeys, and the new rank he holds. He becomes an American by being received in the broad lap of our great *Alma Mater*. Here individuals of all nations are melted into a new race of men, whose labours and posterity will one day cause great changes in the world.

What we find beneath the 'Middle Colonies' label is the force that gave rise to Crèvecœur's observation: the Dutch colony. There were other forces at work too: the Pennsylvania and Rhode Island colonies both became known for religious toleration. But the influence of the Dutch colony would be particularly wide-ranging. Such influence cannot be proved deductively, but evidence to support it comes in many forms. There is, first, the simple fact that the very part of America in which multi-ethnic society first formed was also the region where the Dutch colony had been.

We can further support the connection by looking at other legacies from the colony that also took root first in this region. An example: after Richard Nicolls took charge of New York and had become familiar with the Dutch customs he had allowed the inhabitants to maintain, he found one political office particularly useful. The colony had a law officer, called a *schout*, whose job was to prosecute cases on behalf of the government. The English system at the time had no equivalent; it was the victim of a crime, or his or her relative, who was responsible for seeking justice. The Dutch mechanism enabled the justice system to move more efficiently. Nicolls adopted it – the English records at first took to calling this official the 'scout' – and it spread through the other colonies. The job eventually became known as that of district attorney, and it remains a fixture of local government in

America. (It happens that one of the first 'district attorneys' in America was Adriaen van der Donck, whose original posting was as *schout* of the colony of Rensselaerswyck.) In 1975, Yale law professor A. J. Reiss noted, in an article on the history of the office, that 'The first appearance of public prosecutors in the United States occurred when the Dutch founded the colony of New Netherland,' that '[h]istorical evidence makes it abundantly clear that when this area was taken by the Duke of York in surrender in 1664 ... the Dutch system of public prosecution was maintained where it had been firmly established by then' and that '[h]istorical records demonstrate that the "Schout" was established within five of the 13 original colonies that became the states of the United States of America.'

There are many other telltale legacies – customs and traditions and usages that spread, along with the phenomenon of American pluralism, from what was once Dutch territory. It was in the Dutch colony that an American worker first complained about 'the boss'. It was here that American children first longed for the arrival of 'St. a Claus' (as *Rivington's New York Gazetteer* spelled it in the early 1770s, noting that the saint's feast day would be celebrated 'by the descendants of the ancient Dutch families, with their usual festivities'). It was here that Americans first ate 'cookies' and 'cole slaw'. Of course, nothing is more meaningless than cookies; the reason for mentioning such items is their ubiquity. The blob of slaw on every fixed-price diner meal served from the Depression to the Eisenhower era, riding alongside the baked beans at numberless barbecues, packed into a little plastic tub to offset the grease in a fast food burgers-and-fries meal, ignored or absently consumed, is a modest clue to the pervasive presence of the Manhattan colony. It is a tipoff that in considering its contribution we should be looking not in obscure corners but at what is right in front of us. We won't find it in the form of Dutch pipestems buried in back yards, but in any American town's telephone book, where Singh, Singer, Singleton and Sinkiewicz fall on the same page.

Many inheritances are hard to spot because in the mix and rumble of the centuries they have become layered, altered, embedded in other, larger systems. This stands to reason: we couldn't expect much to last three centuries in pristine form. Rather, we would expect that, if a thing was useful or desirable, it would become part of the blend. Santa Claus may be the perfect example of this. It was a slim fellow in a bishop's hat whose arrival the children of Dutch Manhattan looked forward to on St Nicholas' Eve; typically, he left treats in their shoes, but occasionally (as in a late-century drawing, 'The St Nicholas Celebration', by Cornelis Dusart), in stockings hung from the mantelpiece. As the non-Dutch families adopted him and he gained momentum, bits of other cultural traditions stuck to the ritual; the media (Thomas Nast's cartoons in *Harper's Weekly* plumped the saint and whitened his beard) and corporate advertising (the white-trimmed red suit came compliments of Coca-Cola's iconic ad campaign in the 1930s) refined the image, and the result is a complicated collage, thoroughly American, and rooted in the Manhattan of Stuyvesant and Van der Donck.

The influence of the colony can also be spotted rippling through the layers of political history. After Van der Donck's political crusade helped cement the unique features of the Dutch colony's society, Nicolls's Articles of Capitulation guaranteed that the English would preserve the rights and privileges the residents had come to expect. When in 1686 the New York City Charter, considered by some to mark the launch of the modern city, was signed, it not only made plain those rights and privileges but was clear about their origins, acknowledging that the citizens of the 'ancient Citty . . . Enjoyed . . . sundry Rights Libertyes priviledges [and] ffranchises' that derived not only from its English rulers but from the 'Governours Directors Generalls, and Commanders in Chiefe of the Nether Dutch Nation'.

We can move forward from this charter, and from the rowdy, argumentative, still mostly Dutch-speaking society that stood behind it, straight into the revolutionary period and beyond. In Philadelphia in 1787, New York's delegation to the Constitutional Convention was among those least enamoured of a document that would give so much power to the federal government. Meeting later in Albany, the state's leaders decided that they could not ratify the Constitution unless, among other things, a bill of specific individual rights were attached to it. The names of the twenty-six men who insisted on this were about half English and half Dutch; the new state was already famously contentious, and its pluralistic delegation had a long history of struggling for individual rights to account for its stubbornness.

Of course, when the Bill of Rights was adopted in 1791, no-one looked to the Dutch-led colony that had thrived little over a century earlier as having a hand in it. There had been no written history of the Dutch period, and decades were still to pass before the documents detailing Van der Donck's mission on behalf of the rights of Manhattanites would be unearthed.

The pathways along which the colony's influence spread are also part of the evidence for its lasting importance. Starting from their settlements on the Delaware river, the 'forest Finns' – brought by the Swedes but encouraged to prosper by the Dutch – literally cleared a path down the Appalachian valleys, along which Finnish, Swedish, Dutch and other pioneers travelled, and by the way added the log cabin to America's cultural legacy. But the main route of expansion was to the north. The island of Manhattan became the gateway to America for generations of immigrants, and it was because of this that the legacy of the Dutch colony was amplified. Stepping off the boat, the individuals in those huddled masses, arriving from Naples or Hamburg or Le Havre or Liverpool, breathed in an atmosphere utterly different from what they had left. The smell in the air was one they had hoped to find – a complicated, heady perfume that had in it the big, muscular, fresh odours that came sweeping off the continent, full of green promise; a smell sharpened by the oily tang of industry and good sweat, accented with kielbasa and pasta sauce, horse dung and sawdust and slaughterhouse. The newcomers soaked it in, this odour of promise and of a reblending of peoples into something new, and they called it American. Then they fanned out, and took it with them. Up the Hudson they went, which was to the seventeenth and eighteenth centuries what the Mississippi would be to later eras: the lifeline, the broad highway of commerce and travel.

At Albany, once the site of the fur-trading post of Fort Orange, they cut westward, into the Mohawk river valley. There, in the early nineteenth century, industrial-age politicians discovered what Dutch pioneers had known two centuries earlier: that promise and expansion lay westwards along this valley. In 1825, after eight years of stupendous manual labour, the last yards of a 360-mile trench were carved through the wilderness that Harmen Meyndertsz van den Bogaert had explored on his perilous foray into Iroquois country during the harsh winter of 1634. How the Erie Canal changed the nation is a basic piece of American history. It opened up the interior of the continent, swelled the population, shifted the balance from rural to urban, helped make America an industrial power. America was transformed, and the promise that the first Manhattanites saw in their island came roaring into reality. The stream of people and goods into Manhattan became a flood. From across Europe and around the world they funnelled into the island, then up the river, and so westward along the canal. And with the pipeline of commerce extending into the very heart of the continent, crossroads settlements were transformed into cities, lights winking on in the dusk of the endless landscape, each with its cluster of founding ethnic groups: Toledo, Cleveland, Detroit, Buffalo, Milwaukee, Chicago, Green Bay.

That's why the story of the original Manhattan colony matters. Its impact is so diffuse that it would be perilous to declare and define it too concretely, so here is a modest attempt to encapsulate: it helped set the whole thing in motion. Certainly this isn't evident on the surface: the little village over which

Stuyvesant ruled bears no resemblance to today's metropolis, let alone the vast nation that exploded into existence beyond it, any more than an acorn does to an oak. But the original settlement contributed, and is still there, mixed into the being of the island and the nation.

The legacy of the people who settled Manhattan Island rides below the level of myth and politics. They reshuffled the categories by which people had long lived, created a society with more open spaces, in which the rungs of the ladder were within reach of nearly everyone. They didn't exactly mean to do these things. There was a state policy of tolerance, which helped shape the colony, but there was also ignorance of it and refusal to adhere to it. It was a society that was both haphazard and planned. It didn't have a neat outline of the sort that spawned the Puritan myth. But then, myths have a downside: the shining 'city on a hill' became Manifest Destiny, and too easily twisted into a cheap battle-cry. The first Manhattanites didn't arrive with lofty ideals. They came – farmer, tanner, prostitute, wheelwright, barmaid, brewer, trader – because there was a hope for a better life. There was a distinct messiness to the place they created. But it was very real and, in a way, very modern.

It wasn't until 1908 that a Jewish immigrant, intoxicated by the possibilities, the strength, the progressiveness, the hope for breaking down old hatreds that he found in America's mixed society, wrote a play, which ran for 136 weeks (on Broadway, naturally) called *The Melting Pot*. The phrase entered the lexicon as recently as that; but Israel Zangwill was describing something that had been stewing for a long time. Of course, terms like 'melting pot' and 'pluralism' have long since become weighted and contentious. Should immigrants leave their old ethnicities behind or preserve them and remain in some way apart from the main culture? Instantly, the question becomes 'What is an American?' Or, for that matter, 'Who is English?' 'Who is a German?' Or an Italian, an Israeli, a Turk? In a world of pluralistic societies, the debate is universal.

But the strength in the mixing-of-cultures idea was undeniable for a long time. And the essence of it, the idea of tolerance, may matter more now than ever. The terrorist attack that destroyed the World Trade Center and shook the world in September 2001 struck not only the core of American financial might but also the few square acres of lower Manhattan that were once called New Amsterdam. The fact that the one grew out of the other ought to be proof that the idea of tolerance remains a thing of power. With any luck, it will also remain the mortar of progressive society. Developing it, showing that it could work, was the messy genius of the first Manhattanites.

Epilogue
The Paper Trail

THROUGH ALL THE EVENTS OF THIS STORY, IN A COUNCIL room in Fort Amsterdam and in an administrative office above the gate, the successive secretaries of the Manhattan-based colony of New Netherland did what all secretaries do: took notes and filed records. Lots were sold, houses were built, pigs were stolen, knives were drawn, liquor was taxed, property was damaged. The quill scratched its way softly across the sheets of imported rag paper. The directors issued their decrees and the leaders of the colonists lodged their complaints. Letters streamed out – to Curaçao, Virginia, Boston, Amsterdam. The quill dipped into the ink-pot, then addressed the paper again, row after row of the oddly curling Dutch script of the period.

What happened to these records after Richard Nicolls's troops took possession of them can be summed up in a truism: history is written by the winners. There was probably an element of spite involved in the failure of the English to incorporate the records of the Dutch colony into the first American histories. The bad blood between the two rival nations only intensified with the three wars they fought during the course of the century. The title of one of the many screeds published in England is enough to remind one of the ludicrous levels such animosity could reach: *The Dutch-mens Pedigree, Or, A Relation Shewing How They Were*

First Bred and Descended from a Horse-Turd Which Was Enclosed in a Butter-Box. Another indication of English antipathy towards the Dutch, which America took in with its mother's milk, so to speak, is the tally of 'Dutch' phrases in the language – Dutch treat, Dutch courage, double Dutch, a Dutch bargain, going Dutch, Dutch comfort – all of them derogatory and all coming straight from the seventeenth century.

While the records of other early settlements were being preserved and researched to create the story of America's beginnings, those of the non-English colony were kicked around, fought over, forgotten. Their fitful passage through the next three centuries, during which the archive would be connected to some of the major events and figures in American history, is an ironically dramatic reflection of how the colony itself has been ignored. In 1685, after King James ordered a reorganization of the colonies, the volumes were tossed onto a stagecoach bound for Boston; three years later they made the same rough trip back to New York when the new monarchs, William and Mary, reversed the ruling. It was probably on one or both of these journeys that some volumes were lost (none of the records prior to 1638 remain, and the crucial period of 1649–52, when Van der Donck was presenting the colonists' case before the States General, has also vanished). In 1741 the fort (now called Fort George), in which the records were once again housed, was torched in what was widely considered to be a slave conspiracy. The gatehouse burned, but the records were saved by a diligent secretary tossing them out of the window. It was a blustery day, and many pages blew away, but the bulk of the archive remained intact.

In the build-up to revolution, New York City became a place of chaos and confusion. Bands of radicals did their best to disrupt the British administration; death threats were directed at William Tryon, the royal governor of the colony, so that on 1 December 1775 he found himself trying to conduct business from the lurching deck of a ship, the *Dutchess of Gordon*, in New

York harbour, several hundred yards away from the populace he was supposed to be governing. A new matter of concern came to the governor's attention that morning, involving the same radical who had threatened his life. He wrote a hurried letter to the deputy secretary of the province:

> Sir— As I am credibly informed that Isaac Sears, at the head of a large body of Connecticut people, intends very shortly to march into the city of New-York, to seize and carry off by violence the public records in the secretary's office, I do hereby require you, without loss of time, to put on board the ship Dutchess of Gordon, all such public acts and records under your care, as immediately concern the interests of the crown, until I can advise with his Majesty's council how they may be better secured. The records for patents for land and public commissions are of the first importance to be put on board the above ship. I am, Sir, your obedient servant, WILLIAM TRYON.

The records that Tryon was anxious to protect included not only those of the English colony of New York but those of the earlier Dutch colony as well. They remained for much of the War of Independence in the damp hold of Tryon's ship, where mould set in, the traces of which are still evident on the sheets. Then, according to a letter from the French writer Crèvecœur to none other than Benjamin Franklin, as the fight over the fate of the city and the colonies reached a climax the records were moved to the Tower of London. Eventually, the victorious colonists demanded their return. Miraculously, the papers survived the turmoil of the war, although at its end the secretary of the new State of New York reported that many pages were 'much mill-dewed and greatly injured'; he added, however, that he had exercised 'my best endeavours to preserve them, having frequently exposed them to the sun and air, and several times had them brushed through every leaf'.

With the turn of the century it looked as though the information in the documents would enter the historical record. In 1801 a committee of the New York State Assembly declared that 'immediate measures ought to be taken to procure a translation of the records of this State, now in the Secretary's office, which are written in the Dutch language.' One might expect this directive to have been taken seriously, since it came from Aaron Burr, the most powerful man in the legislature, who was about to leave in order to serve as Thomas Jefferson's vice-president (and would three years later become infamous for killing Alexander Hamilton in a duel). But it wasn't until 1818 that a full-scale translation effort was under way. The man selected for this work – Francis Adrian van der Kemp, an elderly Dutch minister and former soldier who had emigrated to New York – did as he was asked, and in four years produced a translation of the entire twelve thousand pages.

In fact, this episode in the history of the colony's records comes across as a kind of comedy. Such a rate of production is not humanly possible for one man. What's more, Van der Kemp had a faulty grasp of English, he was going blind at the time, and in an effort to save his eyes as he rushed through the documents he stopped intermittently to apply belladonna (a deadly poison). The result of Van der Kemp's *tour de force* was twenty-four volumes of handwritten translations – a fiasco of small errors, howlers and massive, unexplained gaps – that were worse than worthless: worse because they were assumed to be adequate, were housed in the state library in Albany and were used by historians. Eventually, fate occasionally being kind, this entire corpus – which was never published and of which only the original existed – burned in a fire before it could further corrupt history.

The next attempt to bring this chapter of American history to light came in the early twentieth century. A search went out for a translator with a sound understanding of the Dutch language of the seventeenth century, and one was found: a shy, heavy-set,

Dutch-born engineer with a gift for language and a stubborn passion for accuracy. But only two years after A. J. F. van Laer began work on a translation of the records, the infamous fire of 1911 struck the New York Capitol, which housed the state library. Millions of volumes were destroyed. Once again, the Dutch records dodged catastrophe, thanks to the fact that, being considered of lesser importance, they were housed on a bottom shelf, so that when the shelves collapsed, English colonial records that had been stored above protected them from destruction. Nevertheless, some documents were destroyed, others were badly damaged, both by fire and by water, and two years' worth of Van Laer's work was lost. Van Laer himself, seemingly shell-shocked, continued for a long time after the fire to go to work as usual. His workplace was now a smouldering ruin, open to the sky, and he would poke among the debris in search of potential fragments. He continued to be employed in the state archives and after a time produced a translation of four volumes of the Dutch records (which remained unpublished for half a century), but suffered a nervous collapse as a result of the catastrophe, and eventually turned away from the massive, seemingly jinxed project.

And so to the 1970s, to the era of Watergate, when, as I have outlined at the beginning of this book, another effort was launched to crack the code of the Dutch manuscripts. The difficulty was greater than one might imagine. The Dutch language has changed enormously in three hundred years, and in the eighteenth century there was a shift in handwriting style, so that documents written before then are often incomprehensible to modern Dutch speakers. Then there is the vast amount of technical knowledge required: weights and measures, how many *mengelen* in an *aam*, the fact that a *daelder* is worth the same as a Carolus guilder but less than a *rijksdaelder*. The job was a niche within a niche.

It was a shock to both men, then, when Peter Christoph, a senior librarian charged with the task of finding a translator, met

Charles Gehring at a conference. Gehring had finished a dissertation in Germanic linguistics, with a special focus on Netherlandic studies. 'Before I had a chance to say anything,' Christoph said, recalling their meeting for me, 'he asked me, "In your field, do you know of any openings for someone to work with seventeenth-century Dutch documents?" I said, "Boy, do I."'

That was in 1974. Gehring has had only one job since then: translator of the archives of the Dutch colony. In the way of all not-for-profit enterprises, there is a yearly crisis over funding to support the work. Not surprisingly, much of it comes in the way of donations from Americans of Dutch ancestry. There is also a matching grant from the National Endowment for the Humanities. As Gehring's output has been published – there are eighteen volumes in print so far – it has become a central and revolutionary resource for American colonial studies. He is succeeding not only in making the records of America's non-English colony available to researchers, but in broadening the field of colonial studies beyond its historic Anglocentric focus. As a kind of cap to his effort, in 1999 the twelve thousand pages of manuscript records of the colony were declared a national treasure by the US Department of the Interior; besides giving the charred pages a belated dignity, the designation also came with funds to help preserve them.

The historians who in recent years have written dissertations and academic papers on the Dutch colony – further broadening awareness of its significance – owe a lot to Gehring and to Janny Venema, a Dutch historian who has worked as his assistant for the past eighteen years. I too owe them a great deal. Not only have they made the records accessible through their translations, they have allowed me to work alongside them, have answered endless questions, have suggested avenues to explore, and have given me free rein over the shelves and file cabinets of relevant arcana they have collected over the years. Just as valuable, spending time with them has given me a better feel for the people of the colony than I could ever have got from mere books. The New York State Library occupies a soulless 1970s building in downtown Albany, but in the corner where their offices are located it's the age of Rembrandt and Vermeer; for the hours I'm there, life seems richer and wilder. When Charly Gehring holds forth on the hazards of sailing in the seventeenth century, his conversation is sprinkled with Dutch nautical terms not heard in the Netherlands in centuries. He has an appealing habit of talking about people in the present tense: 'Van Tienhoven has a lot of skeletons in his closet, but he's also just about the shrewdest guy on the island,' he will say of a man last seen on Manhattan in 1656.

From them too I've gained a sense of the documents as artefacts, holding stories that don't transfer into type. Sitting with Janny Venema, looking through browned, mould-speckled pages written in the days leading up to the English takeover, I noticed one sheet with a distinctly different writing. The typical scribe's hand is rounded, with intricate little flourishes; this page was filled with thick, jagged, up-and-down strokes. 'Oh, that's Stuyvesant,' she said offhandedly. 'He must have been in a hurry and there was no secretary around.' It was remarkable to see how well the man's handwriting seemed to match his personality, and indeed, the letter – which has yet to be published – brims with immediacy. He is writing to the directors of the West India Company; English frigates are in the harbour, their guns are trained on the city. At the bottom, Stuyvesant adds that he will give the letter to a skipper who hopes to slip undetected through the Hell Gate and out to sea; the fact that I was holding it was proof that the skipper never sailed. Long Island is lost, Stuyvesant informs his bosses, and New Englanders are massing across the river, ready to invade. The town is low on food and gunpowder; the people tell him they aren't willing to fight for a company that has shown no willingness to support them. The anger in the letter is palpable: the corporate bosses had ignored his endless appeals for reinforcements and left him in an impossible situation. It isn't Stuyvesant the pig-headed administrator who comes through in the harsh strokes, but a man rendered powerless by an inept bureaucracy.

One more, smaller example of how these weathered pages reveal fragments of human life. The outpost of Fort Orange (Albany) had its own administration, and for many years a man named Johannes Dijckman acted as secretary, taking minutes of meetings. We know little about him – just an ordinary man, of no account to history – but elsewhere there is a mention of his having a drinking problem. 'Over time, you notice that his handwriting gets harder to read,' Gehring said. 'Then, one day in 1655, right in the middle of a meeting, the handwriting changes. A new hand picks up, and you never see the old one again.' Shortly after, Dijckman appears in the deacon's account books; he's on poor relief, and will stay on the dole until he dies. 'Those last pages of minutes Dijckman takes are covered with stains and blotches,' Venema said. 'Who knows what they are: maybe just water. But maybe it's wine. Maybe tears.'

Notes

Prologue

p. 22 'Original sources of information': Tuckerman, *Peter Stuyvesant*, preface.

p. 24 'measures ought to be taken': Van Laer, *The Translation and Publication of the Manuscript Dutch Records of New Netherland*, 9.

p. 25 'It is impossible': Russell, *A History of Western Philosophy*, 581.

p. 28 'like a great natural pier': Van Rensselaer, *History of the City of New York in the Seventeenth Century*, vol. 1, 49.

p. 28 'best of all His Majties Townes': O'Callaghan and Fernow, *Documents Relative to the Colonial History of the State of New York* [hereafter *Docs Rel.*], vol. 3, 106.

Chapter 1

p. 33 His complicated personality: I have used all of the standard sources in constructing my portrait of Hudson: Hakluyt, *The Principal Navigations*, vol. 3; Purchas, *Hakluytus Posthumus*, vol. 13; Asher, *Henry Hudson the Navigator*; Murphy, *Henry Hudson in Holland*; John Read, *A Historical Inquiry Concerning Henry Hudson*; Powys, *Henry Hudson*; Bacon, *Henry Hudson*. I have also consulted Edwards, *Last Voyages: Cavendish, Hudson, Ralegh*; Donald Johnson, *Charting the Sea of Darkness*; and McNaughton, 'The Ghost of Henry Hudson'.

p. 34 Since we know his destination: The journal of Abacuk Pricket, printed in Purchas, *Hakluytus Posthumus*, vol. 13, confirms that Hudson had a house in London; Powys, *Henry Hudson*, 1, says that it was 'somewhere near the Tower of London'. Muscovy House was originally located in Seething Lane, but, according to Gerson et al. (*Studies in the History of English Commerce during the Tudor Period*, 33, quoting Husting Roll 341, 29), the company moved prior to 1570 to a location 'in the parish of St. Antholin London in or neare a certayne streete since the . . . late dreadfull fire in London called and knowne by the name of Dukes Street'. St. Antholin's was on Budge Row, in Cordwainer Street Ward. In reconstructing Hudson's walk, I have used the 'Agas map', reprinted in Prockter and Taylor, eds, *The A to Z of Elizabethan London*, Claes Jansz Visscher's view of London *c.* 1616, and John Stow's *A Survey of London Written in the Year 1598*.

p. 34 it had numbered several Hudsons on its rolls: The main argument for a line of interrelated Hudsons in the Muscovy Company is made by John Read, *A Historical Inquiry Concerning Henry Hudson*.

p. 34 'Here lyeth': John Read, *A Historical Inquiry Concerning Henry Hudson*, 41.

p. 35 'sturdye Beggers': Browner, 'Wrong Side of the River'; Beier, 'Vagrants and the Social Order in Elizabethan England', 10–11.

p. 35 From the bravado: My sources on the Muscovy Company and the mid-Tudor period are Loades, *The Mid-Tudor Crisis*; Hakluyt, *The Discovery of Muscovy*; Purchas, *Hakluytus Posthumus*; Fell-Smith, *John Dee*; Fisher, *The Russian Fur Trade*; French, *John Dee*; Gerson et al., *Studies in the History of English Commerce during the Tudor Period*; Harrisse, *John Cabot*; Mattingly, *The Armada*; Morison, *The European Discovery of America*, vol. 1: *The Northern Voyages*; Phipps, *Sir John Merrick*; Quinn and Ryan, *England's Sea Empire*; Taylor, *Tudor Geography*; Willan, *The Muscovy Merchants of 1555*; Williamson, *The Age of Drake*.

p. 36 English traders had been excluded: Loades, *The Mid-Tudor Crisis*, 73.

p. 36 *né* Giovanni Cabotto: Morison (*The Great Explorers*, 40–41) says it was probably either Cabotto or Gabote.

p. 37 Some mariners were as confused: Taylor, *Tudor Geography*, 86.

p. 37 the Englishmen's Strait: Taylor, *Tudor Geography*, 34.

p. 38 *fretum arcticum*: Taylor, *Tudor Geography*, 81–5.

p. 38 chipping in twenty-five pounds: Conyers Read, *Mr Secretary Walsingham*, vol. 3, 371.

p. 38 'near the pole the sun shines continually': Powys, *Henry Hudson*, 26.

p. 41 'an age wherein': Albert Gray, 'An Address on the Occasion of the Tercentenary of the Death of Richard Hakluyt'.

p. 42 perpetual clearness of the day': Donald Johnson, *Charting the Sea of Darkness*, 20.

p. 42 six million square miles: 'In the arctic late winter, sea ice covers about 10 million square miles on top of the globe, while in summer the ice pack shrinks to about 6 million square miles, according to Martin Jeffries, an associate research professor of geophysics at the Geophysical Institute': Rozell, 'Sea Ice Reduction May Be Another Climate Change Clue'.

p. 42 the Church of St Ethelburga: Richard Hakluyt, *The Principal Navigations*, vol. 3, 567.

p. 43 'This morning we saw': Purchas, *Hakluytus Posthumus*, vol. 13, 306–7.

p. 44 'We set sayle': Purchas, *Hakluytus Posthumus*, vol. 13, 313.

p. 44 'it is so full of ice': Purchas, *Hakluytus Posthumus*, vol. 13, 329.

p. 44 'out of hope': Purchas, *Hakluytus Posthumus*, vol. 13, 328.

p. 45 'sunk into the lowest depths': Purchas, *Hakluytus Posthumus*, vol. 13, 300.

Chapter 2

p. 51 'a strenuous spirit of opposition': Schama, *The Embarrassment of Riches*, 53.

p. 52 sometimes even buying titles: Van Nierop, *The Nobility of Holland*, 212.

p. 52 'The Originals of the two Republics': Adams, *A collection of state-papers*.

p. 52 he may even have spent: Adriaen van der Donck, in his telling of Hudson's story, says that Hudson had lived in Holland.

Historians have dismissed his account as self-serving to the Dutch claim to New Netherland, but a familiarity with the country would help to explain Hudson's quick decision to sail for the Dutch, as well as his friendships with Plancius and De Hondt.

p. 55 'has found that the more northwards': Asher, *Henry Hudson the Navigator*, 246.

p. 55 'there are also many rich merchants': Asher, *Henry Hudson the Navigator*, 253.

p. 55 'to think of discovering': Powys, *Henry Hudson*, 81.

p. 56 'This is the entrance': Purchas, *Hakluytus Posthumus*, vol. 13, 356.

p. 56 'very pleasant and high': Jameson, *Narratives of New Netherland*, 37.

p. 57 'an abundance of blue plums': Jameson, *Narratives of New Netherland*, 37.

p. 57 the Moravian missionary: Heckewelder, *History, Manners, and Customs of the Indian Nations*.

p. 57 'a very good harbor': Jameson, *Narratives of New Netherland*, 37.

p. 58 'Juan Hudson': Stokes, *Iconography of Manhattan Island*, vol. 2, 44.

p. 59 'as fine a river': Van Meteren, in Asher, *Henry Hudson the Navigator*, 150.

p. 59 '*Vellen . . . Pelterijen*': The English and Dutch versions are in Asher, *Henry Hudson the Navigator*, 150.

p. 60 Even as he was being lowered: All details in this scene come from Abacuk Pricket's account of the mutiny, as printed in vol. 13 of Purchas, *Hakluytus Posthumus*. Pricket's account is skewed and untrustworthy in that he makes himself and his fellow survivors blameless bystanders in the mutiny, conveniently fingering those who had died on the return voyage as the ring-leaders, but there is no reason to mistrust the details regarding weather, dress and so on.

p. 61 'to the great kingdoms': Asher, *Henry Hudson the Navigator*, 255. The charter of the new company was granted in 1612, and the actual trial didn't take place until 1618, after several unsuccessful attempts to navigate the passage the mutineers claimed to have discovered.

p. 61 Arnout Vogels: Information about Vogels comes from Bachman, *Peltries or Plantations*, 3–6.

Chapter 3

p. 63 From Amsterdam the ships made their way: Bachman, *Peltries or Plantations*, 16.

p. 64 'de rivière Hudson': Stokes, *Iconography of Manhattan Island*, vol. 4, 41.

p. 65 'It is obvious': Bachman, *Peltries or Plantations*, 31.

p. 65 'which are the sinews of war': O'Callaghan, *The History of New Netherland*, vol. 1, 31.

p. 66 '12 ships and yachts': *Docs Rel.*, vol. 1, 35–6.

p. 66 'more like princes' palaces': Haley, *The Dutch in the Seventeenth Century*, 158.

p. 67 The councillor who administered: 'Provisional Regulations for the Colonists', Van Laer, *Documents Relating to New Netherland* [hereafter *DRNN*], and also Van Laer's note, p. 256: 'Dr Claes Peterszen was the well-known physician Dr Nicolaes Pietersen Tulp, the central figure in Rembrandt's famous painting called *The Lesson in Anatomy*, which hangs in the Mauritshuis at The Hague. Dr Tulp was from 1622 to his death, in 1674, a member of the council and at different times schepen and burgomaster of the city of Amsterdam. Hans Bontemantel says that he never called himself otherwise than "Claes Pieterss", and that "Tulp" was a nickname, derived from *tulp*, or tulip, which was placed over his front door.'

p. 67 Catalina Trico and Joris Rapalje: Zabriskie, 'The Founding Families of New Netherland, No. 4'.

p. 68 Trico, now in her eighties: Munsell, *A Documentary History of the State of New York*, vol. 3, 32.

p. 68 The records of New Netherland show: References to Rapalje and Trico are scattered throughout the colonial records; the passage of their lives can be traced through the index to O'Callaghan, *Calendar of Historical Manuscripts in the Office of the Secretary of State*.

p. 68 In the 1770s: Bonomi, *A Factious People*, 277.

p. 69 The number of their descendants: Interview with Harry Macy, editor of *The New York Genealogical and Biographical Record* and a Rapalje descendant, 2 April 2003.

p. 69 In modern scientific terms: United States Fish and Wildlife Service, Southern New England–New York Bight Coastal Ecosystems Program, 'Significant Habitats and Habitat Complexes of the New York Bight Watershed'.

p. 69 'reeds': Grumet, *Native American Place Names in New York City*, 24.

p. 69 oysters: Van der Donck, 'A Description of New Netherland', trans. Goedhuys, 74.

p. 69 'hilly island': Grumet, *Native American Place Names in New York City*, 23–24.

p. 70 'Here we found beautiful rivers': Stokes, *Iconography of Manhattan Island*, vol. 4, 60.

p. 70 'It is very pleasant': Jameson, *Narratives of New Netherland*, 77.

p. 71 'hovels and holes': Van Laer, *Annals of New Netherland*, 12.

p. 72 'as high as a man': Jameson, *Narratives of New Netherland*, 76.

p. 74 After more than a decade: Dunn, *The Mohicans and their Land*, 76.

p. 75 'jet-black, quite sleek': Van der Donck, 'A Description of New Netherland', trans. Goedhuys, 91.

p. 75 high cheekbones and aquiline noses: Dyer, *The House of Peace*, 4.

p. 75 'he shall be very careful': Van Laer, *DRNN*, 55.

p. 76 'He shall also see': Van Laer, *DRNN*, 39.

p. 76 His father had taken part: Information about Minuit's family and early life comes from Weslager, *A Man and his Ship*, 14–20.

p. 77 'He shall have Pierre Minuyt': Van Laer, *DRNN*, 44.

p. 79 So he bought it: The order of events is far from clear, and historians debate whether Verhulst or Minuit was the one who purchased Manhattan Island. My account is based on my own reading of all relevant primary source material, as well as the arguments made by various historians. I side against those who in recent decades removed Minuit from his legendary position as purchaser of the island, and with those who reassign him to that position. Reasons: the substance of the 'further instructions' to Verhulst and the dates of Minuit's trip to the Netherlands and of his return suggest the directors were fed up with Verhulst and also realized, perhaps thanks to Minuit's information, that a new central base for the province was needed. Some historians have noted evidence of settlers on Manhattan prior to May 1626, but that doesn't mean the company had already bought the island. More to the point, the whole weight of the events gives a picture of Minuit taking charge and reorganizing the province, something Verhulst, given his weak leadership and position, couldn't have done.

p. 79 '. . . which the Dutch settler': Dave Barry, *Milwaukee Journal–Sentinel*, 26 Dec. 1999.

p. 80 their genetic makeup: Sykes, *The Seven Daughters of Eve*, 279–80.

p. 80 it has been estimated: King, *First People, First Contacts: Native Peoples of North America*, 8.

p. 81 such as one in South Carolina: Banner, 'Manhattan for $24'.

p. 82 sold for scrap paper: *Docs Rel.*, vol. 1, xxv.

p. 84 'carefully note all places': quotations from the Van Rappard documents are taken from Van Laer, *DRNN*, 45–59.

p. 85 a tabard, or cape: Van Laer, *DRNN*, 180.

p. 86 'High and Mighty Lords': The translation of the Schaghen letter is taken from Van Laer, *Annals of New Netherland*.

p. 86 'Received a letter': *Docs Rel.*, vol. 1, 38.

p. 87 'Duffels, Kittles': Melyn, 'The Melyn Papers', 124.

p. 87 'deliver yearly at Christmas': Gehring, *Land Papers*, 8.

p. 88 Andries Hudde sold: Van Laer, *New York Historical Manuscripts: Dutch* [hereafter *NYHM*], vol. 1, 45.

p. 88 a West India Company soldier earned: The Bontemantel Papers include a record of the salaries of New Netherland officials, from the director-general downwards. These documents show that a soldier was paid 8–9 guilders per month.

p. 88 In 1648: Venema, 'The Court Case of Brant Aertsz van Slichtenhorst against Jan van Rensselaer'.

p. 90 'because he is well acquainted': Van Laer, *DRNN*, 176.

p. 92 'the ground in the flat land': Jameson, *Narratives of New Netherland*, 104.

p. 94 'All seafaring persons': Van Laer, *NYHM*, vol. 4, 8.

p. 94 '[E]ach and every one': Van Laer, *NYHM*, vol. 4, 4.

p. 94 'notwithstanding her husband's presence': Van Laer, *NYHM*, vol. 1, 55. In vol. 4 of the same series, Thomas Beech (here called Tomas Bescher) is referred to as an Englishman (p. 5).

p. 95 He complained to the directors: Van Laer, *DRNN*, 188,| 198–9.

p. 96 *Tekel or Balance*: Asher, *Dutch Books and Pamphlets Relating to New-Netherland*, 122–3.

p. 96 'a rundlet of sugar': *Governour Bradford's Letter Book*, vol. 3, 53–4, repr. in Stokes, *Iconography of Manhattan Island*, vol. 4, 70.

p. 96 'a noise of trumpets': *Governour Bradford's Letter Book*, vol. 3, 54–5, repr. in Stokes, *Iconography of Manhattan Island*, vol. 4, 71.

Chapter 4

p. 100 Charles I: The main sources I have used in constructing my portrait of Charles are Carlton, *Charles I*; Gregg, *King Charles I*; Aikin, *Memoirs of the Court of King Charles the First*; and Kenyon, *The Stuarts*.

p. 100 'Essex miles': Hore, *The History of Newmarket and the Annals of the Turf*, vol. 1, 155.

p. 100 William Harvey: Hore, *The History of Newmarket and the Annals of the Turf*, vol. 2, 18.

p. 100 in a single racing season: Lyle, *Royal Newmarket*, 11.

p. 101 couldn't stand French people: Wedgwood, *The Political Career of Peter Paul Rubens*, 45.

p. 101 emigrate to Canada: Carlton, *Charles I*, 184.

p. 101 'but I must tell you': Kenyon, *The Stuarts*, 98–9. Emphasis added.

p. 102 'the enemy': *Docs Rel.*, vol. 1, 55.

p. 104 Rubens also introduced: Carlton, *Charles I*, 125, 144–5.

p. 104 'We cannot perceive': *Docs Rel.*, vol. 1, 49.

p. 105 'this intrigue was set': *Docs Rel.*, vol. 1, 45.

p. 105 'answer of his Majesty': *Docs Rel.*, vol. 1, 49.

p. 107 'brought againe to the torture': East India Company, 'A True Relation Of The Uniust, Cruell, And Barbarous Proceedings against the English at Amboyna In the East-Indies', E3.

p. 107 'the most assured and civill': East India Company, 'A Remonstrance Of The Directors Of The Netherlands East India Company', C2.

p. 107 'Bring more candles': Dryden, *Amboyna: A Tragedy*.

p. 108 'nothing save the balm': *Docs Rel.*, vol. 1, 58.

p. 110 'barber-surgeon': Zumthor, *Daily Life in Rembrandt's Holland*, 155–7.

p. 112 By sheer luck, the journal: My account of Van den Bogaert's journey comes from his journal and the commentary on it published in Van den Bogaert, *A Journey into Mohawk and Oneida Country, 1634–1635*, and on interviews with Charles Gehring and Iroquois scholar Gunther Michelson.

p. 114 'shoot!': This is how Van den Bogaert gives it; Michelson says it actually means 'shoot again'.

p. 114 'As soon as they arrived': Van den Bogaert, *A Journey into Mohawk and Oneida Country*, 10.

p. 116 'This white man': The chant, as recorded by Van den Bogaert: '*ha assironi atsimachkoo kent oyakaying wee onneyatte onaondage koyockwe hoo senoto wanyagweganne hoo schenehalaton kasten kanosoni yndicko*.' The words *kaying wee*, *onneyatte*, *onaondage*, *koyockwe*, *hoo senotowany* refer, respectively, to the Mohawk, Oneida, Onondaga, Cayuga, and Seneca nations. In an interview on 7 Feb. 2002, Gunther Michelson, who translated the Mohawk for the 1988 publication of Van den Bogaert's journal, gave me his rendering of the chant.

p. 116 'man', 'woman', 'prostitute': Van den Bogaert, *A Journey into Mohawk and Oneida Country*, 52–63.

p. 117 an English trader sailed: The account of this incident comes from David de Vries's journal, published in Jameson, *Narratives of New Netherland*, 186–234.

p. 119 Thanks to the wave of scholarship: Jacobs, 'A Troubled Man: Director Wouter van Twiller and the Affairs of New Netherland in 1635'.

p. 119 Ramparts were added: Van Laer, *NYHM*, vol. 1, 108–9.

p. 119 Willem Blauvelt: Van Laer, *NYHM*, vol. 2, 162, 267, 323, 373.

p. 120 'commit adultery': Van Laer, *NYHM*, vol. 4, 89.

p. 120 'what he was doing': Gehring, *Council Minutes, 1655–1656*, 68–9.

p. 120 A man named Simon Root: Van Laer, *NYHM*, vol. 4, 360–1.

p. 121 Jan Premero: Van Laer, *NYHM*, vol. 4, 97–100.

p. 121 The Giant went free: my thanks to Firth Haring Fabend for sharing with me her notion that this case was a form of 'leniency'.

p. 121 'Piere Malenfant': Van Laer, *NYHM*, vol. 4, 269.
p. 122 'dishonorably manipulated': Van Laer, *NYHM*, vol. 4, 49.
p. 123 'her petticoat upon her knees': Van Laer, *NYHM*, vol. 1, 107.
p. 123 Griet was on board too: some details on Reyniers and Van Salee come from Hershkowitz, 'The Troublesome Turk'.
p. 123 It was a hazardous crossing: Van Rensselaer, *History of the City of New York in the Seventeenth Century*, vol. 1, 119.
p. 123 'the shirts of some': Van Laer, *NYHM*, vol. 4, 46.
p. 123 'I have long enough': Van Laer, *NYHM*, vol. 1, 70.
p. 123 measure the penises: Van Laer, *NYHM*, vol. 4, 46.
p. 123 'A Turk, a rascal': Van Laer, *NYHM*, vol. 1, 11.
p. 124 'If you do not know': Van Laer, *NYHM*, vol. 1, 67.
p. 124 'as good neighbors': *Docs Rel.*, vol. 3, 18.
p. 125 exaggerated somewhat: Van Laer, *Van Rensselaer Bowier Manuscripts*, 307.
p. 125 'two days' journey': Van Laer, *Van Rensselaer Bowier Manuscripts*, 166, 181.

Chapter 5

p. 131 by 1622 its population: Van Deursen, *Plain Lives in a Golden Age*, 11.
p. 132 *Treasure of Health*: Schama, *The Embarrassment of Riches*, 557.
p. 134 one-half of all books: Sprunger, *Trumpets from the Tower*, 29.
p. 134 'refuse no honest': Haley, *The Dutch in the Seventeenth Century*, 167.
p. 135 'each person shall': Trans. from Kossman and Mellink, *Texts Concerning the Revolt of the Netherlands*, 165.
p. 135 In the 1620s: On the Dutch tolerance debates, I have relied on Israel, 'The Intellectual Debate about Toleration in the Dutch Republic' and 'Toleration in Seventeenth-Century Dutch and English Thought', and Williams, '"Abominable Religion" and Dutch (In)tolerance'.
p. 135 'Many will be': Mout, 'Limits and Debates', 41.
p. 136 The tolerance advocates: Mout, 'Limits and Debates', 46.
p. 136 His *Discourses*: Sobel, *Galileo's Daughter*, 302.
p. 136 up to a healthy forty gallons of wine: Haley, *The Dutch in the Seventeenth Century*, 118.
p. 137 'in the academic Garden': Lunsingh Scheurleer and

Posthumus Meyjes, *Leiden University in the Seventeenth Century*, 280.

p. 137 Reinier de Graaf: Lunsingh Scheurleer and Posthumus Meyjes, *Leiden University in the Seventeenth Century*, 283.

p. 139 'elegant law': Feenstra and Waal, *Seventeenth-century Leyden Law Professors*, 9–11.

p. 139 'from its conformity': Dumbauld, *The Life and Legal Writings of Hugo Grotius*, 62.

p. 140 Cunaeus: Tuck, *Philosophy and Government*, 166–9.

p. 141 pipe tobacco: Schama, *The Embarrassment of Riches*, 195.

p. 141 'it is not permissible': The quote and analysis of the Dutch home come from Rybczynski, *Home: A Short History of an Idea*, ch. 3.

p. 141 He lived in and around: On Descartes' time in and around Leiden, including his associations and battles with professors there, I am relying on Gaukroger, *Descartes*, 321–86.

p. 142 'as soon as my age': Descartes, *Discourse on Method*, 44.

p. 142-3 'In general, the affairs': Van Laer, *Van Rensselaer Bowier Manuscripts*, 520.

p. 143 Getting experienced workers: Venema, 'Beverwijck', 366–7; Rink, *Holland on the Hudson*, 152.

p. 143 'When convenient': Van Laer, *Van Rensselaer Bowier Manuscripts*, 524.

p. 145 'it is named': Van der Donck, *A Description of the New Netherlands*, trans. Johnson, 7.

p. 146 Gillis Verbrugge: Rink, 'Unraveling a Secret Colonialism', pt I, 14.

p. 146 Dirck de Wolff: Rink, 'Unraveling a Secret Colonialism', pt I, 15.

p. 146 the baker doubled as a ship's captain: Van Laer, *NYHM*, vol. 3, 81.

p. 146 The looseness of Manhattan society: On the 'multitasking' of New Amsterdam residents, I am relying on Maika, 'Commerce and Community', 38–59.

p. 147 Govert Loockermans: Riker, 'Govert Loockermans'.

p. 147 'tortured the chief's brother': Jameson, *Narratives of New Netherland*, 208.

p. 147 home of the pirate: Information on the location of

Loockerman's home comes from Diane Dallal, archaeologist with New York Unearthed.

p. 147 the inventory of his property: Van Laer, *NYHM*, vol. 1, 320–2.

p. 148 perhaps four hundred inhabitants: French priest Isaac Jogues, visiting five years later, estimated the population at between 400 and 500; it is from him that the figure of eighteen languages comes. Jameson, *Narratives of New Netherland*, 259.

p. 148 'a mean barn': Jameson, *Narratives of New Netherland*, 212.

p. 148 the minister's house and stable: Stokes, *Iconography of Manhattan Island*,
vol. 4, 78, 79.

p. 148 Juriaen, who: Van Laer, *NYHM*, vol. 1, 336–7.

p. 149 'a dwelling house': Van Laer, *NYHM*, vol. 1, 338–9.

p. 149 '4 chauldrons' : Van Laer, *NYHM*, vol. 1, 341–2.

p. 149 No sooner had the ship: Commentators have referred to the ship arriving on 20 August 1641. I believe they are relying on De Vries's journal, in which he gives this date (Jameson, *Narratives of New Netherland*, 211). But the fact that the skipper of the ship was in New Amsterdam entering into contract with a merchant for the next delivery on 30 July 1641 doesn't fit with this. My guess is that De Vries got the month wrong, and that perhaps the ship arrived on 20 July.

p. 150 'a silver-plated rapier': Van Laer, *Van Rensselaer Bowier Manuscripts*, 204. The description pertains to the previous, shortlived *schout*; I am assuming that Van der Donck would have received the same badges of office.

Chapter 6

p. 151 inn of Pieter de Winter: Riker, *Revised History of Harlem*, 132.

p. 152 'the just half': Van Laer, *NYHM*, vol. 1, 19.

p. 152 took on a partner: Van Laer, *NYHM*, vol. 1, 93–4.

p. 153 'fumbled at the front': Van Laer, *NYHM*, vol. 1, 55.

p. 153 'black wench': Van Laer, *NYHM*, vol. 1, 57–8.

p. 154 Rembrandt featured his cousin: This family tie was pointed out to me by Willem Frijhoff, who detailed it in his paper 'Neglected Networks: New Netherlanders and their Old Fatherland: The Kieft Case', delivered at the 2001 Rensselaerswijck Seminar in New York City.

p. 154 according to a pamphlet published: 'Broad Advice', in Van der Donck, *Vertoogh van Nieu Nederland, [by A. van der Donck] and, Braeden raedt aende Vereenichde Nederlandsche provintien, [by I. A. G. W. C., pseud. Of C. Melyn]*, 139.
p. 155 It was unique: I am obliged to Jaap Jacobs for this insight, which is developed in his book *Een zegenrijk gewest*.
p. 155 By some estimates: Van den Boogaart, 'The Servant Migration to New Netherland', 55.
p. 158 'I, Willem Kieft': *Docs Rel.*, vol. 12, 19.
p. 159 a new society: The insight into Minuit's desire to found a new society comes from Weslager, *A Man and his Ship*.
p. 161 'Whereas at present': Van Laer, *NYHM*, vol. 4, 107.
p. 162 'Whereas the Company': Van Laer, *NYHM*, vol. 4, 60.
p. 162 'their womenfolk': Van der Donck, 'A Description of New Netherland', trans. Goedhuys, 92.
p. 163 'These savages resemble': Jameson, *Narratives of New Netherland*, 213.
p. 163 'Whereas the Indians': Van Laer, *NYHM*, vol. 4, 115–16.
p. 163 an Indian named Pacham: Jameson, *Narratives of New Netherland*, 211.
p. 165 'Whether it is not just': Van Laer, *NYHM*, vol. 4, 124.
p. 165 'being himself protected': Jameson, *Narratives of New Netherland*, 214.
p. 165 'whereas we acknowledge': Van Laer, *NYHM*, vol. 4, 125.
p. 166 'it will be best': Van Laer, *NYHM*, vol.4, 126.
p. 166 the council of twelve: *Docs Rel.*, vol. 1, 202–3.
p. 166 'And whereas the Commonalty': *Docs Rel.*, vol. 1, 203.
p. 167 The ugliest assault: Jameson, *Narratives of New Netherland*, 226–9.
p. 167 'such work could not be done': Jameson, *Narratives of New Netherland*, 226–9.
p. 169 'Did the Duke of Alva': Jameson, *Narratives of New Netherland*, 228; 'Broad Advice', in Van der Donck, *Vertoogh van Nieu Nederland, [by A. van der Donck] and, Braeden raedt aende Vereenichde Nederlandsche provintien, [by I. A. G. W. C., pseud. Of C. Melyn]*, 149.
p. 170 It also reinforced: For specifics on the development of tolerance in the Dutch psyche, I am relying on Jacobs,

'Between Repression and Approval'.

p. 170 In its very seeding: For this insight I am indebted to Frijhoff, 'New Views on the Dutch Period of New York'.

p. 171 the settlers tried to maintain: Events in this paragraph come from Van Laer, *NYHM*, vol. 2, 21, 33, 34–5, 39–40, 70, 87, 88, 96; vol. 4, 119, 197.

Chapter 7

p. 174 'so much so': Van der Donck, *Beschryvinge van Niew-Nederlant*, 15, trans. Hanny Veenendaal and the author.

p. 174 'The trees are then': Van der Donck, *Beschryvinge van Niew-Nederlant*, 48, trans. Hanny Veenendaal and the author.

p. 175 'Above the highlands': Van der Donck, *A Description of the New Netherlands*, trans. Johnson, 63–4.

p. 175 'none like the gray': Van der Donck, 'A Description of New Netherland', trans. Goedhuys, 59.

p. 175 'soar very high': Van der Donck, *A Description of the New Netherlands*, trans. Johnson, 49.

p. 175 'woodcocks, birch-cocks': Van der Donck, *A Description of the New Netherlands*, trans. Johnson, 51.

p. 175 'the swift and fostering': Van der Donck, *A Description of the New Netherlands*, trans. Johnson, 58.

p. 175 'several kinds of plums': Van der Donck, *A Description of the New Netherlands*, trans. Johnson, 23.

p. 175 'cicerullen, or water-lemons': Van der Donck, 'A Description of New Netherland', trans. Goedhuys, 37–8.

p. 176 'The plants which are known': Van der Donck, *A Description of the New Netherlands*, trans. Johnson, 28.

p. 177 'know of no limits': Van der Donck, *A Description of the New Netherlands*, trans. Johnson, 5.

p. 177 'We, Adriaen van der Donck': Van Laer, *Van Rensselaer Bowier Manuscripts*, 573–4.

p. 178 searching for a young woman: Van Laer, *NYHM*, vol. 4, 173.

p. 178 'It is your duty': Van Laer, *Van Rensselaer Bowier Manuscripts*, 636.

p. 179 'What pleases me': Van Laer, *Van Rensselaer Bowier Manuscripts*, 631.

p. 179 'Your principal fault': Van Laer, *Van Rensselaer Bowier Manuscripts*, 636.

p. 179 'outrageous': Van Laer, *Van Rensselaer Bowier Manuscripts*, 640.

p. 180 'pursued each other': O'Callaghan, *The History of New Netherland*, vol. 1, 460.

p. 180 black stallions: Van Laer, *Minutes of the Court of Rensselaerswyck*, vol. 1, 61, 67–8, 79.

p. 180 'I take it very ill': Van Laer, *Van Rensselaer Bowier Manuscripts*, 616, 649, 650, 666.

p. 180 'From the beginning': Van Laer, *Van Rensselaer Bowier Manuscripts*, 631.

p. 181 'Your Honor may be assured': O'Callaghan, *The History of New Netherland*, vol. 1, 462.

p. 181 'go naked': Schmidt, 'Innocence Abroad', 18.

p. 182 'equal to the average': Van der Donck, 'A Description of New Netherland', trans. Goedhuys, 90.

p. 182 'repel rain': Van der Donck, 'A Description of New Netherland', trans. Goedhuys, 101.

p. 182 'Declension and conjugation': Van der Donck, 'A Description of New Netherland', trans. Goedhuys, 115.

p. 182 'fresh wounds and': Van der Donck, 'A Description of New Netherland', trans. Goedhuys, 119.

p. 182 'devil-hunting': Van der Donck, *A Description of the New Netherlands*, trans. Johnson, 95.

p. 182 'Public authority': Van der Donck, 'A Description of New Netherland', trans. Goedhuys, 133.

p. 183 'Had he written': Thomas O'Donnell, 'Introduction', in Van der Donck, *A Description of the New Netherlands*, trans. Johnson, x.

p. 184 did not appear in print: Van Gastel, 'Van der Donck's Description of the Indians'.

p. 184 'wind, stream, bush': Van der Donck, 'A Description of New Netherland', trans. Goedhuys, 127.

p. 185 'The offering is hung': Van der Donck, 'A Description of New Netherland', trans. Goedhuys, 129.

p. 185 'one of the younger': Van der Donck, 'A Description of New Netherland', trans. Goedhuys, 130.

p. 186 'dishonestly designed': O'Callaghan, *The History of New Netherland*, vol. 1, 338–9.

p. 186 A million acres: Dunn, 'Enlarging Rensselaerswijck'. Dunn says that at its height Rensselaerswyck extended '700,000 or more acres'. I am also including the Van Rensselaer tract called Claverack.

p. 188 Kieft assembled the board: details of the 18 June meeting are taken from *Docs Rel.*, vol. 1, 212–14.

p. 188 he had recently arrived: The New Netherland council minutes for 1644 (Van Laer, *NYHM*, vol. 4, 190), show that on 6 June Van der Donck was in court at Fort Amsterdam.

p. 189 'Almighty God': *Docs Rel.*, vol. 1, 190–1. I am grateful to Dr Willem Frijhoff of the Free University of Amsterdam for elaborating for me his argument that Van der Donck was the author of much of the correspondence generated by the colonists, and that Bogardus was probably responsible for some of what was written in 1643 and 1644. My theory expands on his. His argument is spelled out in his book *Wegen van Evert Willemsz.*, 735–8.

p. 189 expired in August: Van Laer, *Minutes of the Court of Rensselaerswyck*, vol. 1, 10; *Docs Rel.* vol. 1, 431, 532–3.

p. 191 'a coherent vision': Willem Frijhoff, personal communication, 14 March 2002.

p. 191 'The only other candidate': Charles Gehring, personal communication, 14 March 2002.

p. 193 'For the sake of appearances': *Docs Rel.*, vol. 1, 211. The original incorrectly gives the date of the meeting as November 1642.

Chapter 8

p. 196 The island of St Martin: Details of the attack on St Martin are spelled out in Gehring and Schiltkamp, *Curaçao Papers*, 32–5, and in the pamphlet 'Broad Advice', in Van der Donck, *Vertoogh van Nieu Nederland*.

p. 197 'pluck up the skinn': From Peter Lowe's *Discourse on the Whole Art of Chyrurgerie* (1596), as quoted in Leonardo, *History of Surgery*, 153.

p. 197 'Let him prepare': John Woodall, *The Surgeon's Mate* (1617), as quoted in Kessler and Rachlis, *Peter Stuyvesant and his New York*, 48.

p. 198 'did not succeed': Eerdmans, *Pieter Stuyvesant: An Historical Documentation*, 52–5.

p. 198 ferocious micro-management: Gehring and Schiltkamp, *Curaçao Papers*, 37–48.

p. 199 abusing his landlord's: 'Broad Advice', in Van der Donck, *Vertoogh van Nieu Nederland*, 160, refers to Stuyvesant as having 'formerly stolen the daughter of his own landlord at Franiker, and was caught at it, and let off for the sake of his father, otherwise he would have been disgraced.'

p. 200 Carel van Brugge: Gehring, *Council Minutes, 1652–1654*, 223.

p. 200 John Farret: Biographical information comes from J. D. Uhlenbeck, 'Genaelogie van het geslacht Farret'. He appears in most sources as Johan, but the genealogy gives his name at birth as John.

p. 200 correspondence . . . in verse: The poetry exchange between Farret and Stuyvesant is in the collection of the Nederlands Scheepvaart Museum, Amsterdam. I worked from a transcription done by J. P. Puype, librarian of the museum, in the collection of Charles Gehring at the New Netherland Project. Hanny Veenendaal of the Netherlands Center gave me a colloquial translation.

p. 200 which was discovered: Stokes, *Iconography of Manhattan Island*, vol. 4, supplementary addenda for the year 1645.

p. 202 It contained 450 Dutch soldiers: Gehring and Schiltkamp, *Curaçao Papers*, 36–9.

p. 203 He thought he had seen: My thanks to Charles Gehring for suggesting I follow these 450 soldiers who would repeatedly cross paths with Stuyvesant.

p. 203 In one such effort: Abreu, *Chapters of Brazil's Colonial History*, 83.

p. 203 yaws, dysentery: Medical and battle conditions in Brazil come from Guerra, 'Medicine in Dutch Brazil'.

p. 204 'leather, dogs, cats, and rats': Duarte de Albuquerque Coelho, *Memorias diarias de la guerra del Brasil*, quoted in Abreu, *Chapters of Brazil's Colonial History*, 82.

p. 204 '*What mad thunder ball*': My thanks to Elisabeth Paling Funk for translating this poem for me.

p. 205 fell in love with: For some of the information on Stuyvesant's return to the Netherlands I am relying on VanHoevenberg, 'The Stuyvesants in the Netherlands and New Netherland'.

p. 206 'so that the entire country': *Docs Rel.*, vol. 1, 213.

p. 207 Meanwhile, in Scotland: There are many accounts of this scene. I am relying in part on the roundup of the earliest descriptions that appears in chapter 21 of Lees, *St Giles', Edinburgh: Church, College, and Cathedral*.

p. 210 'making a seat': Carlton, *Charles I*, 166.

p. 210 'Some more cavalry': *Docs Rel.*, vol. 1, 127.

p. 210 'News is received': *Docs Rel.*, vol. 1, 127, 133, 134.

p. 211 'Thou shalt not': Exod. 22: 18, King James Version.

p. 211 in an age awash: I am relying on Mowat, 'Prospero's Book', for an understanding of the mix of theology and sorcery in sixteenth- and seventeenth-century England.

p. 212 '[He] came to New England': *Docs Rel.*, vol. 1, 305.

p. 213 Lady Deborah Moody: Winthrop, *Journal of John Winthrop*, 462–3.

p. 213 Anne Hutchinson: For Hutchinson's story, I am relying on Winthrop, *Journal of John Winthrop*, 473-6, and on Selma R. Williams, *Divine Rebel*, chs 1, 9, 14.

p. 214 'Abraham's children': O'Callaghan, *History of New Netherland*, vol. 1, 257.

p. 214 yet another strong-willed creature: Information on the Doughty–Kieft conflict comes from Van der Donck, 'Remonstrance of New Netherland'; *Docs Rel.*, vol. 1, 305; and from the pamphlet 'Broad Advice', in Van der Donck, *Vertoogh van Nieu Nederland*, 159.

p. 214-5 it appears Van der Donck: The dates on which Doughty and Van der Donck were both at court in New Amsterdam are in Van Laer, *NYHM*, vol. 4, 266–74. It's possible that only Van der Donck's opponent, Simon Pos, appeared in person on the dates mentioned in the records, in which case Van der Donck and Mary Doughty could have met later in July, when Van der Donck returned from the north.

p. 215 'Every thing is, by God's blessing': *Docs Rel.*, vol. 1, 157.

p. 216 He came downstairs: The scene involving Agheroense, Van der Donck and Kieft comes from Van der Donck, 'A Description of New Netherland', trans. Goedhuys, 48–9.

p. 217 The gift was to be: Van der Donck, 'A Description of New Netherland', trans. Goedhuys, 129.

p. 217 twenty-four thousand acres: Van der Donck, *A Description of the New Netherlands*, trans. Johnson, xxvii.

p. 218 On 30 August: Details on the Fort Amsterdam peace treaty come from Van Laer, *NYHM*, vol. 4, 232–4.

p. 219 The civil war in England: For my lightning account of the Battle of Naseby I consulted Sprigge, *Anglia rediviva*; Kishlansky, *A Monarchy Transformed*, 165–6; *After the Battle of Naseby* (painting by Sir John Gilbert); and the village of Naseby website.

p. 220 The day of deliverance: Information on Stuyvesant's arrival comes from the pamphlet 'Broad Advice', in Van der Donck, *Vertoogh van Nieu Nederland*, 162–4, and Van der Donck, 'Remonstrance of New Netherland', in *Docs Rel.*, vol. 1, 309–10.

Chapter 9

p. 222 'Peacock like': *Docs Rel.*, vol. 1, 310.

p. 222 'like a father': *Docs Rel.*, vol. 1, 446.

p. 225 A drunken knife-fight: Van Laer, *NYHM*, vol. 4, 365–7.

p. 225 'to be chained': Van Laer, *NYHM*, vol. 4, 369.

p. 228 thick green glass goblets: Pieces of such glasses, which were common in the Dutch Republic at the time, were excavated from New Amsterdam homes dating to precisely this period. Backgammon and cribbage pieces have also been unearthed. See Goodfriend, 'The Sabbath Keeper'; Cantwell and DiZerega Wall, *Unearthing Gotham*, 'Introduction'; Nan Rothschild et al., 'The Archaeological Investigation of the Stadt Huys Block'.

p. 228 'Is he not well aware': *Docs Rel.*, vol. 1, 195–6.

p. 229 'Can he, the Secretary': *Docs Rel.*, vol. 1, 198–9.

p. 231 'Was it ever heard': Van Laer, *NYHM*, vol. 4, 370–1.

p. 232 'with false and bitter poison': *Docs Rel.*, vol. 1, 203–4.

p. 233 magnanimously offered: Van Laer, *NYHM*, vol. 1, 407. The contract is for 450 schepels; a schepel equals 0.764 bushels.

p. 233 Van der Donck comes across: For this insight into Van der Donck as budding politician, I am grateful to Dr Ada Louise van Gastel, who sketches it in chapter 4 of her dissertation, 'Adriaen van der Donck, New Netherland, and America'.

p. 234 'Honorable Gentlemen!': The letter is in *Docs Rel.*, vol. 1, 205–9. I am grateful to Dr Willem Frijhoff for sharing with me his arguments in support of Van der Donck's authorship of the letter.

p. 236 'Thou shalt not revile': Van Laer, *NYHM*, vol. 4, 406–7.

p. 236 'People may think': 'Remonstrance of New Netherland', in *Docs Rel.*, vol. 1, 310.

p. 236 Stuyvesant amended the sentences: Van Laer, *NYHM*, vol. 4, 417–22.

p. 236 The ship *Princess Amelia*: Details regarding the cargo of the *Princess* come from Charles Gehring, 'Wringing Information from a Drowned Princess', and Simon Groenveld, 'New Light on a Drowned Princess: Information from London'.

p. 239 It was largely: Morgan, *The Puritan Dilemma*, 59–61, 103–4.

p. 239 'Honored Sr': Gehring, *Correspondence, 1647–1653*, 6–7.

p. 239 George Baxter: Gehring, *Correspondence, 1647–1653*, 8.

p. 239 'Crazines of my head': Gehring, *Correspondence, 1647–1653*, 8.

p. 239 'hoping all the English': Gehring, *Correspondence, 1647–1653*, 9.

p. 240 He commissioned a detailed report: Gehring, *Delaware Papers: Dutch Period, 1648–1664*, 1–12, and endnote 1.

p. 240 28-stone body: Gehring, 'De Suyt Rivier'.

p. 241 'as if they had been affected': Gehring, *Delaware Papers: Dutch Period, 1648–1664*, 19.

p. 241 'is the greatest insult': Gehring, *Delaware Papers: Dutch Period, 1648–1664*, 18.

p. 242 'My lord': Gehring, *Delaware Papers: Dutch Period, 1648–1664*, 12.

p. 243 'inquire diligently': Gehring, *Delaware Papers: Dutch Period, 1648–1664*, 22.

p. 243 'a school, church': Stokes, *Iconography of Manhattan Island*, vol. 4, 111.

p. 244 'the most notable': Van Laer, *NYHM*, vol. 4, 338–41.

p. 244 A Scotsman named: The Forrester affair is detailed in Van Laer, *NYHM*, vol. 4, 442–5.

p. 246 Sir Edmund Plowden: The Plowden affair is told in Van der Donck's 'Remonstrance of New Netherland', 289, and the broader story is given in Murphy, 'Representation of New Netherland', in New-York Historical Society, *Collections*, 2nd ser., vol. 11, 1849. Plowden's original 1632 petition to King Charles – stating that he and his compatriots are 'willing at their own cost' to plant a colony 'at a remote place, called Manati or Long Isle' – is logged in Public Record Office, Calendar of State Papers, Colonial Series, 1574–1660, vol. 6, 154. I'm also relying here on Pennington, 'An Examination of Beauchamp Plantagenet's Description of the Province of New Albion'.

p. 247 There occurred another: Details of Van den Bogaert's end are found in Van Laer, *NYHM*, vol. 4, 480–1, and Van Laer, *Minutes of the Court of Rensselaerswyck, 1648–1652*, 105. I have also relied on Gehring's introduction to Van den Bogaert, *A Journey into Mohawk Country*, xxi.

p. 248 lawman of the independent fiefdom: Van Laer, *NYHM*, vol. 4, 255; Van Laer, *Minutes of the Court of Rensselaerswyck, 1648–1652*, 11.

p. 249 As he ran across: Gehring, 'Totidem Verbis', in *De Nieu Nederlanse Marcurius*, 4.

p. 250 'Your complaints are unjust': O'Callaghan, *The History of New Netherland*, II, 71–8.

p. 251 Adriaen van der Donck appears again: Van Laer, *Minutes of the Court of Rensselaerswyck, 1648–1652*, entry for 23 July, 1648.

Chapter 10

p. 252 When the *Princess*: Information on the wreck of the *Princess* and survival of Melyn and Kuyter comes from Gehring, 'Wringing Information from a Drowned Princess', Groenveld, 'New Light on a Drowned Princess', and the contemporaneous pamphlet 'Broad Advice'.

p. 254 delivered a letter: The petition is not extant, but Stuyvesant refers to it in Van Laer, *NYHM*, vol. 4, 580.

p. 255 'more closely into consideration': Van Laer, *NYHM*, vol. 4, 489.
p. 256 He catalogued: Van der Donck, 'A Description of New Netherland', trans. Goedhuys, 142.
p. 256 'None of these': Van der Donck, 'A Description of New Netherland', trans. Goedhuys, 141.
p. 256 'the means for the initial settlement': Van der Donck, 'A Description of New Netherland', trans. Goedhuys, 140.
p. 256 led English tobacco farmers: Kupp, 'Dutch Notarial Acts Relating to the Tobacco Trade of Virginia'.
p. 257 They created a variety: Schama, *The Embarrassment of Riches*, 196–7.
p. 257 In 1648: Maika, 'Commerce and Community', 31–6; Kupp, 'Dutch Notarial Acts Relating to the Tobacco Trade of Virginia'.
p. 257 in fact it was: Oliver Rink's *Holland on the Hudson* first made this case in 1986, and since then historians have begun to revise the Anglocentric view of Dutch Manhattan as a muddle; for example, Wayne Bodle, 'Themes and Directions in Middle Colonies Historiography, 1980–1994', notes the new view that the Dutch colony 'rather than languishing in the decade before 1664, had a long-term developmental trajectory broadly parallel to those of many contemporary English colonies' and that this was 'characterized by private enterprise'.
p. 258 Taken together with: Archaeological evidence for the location of the Van der Donck house comes from Rothschild and Matthews, 'Phase 1A-1B Archaeological Investigation of the Proposed Area for the Construction of Six Tennis Courts on the Parade Grounds of Van Cortlandt Park', 13–14; Tieck, *Riverdale, Kingsbridge, Spuyten Duyvil*, 4, 9; Ricciardi, 'From Private to Public: The Changing Landscape of Van Cortlandt Park; Bronx, New York, in the Nineteenth Century', 16; Cantwell and DiZerega Wall, *Unearthing Gotham*, 264.
p. 260 a mandamus: *Docs Rel.*, vol. 1, 250–2.
p. 261 'To Peter Stuyvesant': *Docs Rel.*, vol. 1, 351–2.
p. 261 They would ask the people: 'Remonstrance of New

Netherland', in Jameson, *Narratives of New Netherland*, 349–351.

p. 262 'burned with rage': 'Remonstrance of New Netherland', in Jameson, *Narratives of New Netherland*, 350.

p. 263 'these persons': 'Remonstrance of New Netherland', in Jameson, *Narratives of New Netherland*, 350.

p. 264 'grossly slandered': The arrest of Van der Donck and subsequent council session are detailed in Van der Donck's 'Remonstrance of New Netherland', in Jameson, *Narratives of New Netherland*, 350–2, and Van Laer, *NYHM*, vol. 4, 580–4.

p. 265 gathered in the church: *Docs Rel.*, vol. 1, 321–2, 352–3.

p. 265 Shortly before this: Van Laer, *NYHM*, vol. 4, 584.

p. 266 'so shaped that': *Docs Rel.*, vol. 1, 322.

p. 267 had disembarked: Van Laer, *NYHM*, vol. 3, 85–6; *Docs Rel.*, vol. 1, 321–2.

p. 267 At this moment: 'Remonstrance of New Netherland', in Jameson, *Narratives of New Netherland*; *Docs Rel.*, vol. 1, 311; Van Laer, *NYHM*, vol. 4, 595–7.

p. 268 banned from serving: Van Laer, *NYHM*, vol. 4, 587.

p. 269 He delivered these: *Docs Rel.*, vol. 1, 355–8.

p. 269 'Whereas it is': Van Laer, *NYHM*, vol. 4, 600–1.

p. 270 'Among all the enterprising': *Docs Rel.*, vol. 1, 275.

p. 271 he was in the midst: Gehring, *Correspondence, 1647–1653*, 44–53.

p. 271 and with chiefs: Van Laer, *NYHM*, vol. 4, 607–9.

p. 271 'Whereas the said': Van Laer, *NYHM*, vol. 4, 601.

p. 272 but Captain Blauvelt: Van Laer, *NYHM*, vol. 4, 219, 603, 605; Van Laer, *NYHM*, vol. 3, 114, 121, 151.

p. 273 Van der Donck handed her: *Docs Rel.*, vol. 1, 354–5.

Chapter 11

p. 274 the painting just described: My account of Adriaen Pauw riding into Münster is based on the Gerard ter Borch painting *Entry of Adriaen Pauw and Anna van Ruytenburgh into Münster*, as well as on Alison McNeil Kettering's analysis of the painting in *Gerard ter Borch and the Treaty of Münster*, and on Israel, 'Art and Diplomacy'. Pauw arrived in January but the painting depicts his ceremonial arrival in verdant spring, a liberty ter Borch took, according to Kettering, because it made for a better painting.

p. 275 In the early 1640s: My account of the Peace of Westphalia and its significance relies on Heinz Schilling, 'War and Peace at the Emergence of Modernity'; John Elliott, 'War and Peace in Europe: 1618–1648'; Anja Stiglic, 'Ceremonial and Status Hierarchy on the European Diplomatic Stage: The Diplomats' Solemn Entries into the Congressional City of Münster'; and Volker Gerhardt, 'On the Historical Significance of the Peace of Westphalia: Twelve Theses': all in Bussman and Schilling, *1648*.

p. 275 King Gustavus Adolphus: Gerhardt, 'On the Historical Significance of the Peace of Westphalia', n. 6.

p. 275 the French delegation: Israel, 'Art and Diplomacy', 94.

p. 277 he lived in a castle: Renaud, *Het Huis en de Heren van Heemstede Tijdens de Middeleeuwen*.

p. 277 red-and-white striped tulips: Schama, *The Embarrassment of Riches*, 354.

p. 279 'It appears at first': The quote is from French priest François Fénelon, in White, *Rembrandt*, 27.

p. 279 'I can walk out each day': Gaukroger, *Descartes*, 412–13.

p. 280 'to sell someone eyeglasses': Van der Coelen, *Everyday life in Holland's Golden Age*, 130.

p. 280 women whose whispered sighs: Schama, *The Embarrassment of Riches*, 472–8.

p. 282 'the largest village': Haley, *The Dutch in the Seventeenth Century*, 64.

p. 282 'Remonstrance of New Netherland': *Docs Rel.*, vol. 1, 259.

p. 283 a letter from the board: *Docs Rel.*, vol. 1, 258.

p. 283 'These persons are': *Docs Rel.*, vol. 1, 319.

p. 283 'Manhathans . . . the Capital': *Docs Rel.*, vol. 1, 265.

p. 283 'we may pursue': *Docs Rel.*, vol. 1, 260–1.

p. 283 'It will lose': *Docs Rel.*, vol. 1, 264.

p. 284 'Not that there is any doubt': *Docs Rel.*, vol. 1, 262.

p. 284 Beaver pelts: *Docs Rel.*, vol. 1, 346: 'as well as some samples of the fruits and peltries produced there'.

p. 284 'I have seen rye': Van der Donck, *A Description of the New Netherlands*, trans. Johnson, 31–2.

p. 284 hand-drawn map: *Docs Rel.*, vol. 1, 346: 'a perfect map of the country'.

p.285 This delicately coloured illustration: De Koning, 'From Van der Donck to Visscher'; Robert R. Macdonald, 'The City of New Amsterdam Located on the Island of Manhattan in New Netherland', Museum of the City of New York website (www.mcny.org), 1998.

p. 285 'for the love of New Netherland': *Docs Rel.*, vol. 1, 261.

p. 285 'In our opinion': *Docs Rel.*, vol. 1, 317.

p. 287 fired off a responding pamphlet: The pamphlets debating monarchy are in the Koninklijke Bibliotheek in The Hague (Knuttel catalogue numbers 6377–83); my source on their importance is Geyl, *Orange and Stuart*, 47–8.

p.288 Franciscus van den Enden: Israel, *Radical Enlightenment*, 168–80.

p.288 Pieter Plockhoy: On Plockhoy, see Plantenga, 'The Mystery of the Plockhoy Settlement in the Valley of Swans'; on Plockhoy and Van den Enden, see Israel, *Radical Enlightenment*, 176–9, and Kelver, 'Conflicting "Considerations of State"'.

p. 288 Why American history has: Many historians helped me appreciate this change in the way history is done. For conversations on the topic, my thanks in particular to Joyce Goodfriend of the University of Denver and Cynthia van Zandt of the University of New Hampshire; also to Karen Ordahl Kupperman of New York University and James Williams of Middle Tennessee State University for talks they gave on the subject at the 2001 Gotham History Festival at the Gotham Center.

p. 289 appointed a committee: *Docs Rel.*, vol. 1, 319–20.

p. 291 'a grandeur far beyond': Rowen, *Princes of Orange*, 82.

p. 291 Michiel Stael: Kossmann, *De boekhandel te 's-Gravenhage tot het eind van de 18de eeuw*, 365–6; Keblusek, *Boeken in de hofstad*; Harline, *Pamphlets, Printing, and Political Culture in the Early Dutch Republic*, 126.

p. 292 At the turn of the century: Harline, *Pamphlets, Printing, and Political Culture in the Early Dutch Republic*, 73.

p. 292 *Two Letters of General Cromwell*: The pamphlet titles are taken from Kossman, *De boekhandel te 's-Gravenhage tot het eind van de 18de eeuw*; online catalogue of the Koninklijke Bibliotheek, The Hague.

p. 293 its share price: Israel, *Dutch Primacy in World Trade*, 163.

p. 293 Stael apparently introduced: Vinckeboons et al., *The Origins of New York*, 18.

p. 293 publishing this map: Schmidt, 'Mapping an Empire'; De Koning, 'From Van der Donck to Visscher'; Vinckeboons et al., *The Origins of New York*.

p. 293 The so-called Jansson–Visscher map: Augustyn and Cohen, *Manhattan in Maps*, 32–3.

p. 294 to visit his family: Hoffman, 'Van der Donck–Van Bergen'; Van Gastel, 'Adriaen van der Donck als woordvoerder van de Nieuw-Nederlandse bevolking'.

p. 296 And in what is perhaps: *Docs Rel.*, vol. 1, 369.

p. 297 'Formerly New Netherland': Gehring, *Correspondence, 1647–1653*, 83–4. Vinckeboons et al. (*The Origins of New York*, 17–18), while acknowledging that the rush of interest in the colony in February and March 1650 suggests that the *Remonstrance* was published then, conclude that it must have been published later in the year, because Stael, who gives his address on the title-page as 'on the Buitenhof', did not move there until 10 March. But the sudden popular interest in the colony can only be explained by the publication of the *Remonstrance*, and there are several possible explanations for the information on the title-page. For one, we know that Stael would later move to another address on the Buitenhof, so it's possible that, favouring the neighbourhood, he had an earlier address there as well. Another possibility is that Stael knew he would be moving to the prestigious address, and so set the type for it before he was actually living there, knowing that he would be in residence about the time of publication. There is also no reason why Stael would have delayed publication for several months. The letter of the West India Company directors to Stuyvesant, in which they say that 'now heaven and earth' are interested in the colony, is dated 16 February; Harline (*Pamphlets, Printing, and Political Culture in the Early Dutch Republic*, 92) gives one month as a typical time it took to produce a published pamphlet, which would fit with the

February date, and suggests that the *Remonstrance* hit the streets at the beginning of 1650.

p. 297 He composed: *Docs Rel.*, vol. 1, 376–7.

p. 297 addressing in particular: Jacobs, 'A Hitherto Unknown Letter of Adriaen van der Donck', 4–5.

p. 298 'on the whole subject': *Docs Rel.*, vol. 1, 377–81.

p. 299 'Provisional Order': *Docs Rel.*, vol. 1, 387–91. That the order was read aloud I infer from the paragraph that seems directed to people in the room at the time, beginning: 'We would, therefore, be of opinion that your High Mightinesses do, with the advice and communication of the Directors now summoned from all the Chambers of the West India Company, the major part of whom are in attendance . . .'

p. 300 'Noble, Mighty Lords': *Docs Rel.*, vol. 1, 395.

p. 301 This letter was discovered: Jacobs, 'A Hitherto Unknown Letter of Adriaen van der Donck.' I would like to thank Dr Jacobs for discussing the letter and its significance with me, and for allowing me to reprint his translation of it.

p. 302 'this State . . . alone': *Docs Rel.*, vol. 1, 347.

Chapter 12

p. 304 approximately 300 acres: Stokes, *Iconography of Manhattan Island*, vol. 6, 142.

p. 305 'seditious persons': Gehring, *Correspondence, 1647–1653*, 82.

p. 305 'We suppose that you': Gehring, *Correspondence, 1647–1653*, 88.

p. 305 'We live like sheep': *Docs Rel.*, vol. 1, 452.

p. 305 'He proceeds no longer': *Docs Rel.*, vol. 1, 453.

p. 306 'Many free people': Gehring, *Correspondence, 1647–1653*, 90, 92.

p. 307 fired off a letter: Gehring, *Correspondence, 1647–1653*, 13–14.

p. 307 'For what have I': Gehring, *Correspondence, 1647–1653*, 18–19.

p. 307 the Dutch regarded: See Eaton's letter to Stuyvesant, in Gehring, *Correspondence, 1647–1653*, 21.

p. 308 'Congratulate and reioyce': Gehring, *Correspondence, 1647–1653*, 49–50.

p. 308 'doe your utmost': Ronald Cohen, 'The Hartford Treaty of 1650', 328.

p. 309 The negotiations: On the Hartford Treaty, I have relied on Jacobs, 'The Hartford Treaty', Ronald Cohen, 'The Hartford Treaty of 1650', and Gehring, *Correspondence, 1647–1653.*

p. 310 On 5 June 1650: Rowen, *John de Witt, Grand Pensionary of Holland*, 28–9.

p. 311 put out a pamphlet: Kossmann, *De boekhandel te 's-Gravenhage tot het eind van de 18de eeuw*, 366.

p. 311 'was heard stamping': Rowen, *John de Witt, Grand Pensionary of Holland*, 36.

p. 312 Van Tienhoven vanished: The Van Tienhoven sex scandal is found in *Docs Rel.*, vol. 1, 514–17.

p. 313 some of the most distinguished men: On Pauw and De Witt, see Rowen, *John de Witt, Grand Pensionary of Holland*, 57–60.

p. 314 methodically supporting his case: Van der Donck's 'memorial' to the States General and supporting documents appear in *Docs Rel.*, vol. 1, 438–57.

p. 314 'nothing of the Director': *Docs Rel.*, vol. 1, 453.

p. 315 'The people here': *Docs Rel.*, vol. 1, 446.

p. 315 'Whatever you have done': *Docs Rel.*, vol. 1, 444.

p. 315 'pulled the wool': *Docs Rel.*, vol. 1, 458.

p. 316 'in order that so magnificent': *Docs Rel.*, vol. 1, 464–5.

p. 316 'in order to silence': Gehring, *Correspondence, 1647–1653*, 149.

p. 316 'To Petrus Stuyvesant': *Docs Rel.*, vol. 1, 472.

p. 317 'They make light': Van der Donck, 'A Description of New Netherland', trans. Goedhuys, 108.

p. 317 a resolution granting him: *Docs Rel.*, vol. 1, 470.

p. 317 the de facto Dutch constitution: Mout, 'Limits and Debates', 40–1.

p. 318 Act of Abjuration: Lucas, 'The *Plakkaat van Verlatinge*', 192.

p. 318 He hired several employees: Gemeentearchief, Amsterdam, English Translations of Notarial Documents . . . Pertaining to North America, no. 2279 V, p. 24, notary Jacob de Winter, 15 May 1652.

p. 318 'to hold peaceably': *Docs Rel.*, vol. 1, 473.

p. 319 Oliver Cromwell: My main sources on Cromwell are Hill, *God's Englishman*; Ashley, *The Greatness of Oliver Cromwell*; and Fraser, *Cromwell, the Lord Protector*.

p. 319 seed the American idea: Stephanson, *Manifest Destiny*, ch. 1.

p. 321 Accounts of what happened: My account of the action off Dover is based on the pamphlets 'A declaration of the Parliament of the commonwealth of England, relating to the affairs and proceedings . . .' and 'Nootwendige Observatien op het Antwoort van de Republiicke van Engelant op drie schriften overgelevert by d'Ambassadeurs vande H. Staten Generael . . .', 41–3; Hainsworth and Churches, *The Anglo-Dutch Naval Wars*, ch. 1; and Howarth, *The Men-of-War*, 48–67.

p. 321 Of the two great statesmen: Rowen, *John de Witt, Grand Pensionary of Holland*, 65, and the pamphlet 'De Rechte Beschryvingh van alle het gene den Heer Adriaen Paau Ambassadeur Extraordinary'. Pauw's state of mind is also apparent in his speech before Parliament, 11 June 1652, bound with 'A declaration of the Parliament of the commonwealth of England . . .'

p. 322 John Milton: Miller, *John Milton's Writings in the Anglo-Dutch Negotiations*, 3–13.

p. 323 'The English are about to attack': Hainsworth and Churches, *The Anglo-Dutch Naval Wars*, 17.

p. 323 'their masts and tackles': Howarth, *The Men-of-War*, 60.

p. 324 word had gone out: *Docs Rel.*, vol. 1, 476.

p. 324 'going fast to ruin': *Docs Rel.*, vol. 1, 477.

p. 325 At the end of the book: Van der Donck, 'A Description of New Netherland', trans. Goedhuys, 156–62.

p. 327 'The undersigned': Charles Gehring, *Correspondence, 1647–1653*, 203.

p. 327 'June 4, 1653': Gemeentearchief, Amsterdam, English Translations of Notarial Documents . . . Pertaining to North America, no. 2280, 18–65, notary Jacob de Winter.

Chapter 13

p. 331 'Thou hast received': Fernow, *The Records of New Amsterdam* [hereafter *RNA*], vol. 1, 48.

p. 331 'herewith [to] inform': *RNA*, vol. 1, 49.

p. 332 Roman–Dutch law: Wessels, *History of the Roman–Dutch Law*, 22–5, 124–9.

p. 333 'to this growing town': Seymann, *Colonial Charters, Patents and Grants to the Communities Comprising the City of New York*, 14–19.

p. 333 burst a raucous knot of locals: *RNA*, vol. 1, 51, 53, 58, 59–61.

p. 334 'all apprentices shall again wear blue caps': Gehring, *Correspondence, 1647–1653*, 232.

p. 334 to begin gearing up once again: Gehring, *Correspondence, 1647–1653*, 226.

p. 334 '5 or 6 ordinary': *Docs Rel.*, vol. 1, 484.

p. 334 'certainly informed that': *Docs Rel.*, vol. 1, 487.

p. 334 'to surround the greater part': *RNA*, vol. 1, 65–7, 69, 72–4, 90.

p. 335 replace the gleaming, colonnaded bourse: Schama, *The Embarrassment of Riches*, 348.

p. 336 Second Amboyna: 'The Second Part of the Tragedy of Amboyna'.

p. 336 who had just assumed: Fraser, *Cromwell*, 450–8.

p. 337 'utmost assistance': Thurloe, *A Collection of the State Papers*, vol. 1, 721–2.

p. 337 'Meester Adriaen': Gehring, *Correspondence, 1647–1653*, 220–1.

p. 337 His mother moved: Hoffman, 'Van der Donck–Van Bergen', 233.

p. 338 a member of the gang: *RNA*, vol. 1, 51, 61, 65.

p. 338 The most recent villain: Gehring, *Council Minutes, 1652–1654*, 91–3.

p. 338 The episode has also been used: As an example of this standard dismissing of the Dutch colony, the distinguished historian Dixon Ryan Fox, writing in 1940, recycled the accepted wisdom that 'In New Netherland we do not see Dutch groups insisting on communal privileges, as in New England,' and that 'local self-government came and developed in New Netherland by reason of New England Puritan invasion.' That historians could ignore the long series of petitions crafted by the Dutch colonists, climaxing with Van der Donck's elaborate and impassioned mission to The Hague on behalf of self-government, can only be explained as Anglocentric blindness (Fox, *Yankees and Yorkers*, 71–5).

p. 339 John Brodhead: Brodhead, *The History of the State of New York*, vol. 2, 571.

p. 339 Another early historian: Van Rensselaer, *History of the City of New York in the Seventeenth Century*, vol. 1, 349.

p. 339 was a direct result: My thanks to Dr Willem Frijhoff for helping me to formulate my argument that Van der Donck played a role in the December 1653 remonstrance.

p. 339 was now minister: On Doughty in Flushing, see Brodhead, *The History of the State of New York*, vol. 1, 411, 555, 615.

p. 340 'We do not know': Gehring, *Correspondence, 1654–1658*, 11.

p. 340 'made up of various nations': Gehring, *Council Minutes, 1652–1654*, 92.

p. 340 'natural law': The way it is stated in the supporting petition of the New Amsterdam magistrates is: 'because the laws of nature give to all men the right to assemble for the welfare and protection of their freedom and property' (Gehring, *Council Minutes, 1652–1654*, 100); Stuyvesant in his reply, rejects '"that natural law gives to all men" such rights' (102).

p. 341 The invasion squadron: Thurloe, *A Collection of State Papers*, vol. 2, 418–19.

p. 341 when Manhattan became Manhattan: I am particularly indebted to Dennis Maika, whose 1995 doctoral dissertation, 'Commerce and Community: Manhattan Merchants in the Seventeenth Century', helped change the way historians look at Manhattan under the Dutch. By shifting attention from the West India Company to the new breed of merchant entrepreneurs that came into being on Manhattan, Maika showed that the crucial date for its rise was not 1664, the year of the takeover, but 1653, the year of the municipal charter.

p. 342 These alliances: I owe this insight to Simon Middleton of the University of East Anglia, who outlined it in his talk, 'Artisans and Trade Privileges in New Amsterdam', at the 2001 Rensselaerswijck Seminar in New York City.

p. 342 red and black: Van Rensselaer, *History of the City of New York in the Seventeenth Century*, vol. 2, 138; Stokes, *Iconography of Manhattan Island*, vol. 4, 129.

p. 342 old thatched ones: Gehring, *Council Minutes, 1655–1656*, 186.

p. 342 An order went out: Stokes, *Iconography of Manhattan Island*, vol. 4, 129, quoting Van Rensselaer.

p. 344 Mills, brick yards and tile yards: Venema, 'Beverwijck', 75–81.

p. 344 a thousand residents: Shattuck, 'A Civil Society', 9–11.

p. 344 They are boarders: Gehring, *Fort Orange Court Minutes, 1652–1660*, 354.

p. 344 One shows up: Gehring, *Fort Orange Court Minutes, 1652–1660*, 355.

p. 344 In 1659, two Mohawk chiefs: Gehring, *Fort Orange Court Minutes, 1652–1660*, 463–4.

p. 344 their walls hung: Schama, *The Embarrassment of Riches*, 313, 320–1.

p. 345 products first appearing: Maika, 'Commerce and Community', 128–9; Gehring, *Council Minutes, 1655–1656*, 162.

p. 345 a new, two-tiered system: *RNA*, vol. 7, 150.

p. 345 Nearly every resident: *RNA*, vol. 7, 150–3. On the burgher system, see *RNA*, vol. 7, 149–54. Also, my brief overview of the 'burgher-right' system of New Amsterdam relies on Maika, 'Commerce and Community', especially ch. 3.

p. 346 a looser relationship: Venema, 'Beverwijck', 304.

p. 347 'to bake any more': *RNA*, vol. 3, 391.

p. 347 cookies: Rose, *The Sensible Cook*, 34–5; Simmons, *American Cookery*, 609.

p. 347 *Koolsla*: Rose, *The Sensible Cook*; Kalm, *The America of 1750*, 28. The sample New Amsterdam dishes (pike, meatballs) come from Rose, *The Sensible Cook*.

p. 348 '*Saint Nicholas*': Zumthor, *Daily Life in Rembrandt's Holland*, 185.

p. 348 'In the late 1650s': Personal interview, Albany, 18 June 2002.

p. 349 If they couldn't afford: *RNA*, vol. 7, 200; Maika, 'Commerce and Community', 224.

p. 349 The initial bloc: Riker, *Revised History of Harlem*, 183.

p. 350 in all, a quarter: Goodfriend, *Before the Melting Pot*, 17.

p. 350 Intermarriage also appears: On intermarriage in New Amsterdam, see Purple, ed., *Collections of the New-York Genealogical and Biographical Society*, vol. 1.

p. 351 'thievish, lazy, and useless': Stokes, *Iconography of Manhattan Island*, vol. 4, 74.

p. 351 'laziness and unwillingness': Gehring, *Council Minutes, 1655–1656*, 267–8.

p. 351 But there are also: Christoph, 'The Freedmen of New Amsterdam', 161.

p. 351 'true and free ownership': Charles Gehring, unpublished translation of New Netherland document no. 10(3).332.

p. 351 In its first decades: Swan, 'The Black Presence in Seventeenth-century Brooklyn', 1. Some historians have claimed that Stuyvesant himself owned forty slaves, but I think this figure is too high. It is based on a 1660 account from a minister who reports that 'there are forty negroes' at 'the Bouwery'. But by that time 'the Bouwery' had become a village, and we know that several families of freed blacks owned property there, along what is now Fourth Avenue. So the figure of 'forty negroes' surely included both slaves and free blacks.

p. 351 'by the time of the English takeover': Goodfriend, *Before the Melting Pot*, 13.

p. 352 '724 pine planks': Gehring and Schiltkamp, *Curaçao Papers*, 175.

p. 353 One such shift: On these events of 1651 I am relying on Israel, 'The Intellectual Debate' and *The Dutch Republic*, 706–9; and Williams, '"Abominable Religion" and Dutch (In)tolerance'.

p. 353 'would pave the way': Stokes, *Iconography of Manhattan Island*, 142.

p. 353 In 1654 twenty-three Jews: Hershkowitz, 'New Amsterdam's Twenty-Three Jews'.

p. 353 'for important reasons': Gehring, *Council Minutes, 1655–1656*, 166.

p. 353 'the aversion and disaffection': Gehring, *Council Minutes, 1655–1656*, 81.

p. 353 'consent is hereby': Gehring, *Council Minutes, 1655–1656*, 128.

p. 354 The Jewish community: Gehring, *Council Minutes, 1655–1656*, 261–2; Gehring, *Correspondence, 1654–1658*, 83.

p. 354 'love peace and libertie': *Docs Rel.*, vol. 14, 402–3.

p. 354 But here too: On the historical importance of the Flushing Remonstrance, I am relying on Trebor, *The Flushing Remonstrance* and Voorhees, 'The 1657 Flushing Remonstrance'.

p. 355 'Singing Quakers': *Docs Rel.*, vol. 3, 415.

p. 356 Here he deployed: Details from this scene come from Gehring, *Delaware Papers: Dutch Period, 1648–1664*, 37–47, and from Gehring, '*Hodie Mihi, Cras Tibi*'.

p. 356 'forest Finns': My sources on the forest Finns are Jordan and Kaups, *The American Backwoods Frontier*; Jordan, 'The Material Cultural Legacy of New Sweden on the American Frontier'; Tvengsberg, 'Finns in Seventeenth-century Sweden and their Contributions to the New Sweden Colony'; and Pentikainen, 'The Forest Finns as Transmitters of Finnish Culture'.

p. 357 'restitution of our property': Gehring, *Delaware Papers: Dutch Period, 1648–1664*, 39.

p. 357 'His request was firmly denied': Gehring, *Delaware Papers: Dutch Period, 1648–1664*, 41.

p. 357 '*Hodie mihi*': Gehring, *Delaware Papers: Dutch Period, 1648–1664*, 39.

p. 358 He decided to invite them: Gehring, *Delaware Papers: Dutch Period, 1648–1664*, 46, 54.

p. 359 'Maquas, Mahikanders': Gehring, *Delaware Papers: Dutch Period, 1648–1664*, 35.

p. 359 Such a multicultural: I am indebted to Cynthia J. van Zandt of the University of New Hampshire for this insight, which she outlined in a paper presented at the Annual Meeting of the American Historical Association in 1998 entitled '". . . our river savages . . . betook themselves (unknown to us) and went to Manhattan City, in New Holland, to exact revenge on our behalf": Cross-cultural and Multi-Ethnic Alliances in the 17th-Century Mid-Atlantic'.

p. 361 'had been a good friend': Gehring, *Council Minutes, 1655–1656*, 204.

p. 361 Van der Donck's wife: Hoffman, 'Van der Donck–Van Bergen', 340–1.

p. 362 Croats and Prussians: These nationalities come from marriage records of the colony after 1656.

p. 362 '*So, reader, if you desire*': My thanks to Dr Elisabeth Paling Funk for translating this poem.

p. 362 Three hundred settlers: *Docs Rel.*, vol. 2, 4; supplies: *Docs Rel.*, vol. 2, 643–4.

p. 362 'I have been full': *Docs Rel.*, vol. 2, 17.

Chapter 14

p. 365 Meanwhile, outside the village: Morison, *The Founding of Harvard College*, 257–8; Vaille and Clarke, *The Harvard Book*, 25–32.

p. 366 a 'perfidious rogue': Beresford, *The Godfather of Downing Street*, 150.

p. 366 and blamed his faulty: Beresford, *The Godfather of Downing Street*, 29.

p. 368 literally leaving the man: Brodhead, *The History of the State of New York*, vol. 1, 695; Black, *The Younger John Winthrop*, 209–10.

p. 368 27 pounds of gunpowder: *Docs Rel.*, vol. 2, 460.

p. 368 He spent thirteen days: Black, *The Younger John Winthrop*, 210; Brodhead, *The History of the State of New York*, vol. 1, 695.

p. 368 detailed notes: Quinn, 'Theft of the Manhattans'.

p. 369 comparing notes: O'Callaghan, *Calendar of Historical Manuscripts in the Office of the Secretary of State*, 296.

p. 369 'Four parrots': Gehring and Schiltkamp, *Curaçao Papers*, 115.

p. 369 'He has always shown himself': *Docs Rel.*, vol. 14, 525.

p. 370 for Winthrop later to write: Beresford, *The Godfather of Downing Street*, 128.

p. 370 a map that Winthrop: Quinn, 'Theft of the Manhattans', 29.

p. 370 *Hamlet*, *'Tis Pity She's a Whore*: Samuel Pepys's diary for July to October 1661; Black, *The Younger John Winthrop*, 212.

p. 370 confused with Josiah Winslow: Black, *The Younger John Winthrop*, 244.

p. 370 Charles had given Connecticut: Black, *The Younger John Winthrop*, 225.

p. 371 Winthrop's reply: Black, *The Younger John Winthrop*, 264.

p. 371 'your anxiety over': *Docs Rel.*, vol. 14, 551.

p. 372 Stuyvesant complained: *Docs Rel.*, vol. 2, 230, 484–8; O'Callaghan, *Calendar of Historical Manuscripts in the Office of the Secretary of State*, 307.

p. 372 'a sad and perilous': *Docs Rel.*, vol. 2, 484.

p. 372 'yield obedience': Black, *The Younger John Winthrop*, 268.

p. 372 'unrighteous, stubborn': *Docs Rel.*, vol. 2, 484.
p. 372 the closed islands of Japan would trade: Israel, *Dutch Primacy in World Trade*, 172.
p. 372 other products: Israel, *Dutch Primacy in World Trade*, chs 5, 6.
p. 372 'be instruments of good': Beresford, *The Godfather of Downing Street*, 155. On Downing's attitude and convictions, see Geyl, *Orange and Stuart*, 191.
p. 373 'Go on in Guinea': Feiling, *British Foreign Policy*, 130–1.
p. 373 The second Charles Stuart: My characterization of Charles is based on Fraser, *Royal Charles*; Macleod, *Dynasty: The Stuarts*, chs 8, 9; and Bryant, *The Letters, Speeches, and Declarations of King Charles II*.
p. 373 James Stuart: My characterization of James is based in part on Ashley, *James II*; Haswell, *James II*; and J. S. Clarke, *The Life of James the Second*.
p. 374 Reading the letters, minutes: Feiling, *British Foreign Policy*, 97–131; *Docs Rel.*, vol. 3, 51–66; Royal African Company, 'The several declarations of the Company of Royal Adventurers of England Trading into Africa . . .'
p. 374 In his years of exile: Haswell, *James II*, 104–20.
p. 375 Royal Mint commemorated: Davies, *The Royal African Company*, 181.
p. 375 Reorganized as the Royal African Company: Davies, *The Royal African Company*, 346.
p. 375 'the Royal Company being': Royal African Company, 'The several declarations of the Company of Royal Adventurers of England Trading into Africa . . .'
p. 376 'And pray, what is Cape Verde?': Feiling, *British Foreign Policy*, 125.
p. 376 'What ever injuries': Beresford, *The Godfather of Downing Street*, 170.
p. 376 'Together with all': Christoph and Christoph, *Books of General Entries*, 1–4.
p. 377 a committee at Whitehall: Feiling, *British Foreign Policy*, 124.
p. 377 the next month: Brodhead, *The History of the State of New York*, vol. 1, 736.
p. 377 leave within the month: Black, *The Younger John Winthrop*, 272.

p. 377 James himself took to sea: Ashley, *James II*, 80.
p. 377 'the welfare and advancement': *Docs Rel.*, vol. 3, 61.
p. 377 'putt Mr Winthropp': *Docs Rel.*, vol. 3, 55.
p. 378 'not give us henceforth': *Docs Rel.*, vol. 2, 235–6.
p. 379 'apt to entertaine': Christoph and Christoph, *Books of General Entries*, 25.
p. 379 'in his Majesties Name': Christoph and Christoph, *Books of General Entries*, 26.
p. 379 'These to the Honorable': Christoph and Christoph, *Books of General Entries*, 27.
p. 380 'would be disapproved of': Brodhead, *The History of the State of New York*, vol. 1, 739.
p. 380 pasted back together: *Docs Rel.*, vol. 2, 445–7.
p. 381 There is then: O'Callaghan, *The History of New Netherland*, vol. 2, 525–6.
p. 382 The ministers talked: *Docs Rel.*, vol. 2, 509; O'Callaghan, *The History of New Netherland*, vol. 2, 525–6; John Brodhead, *The History of the State of New York*, vol. 1, 740.
p. 382 'we are oblieged': Christoph and Christoph, *Books of General Entries*, 29.
p. 382 'misery, sorrow, conflagration': *Docs Rel.*, vol. 2, 248.
p. 383 They were now wealthy: Hershkowitz, 'The Troublesome Turk'.
p. 383 the Polish Jew: Hershkowitz, 'New Amsterdam's Twenty-Three Jews'.
p. 383 for the past five years: Charles Gehring, unpublished translation of New Netherland documents no. 10(3):329 and 10(3):330.
p. 383 'I would much rather': Brodhead, *The History of the State of New York*, vol. 1, 741–2.

Chapter 15

p. 385 Starting in the 1660s: Ward, 'The Search for American Identity: Early Historians of New England'.
p. 385 John Adams: McCullough, *John Adams*, 245, 254.
p. 385 'first born of all': The quote is from Urian Oakes, in Wertenbaker, *The Puritan Oligarchy*, 33.
p. 385 ''Tis Satan's policy': Wertenbaker, *The Puritan Oligarchy*, 32.

p. 386 The Puritans' systematic crackdown: The examples in this paragraph come from Wertenbaker, *The Puritan Oligarchy*, 224–40.

p. 386 'the right of our manifest destiny': Stephanson, *Manifest Destiny*, 42.

p. 386 In the early twentieth: On Wilson's expansion of the term, and for the Wilson quotes, I am relying on Stephanson, *Manifest Destiny*, ch. 4.

p. 388 In fact, ships: Koot, 'In Pursuit of Profit: The Netherlands' Trade in Colonial New York, 1664–1688'.

p. 388 Notaries in Amsterdam: Gemeentearchief, Amsterdam, English Translations of Notarial Documents . . . Pertaining to North America, notary Jacob de Winter, nos 2309, 2313, 2326.

p. 389 'they shall continue to enjoy': *Docs Rel.*, vol. 3, 57.

p. 389 'The Dutch here shall enjoy': Christoph and Christoph, *Books of General Entries*, 36–7.

p. 389 'continue as they now are': Christoph and Christoph, *Books of General Entries*, 35–7.

p. 390 'immunities and privileges': Hershkowitz, 'The New York City Charter'.

p. 391 'neglect or treachery': *Docs Rel.*, vol. 2, 420, 491.

p. 392 'take care of the girls': Gehring and Schiltkamp, *Curaçao Papers*, 220.

p. 392 He died: *Docs Rel.*, vol. 3, 363–79, 419–510; Brodhead, *The History of the State of New York*, vol. 2, 131–2.

p. 392 'I saw ye towne': John Winthrop to the Earl of Clarendon, New-York Historical Society, *Collections*, 58.

p. 392 'the best of all': *Docs Rel.*, vol. 3, 106.

p. 392 'You will have heard': Bryant, *The Letters, Speeches, and Declarations of King Charles II*, 168.

p. 393 the Dutch government allowed: *Docs Rel.*, vol. 2, 516–17.

p. 394 as founded on an 'invitation': Israel, 'The Dutch Role in the Glorious Revolution', esp. 124–9.

p. 394 Jacob Leisler: Voorhees, 'The "fervent Zeale" of Jacob Leisler'; Fabend, 'The Pro-Leislerian Dutch Farmers in New York'.

p. 395 the relationships among: Goodfriend, *Before the Melting Pot*, chs 4, 5.

p. 395 What mattered most: Klein, 'Origins of the Bill of Rights in

Colonial New York', 391.

p. 396 French, German, Scottish and Irish: Goodfriend, *Before the Melting Pot*, 16, 56–60.

p. 396 'Our chiefest unhappyness': Lodwick, 'New York in 1692', 244.

p. 396 As late as the 1750s: Tanis, 'The Dutch–American Connection', 24.

p. 397 In fact, the irony: Fabend, *Zion on the Hudson*, esp. ch. 10.

p. 397 'following the example': *Newark Daily Advertiser*, 6 Dec. 1850.

p. 398 'Yielding to no one': John Brodhead, unpublished manuscript, John Romeyn Brodhead Papers.

p. 399 'clamoring for scholarly': *New York Times*, editorial, 7 Aug. 2001.

p. 399 'What then is': Crèvecœur, *Letters from an American Farmer*, 46–7.

p. 400 district attorney: Van Alstyne, 'The District Attorney: An Historical Puzzle'; Reiss, 'Public Prosecutors and Criminal Prosecution in the United States of America'. As with nearly everything in history, the origins of the office of district attorney are open to debate, but the arguments that Reiss and Van Alstyne make show a straightforward chain of influence. The most forceful argument against the district attorney office originating in the office of *schout* is interesting in that it has the classic features of American Anglocentrism. Jack Kress ('Progress and Prosecution') notes that England had no such office, that the Dutch did, that the first district attorneys in English America appeared in precisely the area where the Dutch colony had been, and that those first district attorneys were called 'scout' by the English, seemingly a clear indicator of their Dutch origin. But he then dismisses the argument on the grounds that the Dutch couldn't have made a lasting impact because the Dutch colony was small and the period of Dutch control was 'quite brief, lasting only from 1653 until 1664 and that it is questionable if this was sufficient time for the institution of the *schout* to take root'. Besides getting the date of the colony's founding wrong by thirty years, Kress adopts the classic pattern of reasoning that American history has applied to the Dutch colony: assume the colony had no real presence, then, on the basis of your assumption, dismiss evidence to the contrary.

p. 402 Santa Claus: Elisabeth Paling Funk, 'Washington Irving and the Dutch Heritage', manuscript in progress, ch. 3: 'The Popular Culture of New Netherland'. My thanks to the author for sending me this portion of her work.

p. 402 'ancient Citty': The charter is printed in Schechter, *Roots of the Republic*, 91. My reading of the colony's political legacy comes in part from Hershkowitz, 'The New York City Charter'; Ritchie, *The Duke's Province*, ch. 1; Finkelman, 'The Soul and the State'; Klein, 'Origins of the Bill of Rights in Colonial New York'; Rosenblatt, 'New York State's Role in the Creation and Adoption of the Bill of Rights'.

p. 403 The names of the twenty-six: Rosenblatt, 'New York State's Role in the Creation and Adoption of the Bill of Rights'; 'Albany Committee', *New York Journal and Weekly Register*, 26 April 1788.

Epilogue

p. 408 While the records: My sources on the history, condition and preservation of the colony's records are: The Van Laer Papers, New York State Library; the John Romeyn Brodhead Papers, Rutgers University; the Andrew Elliot Papers, New York State Library; Van Laer, *The Translation and Publication of the Manuscript Dutch Records of New Netherland*; Hopkins, 'The Dutch Records of New York'; New York (State) Secretary of State, 'Inventory of Records and Files'; *Public Papers of George Clinton*, ed. Hugh Hastings, vol. 1, 7–10; Gehring, 'New Netherland Manuscripts in United States Repositories' and 'Translating New York's Dutch Past'; Howard, 'John Romeyn Brodhead'; Christoph, 'Story of the New Netherland Project'; Winne, 'Arnold J. F. van Laer (1869–1955): An Appreciation'; Application Form, US Department of the Interior, 'Save America's Treasures' Program, Project: Dutch Colonial Manuscripts, 1638–1670; interviews with Charles Gehring, Peter Christoph, Christina Holden, Janny Venema.

p. 408 death threats: Information about Tryon comes from Nelson, *William Tryon and the Course of Empire*, and from original documents in the Andrew Elliot Papers at the New York State Library.

p. 409 'Sir — As I am': Yates, 'Report of the Secretary of State', 44.

p. 409 mould set in: Interview with Maria Holden, conservator, New York State Archives, 27 Aug. 2002.

p. 409 according to a letter: It has been assumed the records spent the entire war aboard the *Duchess of Gordon* and another ship, the *Warwick*, but a letter from Crèvecœur to Franklin, written in 1783, provides evidence that they were moved to the Tower late in the conflict. See Crèvecœur, *Letters from an American Farmer*, 341.

p. 409 'much mill-dewed': Yates, 'Report of the Secretary of State', 46.

p. 410 'immediate measures ought': Van Laer, *The Translation and Publication of the Manuscript Dutch Records of New Netherland*.

p. 410 a fiasco of small errors: Historians had long suspected Van der Kemp's translations were flawed. Charles Gehring was able to assess just how bad they were after he discovered two volumes that had escaped destruction in the fire.

p. 414 his having a drinking problem: In fact, it is Stuyvesant, writing to the company directors, who refers to the man as the 'drunkard Johannes Dijckmans'.

p. 414 'Then, one day in 1655': The change in handwriting – the moment at which Dijckman's career ends – occurs on Tuesday, 9 May 1655, and appears on p. 193 of Gehring, *Fort Orange Council Minutes, 1652–1660*.

Bibliography

Letters, Journals, Pamphlets, Maps, Papers, Council Minutes and Other Primary Sources

Adams, John. *A collection of state-papers, relative to the first acknowledgment of the sovereignity of the United States of America, and the reception of their minister plenipotentiary, by their high mightinesses the States-General of the United Netherlands*. The Hague, 1782.

Aglionby, William. *The Present State of the United Provinces of the Low Countries as to the Government, Laws, Forces, Riches, Manners, Customes, Revenue, and Territory of the Dutch*. London: John Starkey, 1671.

'Articles of peace & alliance, between the most serene and mighty prince Charles II, by the grace of God king of England, Scotland, France and Ireland, Defender of the Faith, &c. and the High and Mighty Lords the States General of the United Netherlands, concluded the 21/31 day of July, 1667'. London, 1667.

Asher, G. M. *Dutch Books and Pamphlets Relating to New-Netherland*. Amsterdam: Frederik Muller, 1854.

Asher, G. M., ed. *Henry Hudson the Navigator: The Original Documents in Which His Career Is Recorded*. New York: Hakluyt Society, 1860.

Augustyn, Robert T., and Paul E. Cohen. *Manhattan in Maps, 1527–1995*. New York: Rizzoli, 1997.

Bontemantel, Hans. The Bontemantel Papers. New York: New York Public Library.

Bradford, William. *Of Plymouth Plantation*. New York: Knopf, 1966.

Brodhead, John Romeyn. *An Address Delivered Before the New York Historical Society*. New York: New York Historical Society, 1844.

Brodhead, John Romeyn. The John Romeyn Brodhead Papers. New Brunswick: Alexander Library, Rutgers University.

Bryant, Sir Arthur, ed. *The Letters, Speeches, and Declarations of King Charles II*. London: Cassell, 1935.

Calendar of State Papers, Colonial Series, 1574–1660, Preserved in the State Paper Department of Her Majesty's Public Record Office. London, 1860.

Church of Scotland. *The Booke of Common Prayer, And Administration Of The Sacraments, And other parts of divine Service for the use of the Church of Scotland*. Edinburgh: Robert Young, 1637.

Christoph, Peter R., ed. *New York Historical Manuscripts: English, vol. 22: Administrative Papers of Governors Richard Nicolls and Francis Lovelace, 1664–1673*. Baltimore: Genealogical Publishing, 1980.

Christoph, Peter R., and Florence A. Christoph, eds. *Books of General Entries of the Colony of New York, 1664–1673*. Baltimore: Genealogical Publishing, 1982.

Christoph, Peter R., and Florence A. Christoph, eds. *The Andros Papers*, 3 vols. Vol. 1: *1674–1676*; Vol. 2: *1677–1678*; Vol. 3: *1679–1680*. Syracuse: Syracuse University Press, 1989–91.

Clinton, George. *The Public Papers of George Clinton*, vols. 1 and 8, ed. Hugh Hastings. Albany: State Legislative Printer, 1904.

Connecticut Colony. *The Public Records of the Colony of Connecticut, Prior to the Union with the New Haven Colony*. Hartford: Brown & Parsons, 1850.

Crèvecœur, J. Hector St John de. *Letters from an American Farmer, describing certain provincial situations, manners, and customs . . . of the people of North America*. Philadelphia: Mathew Carey, 1793.

'A declaration of the Parliament of the commonwealth of England, relating to the affairs and proceedings between this commonwealth and the States General of the United Provinces of the Low-Countreys, and the present differences occasioned on the States part. And the answer of the Parliament to three papers from the ambassadors extraordinary of the States General, upon occasion of the late fight between the fleets'. London, 1652.

Descartes, René. *Discourse on Method*. Garden City: Anchor, 1974.

Downing, Sir George. 'A discourse written by Sir George Downing, the king of Great Britain's envoyee extraordinary to the states of the United-Provinces. Vindicating his royal master from the insolencies of a scandalous libel, printed under the title of "An Extract out of the register of the States General of the United Provinces, upon the memorial of Sir George Downing, envoyee, &c." and delivered by the agent de Heyde for such, to several publick ministers: whereas no such resolution was ever communicated to the said envoyee, nor any answer at all returned by their Lordships to the said memorial'. London, 1664.

Dryden, John. *Amboyna: A Tragedy. As it is Acted By Their Majesties Servants*. London, 1691.

Du Moulin, Pierre. *The Monk's Hood Pull'd Off, or, The Capucin Fryar Described*. London: James Collins, 1671.

East India Company. 'A Remonstrance Of The Directors Of The Netherlands East India Company, presented to the Lords States Generall of the united Provinces, in defence of the said Companie, touching the bloudy proceedings against the English Merchants, executed at Amboyna'. London, 1632.

East India Company. 'A True Relation Of The Uniust, Cruell, And Barbarous Proceedings against the English at Amboyna In the East-Indies, by the Neatherlandish governour and Councel there. Also the copie of a Pamphlet, set forth first in Dutch and then in English, by some Neatherlander; falsly entituled, A True Declaration Of The Newes that came out of the East-Indies, with the Pinace called the Hare, which arrived at Texel in June, 1624'. London, 1624.

Edwards, Philip, ed. *Last Voyages: Cavendish, Hudson, Ralegh, The Original Narratives*. Oxford: Clarendon Press, 1988.

Eerdmans, Martha. *Pieter Stuyvesant: An Historical Documentation; compiled upon request of the Provincial Government of Friesland in Commemoration of the Pieter Stuyvesant Festival, Wolvega, Friesland, July 12–16, 1955*. Grand Rapids: Eerdmans, 1957.

Elliot, Andrew. Andrew Elliot Papers, 1767–1785. Albany: New York State Library.

Farret, Johan, and Peter Stuyvesant. Poetry exchange between Johan Farret and Peter Stuyvesant. In the collection of the Nederlands Scheepvaart Museum, Amsterdam. Photocopy, Albany: New Netherland Project, New York State Library.

Fernow, Berthold, trans. and ed. *The Records of New Amsterdam, 1653–1674*, 7 vols. New York: Knickerbocker Press, 1897. Repr. Baltimore: Genealogical Publishing, 1976.

A Friend to this Commonwealth. 'The case stated between England and the United Provinces, in this present juncture. Together with a short view of those Netherlanders in their late practises as to religion, liberty, leagues, treaties, amities. Publish'd for the information and a warning to England'. London, 1652.

Gehring, Charles, trans. and ed. *Correspondence, 1647–1653*. New Netherland Document Series. Syracuse: Syracuse University Press, 2000.

Gehring, Charles, trans. and ed. *Correspondence, 1654–1658*. New Netherland Document Series. Syracuse: Syracuse University Press, 2003.

Gehring, Charles, trans. and ed. *Council Minutes, 1652–1654*. New York Historical Manuscripts Series. Baltimore: Genealogical Publishing, 1983.

Gehring, Charles, trans. and ed. *Council Minutes, 1655–1656*. New Netherland Document Series. Syracuse: Syracuse University Press, 1995.

Gehring, Charles, trans. and ed. *Delaware Papers: Dutch Period, 1648–1664*. New York Historical Manuscripts Series. Baltimore: Genealogical Publishing, 1981.

Gehring, Charles, trans. and ed. *Delaware Papers: English Period, 1664–1682*. New York Historical Manuscripts Series. Baltimore: Genealogical Publishing, 1977.

Gehring, Charles, trans. and ed. *Fort Orange Court Minutes, 1652–1660*. New Netherland Documents Series. Syracuse: Syracuse University Press, 1990.

Gehring, Charles, trans. and ed. *Fort Orange Records, 1656–1678*. New Netherland Documents Series. Syracuse: Syracuse University Press, 2000.

Gehring, Charles, trans. and ed. *Land Papers, 1630–1664*. New York

Historical Manuscript Series. Baltimore: Genealogical Publishing, 1980.

Gehring, Charles, trans. and ed. *Laws and Writs of Appeal, 1647–1663*. New Netherland Documents Series. Syracuse: Syracuse University Press, 1991.

Gehring, Charles T., and J. A. Schiltkamp, trans. and eds. *Curaçao Papers, 1640–1665*. New Netherland Documents. Interlaken, NY: Heart of the Lakes, 1987.

Gemeentearchief, Amsterdam. English Translations of Notarial Documents in the Gemeentearchief in Amsterdam Pertaining to North America. Pocantico Hills, NY: Historic Hudson Valley Collections, Rockefeller Archives.

Grotius, Hugo. *The Jurisprudence of Holland*, trans. R. W. Lee, 2 vols. Oxford: Clarendon Press, 1926.

Hakluyt, Richard. *The Discovery of Muscovy*. London: Cassell, 1904.

Hakluyt, Richard. *The Original Writings & Correspondence of the Two Richard Hakluyts*. London: Hakluyt Society, 1935.

Hakluyt, Richard. *The Principal Navigations Voyages Traffiques and Discoveries of the English Nation*, 12 vols. Glasgow, 1903–5.

Hartgers, Joost. *Beschrijvinghe van Virginia, Nieuw Nederlandt, Nieuw Engelandt en d'Eylanden Bermudes, Berbados, en S. Christoffel*. Amsterdam: Joost Hartgers, 1651.

Hastings, Hugh, ed. *Ecclesiastical Records of the State of New York*, vol. 1. Albany: Lyon, 1901.

Jameson, J. F. *Narratives of New Netherland, 1609–1664*. New York: Charles Scribner's Sons, 1909. Repr. New York: Barnes & Noble, 1937.

Jameson, J. Franklin, ed. *Privateering and Piracy in the Colonial Period: Illustrative Documents*. New York: Macmillan, 1923.

Kalm, Pehr. *The America of 1750: Peter Kalm's Travels in North America; the English version of 1770, revised from the original Swedish and edited by Adolph B. Benson*. New York: Wilson-Erickson, 1937.

Knuttel, W. P. C. *Catalogus van de pamfletten-verzameling berustende in de Koninklijke bibliotheek*. 's-Gravenhage: Algemeene landsdrukkerij, 1889–1920.

Kossman, E. H., and A. F. Mellink, eds. *Texts Concerning the Revolt of the Netherlands*. London: Cambridge University Press, 1974.

Lodwick, Charles. 'New York in 1692: Letter from Charles Lodwick, to Mr. Francis Lodwick and Mr. Hooker, Dated May 20, 1692, Read Before the Royal Society of London'. *Collections of the New-York Historical Society*, 2nd ser., vol. 2. New York, 1849.

Melyn, Cornelis. 'The Melyn Papers, 1640–1699'. In *The New-York Historical Society Collections, 1913*. New York: New-York Historical Society, 1914.

Munsell, Joel, ed. *A Documentary History of the State of New York*, 4 vols. Albany: Weed, Parsons, 1865.

New-York Historical Society. *Collections*. New York: New-York Historical Society, 1869.

New York (State) Secretary of State. 'Inventory of Records and Files in the Office of the Secretary of State, 1818'. Albany: New York State Library.

'Nootwendige Observatien op het Antwoort van de Republiicke van Engelant op drie schriften overgelevert by d'Ambassadeurs vande H. Staten Generael vande Vereenichde Provintien aen den Raedt van Staet, ter occasie van het laetste Zeegevecht tussen de Vlooten van beyde Republiicken'. 1652.

O'Callaghan, E. B. *Calendar of Historical Manuscripts in the Office of the Secretary of State*. Albany: Weed, Parsons, 1865.

O'Callaghan, E. B., trans. *Voyages of the Slavers St. John and Arms of Amsterdam, 1659, 1663, Together with Additional Papers Illustrative of the Slave Trade Under the Dutch*. Albany: Munsell, 1867.

O'Callaghan, E.B., and Berthold Fernow, trans. *Documents Relative to the Colonial History of the State of New York*, 15 vols. Albany: Weed, Parsons, 1856–87.

Olin, John C., ed. *A Reformation Debate: John Calvin and Jacopo Sadoleto, Sadoleto's Letter to the Genevans and Calvin's Reply*. Grand Rapids: Baker Book House, 1979.

Pepys, Samuel. *Diary and Correspondence of Samuel Pepys from his MS Cypher in the Pepysian Library*. New York: Dodd, Mead, 1885.

The Present State of Holland, or a Description of the United Provinces (no author). London, 1745.

Prockter, Adrian, and Robert Taylor, eds. *The A to Z of Elizabethan London*. London: London Topographical Society, 1979.

Purchas, Samuel. *Hakluytus Posthumus or Purchas his Pilgrimes*, 20 vols. Glasgow: MacLehose, 1905–7.

Purple, Samuel, ed. *Collections of the New-York Genealogical and Biographical Society*, vol. 1: *Marriages from 1639–1801 in the Reformed Dutch Church, New York*. New York: New York Genealogical and Biographical Society, 1890.

'De Rechte Beschryvingh van alle het gene den Heer Adriaen Paau Ambassadeur Extraordinary van wegen de Hoog: Moog: Heeren Staten Generael, der Vrye Vereenichde Nederlanden, met het Parlement van Engelant getracteert, heeft nopende een goede Vreede tusschen beyde Republijcquen'. Amsterdam, 1652.

Rijksmuseum te Leiden. *Album studiosorum Academiae lugduno batavae MDLXXV–MDCCCLXXV*. The Hague: Nijhoff, 1875.

Rivington's New York Gazetteer. 23 Dec. 1773; 8 Dec. 1774.

Royal African Company. 'The several declarations of the Company of Royal Adventurers of England Trading into Africa, inviting all His Majesties native subjects in general to subscribe, and become sharers in their joynt-stock. Together with His Royal Highness James duke of York and Albany, &c. and the rest of the said royal companies letter to the Right Honourable Francis lord Willoughby of Parham, &c. Intimating the said companies resolutions to furnish His Majesties American plantations with negroes at certain and moderate rates'. London, 1667.

Schechter, Stephen L., ed. *Roots of the Republic: American Founding Documents Interpreted*. Madison: Madison House, 1990.

'The Second Part of the Tragedy of Amboyna: Or, a True Relation of a Most Bloody, Treacherous, and Cruel Design of the Dutch in the New Netherlands in America. For the total Ruining and Murthering of the English Colonies in New-England. Being extracted out of several Letters very lately written from New-England to several Gentlemen and Merchants in London'. London, 1653.

Seymann, Jerrold. *Colonial Charters, Patents and Grants to the Communities Comprising the City of New York*. New York: Board of Statute Consolidation of the City of New York, 1939.

Snow, Dean R., Charles T. Gehring and William A. Starna, eds. *In Mohawk Country*. Syracuse: Syracuse University Press, 1996.

Sprigge, Joshua. *Anglia rediviva; England's recovery (1647)*. Facs. repr. Gainesville: Scholars' Facsimiles & Reprints, 1960.

Stokes, I. N. P., ed. *Iconography of Manhattan Island, 1498–1909*, 6 vols.

New York: Dodd, 1915–28.

Stow, John. *A Survey of London Written in the Year 1598*. Stroud: Sutton, 1994.

Temple, William. *Observations Upon the United Provinces of the Netherlands*, ed. Sir George Clark. Oxford: Clarendon Press, 1972.

Thurloe, John. *A Collection of the State Papers of John Thurloe, Esq.; Secretary, First, to the Council of State, And afterwards to The Two Protectors, Oliver and Richard Cromwell*, 7 vols. London, 1742.

Van den Bogaert, Harmen Meyndertsz. *A Journey into Mohawk and Oneida Country, 1634–1635*, trans. and ed. Charles T. Gehring, William A. Starna and Gunther Michelson. Syracuse: Syracuse University Press, 1988.

Van der Coelen, Peter, ed. *Everyday life in Holland's Golden Age: The Complete Etchings of Adriaen van Ostade*. Amsterdam: Museum het Rembrandthuis, 1998.

Van der Donck, Adriaen. *Beschryvinge van Nieuw-Nederlant*. Amsterdam: Evert Nieuwenhof, 1655; 2nd edn 1656.

Van der Donck, Adriaen. 'A Description of New Netherland', trans. Diederik Willem Goedhuys (unpublished), 1991.

Van der Donck, Adriaen. *A Description of the New Netherlands*, trans. Jeremias Johnson, ed. Thomas F. O'Donnell. Syracuse: Syracuse University Press, 1968.

Van der Donck, Adriaen. *Remonstrance of New Netherland, and the Occurrences there, addressed to the high and mighty Lords States General of the United Netherlands, on the 28th July 1649; with Secretary van Tienhoven's Answer*, ed. Edmund O'Callaghan. Albany: Weed, Parsons, 1856.

Van der Donck, Adriaen. *The Representation of New Netherland: concerning its location, productiveness and poor condition, presented to the States General of the United Netherlands and printed at the Hague in 1650*, trans. H. C. Murphy. New York: Bartlett & Welford, 1849.

Van der Donck, Adriaen. *Vertoogh van Nieu-Neder-Land, Weghens de Gheleghentheydt, Vruchtbaerheydt, en Soberen Staet desselfs*. 's-Gravenhage: Michiel Stael, 1650.

Van der Donck, Adriaen. *Vertoogh van Nieu Nederland, [by A. van der Donck] and, Braeden raedt aende Vereenichde Nederlandsche provintien, [by I. A. G. W. C., pseud. Of C. Melyn], Two rare tracts, printed in 1649–50, Relating to the administration of affairs in New*

Netherland, trans. H. C. Murphy. New York: Baker, Godwin, 1854.

Van Laer, A. J. F. A. J. F. Van Laer Papers, 1909–1952. Albany: New York State Library.

Van Laer, A. J. F., trans. *Documents Relating to New Netherland, 1624–1626, in the Henry E. Huntington Library*. San Marino: Henry E. Huntington Library and Art Gallery Press, 1924.

Van Laer, A. J. F., trans. and ed. *Minutes of the Court of Rensselaerswyck, 1648–1652*. Albany: University of the State of New York, 1922.

Van Laer, A. J. F., trans. *New York Historical Manuscripts: Dutch, vol. 1: Register of the Provincial Secretary, 1638–1642*. Baltimore: Genealogical Publishing, 1974.

Van Laer, A. J. F., trans. *New York Historical Manuscripts: Dutch, vol. 2: Register of the Provincial Secretary, 1642–1647*. Baltimore: Genealogical Publishing, 1974.

Van Laer, A. J. F., trans. *New York Historical Manuscripts: Dutch, vol. 3: Register of the Provincial Secretary, 1648–1660*. Baltimore: Genealogical Publishing, 1974.

Van Laer, A. J. F., trans. *New York Historical Manuscripts: Dutch, vol. 4: Council Minutes, 1638–1649*. Baltimore: Genealogical Publishing, 1974.

Van Laer, A. J. F., trans. *Van Rensselaer Bowier Manuscripts, being the letters of Kiliaen Van Rensselaer, 1630–1643, and other documents relating to the colony of Rensselaerswyck*. Albany: University of the State of New York, 1908.

Van Strien, Kees. *Touring the Low Countries: Accounts of British Travellers, 1660–1720*. Amsterdam: Amsterdam University Press, 1998.

Van Tienhoven, Cornelis. 'Answer to the Representation of New Netherland'. In *Documents Relative to the Colonial History of the State of New York*, vol. 1, trans. E. B. O'Callaghan and Berthold Fernow. Albany: Weed, Parsons, 1856–87.

Winthrop, John. *Journal of John Winthrop, 1630–1649*, ed. Richard Dunn, James Savage and Laetitia Yaendle. Cambridge, Mass.: Harvard University Press, 1996.

Yates, J. V. N. 'Report of the Secretary of State, relative to the records &c. in his office'. Albany: New York State Senate, 5 Jan. 1820.

Secondary Sources

Abreu, Joao Capistrano de. *Chapters of Brazil's Colonial History, 1500–1800*, trans. Arthur Brakel. New York: Oxford University Press, 1997.

Aikin, Lucy. *Memoirs of the Court of King Charles the First*. Philadelphia: Carey, Lea & Blanchard, 1833.

Akrigg, G. P. V. *Jacobean Pageant, or The Court of King James I*. Cambridge, Mass.: Harvard University Press, 1963.

Archdeacon, Thomas J. *New York City, 1664–1710: Conquest and Change*. Ithaca: Cornell University Press, 1979.

Ashley, Maurice. *The Greatness of Oliver Cromwell*. New York: Macmillan, 1958.

Ashley, Maurice, *James II*. London: Dent, 1977.

Bachman, Van Cleaf. *Peltries or Plantations: The Economic Policies of the Dutch West India Company in New Netherland, 1623–1639*. Baltimore: Johns Hopkins University Press, 1969.

Bacon, Edgar Mayhew. *Henry Hudson: His Times and His Voyages*. New York: Putnam's, 1907.

Bailey, Rosalie Fellows. *Pre-Revolutionary Dutch Houses*. New York: Morrow, 1936.

Baltzell, E. Digby. *Puritan Boston and Quaker Philadelphia*. New York: Free Press, 1979.

Barnes, Donna R., and Peter G. Rose. *Matters of Taste: Food and Drink in Seventeenth Century Dutch Art and Life*. Syracuse: Syracuse University Press, 2002.

Barnet, Sylvan, ed. *The Complete Signet Classic Shakespeare*. New York: Harcourt Brace Jovanovich, 1972.

Beresford, John. *The Godfather of Downing Street: Sir George Downing, 1623–1684*. London: Cobden-Sanderson, 1925.

Bergeron, David M. *King James and Letters of Homoerotic Desire*. Iowa City: Iowa University Press, 1999.

Black, Robert C., III. *The Younger John Winthrop*. New York: Columbia University Press, 1966.

Blackburn, Roderic H., and Ruth Piwonka. *Remembrance of Patria: Dutch Arts and Culture in Colonial America, 1609–1776*. Albany: Albany Institute of History and Art, 1988.

Blakely, Allison. *Blacks in the Dutch World: The Evolution of Racial*

Imagery in a Modern Society. Bloomington: Indiana University Press, 1993.

Bliss, Robert. *Revolution and Empire: English Politics and the American Colonies in the Seventeenth Century*. Manchester: Manchester University Press, 1990.

Blom, J. C. H., and E. Lamberts, eds. *History of the Low Countries*, trans. James C. Kennedy. New York: Berghahn, 1999.

Bogert, Frederick W. *Bergen County, New Jersey, History and Heritage, vol. 2: The Colonial Days, 1630–1775*. Bergen County, NJ: Bergen County Board of Chosen Freeholders, 1983.

Bonomi, Patricia U. *A Factious People: Politics and Society in Colonial New York*. New York: Columbia University Press, 1971.

Bonomi, Patricia U. *Under the Cope of Heaven: Religion, Society, and Politics in Colonial America*. New York: Oxford University Press, 1986.

Boxer, C. R. *The Dutch Seaborne Empire: 1600–1800*. New York: Knopf, 1965.

Brodhead, John Romeyn. *The History of the State of New York, 1609–1691*, 2 vols. New York: Harper & Bros, 1871.

Burrows, Edwin G., and Mike Wallace. *Gotham: A History of New York City to 1898*. New York: Oxford University Press, 1999.

Bussman, Klaus, and Heinz Schilling, eds. *1648: War and Peace in Europe*, 3 vols. Münster: Westfälisches Landesmuseum, 1998.

Calder, Isabel. *The New Haven Colony*. New Haven: Yale University Press, 1934.

Cantwell, Anne-Marie, and Diana diZerega Wall. *Unearthing Gotham: The Archaeology of New York City*. New Haven: Yale University Press, 2001.

Carlton, Charles. *Charles I: The Personal Monarch*, 2nd edn. London: Routledge, 1995.

Ceci, Lynn. 'The Effect of European Contact and Trade on the Settlement Pattern of Indians in Coastal New York, 1524–1665: The Archaeological and Documentary Evidence'. Doctoral dissertation, City University of New York Graduate Center, 1977.

Chiodo, John J. 'The Foreign Policy of Peter Stuyvesant: Dutch Diplomacy in North America, 1647 to 1664'. Doctoral dissertation, University of Iowa, 1974.

Clarke, Desmond, ed. *The Unfortunate Husbandman: an account of the life and travels of a Real Farmer in Ireland, Scotland, England and America, by Charles Varley or Varlo*. London: Oldbourne, 1964.

Clarke, J. S. *The Life of James the Second, King of England, &c. Collected Out of Memoirs Writ of His Own Hand*, 2 vols. London, 1816.

Cohen, David Steven. *The Dutch-American Farm*. New York: New York University Press, 1992.

Commager, Henry Steele. *Jefferson, Nationalism, and the Enlightenment*. New York: George Braziller, 1975.

Cooke, Jacob Ernest, ed.-in-chief. *Encyclopedia of the North American Colonies*, 3 vols. New York: Scribner's, 1993.

Cooper, Victor. *A Dangerous Woman: New York's First Lady Liberty, The Life and Times of Lady Deborah Moody*. Bowie, Md: Heritage, 1995.

Davids, Karel, and Jan Lucassen, eds. *A Miracle Mirrored: The Dutch Republic in European Perspective*. Cambridge: Cambridge University Press, 1995.

Davies, K. G. *The Royal African Company*. London: Routledge, 1999.

Denevan, William, ed. *The Native Population of the Americas in 1492*. Madison: University of Wisconsin Press, 1978.

Dietz, Johann. *Master Johann Dietz, Surgeon in the Army of the Great Elector and Barber to the Royal Court*. New York: Dutton, 1923.

Dodge, Ernest S. *Northwest by Sea*. New York: Oxford University Press, 1961.

Dumbauld, Edward. *The Life and Legal Writings of Hugo Grotius*. Norman: University of Oklahoma Press, 1969.

Dunn, Shirley. *The Mohicans and their Land 1609–1730*. Fleischmans, NY: Purple Mountain, 1994.

Dyer, Louisa A. *The House of Peace*. New York: Longmans, Green, 1956.

Fabend, Firth Haring. *A Dutch Family in the Middle Colonies, 1660–1800*. New Brunswick: Rutgers University Press, 1991.

Fabend, Firth Haring. *Zion on the Hudson: Dutch New York and New Jersey in the Age of Revivals*. New Brunswick: Rutgers University Press, 2000.

Feenstra, R., and C. J. D. Waal. *Seventeenth-century Leyden Law Professors and their Influence on the Development of the Civil Law*.

Amsterdam and Oxford: North-Holland, 1975.

Feiling, Keith. *British Foreign Policy 1660–1672*. London: Macmillan, 1930.

Fell-Smith, Charlotte. *John Dee*. London: Constable, 1909.

Fisher, Raymond H. *The Russian Fur Trade, 1550–1700*. Berkeley: University of California Press, 1943.

Foster, Stephen. *Their Solitary Way: The Puritan Social Ethic in the First Century of Settlement in New England*. New Haven: Yale University Press, 1971.

Fouquet, P. *Oud Amsterdam: Afbeeldingen der Voornaamste Gebouwen en Gezichten uit den Jare 1600–1790*. Amsterdam: Allert de Lange, 1923.

Fox, Dixon Ryan. *Yankees and Yorkers*. New York: University Press, 1940.

Fraser, Antonia. *Cromwell: The Lord Protector*. New York: Knopf, 1973.

Fraser, Antonia. *Royal Charles: Charles II and the Restoration*. New York: Dell, 1979.

Fremantle, Katherine. *The Baroque Town Hall of Amsterdam*. Utrecht: Haentjens Dekker & Gumbert, 1959.

French, Peter J. *John Dee: The World of an Elizabethan Magus*. London: Routledge & Kegan Paul, 1972.

Friedman, Lawrence. *Crime and Punishment in American History*. New York: Basic Books, 1993.

Frijhoff, Willem. *Wegen van Evert Willemsz.: Een Hollands weeskind op zoek naar zichzelf, 1607–1647*. Nijmegen: Sun, 1995.

Funk, Elisabeth Paling. 'Washington Irving and the Dutch Heritage': Manuscript in progress.

Gaukroger, Stephen. *Descartes: An Intellectual Biography*. London: Clarendon Press, 1995.

Gehring, Charles T. *A Guide to Dutch Manuscripts Relating to New Netherland*. Albany: State University of New York, 1978.

Gerson, Armand, Earnest Vaughn and Neva Ruth Deardorff. *Studies in the History of English Commerce during the Tudor Period*. New York: University of Pennsylvania Press, 1912.

Geyl, Pieter. *Orange and Stuart*. New York: Scribner's, 1969.

Goebel, Julius. *Law Enforcement in Colonial New York: A Study in Criminal Procedure*. New York: Commonwealth Fund, 1944.

Goodfriend, Joyce D. *Before the Melting Pot: Society and Culture in Colonial New York City, 1664–1730*. Princeton: Princeton University Press, 1992.

Gregg, Pauline. *King Charles I*. London: Dent, 1981.

Greenberg, Mark. *The Hague*. New York: Newsweek Books, 1982.

Grumet, Robert Steven. *Historic Contact: Indian People and Colonists in Today's Northeastern United States in the Sixteenth through Eighteenth Centuries*. Norman: University of Oklahoma Press, 1995.

Grumet, Robert Steven. *Native American Place Names in New York City*. New York: Museum of the City of New York, 1981.

Hainsworth, Roger, and Christine Churches. *The Anglo-Dutch Naval Wars, 1652–1674*. Stroud: Sutton, 1998.

Haley, K. H. D. *The Dutch in the Seventeenth Century*. London: Thames & Hudson, 1972.

Hall, Michael, Lawrence Leder and Michael Kammen, eds. *The Glorious Revolution in America*. Chapel Hill: University of North Carolina Press, 1964.

Harline, Craig E. *Pamphlets, Printing, and Political Culture in the Early Dutch Republic*. Dordrecht: Martinus Nijhoff, 1987.

Harrisse, Henry. *John Cabot, the Discoverer of North-America, and Sebastian His Son*. New York: Argosy-Antiquarian, 1968.

Hart, Simon. *The Prehistory of the New Netherland Company: Amsterdam Notarial Records of the First Dutch Voyages to the Hudson*. Amsterdam: City of Amsterdam Press, 1959.

Haswell, Jock. *James II, Soldier and Sailor*. New York: St Martin's, 1972.

Heckewelder, John. *History, Manners, and Customs of the Indian Nations*. Philadelphia: Historical Society of Pennsylvania, 1876 (first publ. 1819).

Hill, Christopher. *God's Englishman: Oliver Cromwell and the English Revolution*. New York: Dial, 1970.

Holmes, Martin. *Elizabethan London*. New York: Praeger, 1969.

Hoppin, Charles Arthur. *The Washington Ancestry and Records of the McClain, Johnson, and Forty Other Colonial American Families*, 3 vols. Greenfield, Ohio: privately printed, 1932.

Hore, J. P. *The History of Newmarket and the Annals of the Turf*, 3 vols. London: Baily, 1886.

Howarth, David. *The Men-of-War*. Alexandria, Va: Time-Life Books, 1978.

Hughes, Robert. *Culture of Complaint: The Fraying of America*. Oxford: Oxford University Press, 1993.

Huizinga, Johan. *Dutch Civilisation in the Seventeenth Century*. New York: Ungar, 1968.

Innes, J. H. *New Amsterdam and its People: Studies, Social and Topographical, of the Town under Dutch and Early English Rule*. Princeton: Princeton University Press, 1902.

Israel, Jonathan I. *Dutch Primacy in World Trade, 1585–1740*. Oxford: Clarendon Press, 1989.

Israel, Jonathan I. *The Dutch Republic*. Oxford: Oxford University Press, 1995.

Israel, Jonathan I. *Radical Enlightenment: Philosophy and the Making of Modernity, 1650–1750*. Oxford: Oxford University Press, 2001.

Jacobs, Jaap. *Een zegenrijk gewest: Nieuw-Nederland in de zeventiende eeuw*. Amsterdam: Prometheus, 1999.

Jameson, J. Franklin. *Willem Usselinx*. New York: Putnam, 1887.

Jennings, Francis. *The Ambiguous Iroquois Empire*. New York: Norton, 1984.

Johnson, Amandus. *The Swedish Settlements on the Delaware*, 2 vols. New York: University of Pennsylvania Press, 1911.

Johnson, Donald S. *Charting the Sea of Darkness: The Four Voyages of Henry Hudson*. New York: Kodansha America, 1995.

Jones, Charles W. *Saint Nicholas of Myra, Bari, and Manhattan: Biography of a Legend*. Chicago: University of Chicago Press, 1978.

Jordan, Terry and Matti Kaups. *The American Backwoods Frontier: An Ethnic and Ecological Interpretation*. Baltimore and London: Johns Hopkins University Press, 1989.

Kammen, Michael. *Colonial New York*. New York: Scribner's, 1975.

Keblusek, Marika. *Boeken in de hofstad: Haagse boekcultuur in de Gouden Eeuw*. Hilversum, Neth.: Verloren, 1997.

Kenney, Alice P. *Stubborn for Liberty: The Dutch in New York*. Syracuse: Syracuse University Press, 1975.

Kenyon, J. P. *The Stuarts: A Study in English Kingship*. London: Severn House, 1977.

Kessler, Henry H., and Eugene Rachlis. *Peter Stuyvesant and his New York*. New York: Random House, 1959.

Kettering, Alison McNeil. *Gerard ter Borch and the Treaty of Münster*. The Hague: Mauritshuis, 1998.

King, J. C. H. *First People, First Contacts: Native Peoples of North America*. London: British Museum, 1999.

Kishlansky, Mark. *A Monarchy Transformed: Britain 1603–1714*. New York: Penguin, 1997.

Klooster, Wim. *The Dutch in the Americas, 1600–1800*. Providence: John Carter Brown Library, 1997.

Koolhaas, Rem. *Delirious New York: A Retroactive Manifesto for Manhattan*. Rotterdam: 010, 1994.

Kossmann, E. F. *De boekhandel te 's-Gravenhage tot het eind van de 18de eeuw*. 's-Gravenhage: Nijhoff, 1937.

Kupperman, Karen Ordahl. *Indians and English: Facing Off in Early America*. Ithaca: Cornell University Press, 2000.

Kupperman, Karen Ordahl, ed. *America in European Consciousness, 1493–1750*. Chapel Hill: University of North Carolina Press, 1995.

Kurlansky, Mark. *Cod: A Biography of the Fish that Changed the World*. New York: Walker, 1997.

Lane, Kris E. *Pillaging the Empire: Piracy in the Americas 1500–1750*. Armonk: Sharpe, 1998.

Lees, J. Cameron. *St Giles', Edinburgh: Church, College, and Cathedral, from the Earliest Times to the Present Day*. Edinburgh: Chambers, 1889.

Leonardo, Richard A. *History of Surgery*. New York: Froben, 1943.

Loades, David. *The Mid-Tudor Crisis, 1545–1565*. London: Macmillan, 1992.

Lunsingh Scheurleer, T. H., and G. H. M. Posthumus Meyjes. *Leiden University in the Seventeenth Century*. Leiden: Leiden University Press, 1975.

Lyle, R. C. *Royal Newmarket*. London: Putnam, 1945.

McCullough, David. *John Adams*. New York: Simon & Schuster, 2001.

Macleod, John. *Dynasty: The Stuarts, 1560–1807*. New York: St Martin's, 1999.

Maika, Dennis J. 'Commerce and Community: Manhattan Merchants in the Seventeenth Century'. Doctoral dissertation, New York University, 1995.

Mak, Geert. *Amsterdam*. Cambridge, Mass.: Harvard University Press, 2000.

Mattingly, Garrett. *The Armada*. Boston: Houghton Mifflin, 1959.

Meinig, D. W. *The Shaping of America, A Geographical Perspective on 500 Years of History, vol. 1: Atlantic America, 1492–1800*. New Haven: Yale University Press, 1986.

Merwick, Donna. *Death of a Notary: Conquest and Change in Colonial New York*. Ithaca: Cornell University Press, 1999.

Miller, Leo. *John Milton's Writings in the Anglo-Dutch Negotiations, 1651–1654*. Pittsburgh: Duquesne University Press, 1992.

Milton, Giles. *Nathaniel's Nutmeg*. London: Hodder & Stoughton, 1999.

Morgan, Edmund S. *The Puritan Dilemma: The Story of John Winthrop*. Boston: Little, Brown, 1958.

Morison, Samuel Eliot. *The European Discovery of America*, vol. 1: *The Northern Voyages* (1971); vol. 2: *The Southern Voyages* (1974). New York: Oxford University Press.

Morison, Samuel Eliot. *The Founding of Harvard College*. Cambridge, Mass.: Harvard University Press, 1935.

Morison, Samuel Eliot. *The Great Explorers*. New York: Oxford University Press, 1978.

Morison, Samuel Eliot, Henry Steele Commager and William E. Leuchtenburg. *The Growth of the American Republic*, vol. 1, 7th edn. New York: Oxford University Press, 1980.

Murphy, Henry Cruse. *Henry Hudson in Holland*. The Hague: Nijhoff, 1909.

Murray, David. *Indian Giving: Economics of Power in Indian–White Exchanges*. Amherst: University of Massachusetts Press, 2000.

Nelson, Paul David. *William Tryon and the Course of Empire*. Chapel Hill: University of North Carolina Press, 1990.

Nissenson, S. G. *The Patroon's Domain*. New York: Columbia University Press, 1937.

Nute, Grace Lee. *Caesars of the Wilderness: Medard Chouart, Sieur des Grosselliers and Pierre Esprit Radisson, 1618–1710*. St Paul: Minnesota Historical Society Press, 1978.

O'Callaghan, E. B. *The History of New Netherland*, 2 vols. New York: Appleton, 1848.

O'Callaghan, E. B. *The Register of New Netherland, 1626 to 1674*. Albany: Munsell, 1865.

Otterspeer, Willem. *Groepsportret met Dame*. Amsterdam: Bakker, 2000.

Parks, George Bruner. *Richard Hakluyt and the English Voyages*. New York: American Geographical Society, 1928.

Parr, Charles McKew. *The Voyages of David de Vries, Navigator and Adventurer*. New York: Crowell, 1969.

Patterson, Jerry E. *The City of New York: A History Illustrated from the Collections of the Museum of the City of New York*. New York: Abrams, 1978.

Phipps, Geraldine M. *Sir John Merrick: English Merchant–Diplomat in Seventeenth Century Russia*. Newtonville, Mass.: Oriental Research Partners, 1983.

Powys, Llewelyn. *Henry Hudson*. New York: Harper & Bros, 1928.

Price, J. L. *Holland and the Dutch Republic in the Seventeenth Century: The Politics of Particularism*. Oxford: Clarendon Press, 1994.

Quinn, Arthur. *A New World: An Epic of Colonial America from the Founding of Jamestown to the Fall of Quebec*. Winchester, Mass.: Faber, 1994.

Quinn, David B., and A. N. Ryan. *England's Sea Empire, 1550–1642*. London: Allen & Unwin, 1983.

Read, Conyers. *Mr Secretary Walsingham and the Policy of Queen Elizabeth*, 3 vols. Cambridge, Mass.: Harvard University Press, 1925.

Read, John Meredith, Jr. *A Historical Inquiry Concerning Henry Hudson, his Friends, Relatives, and Early Life, his Connection with the Muscovy Company, and Discovery of Delaware Bay*. Albany: Munsell, 1866.

Regin, Deric. *Traders, Artists, Burghers: A Cultural History of Amsterdam in the 17th Century*. Amsterdam: Van Gorcum, 1976.

Reich, Jerome R. *Leisler's Rebellion: A Study of Democracy in New York, 1664–1720*. Chicago: Chicago University Press, 1953.

Renaud, J. G. N. *Het Huis en de Heren van Heemstede Tijdens de Middeleeuwen*. Heemstede: Vereniging Oud-Heemstede-Bennebroek, 1952.

Ricciardi, Christopher. 'From Private to Public: The Changing Landscape of Van Cortlandt Park; Bronx, New York, in the Nineteenth Century'. Master's thesis, Syracuse University, 1997.

Rietbergen, P. J. A. N. *A Short History of the Netherlands*. Amersfoort, Neth.: Bekking, 1998.

Riker, James. *Revised History of Harlem: Its Origin and Early Annals*.

New York: New Harlem Publishing, 1904.

Rink, Oliver. *Holland on the Hudson: An Economic and Social History of Dutch New York*. Ithaca: Cornell University Press, 1986.

Ritchie, Robert C. *The Duke's Province: A Study of New York Politics and Society, 1664–1691*. Chapel Hill: University of North Carolina Press, 1977.

Rogers, P. G. *The Dutch in the Medway*. London: Oxford University Press, 1970.

Rose, Peter G. *The Sensible Cook: Dutch Foodways in the Old and New World*. Syracuse: Syracuse University Press, 1989.

Rothschild, Nan. *New York City Neighborhoods: The 18th Century*. San Diego: Academic Press, 1990.

Rowen, Herbert H. *John de Witt, Grand Pensionary of Holland, 1625–1672*. Princeton: Princeton University Press, 1978.

Rowen, Herbert H. *John de Witt: Statesman of the 'True Freedom'*. Cambridge: Cambridge University Press, 1986.

Rowen, Herbert H. *The Princes of Orange: The Stadholders in the Dutch Republic*. New York: Cambridge University Press, 1988.

Royal Netherlands Academy of Arts and Sciences. *The World of Hugo Grotius (1583–1645). Proceedings of the International Colloquium Organized by the Grotius Committee*. Amsterdam: APA-Holland University Press, 1984.

Russell, Bertrand. *A History of Western Philosophy*. London: Allen & Unwin, 1946.

Rutkow, Ira M. *Surgery: An Illustrated History*. St Louis: Mosby, 1993.

Ruttenber, E. M. *Indian Tribes of Hudson's River to 1700*. Saugerties, NY: Hope Farm Press, 1992 (first publ. 1872).

Rybczynski, Witold. *Home: A Short History of an Idea*. New York: Viking, 1986.

Savelle, Max. *The Colonial Origins of American Thought*. Princeton: Van Nostrand, 1964.

Schama, Simon. *The Embarrassment of Riches: An Interpretation of Dutch Culture in the Golden Age*. New York: Knopf, 1987.

Scharf, J. Thomas. *The History of Westchester County*. Philadelphia: Preston, 1886.

Schechter, Stephen L., and Richard B. Bernstein, eds. *New York and the Union*. Albany: New York State Commission on the Bicentennial of the United States Constitution, 1990.

Schmidt, Benjamin. 'Innocence Abroad: The Dutch Imagination and the Representation of the New World, *c.*1570–1670'. Doctoral dissertation, Harvard University, 1994.

Shattuck, Martha. 'A Civil Society: Court and Community in Beverwijck, New Netherland, 1652–1664'. Doctoral dissertation, Boston University, 1993.

Shonnard, Frederic. *History of Westchester County, New York, from its Earliest Settlement to the year 1900*. Harrison, NY: Harbor Hill, 1974.

Siefker, Phyllis. *Santa Claus, Last of the Wild Men*. Jefferson: McFarland, 1997.

Simmons, Amelia. *American Cookery*. Albany, NY: Charles & George Webster, 1796.

Sobel, Dava. *Galileo's Daughter: A Historical Memoir of Science, Faith, and Love*. New York: Walker, 1999.

Spencer, Hazelton. *The Art and Life of William Shakespeare*. New York: Harcourt, Brace, 1940.

Sprunger, Keith L. *Trumpets from the Tower: English Puritan Printing in the Netherlands, 1600–1640*. Leiden: Brill, 1994.

Stephanson, Anders. *Manifest Destiny: American Expansion and the Empire of Right*. New York: Hill & Wang, 1995.

Sweetman, Jack. *The Great Admirals: Command at Sea, 1587–1945*. Annapolis: Naval Institute Press, 1997.

Sykes, Bryan. *The Seven Daughters of Eve*. London: Bantam, 2001.

Tantillo, L. F. *Visions of New York State: The Historical Paintings of L. F. Tantillo*. Wappingers Falls: Shawangunk Press, 1996.

Taylor, E. G. R. *Tudor Geography*. New York: Octagon, 1968.

Thompson, Benjamin F. *History of Long Island: From its Discovery and Settlement to the Present Time*, 3 vols. New York: Dodd, 1918.

Thornton, Russell. *American Indian Holocaust and Survival: Population History since 1492*. Norman: University of Oklahoma Press, 1987.

Tieck, William. *Riverdale, Kingsbridge, Spuyten Duyvil: New York City; a Historical Epitome of the Northwest Bronx*. Old Tappan, NJ: Revell, 1968.

Trudel, Marcel. *The Beginnings of New France 1524–1663*. Toronto: McClelland & Stewart, 1973.

Tuchman, Barbara W. *The First Salute*. New York: Knopf, 1988.

Tuck, Richard. *Philosophy and Government, 1572–1651*. Cambridge:

Cambridge University Press, 1993.

Tuckerman, Bayard. *Peter Stuyvesant, Director-General for the West India Company in New Netherland*. New York: Dodd, Mead, 1893.

Vaille, F. O., and H. A. Clarke, eds. *The Harvard Book, A Series of Historical, Biographical, and Descriptive Sketches, by Various Authors*. Cambridge, Mass.: Welch, Bigelow, 1875.

Van den Boogaart, E., ed. *Johan Maurits Van Nassau-Siegen, 1604–1679: A Humanist Prince in Europe and Brazil*. The Hague: Johan Maurits van Nassau Stichting, 1979.

Van den Brink, Herman. *The Charm of Legal History*. Amsterdam: Hakkert, 1974.

Van Deursen, A. T. *Plain Lives in a Golden Age: Popular Culture, Religion and Society in Seventeenth-century Holland*. Cambridge: Cambridge University Press, 1991.

Van Gastel, Ada Louise. 'Adriaen van der Donck, New Netherland, and America'. Doctoral dissertation, University of Pennsylvania, 1985.

Van Gelder, H. E. *'S-Gravenhage in Zeven Eeuwen*. Amsterdam: Meulenhoff, 1937.

Van Nierop, H. F. K. *The Nobility of Holland: From Knights to Regents, 1500–1650*. Cambridge: Cambridge University Press, 1993.

Van Rensselaer, Mariana G. *History of the City of New York in the Seventeenth Century*, 2 vols. New York: Macmillan, 1909.

Venema, Janny. 'Beverwijck: A Dutch Village on the American Frontier, 1652–1664'. Doctoral dissertation, Free University of Amsterdam, 2003.

Vigne, Randolph, and Charles Littleton, eds. *From Strangers to Citizens: The Integration of Immigrant Communities in Britain, Ireland and Colonial America, 1550–1750*. Portland, Or.: Sussex Academic, 2001.

Vinckeboons, Joan, Gunter Schilder and Jan van Bracht. *The Origins of New York*. Zurich: Seefeld, 1988.

Voorhees, David William. *The Holland Society: A Centennial History 1885–1985*. New York: Holland Society, 1985.

Wagman, Morton. 'The Struggle for Representative Government in New Netherland'. Doctoral dissertation, Columbia University, 1969.

Wedgwood, C. V. *The Political Career of Peter Paul Rubens*. London:

Thames & Hudson, 1975.
Wertenbaker, Thomas Jefferson. *The Puritan Oligarchy: The Founding of American Civilization*. New York: Scribner's, 1947.
Weslager, C. A. *A Man and his Ship: Peter Minuit and the Kalmar Nyckel*. Wilmington: Kalmar Nyckel Foundation, 1989.
Weslager, C. A., with A. R. Dunlap. *Dutch Explorers, Traders and Settlers in the Delaware Valley, 1609–1664*. Philadelphia: University of Pennsylvania Press, 1961.
Wessels, J. W. *History of the Roman–Dutch Law*. Grahamstown, Cape Colony: African Book Company, 1908.
White, Christopher. *Rembrandt*. London: Thames & Hudson, 1984.
Willan, T. S. *The Muscovy Merchants of 1555*. Manchester: Manchester University Press, 1953.
Williams, Bernard. *Descartes: The Project of Pure Enquiry*. New York: Penguin, 1978.
Williams, Selma R. *Divine Rebel: The Life of Anne Marbury Hutchinson*. New York: Holt, Rinehart & Winston, 1981.
Williamson, James A. *The Age of Drake*, 5th edn. London: A. & C. Black, 1965.
Wilstach, Paul. *Hudson River Landings*. New York: Tudor, 1933.
Zandvliet, Kees. *Mapping for Money: Maps, Plans, and Topographic Paintings and their Role in Dutch Overseas Expansion During the 16th and 17th Centuries*. Amsterdam: Batavian Lion International, 1998.
Zuckert, Michael P. *Natural Rights and the New Republicanism*. Princeton: Princeton University Press, 1994.
Zumthor, Paul. *Daily Life in Rembrandt's Holland*. New York: Macmillan, 1963.

Articles, Talks, Addresses, Reports

Andrade, Manuel Correia de. 'The Socio-Economic Geography of Dutch Brazil'. In E. Van den Boogaart, ed., *Johan Maurits Van Nassau-Siegen, 1604–1679: A Humanist Prince in Europe and Brazil*. The Hague: Johan Maurits van Nassau Stichting, 1979.
Atkins, T. Astley. 'Adriaen Van der Donck: An Address Delivered Before the Westchester Historical Society'. Yonkers, New York, 1888.

Bankoff, H. Arthur, Frederick A. Winter and Christopher Ricciardi. 'Archaeological Excavations at Van Cortlandt Park, the Bronx, 1990–1992'. Report on file with the New York City Landmarks Preservation Commission.

Banner, Stuart. 'Manhattan for $24: American Indian Land Sales, 1607–1763'. Paper presented to the Law and Economics Workshop, John M. Olin Center for Law and Economics, University of Michigan Law School, 25 Oct. 2001.

Becker, Alfred. 'Mr. Adriaen Van der Donck, the Earliest Lawyer in New York'. *New York State Bar Association Report*, vol. 27, 1904.

Beier, A. L. 'Vagrants and the Social Order in Elizabethan England'. *Past and Present*, no. 64, August 1974.

Berlin, Ira. 'From Creole to African: Atlantic Creoles and the Origins of African-American Society in Mainland North America'. *William and Mary Quarterly*, vol. 53, April 1996.

Bodle, Wayne. 'Themes and Directions in Middle Colonies Historiography, 1980–1994'. *William and Mary Quarterly*, vol. 51, July 1994.

Bonomi, Patricia U. 'The Middle Colonies: Embryo of the New Political Order'. In Alden T. Vaughan and George Athan Billias, eds, *Perspectives on Early American History*. New York: Harper & Row, 1973.

Browner, Jessica A. 'Wrong Side of the River: London's Disreputable South Bank in the Sixteenth and Seventeenth Century'. *Essays in History*, vol. 36, 1994.

Christoph, Peter R. 'The Freedmen of New Amsterdam'. *Journal of the Afro-American Historical Society*, vol. 5, nos 3 & 4, Fall and Winter 1984.

Christoph, Peter R. 'Story of the New Netherland Project'. *De Halve Maen*, vol. 61, Fall 1988.

Cohen, David. 'How Dutch Were the Dutch of New Netherland?' *New York History*, vol. 62, 1981.

Cohen, Ronald D. 'The Hartford Treaty of 1650: Anglo-Dutch Cooperation in the Seventeenth Century'. *New-York Historical Society Quarterly*, Oct. 1969.

Dunn, Shirley, 'Enlarging Rensselaerswijck: 17th Century Land Acquisition on the East Side of the River'. In Nancy Anne

McClure Zeller, ed., *A Beautiful and Fruitful Place: Selected Rensselaerswijck Seminar Papers*. Albany: New Netherland, 1991.

Fabend, Firth Haring. 'The Pro-Leislerian Dutch Farmers in New York: A "Mad Rabble", or "Gentlemen Standing Up for Their Rights"?' *De Halve Maen*, vol. 63, March 1990.

Fabend, Firth Haring. 'What Historians Really Know About New York's History'. Talk prepared for the Annual Meeting, Friends of New Netherland, 22 Jan. 2000.

Finkelman, Paul. 'The Soul and the State: Religious Freedom in New York and the Origin of the First Amendment'. In Stephen L. Schechter, and Richard B. Bernstein, eds, *New York and the Union*. Albany: New York State Commission on the Bicentennial of the United States Constitution, 1990.

Fockema, Andreae, SJ. 'Data on the Dutch Background of Peter Stuyvesant'. *De Halve Maen*, vol. 39, Fall 1964.

Freyre, G. 'Johan Maurits Van Nassau-Siegen from a Brazilian Viewpoint'. In E. Van den Boogaart, ed., *Johan Maurits Van Nassau-Siegen, 1604–1679: A Humanist Prince in Europe and Brazil*. The Hague: Johan Maurits van Nassau Stichting, 1979.

Frijhoff, Willem. 'Dominee Bogardus als Nieuw-Nederlander'. *Jaarboek van het Central Bureau voor Genealogie*. The Hague: Central Bureau voor Genealogie, 1996.

Frijhoff, Willem. 'Identity Achievement, Education, and Social Legitimation in Early Modern Dutch Society: The Case of Evert Willemsz (1622–23)'. International Symposium in Europe, Netherlands, 1999.

Frijhoff, Willem. 'Neglected Networks. New Netherlanders and their Old Fatherland: The Kieft Case'. Paper delivered at the 2001 Rensselaerswyck Seminar, New York City.

Frijhoff, Willem. 'New Views on the Dutch Period of New York'. *De Halve Maen*, vol. 70, Fall 1997.

Gehring, Charles. 'The Founding of Beverwijck, a Dutch Village on the Upper Hudson'. *The Dutch Settlers Society of Albany Yearbook*, vol. 51, 1989–93.

Gehring, Charles. '*Hodie Mihi, Cras Tibi*: Swedish–Dutch Relations in the Delaware Valley'. In Carol E. Hoffecker, Richard Waldron, Lorraine E. Williams and Barbara E. Benson, eds, *New Sweden in America*. Newark: University of Delaware Press, 1995.

Gehring, Charles. 'New Netherland Manuscripts in United States Repositories'. *De Halve Maen*, vol. 57, Aug. 1983.

Gehring, Charles. 'New Netherland: Translating New York's Dutch Past'. *Humanities*, vol. 14, Nov.–Dec. 1993.

Gehring, Charles. 'De Suyt Rivier: New Netherland's Delaware Frontier'. *De Halve Maen*, vol. 65, Summer 1992.

Gehring, Charles. 'Totidem Verbis'. *De Nieu Nederlanse Marcurius*, vol. 4, 1988.

Gehring, Charles. 'Wringing Information from a Drowned Princess'. Paper presented to the Rensselaerswijck Seminar, Albany, 1994.

Gerhardt, Volker. 'On the Historical Significance of the Peace of Westphalia: Twelve Theses'. In Klaus Bussman and Heinz Schilling, eds, *1648: War and Peace in Europe*, 3 vols. Münster: Westfälisches Landesmuseum, 1998.

Goodfriend, Joyce D. 'The Dutch in 17th-Century New York City: Minority or Majority?' In Randolph Vigne and Charles Littleton, eds, *From Strangers to Citizens: The Integration of Immigrant Communities in Britain, Ireland and Colonial America, 1550–1750*. Portland, Or.: Sussex Academic, 2001.

Goodfriend, Joyce D. 'New Netherland in the Atlantic World: Comments and Reflections'. *De Halve Maen*, vol. 70, Winter 1997.

Goodfriend, Joyce D. 'The Sabbath Keeper'. *Seaport*, Fall 2001.

Goodfriend, Joyce D. 'Writing/Righting Dutch Colonial History'. *New York History*, Jan. 1999.

Goosens, Eymert-Jan. 'Monuments to Peace in the Netherlands'. In Klaus Bussman and Heinz Schilling, eds, *1648: War and Peace in Europe*, 3 vols. Münster: Westfälisches Landesmuseum, 1998.

Gray, Albert. 'An Address on the Occasion of the Tercentenary of the Death of Richard Hakluyt'. London: Hakluyt Society, 1917.

Groenveld, Simon. 'New Light on a Drowned Princess'. *De Halve Maen*, vol. 74, Summer 2001.

Grumet, Robert S. 'Hunting Indian History', 'Trade, War and Diplomacy', 'The English Imprint', 'Survival of the Fittest', 'The Diaspora'. Series published in *Hudson Valley*, Jan.–June 1991.

Guerra, F. 'Medicine in Dutch Brazil'. In E. Van den Boogaart, ed., *Johan Maurits Van Nassau-Siegen, 1604–1679: A Humanist Prince in Europe and Brazil*. The Hague: Johan Maurits van Nassau Stichting, 1979.

Heck, Earl Leon. 'A Sketch of Adriaen Van der Donck: Colonizer, Statesman and First Historian of Early New York'. Unpublished typescript presented to the New York State Library, Albany, 1960.

Hershkowitz, Leo. 'New Amsterdam's Twenty-Three Jews: Myth or Reality?' In Shalom Goldman, ed., *Hebrew and the Bible in America: The First Two Centuries*. Hanover, NH: Brandeis University Press, 1993.

Hershkowitz, Leo. 'The New York City Charter, 1686'. In Stephen L. Schechter, ed., *Roots of the Republic: American Founding Documents Interpreted*. Madison: Madison House, 1990.

Hershkowitz, Leo. 'The Troublesome Turk: An Illustration of Judicial Process in New Amsterdam'. *New York History*, Oct. 1965.

Hoetink, H. R. 'Some Remarks on the Modernity of Johan Maurits'. In E. Van den Boogaart, ed., *Johan Maurits Van Nassau-Siegen, 1604–1679: A Humanist Prince in Europe and Brazil*. The Hague: Johan Maurits van Nassau Stichting, 1979.

Hoffman, William. 'Van der Donck–Van Bergen'. *New York Genealogical and Biographical Record*, vol. 67. New York: New York Genealogical and Biographical Society, 1936.

Hopkins, Vivian C. 'The Dutch Records of New York: Francis Adrian Van Der Kemp and De Witt Clinton'. *New York History*, Oct. 1962.

Howard, Ronald. 'John Romeyn Brodhead'. *Dictionary of Literary Biography*, vol. 30, 1984.

Hutchinson, William R. 'Diversity and the Pluralist Ideal'. In William Peter, ed., *Perspectives on American Religion and Culture*. Malden, Mass.: Blackwell, 1999.

Israel, Jonathan I. 'Art and Diplomacy: Gerard Ter Borch and the Münster Peace Negotiations, 1646–8'. In *Conflicts of Empires: Spain, the Low Countries and the Struggle for World Supremacy, 1585–1713*. London: Hambledon, 1997.

Israel, Jonathan I. 'The Dutch Role in the Glorious Revolution'. In Jonathan I. Israel, ed., *The Anglo-Dutch Moment*. Cambridge: Cambridge University Press, 1991.

Israel, Jonathan. 'The Intellectual Debate about Toleration in the Dutch Republic'. In C. Berkvens-Stevelinck, J. Israel and G. H. M. Posthumus Meyjes, eds, *The Emergence of Tolerance in the Dutch*

Republic. Leiden: Brill, 1997.

Israel, Jonathan I. 'Toleration in Seventeenth-Century Dutch and English Thought'. In *Conflicts of Empires: Spain, the Low Countries and the Struggle for World Supremacy, 1585–1713*. London: Hambledon, 1997.

Jacobs, Jaap. 'Between Repression and Approval: Connivance and Tolerance in the Dutch Republic and in New Netherland'. *De Halve Maen*, vol. 71, Fall 1998.

Jacobs, Jaap. 'The Hartford Treaty: A European Perspective on a New World Conflict'. *De Halve Maen*, vol. 68, Winter 1995.

Jacobs, Jaap. 'A Hitherto Unknown Letter of Adriaen van der Donck'. *De Halve Maen*, vol. 71, Spring 1998.

Jacobs, Jaap. 'A Troubled Man: Director Wouter van Twiller and the Affairs of New Netherland in 1635'. Paper presented at the Conference on New York State History, Bard College, Annandale-on-Hudson, New York, 6 June 2003.

Jordan, Terry G. 'The Material Cultural Legacy of New Sweden on the American Frontier'. In Carol E. Hoffecker, Richard Waldron, Lorraine E. Williams and Barbara E. Benson, eds, *New Sweden in America*. Newark: University of Delaware Press, 1995.

Kielty, Bernardine. *The Sidewalks of New York*. Pamphlet published for the Bowman Hotels by the Little Leather Library Corporation, New York, 1923.

Klein, Milton M. 'Origins of the Bill of Rights in Colonial New York'. *New York History*, Oct. 1991.

Klever, Wim. 'Conflicting "Considerations of State". Van den Enden's Opposition against de la Court's Aristocratic Republicanism and its Follow-Up in Spinoza's Work'. *Foglio Spinoziano* (online journal), no. 17, 2001.

Klooster, Wim. 'Winds of Change: Colonization, Commerce, and Consolidation in the Seventeenth-Century Atlantic World'. *De Halve Maen*, vol. 70, Fall 1997.

Koning, Joep de. 'From Van der Donck to Visscher'. *Mercator's World*, vol. 5, no. 4, July–Aug. 2000.

Koning, Joep de. 'Make Governors Island a Beacon of History'. *New York Newsday*, 24 May 2001.

Koot, Christian. 'In Pursuit of Profit: The Netherlands' Trade in Colonial New York, 1664–1688', talk given at conference on New

York City History, CUNY Graduate Center, Oct. 2001.

Kress, Jack. 'Progress and Prosecution'. *Annals of the American Academy of Political and Social Sciences*, vol. 423, 1976.

Kross, Jessica. 'The Dutch and the English in New York'. *Journal of Urban History*, vol. 21, 1994.

Kupp, Jan. 'Dutch Notarial Acts Relating to the Tobacco Trade of Virginia, 1608–1653'. *William and Mary Quarterly*, vol. 30, Oct. 1973.

Kupperman, Karen Ordahl. 'Early American History with the Dutch Put In'. *Reviews in American History*, vol. 21, 1993.

Lovejoy, David S. 'Equality and Empire: The New York Charter of Libertyes, 1683'. *William and Mary Quarterly*, vol. 21, 1964.

Lucas, Stephen E. 'The *Plakkaat van Verlatinge*: A Neglected Model for the American Declaration of Independence'. In Rosemarijn Hoefte and Johanna C. Kardux, eds, *Connecting Cultures: The Netherlands in Five Centuries of Transatlantic Exchange*. Amsterdam: Free University Press, 1994.

McNaughton, Douglas. 'The Ghost of Henry Hudson'. *Mercator's World*, May–June 1999.

Martinez, Jeanette. 'New Netherland Documentary Projects'. *De Halve Maen*, vol. 66, Spring 1993.

Matson, Cathy. '"Damned Scoundrels" and "Libertisme of Trade": Freedom and Regulation in Colonial New York's Fur and Grain Trades'. *William and Mary Quarterly*, vol. 51, July 1994.

Middleton, Simon. 'Artisans and Trade Privileges in New Amsterdam'. Paper presented to the 2001 Rensselaerswijck Seminar, New York City.

Middleton, Simon. '"How it came that the bakers bake no bread": A Struggle for Trade Privileges in Seventeenth-Century New Amsterdam'. *William and Mary Quarterly*, vol. 58, April 2001.

Mout, M. E. H. N. 'Limits and Debates: A Comparative View of Dutch Toleration in the Sixteenth and Early Seventeenth Centuries'. In C. Berkvens-Stevelinck, J. Israel and G. H. M. Posthumus Meyjes, eds, *The Emergence of Tolerance in the Dutch Republic*. Leiden: Brill, 1997.

Mowat, Barbara. 'Prospero's Book'. *Shakespeare Quarterly*, vol. 52, no. 1, 2001.

Murrin, John. 'English Rights as Ethnic Aggression: The English

Conquest, the Charter of Liberties of 1683, and Leisler's Rebellion in New York'. In W. Pencak and C. Wright, eds, *Authority and Resistance in Early New York*. New York: New-York Historical Society, 1988.

Murrin, John. 'The New York Charter of Liberties, 1683 and 1691'. In Stephen L. Schechter, ed., *Roots of the Republic: American Founding Documents Interpreted.* Madison: Madison House, 1990.

New York City Landmarks Preservation Commission. 'Street Plan of New Amsterdam and Colonial New York'. Report no. LP-1235, 14 June 1983.

New York City Landmarks Preservation Commission. 'Van Cortlandt Mansion'. Report no. LP-0890, 22 July 1975.

Page, Willie F. 'By Reason of their Colour: Africans in New Netherland, 1626–1674'. *De Halve Maen*, vol. 71, Winter 1998.

Pennington, John. 'An Examination of Beauchamp Plantagenet's Description of the Province of New Albion'. In *Memoirs of the Historical Society of Pennsylvania*, vol. 4, pt I. Philadelphia: McArty & Davis, 1840.

Pentikainen, Juha. 'The Forest Finns as Transmitters of Finnish Culture from Savo Via Central Scandinavia to Delaware'. In Carol E. Hoffecker, Richard Waldron, Lorraine E. Williams and Barbara E. Benson, eds, *New Sweden in America*. Newark: University of Delaware Press, 1995.

Plantenga, Bart, 'The Mystery of the Plockhoy Settlement in the Valley of Swans'. *Mennonite Historical Bulletin*, April 2001.

Postma, Johannes. 'A Monopoly Relinquished: The West India Company and the Atlantic Slave Trade'. *De Halve Maen*, vol. 70, Winter 1997.

Quinn, Doris C. 'Theft of the Manhattans'. *De Halve Maen*, vol. 66, Summer 1993.

Reiss, A. J. 'Public Prosecutors and Criminal Prosecution in the United States of America'. *Juridical Review*, vol. 1-21, April 1975.

Riker, David M. 'Govert Loockermans: Free Merchant of New Amsterdam'. *De Halve Maen*, vol. 62, Sept. 1989.

Rink, Oliver A. 'Unraveling a Secret Colonialism'. *De Halve Maen*, vols 59 and 60, Spring and Summer 1987.

Rosenblatt, Betsy L. 'New York State's Role in the Creation and Adoption of the Bill of Rights'. *New York History*, Oct. 1991.

Rothschild, Nan A. and Christopher N. Matthews. 'Phase 1A-1B Archaeological Investigation of the Proposed Area for the Construction of Six Tennis Courts on the Parade Grounds of Van Cortlandt Park, the Bronx, New York'. Report submitted to the City of New York Department of Parks and Recreation (n.d.).

Rothschild, Nan A., and Arnold Pickman. 'The Archaeological Excavations on the Seven Hanover Square Block'. Report on file with the New York City Landmarks Preservation Commission, 1990.

Rothschild, Nan A., Diana DiZerega Wall and Eugene Boesch. 'The Archaeological Investigation of the Stadt Huys Block: A Final Report'. Report on file at the New York City Landmarks Preservation Commission, 1987.

Rowen, Herbert H. 'The Revolution that Wasn't: The *Coup d'État* of 1650 in Holland'. In Craig E. Harline, ed., *The Rhyme and Reason of Politics in Early Modern Europe: Collected Essays of Herbert H. Rowen*. Dordrecht: Kluwer, 1992.

Rozell, Ned. 'Sea Ice Reduction May Be Another Climate Change Clue'. *Alaska Science Forum*, 5 Oct. 1995.

Schmidt, Benjamin. 'Mapping an Empire: Cartographic and Colonial Rivalry in Seventeenth-Century Dutch and English North America'. *William and Mary Quarterly*, vol. 54, 1997.

Shattuck, Martha Dickinson. 'The Dutch and the English on Long Island: An Uneasy Alliance'. *De Halve Maen*, vol. 68, Winter 1995.

Sieber, Harry. 'The Magnificent Fountain: Literary Patronage in the Court of Philip III'. *Cervantes: Bulletin of the Cervantes Society of America*, vol. 18, no. 2, 1998.

Swan, Robert J. 'The Black Presence in Seventeenth-century Brooklyn'. *De Halve Maen*, vol. 63, Winter 1990.

Tanis, James R. 'The Dutch–American Connection: The Impact of "The Dutch Example" on American Constitutional Beginnings'. In Stephen L. Schechter and Richard B. Bernstein, eds, *New York and the Union*. Albany: New York State Commission on the Bicentennial of the United States Constitution, 1990.

Trebor, Haynes. *The Flushing Remonstrance*. Pamphlet commissioned by Bowne House, Flushing, New York, 1957.

Tvengsberg, Per Martin. 'Finns in Seventeenth-century Sweden and their Contributions to the New Sweden Colony'. In Carol E.

Hoffecker, Richard Waldron, Lorraine E. Williams and Barbara E. Benson, eds, *New Sweden in America*. Newark: University of Delaware Press, 1995.

Uhlenbeck, J. D. 'Genealogie van het geslacht Farret'. *De Nederlandsche Leeuw*, vol. 55, 1937.

United States Fish and Wildlife Service, Southern New England–New York Bight Coastal Ecosystems Program. 'Significant Habitats and Habitat Complexes of the New York Bight Watershed'. Charlestown, Rhode Island, 1997.

Van Alstyne, W. Scott, Jr. 'The District Attorney: An Historical Puzzle'. *Wisconsin Law Review*, vol. 1952, Jan. 1952.

Van den Boogaart, Ernst. 'The Servant Migration to New Netherland, 1624–1664'. In P. C. Emmer, ed., *Colonialism and Migration; Indentured Labour Before and After Slavery*. Dordrecht: Nijhoff, 1986.

Van Gastel, Ada. 'Adriaen van der Donck in Rensselaerswyck: 1641–1643'. *De Halve Maen*, vol. 60, Winter 1987.

Van Gastel, Ada. 'Adriaen van der Donck als woordvoerder van de Nieuw-Nederlandse bevolking'. *Jaarboek van het Central Bureau voor Genealogie*. The Hague: Central Bureau voor Genealogie, 1996.

Van Gastel, Ada. 'Van der Donck's Description of the Indians: Additions and Corrections'. *William and Mary Quarterly*, vol. 47, July 1990.

Van Hoevenberg, Alma R. 'The Stuyvesants in the Netherlands and New Netherland'. *The New-York Historical Society Quarterly Bulletin*, vol. 10, April 1926.

Van Laer, A. J. F. *Annals of New Netherland: The Essays of A. J. F. Van Laer*, ed. and ann. Charles Gehring. Pamphlet. Albany: New Netherland Project, 1999.

Van Laer, A. J. F. *The Translation and Publication of the Manuscript Dutch Records of New Netherland, with an Account of Previous Attempts at Translation*. Pamphlet. Albany: University of the State of New York, 1910.

Van Winkle, Edward. 'The Stuyvesant Family Bible'. *The New-York Historical Society Quarterly Bulletin*, vol. 18, April 1934.

Van Zandt, Cynthia J. '". . . our river savages . . . betook themselves (unknown to us) and went to Manhattan City, in New Holland, to exact revenge on our behalf": Cross-cultural and Multi-ethnic Alliances in the 17th-Century Mid-Atlantic'. Paper presented to the American Historical Association Annual Meeting, 10 Jan. 1998.

Van Zwieten, Adriana. 'On Her Woman's Troth: Tolerance, Custom, and the Women of New Netherland'. *De Halve Maen*, vol. 72, Spring 1999.

Venema, Janny. 'The Court Case of Brant Aertsz van Slichtenhorst against Jan van Rensselaer'. *De Halve Maen*, vol. 74, Spring 2001.

Voorhees, David William. 'The "fervent Zeale" of Jacob Leisler'. *William and Mary Quarterly*, vol. 51, July 1994.

Voorhees, David William. 'First Families'. *Seaport*, Fall 2001.

Voorhees, David William. 'In the Republic's Tradition: The Persistence of Dutch Culture in the Mid-Atlantic Colonies after the 1664 English Conquest'. *De Halve Maen*, vol. 74, Fall 2001.

Voorhees, David William. 'The 1657 Flushing Remonstrance in Historical Perspective'. Remarks delivered at the Unveiling Ceremonies of the Flushing Remonstrance Queens Borough Public Library, Flushing, 19 Nov. 1999.

Wagman, Morton. 'The Origin of New York City's Government: From Proprietary Control to Representative Democracy'. *De Halve Maen*, vol. 57, Feb. 1983.

Ward, Harry M. 'The Search for American Identity: Early Historians of New England'. In Alden T. Vaughan and George Athan Billias, eds, *Perspectives on Early American History*. New York: Harper & Row, 1973.

White, Philip. 'Municipal Government Comes to Manhattan'. *New-York Historical Society Quarterly*, vol. 37, April 1953.

Williams, James Homer. '"Abominable Religion" and Dutch (In)tolerance: The Jews and Petrus Stuyvesant'. *De Halve Maen*, vol. 71, Winter 1998.

Winne, Charles K., Jr. 'Arnold J. F. van Laer (1869–1955): An Appreciation'. In Van Laer, *New York Historical Manuscripts: Dutch*, vol. 1.

Wright, Langdon G. 'Local Government and Central Authority in New Netherland'. *New-York Historical Society Quarterly*, vol. 57, Jan. 1973.

Zabriskie, George Olin. 'The Founding Families of New Netherland, No. 4: The Rapalje-Rapelje Family'. *De Halve Maen*, vol. 46, Jan.,

April, July 1972.
Zabriskie, George Olin, and Alice P. Kenney. 'The Founding of New Amsterdam: Fact and Fiction'. *De Halve Maen*, vols 50, 51, 52, 1976 and 1977.
Zeller, Nancy Anne McClure, ed. *A Beautiful and Fruitful Place: Selected Rensselaerswijck Seminar Papers*. Albany: New Netherland, 1991.

Picture Credits

Illustration to part-titles: the earliest view of Dutch Manhattan, dated two years after Minuit's purchase, shows the fort, windmill, a cluster of dwellings and Indians as a regular presence. Engraving by Joost Haartgers from *Beschryvinghe van Virginia, Niew Englandt . . .*, 1651.

PLATE SECTION

Pieter Schaghen's letter, 1626. National Archives, The Hague.

Leiden University from *A Dutch Athens* by J. Meursius, 1625; portrait of René Descartes after Frans Hals. © Archivo Iconografico, S.A./Corbis; portrait of Grotius by Michiel Mierevelt, 1631. Vredespaleis, The Hague; title page of *Vryheden, by de vergaderinghe van de Negenthiene vande . . . West-Indische Compagnie vergunt aen allen den ghenen, die eenighe Colonien in Nieuw Nederlandt sullen planten*, 1630. National Library of the Netherlands; engraved portrait of David de Vries by Cornelis Visscher, 1653. New York State Library; anonymous portrait of Adriaen van der Donck [?]. National Gallery of Art, Washington, D.C.; portrait of Peter Stuyvesant by Hendrick Couturier, c. 1660 © New-York Historical Society/Bridgeman Art Library, London.

Map: *Novi Belgii novaeque Angliae nec non partis Virginiae tabula*, Nicholas Visscher after an earlier map by Janzoon Blaue, c. 1651. Collection of Joep de Koning.

Picture Credits

View of New Amsterdam, possibly by Augustin Herrman. Austrian National Library; manuscript page, New York State Library; title page of *Description of New Netherland* by Adriaen van der Donck, 1655. New York State Library; plan of New Amsterdam, 1660. Collection of the New-York Historical Society; Dutch attack on New York in 1673. Library of Congress, Washington, D.C.

Anonymous seventeenth-century Dutch engraving of New Amsterdam, © Bettmann/Corbis; title page and frontispiece of *A True Relation of the Unjust, Cruell, and Barbarous Proceedings against the English at Amboyna . . .*, 1665.

Index

Note on names: these have been indexed under the last element, e.g. Donck, van der, except in sub-entries where they appear as in the text, e.g. Van der Donck.

THE CONFIDENT HOPE OF A MIRACLE
The True Story of the Spanish Armada
by Neil Hanson

'Continual destruction in the foretop, the pox above board, the plague between decks, hell in the forecastle and the devil at the helm.'

It is the summer of 1588, and the fate and future of England hangs in the balance. Obsessed by the dream of reclaiming England for the Catholic Church, Philip II of Spain has assembled a huge fleet of castle-crowned galleons ripe for the task. Lying in wait in the Netherlands lies a battle-hardened Spanish army, ferocious professionals with a taste for rape, looting and atrocity.

Across the Channel the English are scraping together bands of barely trained men, many armed only with scythes, stakes or longbows. Great warning beacons stand all along the coast of England. Their only hope lies in the English Navy.

But Philip's Armada is doomed before it even leaves port. As soon as it engages with the English fleet, its shortcomings are clear in the face of superior tactics and firepower. Within hours, the mightiest fleet ever assembled is mercilessly harried into fleeing north, at the mercy of the elements and the dream of subduing the Protestant English lies in tatters.

A triumphant combination of historical detail and storytelling flair, *The Confident Hope of a Miracle* draws on undiscovered and little known personal papers and records to tell the epic story of the Spanish Armada in all its scope.

'The finest ever recreation of a monumental battle . . . Riveting stuff'
Sunday Times

0 552 14975 6

CORGI BOOKS

ARBELLA
England's Lost Queen
by Sarah Gristwood

'I must shape my own coat according to my cloth, but is shall not be after the fashion of this world, but fit for me'

Niece to Mary, Queen of Scots, granddaughter to the great Tudor dynast Bess of Hardwick, Lady Arbella Stuart was brought to the court as a young girl and acknowledged as her heir by her cousin Elizabeth I – her right to the throne equalled only by James VI of Scotland. Arbella could have been Queen. But her fate was to make her own forbidden marriage, to die a lonely, squalid death in the Tower and to be written out of history . . .

Drawing on a wide range of contemporary sources, including Arbella's own extraordinary, passionate letters, Sarah Gristwood's acclaimed biography paints a vivid and powerful portrait of a woman forced to tread a precarious path through one of the most turbulent, treacherous periods in British history, and in so doing rescues this 'lost queen' from obscurity.

'Utterly compelling and a thumping good read . . . an exquisite jewel of a book' Alison Weir

'Fresh, vivid and beautifully detailed . . . conveyed with exactly the right mixture of suspense and sympathy. All her details tell' *Independent*

'She teases out some vivid threads...and deftly weaves them into a startling, "pattern of misfortune" . . . The delights are in the detail, and Gristwood makes the most of them' *Daily Telegraph*

'Carrying her learning lightly, Sarah Gristwood presents a powerful story of the dynastic insecurity of the Tudors and Stuarts . . . This life of Arbella gives us perhaps what she was: a Stuart at the centre of the historical canvas, but a woman who lived on the fringes' *Sunday Times*

'Sarah Gristwood succeeds triumphantly . . . an enthralling account of an extraordinary life' *Spectator*

A SHORT HISTORY OF NEARLY EVERYTHING
Bill Bryson

'IT DESERVES TO SELL AS MANY COPIES AS THERE ARE PROTONS IN THE FULL STOP THAT ENDS THIS REVIEW (AT LEAST 500,000,000,000.' Craig Brown, *Mail on Sunday*

'THE VERY BOOK I HAVE BEEN LOOKING FOR MOST OF MY LIFE . . . TRUNKLOADS OF INFORMATION, AMAZING STORIES AND EXTRAORDANARY PERSONALITIES'
Christopher Matthew, *Daily Mail*

Bill Bryson describes himself as a reluctant traveller, but even when he stays safely at home he can't contain his curiosity about the world around him. *A Short History of Nearly Everything* is his quest to understand everything that has happened from the Big Bang to the rise of civilization – how we got from there, being nothing at all, to here, being us. The ultimate eye-opening journey through time and space, revealing the world in a way most of us have never seen it before.

'BRIMS WITH STRANGE AND AMAZING FACTS . . . DESTINED TO BECOME A MODERN CLASSIC OF SCIENCE WRITING'
Ed Regis, *New York Times Book Review*

'THE AMOUNT OF GROUND COVERED IS TRULY IMPRESSIVE . . . IT'S HARD TO IMAGINE A BETTER ROUGH GUIDE TO SCIENCE' John Waller, *Guardian*

'A THOROUGHLY ENJOYABLE, AS WELL AS EDUCATIONAL, EXPERIENCE. NOBODY WHO READS IT WILL EVER LOOK AT THE WORLD AROUND THEM IN THE SAME WAY AGAIN'
William Hartston, *Daily Express*

'A TRAVELOGUE OF SCIENCE, WITH A WITTY, ENGAGING, AND WELL-INFORMED GUIDE WHO LOVES HIS PATCH AND IS DESPERATE TO SHARE ITS DELIGHTS WITH US'
Peter Atkins, *The Times*

0 552 99704 8

BLACK SWAN

THE RIGHTEOUS
The unsung heroes of the Holocaust
Martin Gilbert

'A TIMELY BOOK FOR A NEW CENTURY . . . THE QUESTIONS RAISED IN THIS BOOK LIE AT THE HEART OF OUR HUMANITY' *Guardian*

'He who saves one life, it is as if he saved an entire world'

The Holocaust will be forever numbered amongst the darkest of days in human civilisation. Yet even in that darkness, there were sparks of light Many will recognise the names of Oskar Schindler, Raoul Wallenberg and Miep Gies, But there were thousands of others throughout Europe who risked their own lives to save Jews from the Nazis and their horrific campaign of obliteration that was the Holocaust.

By the beginning of 2002, more than 19,000 non-Jews had been recognized as Righteous (Among the Nations) by Yad Vashem, the Holocaust museum in Jerusalem, some were officials, some were clergy; others were citizens of countries who united in their efforts to protect Jews. Many were merely individuals who had the courage to stand up against a growing tide of collaboration and simply say: 'We did what we had to do'.

Martin Gilbert, the foremost British historian of the Holocaust, here presents the evidence collected over many years. Cumulatively, these accounts, from every occupied country in Europe, from the Baltic to the Mediterranean, from the Atlantic to the Black Sea, and from inside the Third Reich itself, form an inspiring tribute to those heroic individuals who, without thought to the risk to their own lives, dared to challenge barbarism, and hold out the hand of rescue to the Jews of Europe.

'MARTIN GILBERT BRINGS TOGETHER SOME REMARKABLE STORIES OF COURAGE AND INGENUITY'
Matthew J. Reisz, *Independent*

0 552 99850 8

BLACK SWAN